PETERSON INSTITUTE FOR INTERNATIONAL ECONOMICS

The Arab Economies
in a Changing World, 2nd edition

MARCUS NOLAND AND HOWARD PACK

Washington, DC
November 2011

MIX
Paper from
responsible sources
FSC® C005010
FSC
www.fsc.org

Marcus Noland, senior fellow, became deputy director of the Peterson Institute in September 2009. He has been associated with the Institute since 1985. He is concurrently a senior fellow at the East-West Center. He was a senior economist for international economics on the Council of Economic Advisers (1993–94); visiting professor at Yale University, Johns Hopkins University, the University of Southern California, Tokyo University, Saitama University (now the National Graduate Institute for Policy Studies), and the University of Ghana; and a visiting scholar at the Korea Development Institute. He is author, coauthor, or editor of *The Arab Economies in a Changing World* (2007), which was selected as Choice Outstanding Academic Title for 2007, *Witness to Transformation: Refugee Insights into North Korea* (2011), *Famine in North Korea: Markets, Aid, and Reform* (2007), *Korea after Kim Jong-il* (2004), *Industrial Policy in an Era of Globalization: Lessons from Asia* (2003), *No More Bashing: Building a New Japan–United States Economic Relationship* (2001), *Avoiding the Apocalypse: The Future of the Two Koreas* (2000), which won the 2000–01 Ohira Memorial Award, and *Economic Integration of the Korean Peninsula* (1998).

Howard Pack, visiting fellow, has been a professor of business and public policy and professor of economics at the Wharton School, University of Pennsylvania, since 1986. He was a fellow at the Harry S. Truman Institute for Peace Research, the Hebrew University, Jerusalem. He has been a consultant to the World Bank, the UN Conference on Trade and Development, and many other international development agencies. He is author or coauthor of *The Arab Economies in a Changing World* (2007), which was selected as Choice Outstanding Academic Title for 2007, *Industrial Policy in an Era of Globalization: Lessons from Asia* (2003), *Productivity, Technology and Industrial Development* (Oxford University Press, 1987), and *Structural Change and Economic Policy in Israel* (Yale University Press, 1971).

PETER G. PETERSON INSTITUTE FOR INTERNATIONAL ECONOMICS
1750 Massachusetts Avenue, NW
Washington, DC 20036-1903
(202) 328-9000   FAX: (202) 659-3225
www.piie.com

C. Fred Bergsten, *Director*
Edward A. Tureen, *Director of Publications, Web Development, and Marketing*

Printing by Versa Press, Inc.
Typesetting by BMWW
Cover Photo: Nasser Nouri—Corbis

Printed in the United States of America
13 12 11   5 4 3 2 1

Second Edition reprinted in October 2011.
New ISBN 978-0-88132-628-4

Library of Congress Cataloging-in-Publication Data

Noland, Marcus, 1959–
   The Arab economies in a changing world /
   Marcus Noland and Howard Pack.
      p. cm.
   Includes bibliographical references and index.
   ISBN 978-0-88132-393-1 (alk. paper)
   1. Arab countries—Economic conditions.
   2. Arab countries—Economic policy.
   3. Arab countries—Politics and government.
   4. Arab countries—History.   5. Arab countries—Social conditions.
   6. Globalization.   I. Pack, Howard.
   II. Title.

   HC498.N56 2007
   330.917'4927—dc22   2007004018

Contents

Tables

Figures

Boxes

Preface

The Arab countries confront a major challenge: how to successfully employ a large cohort of young people reaching working age. The stakes are high: Apprehensions about the availability of jobs together with disaffection with the region's undemocratic political regimes raise fundamental questions regarding political stability. Terrorism, whether aimed at targets foreign or domestic, raises the risk profile of the region and thus has significant implications for its economic performance. In short, the Arab countries risk being left behind in global competition precisely when they need to accelerate growth to create jobs.

This book, *The Arab Economies in a Changing World* by Marcus Noland and Howard Pack, directly addresses this range of issues. It brings to bear a strong comparative perspective on the historical performance of the Arab economies and, crucially, their future prospects. Noland and Pack demonstrate that, while the problems facing the Arab economies can be largely comprehended in conventional economic terms, the particular social and political sensitivities of the region present policymakers with unusually complex challenges in terms of devising and implementing solutions.

The authors directly confront the notion that Islam, the dominant religion of the region, is itself an inhibitor to economic performance. They conclude that, while the evidence does not support the notion that Islam impedes growth, it is relevant to understanding the discomfort that some in the region express about globalization and the constraints its governments face in formulating their external engagement policies.

In this regard, the book follows earlier Institute studies by Robert Z. Lawrence, *A US–Middle East Trade Agreement: A Circle of Opportunity?* and Ahmed Galal and Lawrence, *Anchoring Reform with a US-Egypt Free Trade Agreement*, on how trade agreements could serve as precommitment mechanisms to "lock in" reforms and reduce policy uncertainty.

The Arab Economies in a Changing World concludes that, if the region's employment challenge can be successfully addressed, the Arab world could look forward to a "demographic dividend" as the new generation enters its most productive working years—a phenomenon that contributed to the outstanding performance of East Asia over the past four decades or so. In the context of growing prosperity, increasing political and social liberalism could translate into a virtuous circle of enhanced cross-border economic integration, economic efficiency, rising incomes, self-confidence, and satisfaction. If this is the case, the region's young demographic could turn from a potential liability to a bonus.

There is no guarantee that this positive vision will be obtained, however. An alternative outcome is a vicious circle in which impoverishment, discontent, militancy, and repression feed upon one another, deterring reform and impeding growth. The fact that neither of these scenarios can be dismissed underscores the extraordinary salience of Noland and Pack's analysis for today's global geopolitical as well as economic development debate.

The Peter G. Peterson Institute for International Economics is a private, nonprofit institution for the study and discussion of international economic policy. Its purpose is to analyze important issues in that area and to develop and communicate practical new approaches for dealing with them. The Institute is completely nonpartisan.

The Institute is funded by a highly diversified group of philanthropic foundations, private corporations, and interested individuals. About 30 percent of the Institute's resources in our latest fiscal year were provided by contributors outside the United States, including about 12 percent from Japan. Major support for this study was provided by the Carnegie Corporation, The Olayan Group, and JER Partners, reflecting its major interest in the Middle East and in economic relations between the United States and that region.

The Institute's Board of Directors bears overall responsibilities for the Institute and gives general guidance and approval to its research program, including the identification of topics that are likely to become important over the medium run (one to three years) and that should be addressed by the Institute. The director, working closely with the staff and outside Advisory Committee, is responsible for the development of particular projects and makes the final decision to publish an individual study.

The Institute hopes that its studies and other activities will contribute to building a stronger foundation for international economic policy around the world. We invite readers of these publications to let us know how they think we can best accomplish this objective.

C. Fred Bergsten
Director
March 2007

Introduction to the Second Edition

MOHAMED A. EL-ERIAN

The Arab world has experienced more internal political upheaval in the past five months than the previous 50 years. While it is still too early to predict confidently how this will all play out, Marcus Noland and Howard Pack have provided an insightful analysis of the drivers of change in *Arab Economies in a Changing World*.

The book, published in 2007, was remarkably prescient in delineating the factors that they said would inevitably produce the kind of economic discontent that can lead to political instability. That analysis is more relevant than ever to understanding the changes under way in the region; and, given economic, financial, social, and geopolitical realities, these are changes that are consequential not only for the region but also the entire world.

One of the fundamental challenges facing the region is demographic in nature, including linkages to economic prospects, social pressures and political empowerment.

According to the World Bank, the region will have to create 40 million jobs over the next decade to absorb the legions of young people entering the labor market. And the initial conditions are far from favorable.

Mohamed A. El-Erian is co-chief executive officer and co-chief investment officer of Pacific Investment Co. (Pimco) and a member of the Peterson Institute for International Economics Board of Directors.

Already, one-quarter of the region's young people are estimated to be unemployed. In Egypt alone, the likelihood of a young college graduate being unemployed is nearly 10 times that of peers who only made it through elementary school. As youth unemployment mounts, the prospect of going from unemployed to unemployable becomes even more distressing, especially for restless segments of the population. In the meantime, skill erosion accelerates, the pressures on already weak social safety nets increase, and future productive capabilities are impaired.

Egypt is the most notable case but the same pattern is evident throughout the region. Youth unemployment—including unemployment among urban, educated youth—is likely to influence the response to the uprising confronting the region's rulers. Whether they will make the right choices is, unfortunately, anything but clear.

Judging from the experience of other developing countries, one way of rapidly generating commercially sustainable employment is through a successful process of linkages into the global economy. In essence, the trick is to use the global marketplace to enhance your employment creation capabilities and improve the welfare of your populations (including, critically, to reduce the incidence and severity of poverty), and then gradually increase the contribution of domestic demand to a rapidly growing pie.

Policy reforms and the rise of commodity prices over the past decade have contributed to an increase in cross-border trade and investment, but these gains have not been sufficient to absorb all the labor entering the market. Indeed, over a broader 50 year horizon, too many metrics suggest that the Arab world has essentially stagnated in this area while the rest of the world has rapidly integrated into the world economy. Now the region must play catch-up at a time when the global economy is less accommodating.

The situation is ironic in certain respects. Over the last two generations the region has achieved improvement on a wide range of social indicators, such as life expectancy, infant mortality, literacy, and educational attainment—spectacularly so in some cases. Neither absolute poverty nor inequality (except for the outsized wealth of the major energy exporters) appeared high by the standards of some other regions. Indeed, these indicators led to a damaging sense of complacency, both within and outside the regions. Yet recent events have borne out Noland and Pack's contention that what appeared to be stability masked "brittleness."

In the short-term, all the countries experiencing political instability, particularly those without oil resources, could face a higher risk of financial disruptions, capital flight, economic stagnation, and the need for external balance of payments support. Moreover, sustained efforts—implemented over a number of years and in an inclusive, transparent, and well communicated fashion—are needed to address the underlying structural challenges.

There are two broad possibilities as to how these regimes might respond.

The inevitable economic and financial disruptions associated with popular uprisings could derail recently implemented reforms, particularly in the trade and financial sector. The long-run fiscal situation could also come under greater pressure as some governments use civil service hiring and wages to mollify disaffected unemployed educated youth.

Fortunately, a more optimistic outcome is also possible, and should be advocated and hopefully will materialize. Enhanced political legitimacy and greater participation could create the political space for reform, enabling governments to move aggressively in dismantling the web of rent-creating economic distortions that have been used to buttress political elites who have governed many of the countries of the region for decades. This, along with political reform and greater personal freedom, could unleash entrepreneurship and dynamism, reversing the brain drain and drawing in new foreign investment and technology.

While my hope and aspirations are for this second, more optimistic outcome, I also recognize that no one can forecast with any confidence how the epochal events in the Arab world will unfold. Fortunately, *Arab Economies in a Changing World* provides us with a uniquely valuable framework and analysis to assess developments as the region moves forward through this critical moment of its history.

Acknowledgments

In writing this book we have benefited tremendously from the opportunity to present this study or its background papers at conferences or seminars sponsored by the Aboitiz Foundation, Cebu, the Philippines; the Ateneo de Davao, Davao, the Philippines; the East Asian Economic Association conferences in Kuala Lumpur, Malaysia, and Hong Kong; Egypt's International Economic Forum, Cairo, Egypt; the Gulf Research Center, Dubai, the United Arab Emirates; the Gulf University for Science and Technology, Kuwait City, Kuwait; Harvard University, Cambridge, MA; the Peterson Institute for International Economics, Washington, DC; the Korea Development Institute Graduate School, Seoul, Korea; the Middle Eastern Technical University, Ankara, Turkey; and the US Agency for International Development mission in Cairo, Egypt.

We also wish to acknowledge Patrick Clawson, Bernard Hoekman, Farrukh Iqbal, Mohsin S. Khan, Jacob Funk Kirkegaard, and Mustapha Nabli for valuable comments on drafts.

We owe a considerable debt to Paul Karner, Ketki Sheth, and Erik Weeks, who ably assisted us with the research at various stages of this project, and to Madona Devasahayam and Marla Banov for turning our prose into an actual book.

Historian Walter Rodney once argued that the remedying of shortcomings is a collective responsibility. Perhaps. But in light of all of the assistance noted above, at the risk of being labeled bourgeois subjectivists, we will shoulder responsibility for the remaining errors.

MARCUS NOLAND
HOWARD PACK
March 2007

Introduction

The economic performance of the Arab countries of the Middle East has been middling over the past four decades. It has been worse than East Asia, better than sub-Saharan Africa—the other region most profoundly marked by arbitrary borders and weak states—and about the same as Latin America and South Asia: in a nutshell, not the worst, not the best, falling behind the West (see figures 1.1 and 1.2 and box 1.1). While the region has suffered no major crisis, it now faces a major imminent challenge, namely the demographic imperative to create jobs for the large cohort of young people reaching working age. The stakes are high: Rapid labor force growth in many Arab countries has contributed to despair among young men about their job prospects and consequent worries about political stability.

The fact that economic performance slipped over the past quarter century relative to a broad set of comparators heightens concern about this fundamental challenge. In part due to relatively high population growth rates, living standards in the Arab countries as a whole stagnated during the 1980s and 1990s, with per capita income in 2000 at roughly the same level as 20 years earlier. The average disguises considerable intragroup variation, however: Growth in countries such as Egypt and Tunisia has been sustained if modest, while income levels in major oil exporters such as Algeria, Kuwait, and Saudi Arabia have exhibited greater volatility, largely mirroring movements in the price of oil. With the real price of oil nearing record levels, these countries are currently riding high (figure 1.3 and box 1.2). This heterogeneity complicates the analysis: While investment bankers understandably focus on the Persian Gulf oil exporters that have earned more than $1 trillion of petrodollars this decade, for those more concerned with generating employment, alleviating poverty, or at-

Figure 1.1   Rate of growth of GDP per capita in constant prices, 1960–2004

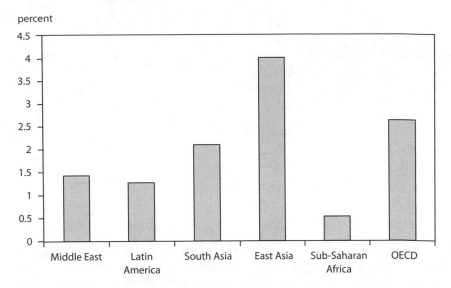

percent

OECD = Organization for Economic Cooperation and Development

Notes: Figure shows simple regional averages for compound annual growth rates. Middle East includes Algeria, Bahrain (1982–2003), Egypt, Jordan (1975–2004), Kuwait (1962–2003), Lebanon (1988–2004), Libya, Morocco, Oman (1960–2003), Saudi Arabia (1968–2003), Syria, Tunisia (1961–2004), United Arab Emirates (1973–2002), and Yemen (1990–2004).

Source: World Bank, *World Development Indicators,* various years; *Taiwan Statistical Databook,* 2004.

tenuating political violence, the more populous lower-income countries such as Egypt or Morocco may be of greater salience. This division is not hermetic: Most of the 9/11 hijackers were Saudis, and the lower-income countries have plenty of business opportunities. In short, the region embodies considerable diversity and complexity, features that this book explicitly takes into account.

Internal pressure across the region stems primarily from demographic patterns. Mortality rates have fallen, life expectancy is rising, and fertility rates have begun to decline. During this transition, population growth has been surging, and children and young people outnumber adults by a very large margin. Eventually fertility will fall far enough so that population growth slows, but the interim period of transition is generating a large "demographic bulge" cohort that is slowly working its way through the population age profile. Between 1980 and 2000, life expectancy in the region increased by more than eight years, and infant mortality was cut in half. Fertility rates fell dramatically—by more than two births per woman—but not quickly enough to preclude the emergence of a sizable demographic bulge. The three most populous Arab countries—Egypt, Algeria, and Mo-

Figure 1.2   Map of the Arab economies

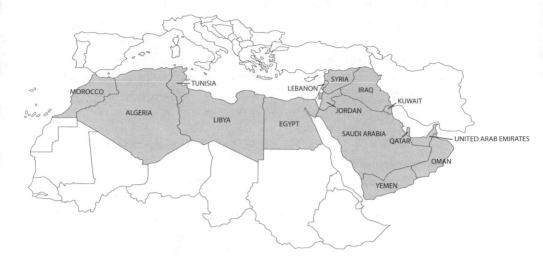

rocco—have median ages of 20, 20, and 21, respectively. Only in the United Arab Emirates, a small country on the Persian Gulf, is the median age 30 or more. According to the UN Development Program's (UNDP) *Arab Human Development Report 2002*, the population of the Arab region, narrowly defined, is expected to increase by around 25 percent between 2000 and 2010 and by almost 50 percent by 2020—or by perhaps 150 million people, a figure equivalent to more than two additional Egypts. Even under the UNDP's more conservative scenario, in 2020, Bahrain, Kuwait, Qatar, and the United Arab Emirates will be the only Arab countries with median ages projected to exceed 30.

These figures suggest that the region as a whole will experience labor force growth of more than 3 percent for roughly the next 15 years or so. According to the Arab League, unemployment in the region could rise from 15 million to 50 million over this period. Under these circumstances the imperative is to create jobs.

Besides the internal demographic pressures, the region faces an external challenge as well: The successful ongoing globalization of China, India, and smaller rivals is creating an ever more competitive global economic environment in which the Middle East has to operate. The global marketplace embodies increasingly stringent competitive pressures and less tolerance of substandard policies and practices than existed 20 or even 10 years ago.

Yet it is almost impossible to imagine sustained generation of needed employment opportunities without successful globalization and cross-border economic integration. While the benefits (and losses to some) of globalization have become clichés, it is critical to solve myriad problems.

Box 1.1   What is the Middle East?

There is no commonly accepted definition of the Middle East (see map in figure 1.2). This book focuses on the Arab countries from Morocco in the west to Iraq in the east. Due to data availability constraints we concentrate on eight countries: Algeria, Egypt, Jordan, Kuwait, Morocco, Saudi Arabia, Syria, and Tunisia, which together account for more than half of the region's population and economic output. We refer to the other economies of the region as circumstances permit.

A number of countries on the periphery of this region (as we define it) are sometimes treated as part of the region, though we believe that the divergences outweigh the commonalities and are not of central interest to understanding the dynamics of the region. For example, Israel, geographically part of the region, is distinct both economically and politically. To the east, Iran shares certain common historical, religious, and economic characteristics of parts of the Middle East; in the classification scheme of the Bretton Woods institutions it is part of the Middle East North Africa (MENA) region, though it is not considered part of the Middle East by the United Nations system, whose individual agencies do not follow a common definition. Similarly, countries on the African periphery such as Djibouti, Mauritania, Somalia, and the Sudan are members of the Arab League and included in the *Arab Human Development Report* (despite not being classified as part of the Middle East by its sponsor the UN Development Program [UNDP]). Like Iran, Turkey shares many links to the region but is not classified as a Middle Eastern country and is a member of only the broader pan-Islamic organizations. Classifications and memberships according to the World Bank, International Monetary Fund, UNDP, UN Educational, Scientific and Cultural Organization, Arab League, Arab Bank for the Economic Development of Africa, the Islamic Development Bank, the Organization of the Islamic Conference, and the Organization of Petroleum Exporting Countries are reported in appendix table 1A.1.

Even though for reasons of data availability we often consider only a subset of all Arab countries in our analysis, occasionally for convenience they are referred to as Arab, Middle Eastern, or MENA countries with the understanding that we are referring specifically to the more limited core set, though we believe that their experiences are broadly representative of the region in its entirety.

Unlike public-sector employment programs, expansion of labor-intensive export activity can absorb many new labor force entrants on a commercially sustainable basis. Imports of new equipment and intermediate materials can improve productivity, which can both lower prices of domestic goods and enhance exports. Foreign direct investment (FDI) can add to domestic savings, thus increasing the national saving rate, and provide

Figure 1.3   Commodity price series for petroleum, spot

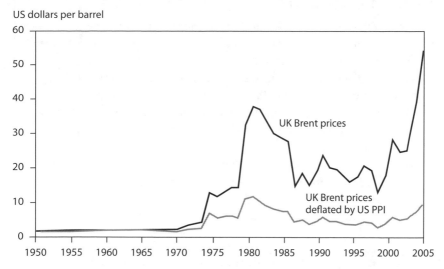

US dollars per barrel

Source: IMF, *International Financial Statistics*, February 2006, June 2006.

technological knowledge and ready-made distribution networks, thereby reducing the need for the time-consuming and expensive process of developing such networks. However, the greater social openness required to realize these benefits will disrupt established practices and mores.

To date, the region's performance on numerous indicators of economic opening to the rest of the world has been unimpressive, and looking forward there is cause for concern as to the region's ability to successfully globalize and generate the necessary growth in employment. For example, in 2003, the Philippines had more manufactured exports than the entire Middle East and North Africa (MENA) region combined. Until the recent oil-fueled expansion of FDI, the region attracted less FDI than some small Scandinavian economies. The Middle East risks being left behind, precisely when it needs to accelerate growth to create jobs for its growing labor force.

Deep uncertainty about the future of many of the region's political regimes impedes successful globalization and sustained employment growth. While the region's contemporary economic performance may not be distinctive, on the whole, its political regimes are. According to Freedom House, the only Arab League member government classified as a democracy is the small Red Sea enclave of Djibouti. Enduring authoritarian regimes are instead the norm (figure 1.4). All received negative assessments on the Polity IV Project ratings that range from 10 (most democratic) to −10 (least democratic), based inter alia on the relative competitiveness of the head of government's recruitment, constraints on him or her, and competitiveness of political participation. The individual country scores range from –2 in the cases of Jordan and Yemen to –10, the absolute minimum, in the cases of Qatar and Saudi Arabia. Similar results are obtained with measures of repression such as the degree of extralegal political terror (de Soysa and Nordås 2006). Moreover, this authoritarianism is enduring: According to the Polity IV scoring, only the industrialized democracies of the Organization for Economic Cooperation and Development (OECD) experienced fewer regime changes on average for the period 1960–2000—no developing area was as unchanging as the Middle East (figure 1.5). In developed democracies, the absence of abrupt change is unsurprising, but in poorer countries it often signifies a closed political system in which elections are infrequent and more closely resemble staged acclamations than a genuine contest of power. There is modest evidence of democratization in the Middle East data: Five countries exhibit increases in democratization scores over the sample period, two exhibit declines, and the scores of the remainder are unchanged or exhibit fluctuations without any obvious trend. This combination of authoritarianism and stability is indeed unique.

This is not to say that the region's political regimes are alike: Some such as Morocco, Saudi Arabia, and Jordan are monarchies of varying historical duration and liberalism; others such as Algeria, Tunisia, and Yemen are authoritarian states with security services forming the core; and Syria, Egypt, Libya, and Iraq (under Saddam Hussein) combine both authoritarian and dynastic tendencies. Lebanon is sui generis, a fragmented democracy subject to Syrian influence that has varied over time. The Palestinian Authority might similarly be described as an unconsolidated democracy in a state of semiautonomy in relation to Israel. Needless to say, the political trajectory of post-Saddam Iraq is highly uncertain. Whatever their formal institutional characteristics, a number of these regimes are dominated

Figure 1.4 Average polity score, 2003

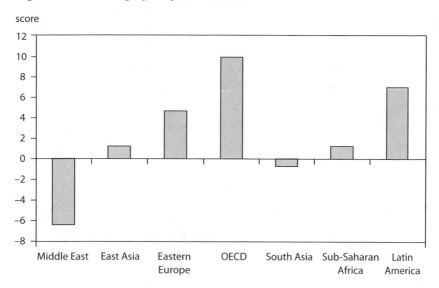

score

Note: Middle East includes Algeria, Bahrain, Egypt, Iraq, Jordan, Kuwait, Libya, Morocco, Oman, Qatar, Saudi Arabia, Syria, United Arab Emirates, and Yemen.

Source: Polity IV Project, www.cidcm.umd.edu/polity (accessed January 24, 2007).

by religious or tribal minorities. Lacking popular legitimacy, they resort to coercion to obtain compliance.

Popular dissatisfaction associated with lack of political voice appears to be reinforced by dismal prospects for employment over the next decades and an appreciation of the better performance that was forgone. In a 2002 poll of Arab attitudes conducted by the American pollster James J. Zogby, in most countries surveyed, respondents among the young and educated were generally more pessimistic about their economic future. This pessimism was particularly acute in countries like Saudi Arabia and Kuwait, which witnessed large declines in per capita income in previous years (Zogby 2002). While this discontent may have been mitigated by benefits from the recent increase in the price of oil and associated trickle down, the long-term structural concerns remain. And in countries such as Syria and Yemen, revenues from oil sales, which have enabled the continuance of substandard economic practices and associated political regimes, are expected to be exhausted within a decade (World Bank 2006a).

This situation is enormously important, most directly for the region's residents who endure repressive governance or the many who emigrate. Yet it goes without saying that both internally and externally there are other, noneconomic stakes as well. It is often argued that authoritarian governments typically have difficulty making credible policy commitments because the lack of democratic accountability facilitates capriciousness. As

Figure 1.5   Average number of regime changes, 1960–2003

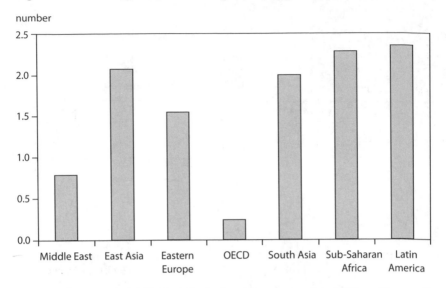

number

Note: Middle East includes Algeria, Bahrain, Egypt, Iraq, Jordan, Kuwait, Libya, Morocco, Oman, Qatar, Saudi Arabia, Syria, United Arab Emirates, and Yemen.

Source: Polity IV Project, www.cidcm.umd.edu/polity (accessed January 24, 2007).

a consequence, credibility in authoritarian regimes is, to a greater extent than in democracies, a function of reputation, which is hard to gain and easily lost. This credibility deficit can manifest itself in a variety of ways. For example, if economic reforms are introduced, supply response may be lacking if entrepreneurs are unsure if the policies will be sustained, and as a consequence they are reluctant to make irreversible investments if they believe that the government could easily undo the reforms.

Rather than excessive policy instability, however, the region appears to be afflicted with a stultifying policy inertia, and the political issues confronting the region would appear to run deeper than mere reputational effects. Across the region there is a tendency to rely on centralized regulatory intervention to facilitate the creation of economic rents and their channeling to politically preferred groups. By implication, cross-border economic integration, whether globally or regionally, is discouraged: Opening up would imply a loss of control and the concomitant ability to rig the local market to the benefit of regime supporters. All of this militates against a vibrant private sector that could promote increased productivity, employment, and growth. This combination of political illegitimacy and policy intervention makes it difficult for these economies to liberalize: Reform and the erosion of rents could undermine the very basis for political loyalty. In the words of one observer, "Only by altering the political logic that sustains these regimes, moving from a base built on the discretionary distribution of patronage to one grounded in the legitimacy that comes with procedural legality and political accountability, will political elites ever be persuaded to undertake economic reform" (Bellin 2006, 137–38). Ironically, though many speak of a "resource curse" associated with the oil industry, the availability of "natural" rents created by the energy sector may actually reduce the political incentives to create rents through efficiency-inhibiting policy interventions in other sectors such as manufacturing or publicly financed construction of infrastructure. Sufficient payoffs to cronies are feasible with the oil rents alone.

This lack of political dynamism in the face of underlying social change together with the increasingly religious orientation of the political opposition paradoxically raises the possibility of abrupt transitions or regime changes. Such deep political uncertainty discourages behavior that necessitates irreversibility, from investment by foreigners or local residents to return on the part of skilled émigrés, and creates a self-reinforcing downward spiral: Political uncertainty impedes investment and growth, which in turn contributes to popular discontent and intensified uncertainty.

None of this is to say that undemocratic governance is an insurmountable obstacle to development—South Korea and Taiwan in the 1960s and 1970s and China in the last quarter century spring to mind as obvious counterexamples—or that evolutionary political change is impossible, as the South Korean and Taiwanese examples demonstrate. Yet despite considerable external threats, in South Korea and Taiwan both governments sought legitimacy through economic prosperity. South Korean strongman Park Chung-hee once remarked, "In human life, economics precedes politics or culture" (SaKong 1993, 24). We know of no equivalent statement by an Arab autocrat elevating economics above political or cultural or foreign policy concerns. Instead, in the Middle East authoritarian governments have tended to encourage the externalization of discontent associated with relatively poor economic performance or to channel it into quixotic pan-Arab projects.

In the wake of 9/11, it may be tempting to parse the analysis that follows for insights into the relation between economic performance and terrorism, which, following Boaz Ganor (2002), can be defined as the intentional use of, or threat to use, violence against civilians or civilian targets to attain political aims. Many diagnoses of the sources of terrorism have emerged. Some have emphasized discontent with the rulers of Arab countries, while others locate the cause in hostility to aspects of Western culture such as women's rights. The list of causes is as varied as the intellectual background of the writers. Among the favorite explanations is that poverty and economic stagnation have provided a fertile recruiting ground for terrorists, a view that presupposes that the economic and social performance of these countries has been worse than that of other comparably situated nations—an assumption that finds little support in the evidence reported in the succeeding chapters. Yet whatever its origins, terrorism has significant implications for economic performance in the region. It raises the risk premium in the calculus of both internal and external investors, reducing and distorting both physical and portfolio investment as well as contributing to capital flight.

Such concerns have contributed to a revival of the neo-Weberian attribution of economic prosperity to religious tradition, though in this new rendition, instead of Calvinism acting as a catalyst, Islam is recast as an inhibitor. This notion has some surface plausibility: Muslims around the world are, on the whole, poorer than non-Muslims, and Islam is associated with distinct institutions and practices that could serve as the causal links between theological belief and economic performance. Some have also argued that the all-encompassing nature of Islamic belief may also contribute to political cultures that give rise to unresponsive authoritarian governments, which ultimately impede economic development. We explicitly address these ideas and conclude that while the evidence does not support the notion that Islam is a drag on growth, it is relevant to understanding the discomfort that some in the region express about globalization and the constraints governments in the region face in formulating their external engagement policies, which we argue are critical to the region's economic prospects.

That said, the role of Islam or other cultural factors should not be overstated. Obstacles to change governments face throughout the region may not be unique, and comprehending the difficulties of implementing reform may not require an analysis of spiritual evolution in the last millennium. Consider the region's largest nation in terms of population, Egypt. Over the past quarter century, it has experienced sustained growth, not particularly low relative to comparable countries outside the region but insufficient to absorb its rapidly increasing labor force. Acceleration of growth may require policy changes that could pose serious short-term political challenges with no guarantee of success. Incumbent politicians and the many workers who benefit from the current system may not support such changes any more than American textile workers support further reduction in barriers to cheap imports. In some respects the mix of collective action problems and entrenched interest group politics that currently impedes Egyptian economic reform resembles that in present-day Argentina or in India two decades ago, though the rigidity of the political system and popularity of groups such as the Muslim Brotherhood create the possibility of abrupt political transitions and raise the political stakes of economic reform. The latter two cases are relevant to the Middle East in that their divergent paths dramatically underline that outcomes are not preordained and that policy can have a significant impact—for good or ill.

In sum, the region faces a demographic imperative, a globalization challenge, and a deep uncertainty surrounding its politics. Responses to these forces are to varying degrees conditional on the price of oil determined in global markets. Contrary to rhetoric that claims the Arab countries of interest are sui generis, closer scrutiny employing standard modes of economic analysis suggests they share important commonalities with appropriately identified comparators from outside the region. Nothing immediately suggests that the Arab economies of the Middle East have a particularly onerous heritage that is inimical to successful development. In this light, the reform experiences of other countries are germane, from those of some relatively successful Asian countries to examples from Latin America, Eastern Europe, and other regions with more varied experiences.

Addressing the Challenge

The Arab economies are squeezed by the demographically preordained imperative to create jobs on the one hand and the increasingly competitive nature of the global economy on the other. For the region's more successful countries, the "crisis" is partly comparative—how will they fit into a rapidly evolving world economy in which some of the channels of development such as manufacturing exports pursued by recent success stories in Asia will be hard to replicate given the high competence built up by low-cost rivals such as China and India, as well as their now more advanced predecessors. And as attention increasingly turns to services, countries such as India and the Philippines are already establishing themselves as formidable centers for offshoring back-office activities and other business services.

To successfully meet this looming challenge, three intertwined questions arise:

- Can the underlying problems be diagnosed and the relevant policy levers identified?
- Will reform be blocked by elite and popular resistance?
- Will the requisite supply response to the policy change be forthcoming, i.e., will the economy actually respond to policy change?

The first task is, to borrow a medical metaphor, to form a proper diagnosis. In order to accelerate growth, the most important constraints impinging on the economy must be identified. Weak links to the global economy, low levels of FDI, lack of technology transfer, industrial incompetence, high levels of government investment and ownership, and high costs of doing business are among the difficulties that have been extensively documented, for example, by a series of World Bank volumes (2003a, 2003b, 2004c). All of these affect the critical issue of the incentives facing individuals and the farms and firms they manage.

Chapters 2 and 3 present evidence from 1960 to the present on both economic and social indicators within a framework that allows comparison with other countries at comparable stages of development. Concentrating on this period allows us to focus on some of the structural features of the Arab economies, including the rise and then fall of oil prices in the 1970s and 1980s, which is obviously relevant to the present situation, where the permanence of the rise in oil prices is unknown. The comparative perspective is useful for a variety of reasons: It enables us to benchmark the performance of the Arab economies historically and allows us to situate their current position within the global economy today, and the experiences of other regions may also provide insights into the dynamics of reform. The reform experiences of relatively successful comparators from outside the region document the opportunities forgone but more importantly point to the potential future gains if opportunities are seized.

In chapter 4 we examine the evidence on the magnitude of the challenge and address two issues that are central to our diagnosis of the future problems of the Arab countries: (1) the challenge presented by the need to absorb the looming bulge in the labor force and the absence of globalization as measured by FDI, financial-market development, international trade, and other indicators and (2) the adverse effect of globalization's absence on the efficiency of the economy and on the ability to absorb labor and simultaneously to increase per capita income.

This diagnosis is followed by an analysis in chapters 5 and 6 of the region's institutions and policies, including consideration of the impact of the region's Islamic legacy on institutional development. In this context we demonstrate that macroeconomic policy deficiencies that have been frequently cited in the past have been addressed in recent years and note the positive progress in other dimensions such as the quality of the legal system. Yet the rates of income and employment growth remain far from those needed to solve the looming unemployment problem and provide higher living standards, suggesting that still other reforms are needed or that some kind of shortcoming is inhibiting the economy's response to these stimuli. We find that much of what appears to be problematic in the Arab economies revolves around more difficult issues of institutional effectiveness and technological competence, which require public policy interventions of nontrivial complexity. We also find that there is considerable intraregional variation, particularly with respect to progress on institutional reform. This is important insofar as it suggests that at least across a variety of relevant characteristics, outcomes are not determined by deep cultural or religious factors—if it takes 27 days to enforce a contract in Tunisia, it is not obvious why it should take 410 in Egypt.

The analysis of institutions and policies is extended in chapters 7 and 8 from the domestic to the international sphere and how local attitudes toward globalization condition the commitment to and intensity of economic reform in this dimension. This is a particularly acute set of issues because one of the basic challenges for the region is that it is regarded as a risky business environment for a variety of reasons already touched upon.

The conventional indicators of the unfinished efforts at policy reform are useful in indicating the directions in which the countries probably need to move to improve their chances for more rapid growth of income and employment. Many of these reflect inadequate integration into both formal international trade institutions such as the World Trade Organization (WTO) and informal private-sector supply networks. Even in the latter case, there is a policy dimension insofar as the extent of private-sector cross-border integration may be encouraged or impeded by a host of local policies, beyond those directly concerning trade and investment.

In this context, we consider how commitments through the WTO or bilateral agreements might act as a credible precommitment mechanism to "lock in" reforms and at least reduce policy uncertainty if not other risks and leverage domestic support for complementary policy changes necessary to realize more fully the potential benefits of greater international orientation to address the imperative to create jobs detailed in chapter 4.

Economists are social scientists, not physicians, however, and even if they diagnose the "illness" and suggest the correct set of remedies or policy interventions, they encounter an additional—political economy—hurdle of actually getting the policies implemented. Opposition to reform by entrenched special interests or risk aversion by policymakers facing uncertainty with respect to putative benefits and cognizant of political costs may pose a greater obstacle to long-run success than correctly designing policy interventions—that is, political resistance may constitute the most binding constraint. The contemporary Middle East poses particularly difficult challenges in this respect, given the profound uncertainty surrounding the future trajectory of a number of the region's political regimes and the possibility of abrupt transitions.

These political economy constraints are considered in chapters 9 and 10, with emphasis on the roles of uncertainty and risk in both the economic and political spheres: If policies and practices are reformed, will a supply response be forthcoming? If the needed policies are put in place, will local or foreign entrepreneurs or in some cases state-owned enterprises respond to a changed incentive structure, and do they have the technical capacity to do so?

Conclusion

If the region's employment challenge can be successfully addressed, the Middle East could look forward to a complementary period of "demographic dividend" as this generation enters its most productive working years—a phenomenon that contributed to the outstanding performance of East Asia over the past four decades or so. With fertility now dropping rapidly, the region may well be through the process of demographic transition, and as the size of the cohorts entering adulthood begins to shrink, there will be a concomitant diminution in the problems that all societies face socializing young adult males. This process of absorbing a rapidly growing labor force, while prolonged, is self-terminating. In the context of growing prosperity, increasing political and social liberalism could translate into a virtuous circle of enhanced cross-border economic integration, economic efficiency, rising incomes, self-confidence, and satisfaction. If this is the case, the region's young demographic could turn from a potential liability to a bonus.

Yet demography is not destiny, and there is no guarantee that this happy outcome will be achieved: An alternative is a vicious circle in which political uncertainty impedes investment and growth, fueling political discontent and a reluctance to reform. In the Middle Eastern context, authoritarianism enables countries to neglect economic issues in the quest for their own stability and simultaneously may help generate radicalism that engenders still more repression, all of which discourages economic activity. This dynamic is complicated by the possibility that high oil prices, if sustained, may permit the continuation of such repression (and a reluctance to undertake reforms that would benefit the nonoil sectors) while having significant short-term economic benefits. These are not purely theoretical ruminations: For more than a quarter century, Venezuela, a country comparable in certain respects to the oil producers of the Middle East, has managed to combine the favorable demographic of a declining dependency ratio with falling per capita income (until the recent spike in oil prices) and rising political instability. Russia suffers from much of the same syndrome.

Clearly no answer can be given to whether optimism is warranted or the disabling dynamic will prevail. We can contribute to a more sophisticated understanding of the workings of these economies and the measures that might be undertaken, primarily by Arab governments but by the international community as well; note their potential benefits and costs; and suggest the deeper trepidation that they might exacerbate. Solely emphasizing the fears would consign a whole region to languish in serious economic turmoil, as the labor force growth is not a forecast but the movement into the labor force of those already born. Our concluding observations along these lines are summarized in chapter 11.

Appendix 1A

Table 1A.1 Classifications and memberships

Country	MENA (World Bank)	UNDP Country Office	UNESCO	Arab League	Islamic Development Bank	Arab Bank for Economic Development in Africa	Organization of the Islamic Conference	OPEC
Afghanistan					X		X	
Albania					X		X	
Algeria	X	X	X	X	X	X	X	X
Azerbaijan					X		X	
Bahrain	X	X	X	X	X	X	X	
Bangladesh					X		X	
Benin					X		X	
Bosnia and Herzegovina							Observer	
Brunei					X		X	
Burkina Faso							X	
Cameroon					X		X	
Central African Republic							Observer	
Chad					X		X	
Comoros				X	X		X	
Côte d'Ivoire					X		X	
Djibouti	X	X	X	X	X		X	
Egypt	X	X	X	X	X	X	X	
Gabon					X		X	
Gambia					X		X	
Guinea					X		X	

(table continues next page)

Table 1A.1 Classifications and memberships *(continued)*

Country	MENA (World Bank)	UNDP Country Office	UNESCO	Arab League	Islamic Development Bank	Arab Bank for Economic Development in Africa	Organization of the Islamic Conference	OPEC
Guinea-Bissau					×		×	
Guyana							×	
Indonesia					×		×	×
Iran	×				×		×	×
Iraq	×	×	×	×	×	×	×	×
Israel	×							
Jordan	×	×	×	×	×	×	×	
Kazakhstan					×		×	
Kuwait	×	×	×	×	×	×	×	×
Kyrgyz Republic					×		×	
Lebanon	×	×	×	×	×	×	×	
Libya		×	×	×	×	×	×	×
Malaysia					×		×	
Maldives					×		×	
Mali					×		×	
Malta			×					
Mauritania			×	×	×	×	×	
Morocco	×	×	×	×	×	×	×	
Mozambique					×		×	
Niger					×		×	
Nigeria							×	×
Oman	×		×	×	×	×	×	
Pakistan					×		×	

Country						
Palestinian Authority territories	X	X	X		X	
Qatar	X	X	X	X	X	X
Saudi Arabia	X	X	X	X	X	X
Senegal			X	X	X	
Sierra Leone			X	X	X	
Somalia	X	X	X	X	X	
Sudan	X	X	X	X	X	
Suriname			X	X	X	
Syria	X	X	X	X	X	
Tajikistan			X	X	X	
Thailand			Observer		X	
Togo			X	X	X	
Tunisia	X	X	X	X	X	
Turkey			X	X	X	
Turkmenistan			X	X	X	
United Arab Emirates	X	X	X	X	X	X
Uganda			X	X	X	
Uzbekistan			X	X	X	
Venezuela				X	X	X
Yemen	X	X	X	X	X	X

MENA = Middle East and North Africa
UNDP = UN Development Program
UNESCO = UN Educational, Scientific and Cultural Organization
OPEC = Organization of Petroleum Exporting Countries

Note: The *Arab Human Development Report* (UNDP) definition of MENA is identical to the Arab League definition reported here.

2

Growth, Productivity, and Income

The aggregate growth and productivity performance of the Arab economies is of interest for at least two reasons. First, in light of the challenges the Middle East faces, it is helpful to get a sense of the region's history as a starting point for forming expectations about its future. However, as investment advisers endlessly caution, past performance is no guarantee of future results. For most countries, not only the Middle East, performance over decades varies significantly—good in one, bad in the next (Easterly et al. 1993). Only a handful of countries in Asia have been able to realize sustained growth decade after decade. The Middle East has not, but it is not unusual in this respect.

Second, economic performance may be related to a widespread sense of disaffection of significant parts of the population, which is often remarked upon in Arab as well as Western sources (UNDP 2002, 2003). Dissatisfaction with current performance, if channeled constructively, might yield political pressure for reform, or it can be externalized unproductively (Lust-Okar 2004). In this regard, one can view economic performance in two relevant ways. The first is in an absolute sense: Has the economy delivered increasing levels of material prosperity and if so at what rate? The second is in a relative sense internationally: Have incomes risen more or less quickly than those of other countries to which Middle Eastern citizens and policymakers might compare themselves?

This chapter focuses on economic development in some of the major countries of the Middle East. Given the current intense focus on the Arab economies and assertions that terrorism has its source in poverty and a lack of improvement in social well-being (Lugar 2004), we first consider the economic performance of the Arab nations in terms of their income in purchasing power units relative to that of the advanced industrial countries of the Organization for Economic Cooperation and Development (OECD) and then analyze the change in absolute living standards over time within the Arab countries themselves. The main findings are that (1) as a group, the Arab countries grew fairly rapidly in the 1960s and 1970s but, like almost all developing nations, were not able to close the relative gap with the OECD economies; (2) their performance was much weaker in the 1980–2000 period than in the preceding two decades; and (3) despite the increased gap relative to rich countries, in a number of Arab countries for which data are available, the absolute standard of living improved, measured in local constant prices. Local residents could afford more calories and clothing, just not as many more as citizens of the OECD countries. However, in some of the highly oil-dependent economies, a decline in real income may have negated, in local perception, improved education and health. The recent spectacular increase in oil prices has changed some of these results not only for producers of oil but also for surrounding economies with which they have considerable interactions, particularly in employing expatriates. But the persistence of high prices is not assured, and we focus on the longer record from 1960 to the present.

The chapter begins by providing a number of descriptive measures in a comparative international framework. We consider the evolution of a few Arab economies relative to the advanced industrial economies of the OECD. These comparisons are carried out using internationally comparable measures that adjust for differences in purchasing power across nations. Even one of the best performing economies, Egypt, has not closed the gap between itself and the OECD nations over the last quarter century, while Saudi Arabia declined dramatically until the upsurge in oil prices in 2004, the sustainability of which is unknown. However, by another measure, namely the growth of per capita income within a country at local constant prices, the performance of Egypt and several (but not all) of the Arab countries is not very different from many other developing countries. In our view, this measure is likely to be more informative about how individuals perceive their own progress, though international comparisons are of interest in other dimensions.

We then analyze some of the proximate determinants of differences in growth over time and consider them in an international context. Contrary to what is usually claimed by those who focus solely on the Middle East, the achievements of the non–oil dominated Arab economies are not systematically worse than countries in other regions except for the East Asian countries. For nations such as Kuwait and Saudi Arabia, however, their near collapse since the peaking of oil prices in the 1980s has been notable (as is their more recent rise). While this failure has had ramifications for other countries, such as Jordan, ranging from reduced repatriation of earnings of expatriates to smaller export purchases, these effects have not precluded continued growth in the nations that are not resource rich. Now with oil prices rising, these indirect impacts have been partly reversed.

Identifying the Comparators

We focus on Egypt, Jordan, Saudi Arabia, Kuwait, Tunisia, Morocco, Algeria, and Syria, which account for more than half the population and GDP of the Middle East and reflect the many factors that determine economic performance in the region (table 2.1). Data availability even for this group is uneven but is better than that for other Arab countries. Even though, for reasons of data availability, we will often consider only a subset of all Arab countries in our analysis, occasionally for convenience they will be referred to as Arab, Middle Eastern, or Middle East and North Africa (MENA) countries with the understanding that sometimes we are analyzing the more limited set.

Obviously even this small group is disparate both economically and historically. Unlike the others, Egypt has a millennia-long national history, a strong sense of Egyptian national identity, a substantial cosmopolitan heritage predating colonialism, and was home to non-Arab minorities, including Copts, Greeks, and Jews who figured prominently among the entrepreneurial class.[1] French colonization of Algeria, Morocco, and Tunisia left a number of legacies including a greater identification with Europe than is true of some of the other countries. Algeria, Kuwait, and Saudi Arabia are resource rich, the others less so. The economic systems range from Soviet-style state intervention in Algeria to the freer economy of Jordan. In contrast, countries such as Kuwait, Jordan, Saudi Arabia, and Syria were the creation of the post–World War I victors who disposed of the territories of the Ottoman Empire. Thus, the countries considered are not a monolithic entity—they are all Arab but different in significant dimensions from each other. Nevertheless, their economic destinies are closely linked through population and financial flows. Compared with other regional groupings, they exhibit much greater similarities than differences, for example, in their being much less part of emerging trends in many aspects of international economic transactions.

We take account of many of the major economic differences as we search for comparable countries. It is difficult and arguably not helpful to search for correspondence in all dimensions such as colonial history. There is a great divergence across countries throughout the world yet many similarities in economic performance and the policies that nations with varying legacies have followed. To cite one example, almost all countries pursued a policy of import-substituting industrialization, neglect of

---

1. See, for example, the Alexandria quartet of novels of Lawrence Durrell or the memoir of Alhadeff (1998).

Table 2.1   GDP and population of the Middle East, 2004

Country	GDP (billions of current US dollars)	Population (millions)
Algeria	84.65	32.36
Bahrain	11.01	0.72
Djibouti	0.66	0.78
Egypt	78.80	72.64
Iran	163.44	67.01
Iraq	12.60	n.a.
Israel	116.88	6.80
Jordan	11.51	5.44
Kuwait	55.72	2.46
Libya	21.77	3.54
Lebanon	29.12	5.74
Morocco	50.03	29.82
Oman	24.28	2.53
Palestinian Authority territories	3.45	3.51
Qatar	20.43	0.78
Saudi Arabia	250.56	23.95
Syria	24.02	18.58
Tunisia	28.18	9.93
United Arab Emirates	104.20	4.32
Yemen	12.83	20.33
Total	1,104.16	311.23
Share of Middle East:		
Algeria	0.08	0.10
Egypt	0.07	0.23
Jordan	0.01	0.02
Kuwait	0.05	0.01
Morocco	0.05	0.10
Saudi Arabia	0.23	0.08
Syria	0.02	0.06
Tunisia	0.03	0.03
Total	0.53	0.63

n.a. = not available

Note: GDP data for Iraq, Qatar, and Palestinian Authority territories are from 2003.

Source: World Bank, *World Development Indicators,* May 2006.

agriculture, and intensive attempts by government to foster industrial development. Most efforts failed or resulted in slow growth, but a handful of Asian countries hit upon an improved version of these formulas that emphasized the role of exports while not abandoning the protection of the home market for a long period. Nevertheless, compared with other regions of the world, there are strong similarities among the Arab countries we consider, particularly their much lower integration into the world economy in a number of critical dimensions including a paucity of non-primary product exports, low inflows of both portfolio and foreign direct investment, and tiny technology transactions. Moreover, they all will face, to varying degrees, a much more rapid growth in their labor force than any nation outside of sub-Saharan Africa.

For most of these countries, data from the 1950s and 1960s are sketchy, but Robin Barlow's (1982) attempt to construct consistent time series for the period 1950–72 suggests that, if anything, the countries of the Middle East exhibited slightly more rapid growth than comparable developing countries over this period. This would be consistent with the fairly rapid expansion of education evidenced by rising rates of school attendance and literacy. Data availability problems are less severe for the 1960s. Though consistent data are typically in local prices, it is now well understood that measures in Egyptian pounds or Saudi dinars converted to dollars at the official exchange rate may be misleading because of both exchange rate misalignment and the systematically lower costs in poor countries of internationally nontraded goods like haircuts and housing. Purchasing power parity (PPP)–adjusted national income data constructed using international price comparisons permit more informative comparisons of living standards across countries.

The question of what is the relevant set of countries to compare with the Arab countries can be answered in multiple ways. In one sense one wants to compare them with the best contemporaneous performers because it indicates the maximum that one might have expected from them or alternatively the upper bound of the opportunities forgone. In this regard South Korea and Taiwan are the exemplars. Admittedly from an Arab perspective, the comparison with South Korea and Taiwan may not seem an entirely fair one. Fifty years ago the Asians may have been "deceptively poor": Contemporary income was low because of small physical capital stocks (due to war devastation in the case of South Korea and a lack of investment on the island of Taiwan prior to the decampment of the Kuomintang from mainland China), but in the mid-1950s the ratio of human capital to income was among the highest in the world (Noland and Pack 2003, table 2.1). These were countries with considerable social capacity but lacking physical capital, which was rapidly accumulated, some of it financed by US aid in the context of the Cold War.[2] Nevertheless, in establishing the upper limits of opportunities forgone, these countries set the standard.

Another set of comparators would be large developing countries insofar as the familiarity with these countries engendered by political or eco-

---

2. It is worth debunking one frequently made assertion that the major source of South Korean and Taiwanese growth was foreign aid, particularly from the United States. Such aid can be viewed as akin to remittances by expatriate workers, foreign aid, and rents from natural resource revenue. As shown in chapter 4, some Arab countries received very large amounts in these dimensions, dwarfing the Asian aid inflows of the earlier period. Even aid alone, including debt forgiveness, was larger in some Arab countries than in South Korea or Taiwan.

nomic prominence would invite self-comparisons both by residents and policymakers in the Middle East. In this respect the obvious reference nations would be India and China, both of which exhibited slow growth for decades but have grown rapidly in the last two and three decades, respectively.

Lastly, we compare the Arab countries with other intrinsically similar economies. Here the heterogeneity within the Middle East itself suggests two separate groups of comparators: one set for the major oil producers and the other for countries less abundant in natural resources. Scatterplots of data on labor, physical capital, human capital, and arable land endowments for 83 countries in 1961 are shown in figures 2.1a and 2.1b. The country sample was determined on the basis of data availability; the countries of the Eastern Bloc and most major oil producers are missing. The absence of the former is not really a problem for identifying relevant historical comparators—they were operating in a fundamentally different system for most of the period under consideration so the comparisons would have been questionable in any case. (The experience of Eastern Europe may be more relevant with respect to policy reform and associated supply responses, however, and we examine that experience in chapter 7.) The oil producers are discussed separately below.

Each panel shows a two-dimensional barycentric projection of three endowments in 1961, roughly the starting year of our analysis. Every endowment point on a ray emanating from one corner of the triangle has the same ratio as the other two factors; points lying closer to the corner of the triangle have a larger relative endowment of that factor. The point where the three rays emanating from each vertex intersect in the middle of the triangle indicates the average endowment bundle of the sample. The endowments are physical capital, labor force, human capital, and arable land. It is arguable that a more inclusive measure should include mineral endowments including oil. On the other hand, the price per barrel of oil was still less than $3 as late as 1973 and the real price, after the 1970s spike, declined through most of the 1980s and 1990s. Similarly, the price of a number of primary metals declined for periods of varying length. Allowing for natural resource–based production other than agriculture would thus entail another kind of analysis, perhaps such barycentric projections every five years, but even that would be arbitrary. We believe the main points can be derived from the starting point that we use, and results that are sensitive to the 1961 grouping will be noted.

In figure 2.1a, the five Arab countries in the sample—Algeria, Egypt, Jordan, Morocco, and Tunisia—all fall into the triangle defined by the land (A) and labor (B) vertices together with the center point (C) representing the sample average—i.e., they were all human capital–scarce. In figure 2.1b, arable land is replaced by physical capital. The five Arab countries fall into quadrilateral $ABCD$, indicating their relative labor abundance. Twenty-six countries constitute the Arab group's "neighbors" in these two

Figure 2.1a   Endowment triangle of human capital, land, and labor, 1961

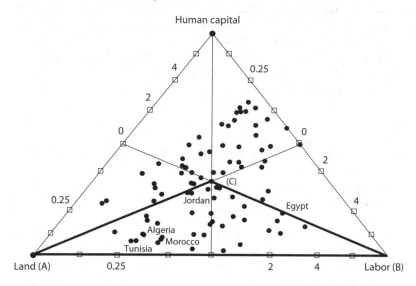

Figure 2.1b   Endowment triangle of physical and human capital and labor, 1961

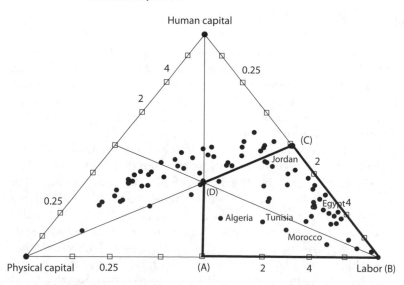

□ axis point

● countries

Note: Sample: n = 83

Source: Data from Bosworth and Collins (2003).

projections; most of these countries are relatively small African or Caribbean Basin economies. Seven are relatively large countries, however: Bangladesh, Brazil, India, Indonesia, Nigeria, Pakistan, and Turkey. It is an interesting and geographically diverse set of comparators. Four of the seven
(Bangladesh, Indonesia, Pakistan, and Turkey) are predominantly Muslim,
with Indonesia and Pakistan accounting for the largest Muslim populations in the world. Muslims make up a considerable share of Nigeria's population, while India's Muslims, though much smaller in percentage terms,
constitute the third largest Muslim population in the world behind Indonesia and Pakistan. The four Muslim-majority countries plus Nigeria
are members of the Organization of the Islamic Conference. Indonesia and
Nigeria are members of the Organization of Petroleum Exporting Countries (OPEC), and their oil endowment could be viewed as justifying their
inclusion in the natural resource–rich grouping. On the other hand, their
per capita endowment of oil is much smaller than those of Kuwait or Saudi
Arabia.

Thus we have identified a small group of comparators for the Arab
economies: Some have been high performers, some are large and prominent, and some were similarly endowed. India is included on both of the
latter two criteria, and Indonesia does double duty as a comparator to
both Middle East oil producers (or at least to Algeria, which has a large
population) as well as its less resource-abundant economies.

Natural Resources and Physical Capital

The relevant issues for the oil-centered economies are distinct. The economies of the Arabian Gulf, built around the export of a single commodity,
are characterized by the generation of large oil rents and boom and bust
cycles driven by the world price of their sole export. Table 2.2 reports the
share of rents—defined as property income, grants from abroad, and state
entrepreneurial income—in government revenue and GDP for seven Arab
economies and four resource-abundant comparators. (It might be desirable to exclude state-owned enterprise income from this definition, but the
reporting convention used by the International Monetary Fund [IMF]
does not permit this.) As is immediately obvious, the Middle East oil producers represent extreme varieties of the species: It is difficult to identify
other economies that are as rent-dependent. In terms of rentier status, diamond producer Botswana comes the closest; Nigeria and Venezuela, two
other oil producers, rely significantly on rents for government revenue,
though they have more broadly diversified economies than Kuwait, Saudi
Arabia, and the smaller Gulf states, subject to the proviso that the Nigerian data are not the most current and almost certainly understate the contemporary centrality of oil to the Nigerian economy. Indonesia, another oil
producer and predominantly Muslim country, is far less dependent on oil

Table 2.2   Rents (percent)

Country	Year	Share of government revenue	Share of GDP
Middle East			
Algeria	2000	70.0	24.9
Bahrain	2000	72.9	25.5
Kuwait	1999	85.2	29.4
Oman	2000	83.0	36.6
Qatar	2000	79.2	30.5
Saudi Arabia	2000	83.0	30.3
United Arab Emirates	2000	74.2	33.0
Resource-rich comparators			
Botswana	1996	66.2	30.4
Indonesia	1999	21.2	7.0
Nigeria	1978	30.0	4.9
Venezuela	2000	33.6	6.9

Note: Rents consist of entrepreneurial and property income (which includes income from state-owned enterprises) and grants (from abroad, including from supranationals, and from other general government units). Data for Bahrain and Saudi Arabia correspond to oil revenue only.

Sources: International Monetary Fund (IMF), *Government Finance Statistics,* various years; World Bank, *World Development Indicators,* various years; IMF Article IV Consultations.

than the major Arab producers, more closely resembling Algeria. Obviously the comparisons are imperfect: Botswana is subject to a different set of commodity price shocks, and Nigeria and Venezuela are less dependent on oil. Nevertheless they at least approximate the economic structures of the Middle Eastern oil producers.[3]

In these economies there is a macroeconomic tendency to save insufficiently during the booms and to overinvest in the export sector and local real estate, and as a consequence both individual financial institutions and the financial sector as a whole tend to be insufficiently diversified and subject to considerable systemic risk. For example, only one Gulf bank established following the second oil shock has survived.[4] The outstanding issue is for the government and local financial institutions to efficiently allocate the windfalls during the booms and maintain solvency during the busts, a task that is easier said than done.

A crude descriptive indicator of the efficiency of the capital allocation mechanism is the incremental capital-output ratio (ICOR), which measures

---

3. Colleagues have suggested that Angola, Equatorial Guinea, and Gabon might be appropriate comparators. Appropriate or not, lack of data prevents their consideration.

4. Roula Khalaf, "Sea of Cash Flooding into the Gulf Brings an Explosion of Investment Companies," *Financial Times*, October 19, 2006.

the investment necessary to produce an additional unit of output, a lower ratio being one indicator of better performance.[5] ICORs for some resource-rich economies are reported in table 2.3. For many countries, the available investment data include residential housing. In order to maximize the country sample we have computed the ICORs from these data; where available, ICORs derived from fixed business investment data alone are quantitatively quite similar. In a conventional neoclassical growth model one would expect the ICORs to rise gradually over time as capital deepening occurred and the marginal product of capital declined unless capital deepening were offset by growth in total factor productivity (TFP), the amount of output obtainable from a combined unit of labor and capital.

As seen in table 2.3, the ICORs in the resource-rich Middle Eastern countries are quite low in the 1960s, lower than in the comparator countries, arguably signaling an efficient allocation and use of investment. They rise in the 1970s but remain comparable to the comparators from outside the region. However in the 1980s, the ICORs in several of the oil producers explode. The ICORs of Kuwait and the United Arab Emirates—and over a more limited sample period, Bahrain and Libya—turn negative because income actually fell. By the turn of the millennium, the ICORs had clearly declined (i.e., capital was used more efficiently),[6] though Saudi Arabia's was relatively high, similar to Nigeria's, which in turn is often cited as exceptionally inefficient (Bevan, Collier, and Gunning 1999). Other countries such as Algeria and Oman had ICORs similar to those of Botswana and Indonesia, while Venezuela stands out as a relatively unsuccessful outlier. All in all, the data do not suggest that the identified economies are an unreasonable set of comparators for the Middle East's resource-abundant countries. ICORs for a larger group of countries are more systematically discussed later in this chapter in the section on investment and growth.

For economies that are more diversified than those of say the Gulf states, the presence of oil complicates exchange rate management. The tendency for the real exchange rate to appreciate during commodity booms and thereby render other industries uncompetitive in international markets is known as "Dutch disease," or more loosely the natural resource curse, named for the experience of the Netherlands after the discovery of natural gas in the 1970s. This phenomenon could also afflict neighboring economies that experience large capital inflows associated with remittances

---

5. The ICOR is proportional to the inverse of the marginal product of capital. In the Cobb-Douglas production function $Q=AK^\alpha L^{1-\alpha}$, the marginal product of capital is $\alpha Q/K$ while the ICOR is $\Delta K/\Delta Q$, where Q is gross domestic product, K is the quantity of capital, and L the amount of labor. ΔK is roughly equal to the value of investment in a year. The value of $\Delta K/\Delta Q$ is affected by the level of total factor productivity (TFP), A, in the individual sectors of the economy, and by the efficiency of the allocation of capital across sectors insofar as the marginal product of capital varies among sectors. These are discussed in the next section.

6. The ICORs declined due to better allocation across sectors and/or more efficient use within sectors.

Table 2.3 Incremental capital-output ratios (ICORs)

Country	1960s Period	1960s ICOR	1970s Period	1970s ICOR	1980s Period	1980s ICOR	1990s Period	1990s ICOR	2000s Period	2000s ICOR
MENA										
Algeria	1960–69	4.0	1970–79	2.9	1980–89	8.0	1990–99	8.9	2000–2004	4.4
Bahrain		n.a.		n.a.	1980–85	−27.9		n.a.		n.a.
Kuwait	1962–69	0.5	1970–79	2.0	1980–88	−5.2	1995–99	12.6	2000–2003	3.5
Libya	1960–69	0.6	1970–79	5.7	1980–83	−3.5		n.a.		n.a.
Oman		n.a.		n.a.	1980–85	2.4	1990–99	3.3	2000–2004	4.7
Saudi Arabia		n.a.		n.a.		n.a.	1997–99	24.9	2000–2003	8.6
United Arab Emirates		n.a.	1975–79	2.9	1980–89	−9.2	1993–99	6.8	2000–2004	3.3
Comparators										
Botswana		n.a.	1975–79	2.9	1980–89	1.5	1990–99	4.3	2000–2004	4.8
Indonesia	1960–69	1.3	1970–79	1.2	1980–89	2.6	1990–99	5.0	2000–2004	4.7
Nigeria	1960–69	3.9	1970–79	6.0	1980–89	51.7	1990–98	6.7	2001–2004	9.9
Venezuela	1960–69	2.6	1970–79	4.7	1980–89	62.5	1990–99	5.6	2000–2004	38.6

MENA = Middle East and North Africa

n.a. = not available

Source: World Bank, *World Development Indicators*, 2004, 2006.

from workers in the oil patch. Indonesia, with its diversified economy, including oil, timber, and manufactures, is the obvious comparator in this dimension.

It is frequently argued that beyond narrow issues of economic management, the presence of large rents associated with extractive industries has a negative impact through a variety of channels. The allocation of those rents is an intrinsically political action whether it occurs in Riyadh, Moscow, or Austin. In the case of the Arabian Gulf oil producers, those rents are so vast that the state does not need economic policy, only expenditure policy (Luciani 1990). In fact, a constant theme of the IMF's interactions with Saudi Arabia has been the clarification of the definition of the public sector and the introduction of more orderly and transparent budgetary procedures (IMF 2001, 2002, 2003).

At the level of the individual, the generation of massive oil rents means that few are directly involved in the production of wealth—the majority are involved in its distribution and consumption. Indeed one commentator goes so far as to argue that in what he describes as the allocation states of the Middle East, the rentier mentality embodies a disconnect in the work-reward causation (Beblawi 1990). It is almost always more remunerative to maneuver for a larger rent allocation than to engage either in directly productive economic activity or in political activism to construct a more rational system of allocation.

And while money cannot buy happiness, as discussed in chapter 3, it helps. From the standpoint of the political cultures and stability of the rentier states, the positive effect of high incomes on personal well-being has to be set against potentially destabilizing concerns about distribution: The absence of any transcendently rational or objective ground for determining who receives a share of the rents could manifest itself in dissatisfaction.[7]

Authoritarianism is an understandable, though regrettable, response of a political leadership confronting this conundrum and a potentially aggrieved populace. The existence of oil rents acts as an emollient through multiple channels. First, the existence of rents may absolve governments from taxation and as a consequence relieve pressure for accountability through what might be called the "accountability effect" (Ross 2001). Second, rents may furnish governments with revenues for patronage and again relieve discontent or undercut the formation of social groups independent of the state. As Lisa Anderson (2001, 56) observes, in MENA "the

---

7. Clement M. Henry and Robert Springborg (2001, 107–108) describe the opaque carving up of rents in Algeria, underpinned by oil, with "little or no economic rationale" by internal factions likened to the "Mafiosi." In Syria, under the alliance of convenience between the Alawite-dominated security services and the Sunni merchant class, "the differences between 'Arab Socialism' and 'Mafya-Kapitalism,' Russian-style, have blurred considerably" (Richards 2001, 48).

Table 2.4 Polity scores

Country	1960–69	1970–79	1980–89	1990–99	2000–2003
Middle East					
Algeria	–8.6	–9.0	–8.3	–4.0	–3.0
Bahrain	n.a.	–9.3	–10.0	–9.3	–7.8
Kuwait	–8.7	–8.9	–9.0	–7.2	–7.0
Oman	–10.0	–10.0	–10.0	–9.1	–8.5
Qatar	n.a.	–10.0	–10.0	–10.0	–10.0
Saudi Arabia	–10.0	–10.0	–10.0	–10.0	–10.0
United Arab Emirates	n.a.	–8.0	–8.0	–8.0	–8.0
Resource-rich comparators					
Botswana	6.3	7.0	7.3	8.3	9.0
Indonesia	–5.7	–7.0	–7.0	–5.4	7.0
Nigeria	1.8	–5.4	–1.2	–4.4	4.0
Venezuela	6.4	9.0	9.0	8.1	6.3

n.a. = not available

Source: Polity IV Project, 2003, www.cidcm.umd.edu/polity (accessed January 24, 2007).

public sector accounts for over half the labor force: Government employment is a form of social security." (On the other hand, as seen in later chapters, a large public sector may reduce the flexibility of the government in addressing serious economic problems.) A third channel through which rents may impede democracy would be by financing the development and maintenance of institutions of internal repression.

In fact, the Polity IV scores of the quality and nature of government in the resource-abundant Middle Eastern countries are appalling (table 2.4).[8] On a scale from –10 to 10, all are negative, with Qatar and Saudi Arabia flat-lining at the minimum –10.[9] Not all the news is bad—the Algerian scores show an upward trend as do the scores for Kuwait. These data do not capture post–sample period liberalizing openings in a number of countries including Lebanon, Palestinian Authority territories, Saudi Arabia, Kuwait, and Egypt, with post-Saddam Iraq representing an obviously special case. Even so, the resource-rich Middle Eastern countries appear

---

8. For definitions and numerical results, see Polity IV Project, www.cidcm.umd.edu/polity (accessed January 24, 2007).

9. In addition to Qatar and Saudi Arabia, eight other countries scored –10 at some point between 1970 and 2000: Bahrain, Haiti, Iran, Jordan, Kuwait, Oman, Qatar, and Swaziland. Saudi Arabia alone scored –10 for the entire sample period, though. On average, the Arab countries experienced 1.1 regime changes during this period. Algeria was the least stable with three regime changes, while Kuwait and Saudi Arabia experienced no regime changes during this period.

Figure 2.2 Savings and investment ratios, 1960–2004

percent of GDP

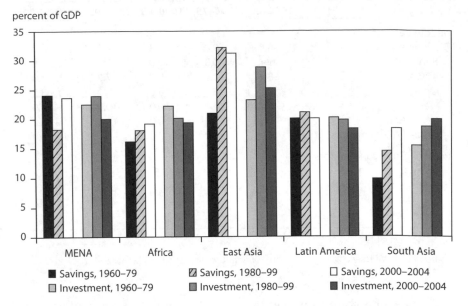

Savings, 1960–79   Savings, 1980–99   Savings, 2000–2004
Investment, 1960–79   Investment, 1980–99   Investment, 2000–2004

Note: Annual averages of gross domestic savings and gross fixed capital formation as a share of GDP. Average of available data.

Sources: World Bank, World Development Indicators, 2004, 2006; Taiwan Statistical Databook, 2006.

remarkably undemocratic, even in comparison with other resource-abundant economies in other parts of the world.

At least at the regional level, capital accumulation patterns in the Middle East have exhibited episodic shifts associated significantly with movements in the price of oil. During the 1960s and 1970s capital accumulation in the Middle East, financed in large part by oil revenues, was as rapid as in Asia and more rapid than in other developing areas (figure 2.2).

However, the Middle East's rate of capital accumulation slowed after 1980, largely due to declining saving in Kuwait and Saudi Arabia, while Asia surged ahead as rates of saving and investment rose across the region, particularly in China. However, weakness in the institutional environment, specifically fear of expropriation, may have encouraged local entrepreneurs to focus on trading and services and eschew illiquid investments in fixed capital. The upshot was to encourage the Arab states to assume a leading role in capital-intensive sectors, ultimately saddling the economy with inefficient public enterprises and a public employment share twice the world average. This may be one explanation for the falloff in the efficiency of capital investment, as discussed in greater detail below, though there is considerable intraregional variation in this regard.

Regional capital accumulation surged in the most recent period, driven by the increase in the price of oil. Although many in the region are determined that the free-spending, low-efficiency pattern of investment will not be reproduced again, concerns remain, as discussed in greater detail below (box 2.1). Slow capital accumulation does not appear to be the only explanation of the region's deteriorating relative performance, though there are reasons for concern with respect to both quality and in some nonoil producers, quantity. As seen below, despite the respectable investment rates, rapid growth in the labor force led to relatively slow growth or decline of the capital-labor ratio in a number of countries in the 1990s.

Human Capital

Economists increasingly regard investment in education and skills—human capital—as an important determinant of economic performance. As shown in figure 2.3a, South Korea and Taiwan started out with more human capital than the other comparators, at least as measured by years of schooling embodied in the labor force, and widened that lead over most of these countries over the succeeding four decades.[10] A noticeable exception was Jordan, which surpassed Brazil and China and had nearly caught up with Taiwan by the turn of the millennium. Egypt, which started the period with an educational attainment similar to that of India, Pakistan, and Bangladesh, accumulated human capital more quickly than the South Asian trio and on this measure by the end of the period had passed Turkey and had caught up with Brazil and China. Tunisia also started out behind the South Asian countries, passed Bangladesh and Pakistan, and had nearly caught up to India by 2000.

Figure 2.3b presents the same series for some resource-rich countries. Algeria started out the period a bit behind Indonesia but virtually closed the gap by the end of the period. In 1960 Iraq was comparable to Algeria, though as discussed in the next chapter it deteriorated significantly during the past 30 years. These three countries are bracketed by Venezuela, which began the period at a higher level of educational attainment and accumulated it more quickly, and Nigeria, which lagged from the start.

For late developers trying to adapt to local circumstances technology developed abroad, science and engineering education could have a particularly large impact (table 2.5). Again, the Middle East does not look distinct—its 13 percent share of tertiary graduates receiving science or engineering degrees during the late 1950s and 19 percent share in the late 1990s are both well within the norms of the comparator group. China and Taiwan had particularly high shares in the 1950s. South Korea did not,

---

10. Mean years of education are only a first approximation as quality measures discussed in the next chapter indicate that the Arab countries may have weak education outcomes.

Box 2.1   An oil-driven revival?

The Arab economies directly and indirectly benefit from increases in the price of oil. Obviously exporters of oil benefit immediately while contiguous resource-poor nations realize greater repatriated earnings, increased tourism from other oil-based countries, and perhaps financial inflows that allow the expansion of real investment in the recipient. In the past, such short-term gains have not been transformed into sustained growth as much of the new investment went into nontraded sectors or into inefficient investment in traded goods. It is obviously too early to tell whether, as the financial community often says in the face of a bubble, "this time it's different." The following table shows two measures of interest, namely, the total growth of per capita GDP at constant US prices and the growth of manufacturing value added at the same prices. The United States is included to allow a benchmark.

The oil-rich countries, as expected, do best, but Jordan and Tunisia exhibit very rapid growth—with Jordan partly reflecting the impact of trade agreements with the United States and Tunisia the effects of continuing economic reform. Both of these nations also experienced rapid growth in manufacturing, which augured well for the future. Thus, these examples provide some basis for optimism about the effect of an oil boom superimposed on trade agreements and policy reform (discussed in chapter 8).

Cumulative percent change in GDP per capita and manufacturing value added, 2003–05

Country	GDP per capita	Manufacturing value added
Algeria	7.4	6.2
Egypt	5.2	6.3
Jordan	9.5	30.1
Kuwait	8.9	n.a.
Morocco	1.1	6.1
Saudi Arabia	6.5	n.a.
Syria	3.1	n.a.
Tunisia	8.5	9.0
United States	5.8	n.a.

n.a. = not available

Source: World Bank, World Development Indicators, 2006.

Figure 2.3a   Human capital accumulation, normally endowed countries, 1960–2000

education (years)

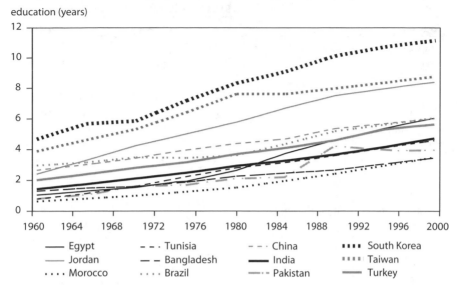

Note: Mean years of total education of the population age 15 and over.

Source: Bosworth and Collins (2003).

Figure 2.3b   Human capital accumulation, resource-rich countries, 1960–2000

education (years)

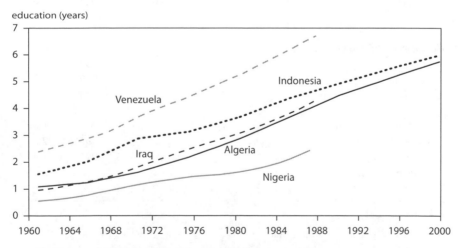

Note: Mean years of total education of the population age 15 and over.

Sources: Iraq, Nigeria, and Venezuela: Nehru and Dhareshwar (1995); Others: Bosworth and Collins (2003).

Table 2.5 **Share of science and engineering tertiary graduates**
(percent)

Country	1950s and 1960s Year	1950s and 1960s Share	1990s Year	1990s Share
Middle East (aggregated)		13.1		18.6
Algeria		n.a.	1995	43.2
Bahrain		n.a.	1994	28.1
Egypt	1957	11.4	1995	10.2
Jordan	1962	0.0	1996	19.4
Lebanon	1961	18.6	1995	14.3
Libya	1960	16.4		n.a.
Morocco	1964	37.3	1995	27.8
Tunisia	1961	5.5	1996	16.7
Oman		n.a.	1995	10.4
Palestinian Authority territories		n.a.	1995	18.7
Qatar		n.a.	1997	3.0
Saudi Arabia		n.a.	1996	14.3
Syria	1957	6.6	1995	27.5
United Arab Emirates		n.a.	1997	19.4
Yemen		n.a.	1992	4.0
High-performing comparators				
Taiwan	1957	30.6	1997	32.2
South Korea	1957	15.9	1997	39.4
Large comparators				
China	1960	40.0	1994	29.9
India	1957	3.7	1991	16.3
Normally endowed comparators				
Brazil	1957	10.5	1993	12.3
Pakistan[a]	1957	22.4	1992	11.2
Turkey	1957	16.2	1994	23.6
Resource-rich comparators				
Botswana		n.a.	1997	22.0
Indonesia		n.a.	1996	17.2
Nigeria	1961	23.3	1990	16.7
Venezuela	1958	15.7		n.a.

n.a. = not available

a. 1957 figure for Pakistan includes Bangladesh.

Sources: UN Educational, Scientific and Cultural Organization, *Statistical Yearbook*, 1970, 1998; *Taiwan Statistical Data Book,* 1997.

though its proportion of science and engineering graduates rose dramatically in the 1960s.

However, there is some evidence that the quality of Middle Eastern education, at least in the contemporary period, has been substandard.[11] For example, in international tests in mathematics and science for fourth graders, Morocco and Tunisia had the lowest scores in both disciplines. In reading literacy scores, Kuwait (not included in the science and mathematics tests) and Morocco exceeded only Belize and were far below Moldova, Turkey, Macedonia, and Argentina (National Center for Education Statistics 2004). And the experience in the United States and other countries is that such differentials usually widen as children progress through the school system.

Indeed, in separate surveys conducted by the *Times of London* and Shanghai Jiao Tong University, no Arab university ranked among the top 200 in the *Times* survey and the top 500 in the Shanghai survey, the only region to achieve this dubious distinction.[12] The *Times* survey was based on a combination of peer reviews by 1,300 academics worldwide and objective indicators such as faculty publication and citation counts; the Shanghai survey relies exclusively on objective indicators such as citation counts and Nobel Prize winners among faculty and alumni to form these rankings—that is, neither survey is purely a beauty contest. The rankings do not prove that there are no good universities in the Middle East—the results could be interpreted as reflecting lack of integration into peer networks rather than the quality of output per se—and there may well be pockets of excellence within individual institutions that do not get picked up in these kinds of aggregate data. But even the more generous "lack of peer recognition" interpretation suggests that Middle East academics are relatively isolated from world intellectual developments, a theme to which we return in chapter 7. The bottom line is that as with the accumulation of physical capital, with respect to investment in human capital, the Middle East does not look very different from other developing areas, save Asia, but there are reasons for concern, especially with regard to quality.

Relative International Performance

The citizens of a nation are obviously concerned with their standards of living. They may be interested in how they fare relative to citizens of other

---

11. On the quality of Arab education systems, see the *Arab Human Development Reports* (UNDP 2002, 2003) and Iqbal (2006).

12. See *Times Higher Education Supplement*, www.thes.co.uk (accessed April 22, 2005) and Institute of Higher Education, Shanghai Jiao Tong University (http://ed.sjtu.edu.cn) for rankings and links to the study methodologies.

Box 2.2   The Mediterranean shores

In 1950, with the end of colonization imminent in Algeria, Egypt, Morocco, and Tunisia, local leaders might have envisioned a decline in the income gap and a move toward a European standard, but by 2000 it had become clear that whatever dreams that existed were now unattainable. Combined with the failure of the societies to modernize in so many dimensions delineated in the *Arab Human Development Reports,* the dismay voiced in those reports and elsewhere becomes more understandable.

Yet the absolute performance of these and other Arab economies has not been very different from those of many other developing economies, and in some aspects such as income distribution it has been quite good. But if the relevant comparison group is indeed the Southern European countries of the northern shore of the Mediterranean, as may well have been the case for the postwar Egyptian middle class depicted in the novels of the expatriate Lawrence Durrell, the disenchantment of the current descendants of that group may become more comprehensible.

Gap in GDP per capita (purchasing power parity) (dollars)

Country	1950	2000
Average GDP per capita of Greece, Portugal, and Spain	2,063	13,778
Difference between this average and local income in		
Algeria	698	10,986
Egypt	1,153	10,858
Morocco	608	11,120
Tunisia	948	9,240
Saudi Arabia	−168	5,776

Source: Calculated from Maddison (2003).

countries—an increasingly likely comparison given the growth of satellite television and the Internet. But perhaps of more importance is the growth in the local standard of living regardless of how the country performs relative to others. The former comparative perspective has led to widespread dismay among Arab analysts about the perceived poor performance of their countries and to a search for its proximate causes, for example in the various *Arab Human Development Reports* (UNDP 2002, 2003, 2004a). Even if this perception is incorrect, it is clearly widely held and has motivated a search for explanations (see box 2.2).

Considerable literature predicts per capita income convergence across countries in terms of purchasing power parity. Egypt, the major nonoil country in the region, is one among many poorer countries that did not converge. On this purchasing power–adjusted measure, over the period 1960–2000, Egyptian incomes fell slightly relative to the industrial countries of the OECD while the absolute difference in per capita incomes widened from roughly $7,000 in 1960 to nearly $20,000 in 2000 (table 2.6).

In marked contrast, incomes in South Korea and Taiwan, which in 1960 were similar to those in Egypt, rapidly converged to the OECD average. (Indeed, South Korea joined the OECD in 1996, and given the "normal" requirements for membership Taiwan would have joined the organization had it not been for its peculiar diplomatic status.) Their performance is not cited as a cudgel but to underline the opportunities that have existed in the world over the period considered, opportunities forgone by the key Arab countries (and most other less developed countries as well). To wit, China, one of the populous developing countries, experienced rapid convergence in the latter part of the sample period, while India's relative status during the period as a whole remained unchanged as in Egypt. Among the similarly situated economies, income converged on the OECD average in Indonesia after economic reforms were initiated in the 1970s, showed no trend in Brazil and Pakistan, and worsened in Bangladesh and Turkey. Despite the predictions of theoretical models, most countries outside of East Asia did not converge on the OECD, and in a much larger group of nations divergence has been standard (Pritchett 1997). While the Middle East was not alone in its relative misery, this outcome was not preordained. As indicated in table 2.6, of the six similarly endowed countries that began the period at income levels similar to or lower than Egypt, Morocco, and Syria, three of them experienced substantial convergence (Botswana, China, and Indonesia), and the two high-performing Asian economies outstripped the Middle Eastern countries in absolute terms by a huge margin. Tunisia stands alone among the larger Arab countries in having significantly narrowed the gap in relative terms.

The convergence of South Korea with respect to the OECD offers an important benchmark for the forgone achievement of Egypt and others. In 1960 South Korea had roughly the same population and per capita income as Egypt. Both are poor in natural resources, though South Korea possessed considerably more human capital. In the natural resources dimension, if anything, Egypt is better endowed—it benefits from tourist attractions such as the Pyramids, revenue from the Suez Canal, natural irrigation from the Nile River, and is a few hundred miles by ship from the European market. Moreover, given the rapid growth in income in the oil states, similar language and religion led to considerable growth in Egyptians being employed abroad and substantial repatriation of earnings after the oil price boom of the 1970s. Contrast this with South Korea's largely poor agricultural land, dearth of tourist attractions, lack of overland

Table 2.6 GDP per capita (PPP)

Country	Constant 1996 international dollars					Share of OECD				
	1960	1970	1980	1990	2000	1960	1970	1980	1990	2000
Middle East										
Algeria	2,693	3,428	4,745	4,965	4,894	0.32	0.28	0.30	0.25	0.20
Egypt	1,476	1,977	2,419	3,241	4,184	0.17	0.16	0.15	0.16	0.17
Jordan	2,305	2,248	4,051	3,472	3,892	0.27	0.18	0.26	0.18	0.16
Kuwait	n.a.	n.a.	18,319	11,352	14,545	n.a.	n.a.	1.13	0.58	0.58
Lebanon	n.a.	n.a.	n.a.	3,244	5,780	n.a.	n.a.	n.a.	0.16	0.24
Morocco	1,322	2,245	2,976	3,547	3,720	0.16	0.18	0.19	0.18	0.15
Saudi Arabia	n.a.	n.a.	21,120	11,028	11,716	n.a.	n.a.	1.30	0.55	0.47
Syria	1,388	1,648	2,965	3,113	4,094	0.16	0.13	0.19	0.16	0.17
Tunisia	n.a.	2,550	4,354	4,937	6,777	n.a.	0.21	0.27	0.25	0.28
Yemen	n.a.	n.a.	n.a.	1,098	818	n.a.	n.a.	n.a.	0.06	0.03
High-performing comparators										
South Korea	1,571	2,777	4,830	9,959	15,881	0.18	0.22	0.30	0.51	0.65
Taiwan	1,468	2,809	5,850	10,995	17,056	0.17	0.23	0.37	0.56	0.74
Large comparators										
China	685	820	1,072	1,790	3,747	0.08	0.07	0.07	0.09	0.15
India	838	1,077	1,162	1,675	2,480	0.10	0.09	0.07	0.08	0.10
Normally endowed comparators										
Bangladesh	1,057	1,100	967	1,278	1,685	0.12	0.09	0.06	0.06	0.07
Brazil	2,395	3,600	6,327	6,212	7,185	0.28	0.29	0.40	0.32	0.29
Pakistan	639	945	1,159	1,748	2,007	0.08	0.08	0.07	0.09	0.08
Turkey	2,700	3,625	4,325	5,741	6,838	0.32	0.29	0.27	0.29	0.28

Resource-rich comparators

Botswana	984	1,208	3,462	5,417	7,541	0.12	0.10	0.22	0.27	0.32
Indonesia	960	1,097	1,891	2,851	3,637	0.11	0.09	0.12	0.14	0.15
Nigeria	1,035	1,113	1,209	1,096	713	0.12	0.09	0.08	0.06	0.03
Venezuela	7,751	10,342	7,905	6,974	6,420	0.91	0.84	0.50	0.35	0.26
Memoranda:[a]										
Middle East (6)	1,837	2,349	3,585	3,879	4,594	0.22	0.19	0.23	0.20	0.19
OECD	8,508	12,384	15,885	19,718	24,418	1.00	1.00	1.00	1.00	1.00
East Asia	1,644	2,950	5,456	9,030	11,044	0.19	0.24	0.34	0.46	0.45
Latin America	3,814	5,031	6,357	5,773	7,527	0.45	0.41	0.40	0.29	0.31
South Asia	845	1,041	1,096	1,567	2,057	0.10	0.08	0.07	0.08	0.08
Sub-Saharan Africa	1,839	2,429	2,984	3,482	4,210	0.22	0.20	0.19	0.18	0.17

n.a. = not available

OECD = Organization for Economic Cooperation and Development

PPP = purchasing power parity

a. Regional averages composed of Middle East: Algeria, Egypt, Jordan, Morocco, Syria, and Tunisia (except 1960); OECD: Current members excluding Czech Republic, Hungary, Mexico, Slovakia, South Korea, and Turkey; East Asia: China, Hong Kong, Indonesia, Philippines, Singapore, South Korea, Taiwan, and Thailand; Latin America: Argentina, Brazil, Chile, Colombia, Costa Rica, Mexico, and Peru; South Asia: Bangladesh, India, and Pakistan; sub-Saharan Africa: Ghana, Kenya, Mauritius, Nigeria, South Africa, and Tanzania.

Notes: Data for Botswana reported for 2000 are from 1999; Kuwait for 1990 are from 1989; Taiwan for 2000 are from 1998.

Sources: Penn World Tables, v6.1 (Laspeyres series, reference year 1996); for Kuwait and Saudi Arabia: World Bank, *World Development Indicators*, 2004 (constant 1995 PPP dollars). Original source does not report data after 2000.

transportation routes to Europe and Asia due to the division of the Korean peninsula, and a 7,000-mile distance from its major market, the United States. (The closer, but smaller, Japanese market was only semiaccessible because of trade barriers for most of the period.) But as evidenced by the quote from South Korean leader Park Chung-hee in the previous chapter, the South Korean government from 1961 onward decided that its legitimacy was dependent on delivering growing living standards and oriented its policies to achieve this (see also Mason et al. 1980, Haggard 1990). In contrast, during the 1950s and 1960s Gamal Abdel Nasser attempted to obtain legitimacy by playing a leadership role first in the nonaligned movement and then by his advocacy of pan-Arabism, including a short-lived union with Syria that did not benefit either country. Moreover, he fought a proxy war in Yemen with Saudi Arabia in the 1960s and two wars with Israel in 1956 and 1967. In the more than two decades in which he has been the leader since the assassination of Anwar Sadat, Hosni Mubarak has not evinced any overriding concern with accelerating growth.

Even if one dismisses the results for South Korea and Taiwan as reflecting transitorily low incomes at the beginning of the sample period for reasons previously elaborated, and that of China as embodying an unsustainable recovery from the aberrant effects of self-imposed Maoism, from the perspective of the Middle East it would seem difficult to dismiss the experience of Indonesia: postcolonial, multiethnic, predominantly Muslim, similar level of human capital, oil producing, historically authoritarian, and occasionally in conflict with its neighbors. Perhaps in a big enough sample it represents the anomalous case that just got lucky—alternately it reflects the effect of good policymaking for much of the period (Hill 1996).[13]

With respect to the resource-rich countries, the results are more ambiguous: While Saudi Arabia experienced a tremendous decline in income relative to the OECD, the other two large oil producers, Nigeria and Venezuela, did as well. Incomes in Botswana and Indonesia converged on the OECD, but Botswana is subject to different commodity price shocks, and Indonesia is far less reliant on oil. Both have also benefited from good macroeconomic policies that have helped to contain potential "Dutch disease" problems.

Saudi Arabia, whose pattern roughly parallels that of other oil-producing economies in the Middle East, exhibited growing divergence from the OECD nations. Between 1980 and 2000, its relative per capita income

---

13. Nor can one dismiss the Indonesian (and Malaysian) experiences as simply reflecting the influence of the ethnic Chinese business community. In Indonesia, the Chinese make up less than 4 percent of the population. Between 1960 and 2000, the value-added share of industry tripled. Employment data are only available beginning in 1980, but between 1980 and 2000 nonagricultural employment more than doubled, increasing by 29 million jobs. Even if the ethnic Chinese are vastly overrepresented in the business community, it is difficult to imagine that structural transformation of this magnitude could have occurred without substantial input from, and impact on, the indigenous population.

(PPP) declined dramatically from 1.30 to 0.47. From an average living standard of Lyon or Geneva, income declined to that of Sao Paolo, Brazil. Similar declines occurred in other oil economies like Kuwait and Oman. Not only was there a decline vis-à-vis the OECD and some fast-growing poorer countries but also the absolute level of GDP per capita (in purchasing power–adjusted terms) in Saudi Arabia declined by roughly 40 percent. Unlike Egypt, where weak growth relative to the OECD was nevertheless accompanied by an increase in the absolute standard of living, Saudi Arabia suffered both absolutely and relatively—not a prescription for domestic tranquility. The recent boom in oil prices has reversed much of this decline, the sustainability of which is far from assured in the absence of a major change in economic policies.

Despite the continued growth in countries such as Egypt, it is nevertheless true that the absolute income gaps with respect to the OECD have continued to grow. The absolute gap in PPP income per capita between Egypt and the OECD average was $2,030 in 1960, $13,466 in 1980, and $20,234 in 2000. The absolute gap has increased dramatically even for an economy that has been growing steadily. At a time when knowledge of international consumption patterns is widely disseminated through film, satellite television, and the Internet, such growing absolute disparities are likely to have generated envy and perhaps some resentment toward both the richer countries and the local governments that have not been able to close these gaps. Whether growing absolute levels of income over time in individual countries will assuage discontent is unknowable, but many observers believe it is one component of the dissatisfaction in many Arab countries.

Domestic Growth over Time

Having set out an international prism through which to view the comparative development of the major Arab economies, we now turn to the absolute performance measured in constant local prices. While international comparisons of levels of real income are important, showing the best performance possible given the extant international conditions and the forgone income in not achieving this frontier, levels of real domestic living standards are probably more important in characterizing any economy. People's perception of their welfare may depend more on how they are doing this year relative to five years ago than how they compare with residents of London, Silicon Valley, Seoul, Shanghai, or Côte d'Azur. The evolution of GDP per capita in constant local prices (figures 2.4a and 2.4b) is shown for two separate groups, the resource-rich and resource-poor countries, as different factors affect their growth.

Of the poorer countries (figure 2.4a), Tunisia has done much better than the others, though Egypt, often described as a weak economy, has in fact experienced more rapid growth since 1980. But growth in Jordan declined

Figure 2.4a   GDP per capita, normally endowed countries, 1960–2004

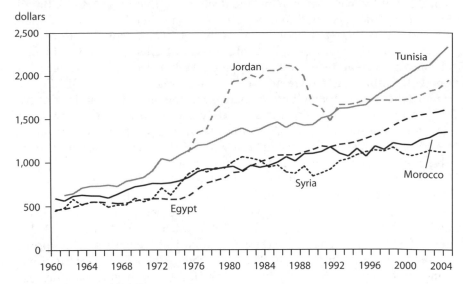

Note: Constant 2000 US dollars.

Source: World Bank, *World Development Indicators,* 2004, May 2006.

Figure 2.4b   GDP per capita, resource-rich countries, 1960–2004

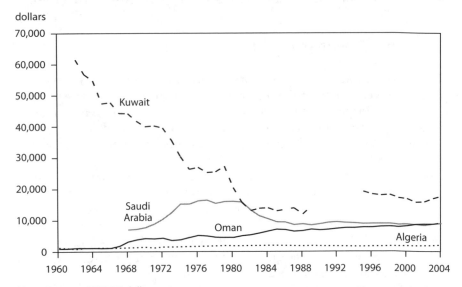

Note: Constant 2000 US dollars.

Source: World Bank, *World Development Indicators,* 2004, May 2006.

(perhaps surprisingly given its significant economic reforms and relatively high human capital), while Morocco has had relatively slow growth. Despite its oft-cited rigidities, Syria exhibited a small positive growth rate, though its data are more uncertain than those of the other countries we consider. Its performance is largely due to oil exports (small relative to the oil-rich countries), a rapidly diminishing resource.

Turning to the oil-rich countries, Algeria stagnated for roughly two decades before the reversal of oil prices in 2003, and the other major oil-rich nations (figure 2.4b) were also not able to transform their oil riches into sustained growth. Kuwait underwent a precipitous decline over 30 years, while over the past generation Saudi Arabia has witnessed a decline of almost 50 percent in per capita income measured in constant dollars. As noted earlier, the reversal since 2003 in oil prices is too short-lived to allow strong inferences. Thus, these Middle Eastern countries resemble Nigeria and Venezuela rather than Indonesia, three other oil-rich countries with widely divergent paths. Nigeria and Venezuela suffered declines in per capita income since the mid-1970s despite vast oil revenues (and in the case of Venezuela, a demographically favorable declining dependency ratio), while Indonesia has been a success despite recent problems. These differences can be accounted for by appalling government policies in the former and rather good ones in the latter (Bevan, Collier, and Gunning 1999).

Major wars have had very limited effects in the poorer countries. For example, in Egypt the intensive war in Yemen against the Saudis and Yemeni factions from 1962 to 1967, immediately followed by the Six Day War of 1967, the War of Attrition in the late 1960s, and the October War of 1973 had no major effect. In 1974 growth resumed, albeit at a slow rate. In most wars the lost military equipment and infrastructure were replenished by foreign patrons, particularly the Soviet Union, thus precluding the need for major expenditures in this sphere.

As shown in figures 2.4a and 2.4b, the effect of the Gulf War of 1990–91 did not affect trends in the countries not directly involved, although Kuwait sustained significant damage during the Iraqi invasion in the summer of 1990. The low growth of Jordan in the 1990s may have been partly attributable to its proximity to Iraq and the effects of the Iraq-Iran war of the 1980s and the Gulf War of 1990–91. Although the Gulf War was of limited duration and Jordan did not suffer any material damage, the cost of absorbing the Palestinians expelled from Kuwait, Saudi Arabia, and other countries may have been significant though many repatriated their assets. In addition, Jordan lost some entrepôt rents as international trade with Iraq declined. Even the assassination of President Anwar Sadat in 1981, an event that might have shaken confidence in the Egyptian economy, did not have any lasting effect on growth.

While the downside effect of political turbulence has not been quantitatively significant, it is notable that international expansion also has scant

Table 2.7 Cumulative percent change of constant price GDP per capita and exports, 1995–2000

Country	Exports	GDP per capita
Algeria	34.0	8.5
Egypt	13.6	19.8
Jordan	−5.4	3.3
Kuwait	−4.3	−9.6
Morocco	27.2	12.5
Saudi Arabia	n.a.	−1.3
Syria	64.7	−3.8
Tunisia	28.6	23.0
OECD	45.7	10.8

n.a. = not available

Source: World Bank, World Development Indicators, 2006.

spillover effect. As can be seen from figures 2.4a and 2.4b and table 2.7, there was no particular benefit in the late 1990s from the unusual prosperity in the world economy. All of the countries except Syria lagged the OECD increase in export growth, and only Egypt, Morocco, and Tunisia exceeded the OECD growth in GDP.

This is not surprising given that much of the boom of the late 1990s was due to investment in information technology (both hardware and software) and the telecommunication sectors. In some of the OECD countries such as the United States, the purchase of domestically produced hardware and software led to a rapid growth in aggregate demand while their adoption may have led to an acceleration of the rate of growth of potential supply. In contrast, the Arab countries had little ability to produce these goods or their components and thus did not benefit significantly from growing international demand for them. And they also had only modest ability to take advantage of the growth in income of potential trading partners, which led to an enormous increase in demand for all consumer and producer goods, not just those in information and communication technology. Unlike India and the Philippines, nations that are considerably poorer than many of those considered here, there was meager success at even partly transforming the structure of production to take advantage of low-wage costs to export software and other services.

Comparative data for a number of relevant countries are given in table 2.8. From 1960 to 1980 growth in the Middle East was comparable to other developing areas, superior to many, consistently inferior only to the high-performing Asian countries. In the 1980s, performance in the Arab countries deteriorated, as it did in many other less developed countries. Growth lagged not only the high-performing Asian countries but also the large

Table 2.8   Growth rate of GDP per capita (percent)

Country	1960–70	1970–80	1980–90	1990–2000
Middle East				
Algeria	1.2	2.8	–0.2	–0.3
Egypt	2.9	4.4	2.9	2.3
Jordan	n.a.	n.a.	–1.8	0.6
Kuwait	–4.9	–6.5	–3.8	1.3
Lebanon	n.a.	n.a.	n.a.	5.3
Morocco	2.0	2.7	1.6	0.4
Saudi Arabia	n.a.	7.9	–5.7	0.0
Syria	2.0	6.4	–1.1	2.1
Tunisia	3.2	5.0	1.1	3.1
Yemen	n.a.	n.a.	n.a.	1.7
High-performing comparators				
South Korea	5.6	5.5	7.4	5.1
Taiwan	6.9	6.9	6.9	5.0
Large comparators				
China	1.5	4.3	7.7	8.9
India	1.7	0.7	3.6	3.6
Normally endowed comparators				
Bangladesh	1.4	–1.0	1.1	3.0
Brazil	3.2	5.9	–0.4	1.3
Pakistan	4.3	1.5	3.5	1.4
Turkey	n.a.	1.7	2.8	1.7
Resource-rich comparators				
Botswana	5.6	11.1	7.1	1.9
Indonesia	1.8	5.4	4.4	2.7
Nigeria	1.7	1.7	–1.9	–0.1
Venezuela	1.5	–0.8	–1.7	–0.1
Memoranda:[a]				
Middle East (6)	2.2	4.3	0.4	1.4
OECD	4.4	2.6	2.5	1.7
East Asia	2.4	4.6	5.6	6.4
Latin America	2.5	3.4	–0.9	1.6
South Asia	1.9	0.7	3.3	3.3
Sub-Saharan Africa	2.6	0.7	–1.1	–0.4

n.a. = not available

a. Composition of regional averages follows the World Bank's definition except for the Middle East and North Africa (MENA), which includes Algeria, Egypt, Jordan (1980–90 and 1990–2000), Morocco, Syria, and Tunisia.

Note: Compound annual growth rates for the period. Data for Kuwait are for 1962–70 and 1980–89, and Tunisia are for 1961–70.

Sources: World Bank, *World Development Indicators,* 2004 (constant 1995 US dollars); and *Taiwan Statistical Databook,* 2004 (per capita national income, constant 1996 local currency). Index is no longer reported in the *World Development Indicators.*

comparators of India and China, though it remained superior to that in Africa and the Latin American nations that were strongly affected by the debt crises that began in the early 1980s. But the divergence widened during the 1990s, when many Middle Eastern economies continued to have slow or negative growth while most other regions resumed or accelerated growth. There was some intragroup variation in all regions, but the poor performance in the Arab countries was largely, though not exclusively, due to the major oil producers. This underlies our point that even in the worst decades, much of the bad international performance was concentrated in the oil producers, and the more diversified economies often performed similar to Latin America and typically better than Africa. Of course, judged by the standards of East Asia, even the better-performing Middle Eastern countries did weakly. Moreover, they did poorly relative to the heretofore weak, and arguably more comparable, economies of South Asia such as India and Bangladesh, two nations that considerably lagged the Arab countries in the 1960–80 period but whose reforms facilitated improving performance in the 1990s.

Investment and Growth

Having examined the growth of per capita income in domestic prices in the previous section and noting the fact that many of the countries had fairly good performance for varying periods, we consider a particularly simple relation between GDP growth and investment to GDP ratio.[14] While these two series are subject to some uncertainty, the simple relationship is helpful. In the next section we amplify the determinants of growth by including the impact of labor force and TFP. Figures 2.5a, 2.5b, and 2.5c show the investment to GDP ratio and GDP growth rates for three decades. These figures are a graphic representation of the ICORs discussed above.

In the 1970s most of the Arab countries exhibited either average or superior performance: They had better than average investment ratios and for a given investment ratio, GDP growth was equal or superior to that of other nations or regions, being close to or to the right of the regression

---

14. Barry Bosworth and Susan Collins (2003) find that there is a low correlation between investment to GDP ratios and capital stock growth rates that have been calculated for individual countries using perpetual inventory. The investment to GDP ratio is of interest as the underlying 1960–90 capital stock series built up by Vikram Nehru and Ashok Dhareshwar (1995) and the 1990 to 2000 additions by Bosworth and Collins assume an identical depreciation rate across countries. In contrast, significant literature argues the lower cost of skilled labor in poorer countries militates in favor of longer life for capital. Different depreciation rates across countries, which may also vary over time, imply that the absence of a significant relation between investment to GDP ratios and the Nehru-Dhareshwar—Bosworth-Collins capital stock series is not surprising.

Figure 2.5a   Investment ratio and GDP growth, 1970–80

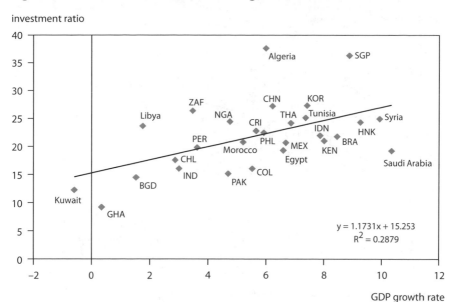

Source: World Bank, *World Development Indicators*, various years.

Figure 2.5b   Investment ratio and GDP growth, 1980–90

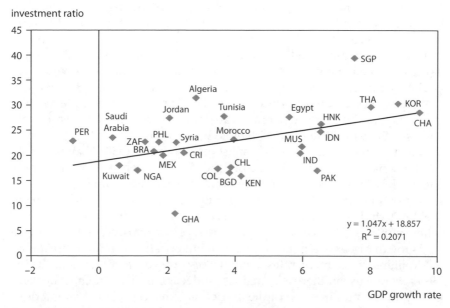

Source: World Bank, *World Development Indicators*, various years.

Figure 2.5c   Investment ratio and GDP growth, 1990–2000

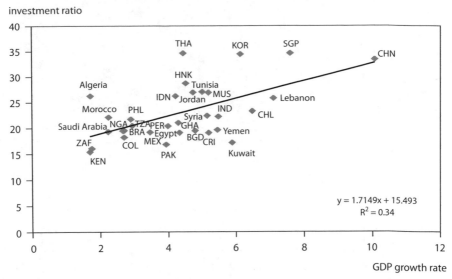

Source: World Bank, *World Development Indicators*, various years.

line. Morocco, Egypt, Tunisia, Syria, and Saudi Arabia fall into this group. Saudi Arabia in particular exhibited extraordinary performance, achieving 10 percent growth with a relatively low investment to GDP ratio. At the other extreme, even in a boom, Algeria had Soviet-style outcomes, very high investment not accompanied by spectacular growth. The only country in the graph with a similar (though somewhat lower) investment ratio, Singapore, achieved a growth rate of 10 percent compared with Algeria's 6 percent. Singapore's rate also led to a much higher growth in per capita income given its slower population growth rate. Though obviously per capita income growth differs from GDP growth, the simple relation suggests that the oil price boom decade was accompanied by reasonably successful deployment of considerable investment.

However, the picture changed substantially in the 1980–2000 period. In the 1980s many countries outside of East Asia experienced slower growth. Clearly, low investment was not the source of poor economic performance in this period. Most of the Arab countries lie above the regression line in the 1980s, indicating lower gross average returns than those realized in other countries. The weakening performance was partly due to a drop in TFP growth discussed in the next section but certainly cannot be attributed to declining investment rates though these played a minor role. In the 1990s there was another twist, namely, a decline in investment ratios and GDP growth rates in some of the oil-rich nations, especially Saudi Arabia (figure 2.5c). At the same time some Arab countries such as Egypt and Tunisia achieved a growth rate greater than would be predicted from their investment ratio. The problems of the 1990–2000 period occur most clearly in several of the oil-rich countries. Algeria and Saudi Arabia invested 40 and 19 percent of GDP, respectively, yet realized very little growth. In Algeria there were sufficiently small returns so that per capita income was declining. Such low gross returns from investment are unusual though some Communist countries such as Cuba and North Korea have had similar experience. The ICORs shown in these figures belie the assertions often made of Arab exceptionalism. Performance of Arab countries, excluding oil-rich ones, was not notably worse (or better) than other countries or regions. Other countries had either lower investment rates or lower gross returns. Indeed in the 1990s, Egypt had an investment-growth performance similar to Mexico despite the latter's benefiting from the newly signed North American Free Trade Agreement, partly offset by the peso crisis of 1994–95.

Although figures 2.5a, 2.5b, and 2.5c provide a gross picture, it is necessary to consider more focused measures that take account simultaneously of the growth in the labor force and TFP rather than the simple ICOR relation shown for expository purposes.

Sources of Differences in Growth Rates

In the previous section, we looked at the simple relation between the investment to GDP ratio and GDP growth rate to determine whether low investment has been the key issue for a large sample of countries. In this section we examine TFP, which measures the growth in production after the growth of capital and labor inputs are taken into account. It is essentially a measure of growing efficiency of resource use. TFP estimates by Collins and Bosworth (1996) and Bosworth and Collins (2003) for a handful of Middle Eastern countries imply that over the 1960–73 period (i.e., before the run-up in oil prices), they achieved similar TFP growth rates to other developing countries, registering modest positive TFP growth prior to 1973, and like other developing countries turning slightly negative (–0.1 percent) afterward (i.e., after the first oil shock and the possible onset of "Dutch disease" and, more plausibly, the economic and political challenges associated with the need to allocate the massive oil-derived windfall). The impression one gets is of countries that had done a reasonable job of mobilizing labor and capital, developed human capital from a low base, achieved a modicum of technological efficiency up until a turning point roughly a generation ago, and stagnated afterward.

One reason the preceding section focused on the investment-growth relationship is because it is difficult to measure both labor force and TFP. All recent measures of TFP growth have used labor force rather than employment or total hours. However, the labor force is subject to error, e.g., calculating the total employment in rural activities and the urban informal sector. This difficulty is compounded when neither unemployment rates nor hours are available with any precision. And as is well known the measures of constant price capital contain a considerable degree of arbitrariness. Moreover, TFP is calculated as a residual from a posited aggregate production function relationship and hence specific estimates are dependent on the form of the assumed production function. Thus, the TFP growth calculations for all nations need to be taken with caution.

Bosworth and Collins (2003) present systematic estimates of TFP growth for a large number of countries, based on growth accounting.[15] They have attempted to use consistent data and utilize an identical assumed international production function. Of the countries of interest in this book, they undertake calculations for five—namely, Algeria, Egypt, Jordan, Morocco, and Tunisia. Data for Kuwait, Saudi Arabia, and Syria and others are not available. Their calculations for these and other countries and regions are graphically represented in figures 2.6a, 2.6b, and 2.6c.[16]

The data are broadly consistent with the implications of the simple investment-to-GDP ratio/GDP growth rate graphs. Egypt and Tunisia (and Morocco to a lesser extent) have realized sustained growth output per worker and only a rare decade of declining TFP. In contrast, Algeria and Jordan experienced two decades of negative growth in output per worker. In Algeria both negative TFP growth and a declining capital intensity contributed to the downturn whereas in Jordan a decrease in capital intensity played some role, but the decline was due mainly to negative TFP growth rates. Despite Algeria's high investment rates, its labor force growth of 3.7 percent in these decades offset it. As seen in chapter 4, the rapid labor force growth of nations like Algeria will be a principal source of the problems facing many of the Arab nations.

As shown in earlier studies (for example, Easterly et al. 1993), there is very little stability across decades, in the case of the Arab countries as well. Jordan was the leader in the 1970s in both growth in per worker

---

15. TFP estimates using growth accounting have a number of limitations compared with econometric estimates of production functions (Nelson and Pack 1999, Pack 2001). However, growth accounting estimates provide notional orders of magnitude and are unlikely to have systematic biases that would reverse the findings of econometric estimates.

16. In addition to the TFP growth rates assuming that growth in physical capital is the only other source of growth, Bosworth and Collins (2003) also calculate one that allows for human capital, but it is more problematic in our context as identical international elasticities of output with respect to human capital are employed to calculate its contribution to growth in output per worker. In the Arab countries the measure they employ, whether years of education or one using wage information, is widely viewed as a weak proxy for labor force quality due to the declining quality of education (UNDP 2003 and Richards and Waterbury 1996 for detailed discussions). Thus, their narrower measure, which allows only for the growth of physical capital, is arguably more informative.

Figure 2.6a   Accounting for economic growth, 1970–80

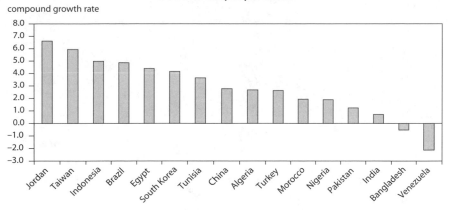

Growth in output per worker

compound growth rate

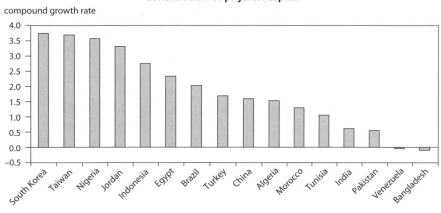

Contribution of physical capital

compound growth rate

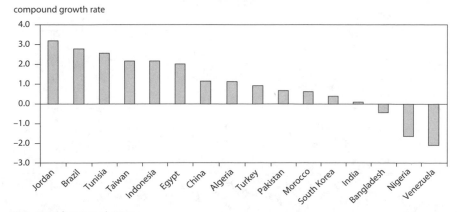

Contribution of TFP

compound growth rate

TFP = total factor productivity

Source: Bosworth and Collins (2003).

Figure 2.6b Accounting for economic growth, 1980–90

Growth in output per worker

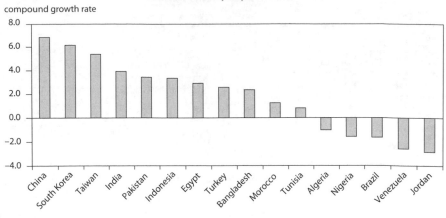

Contribution of physical capital

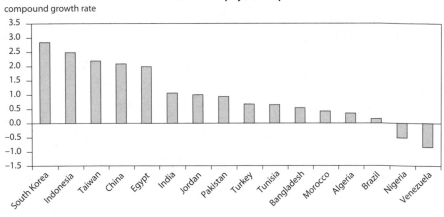

Contribution of TFP

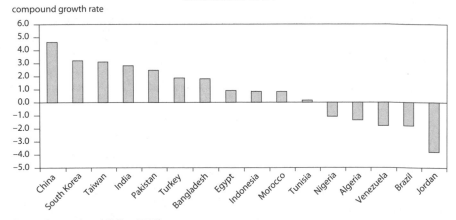

Source: Bosworth and Collins (2003).

Figure 2.6c   Accounting for economic growth, 1990–2000

Growth in output per worker

compound growth rate

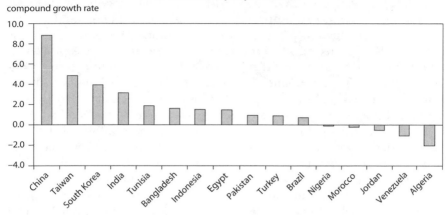

Contribution of physical capital

compound growth rate

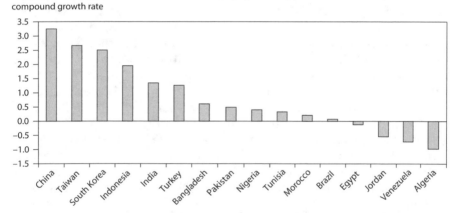

Contribution of TFP

compound growth rate

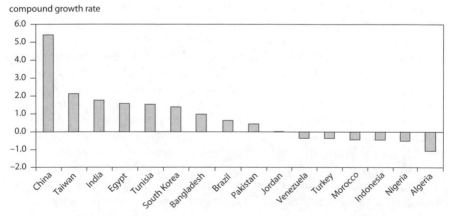

Source: Bosworth and Collins (2003).

income and in TFP and was at the bottom in the 1980s. As can be seen in the figures, the 1980s witnessed much slower growth than the preceding decade. However, in much of the world there was a rebound in the 1990s as various policies were improved and the United States (and China) grew rapidly, propelling a boom in the international economy despite the Asian crisis that affected a few countries from 1997 to 1999. Despite widespread views that Egypt and Tunisia are authoritarian and ossified economies, their TFP performance in the 1990s was among the best in the entire group. Journalistic and popular views are not supported by systematic studies—they are too anecdotal and don't easily generalize.

In the countries with low TFP growth, one contributory factor may have been the very high youth dependency ratio across the region during this period. Some empirical support exists for the notion that a high youth age dependency ratio may depress the growth of both income and TFP (Kögel 2004). The argument is that large numbers of children depress aggregate household saving and, in the presence of international capital market imperfections, national saving. The result is less investment and thus lower capital-embodied technical change, which is not explicitly allowed for in the Bosworth-Collins calculations but instead is manifested as slower measured TFP growth. Yet this cannot be the whole story as Algeria with high investment had low TFP growth. Several observations stem from these graphs. The Arab economies were not very different from other countries or regions in the 1970s, but there was a significant decline, particularly in TFP growth rates in the 1980s and 1990s. In the 1990s, the decline in the rate of growth of capital per worker was an important source of the slowdown in the growth of income per worker despite the still relatively high investment rate shown in figures 2.6a, 2.6b, and 2.6c. This reflected the rapid growth of the labor force in most countries. This trend, which is likely to continue, is particularly problematic, as seen in chapter 4.

Persistent slow TFP growth presents a substantial problem. If productivity growth could be accelerated, greater output growth could be obtained with a given deployment of resources. An acceleration of productivity growth also implies that a given level of growth of real income per capita could be achieved with lower investment-GDP ratios, resulting in less immediate dissatisfaction compared with one in which short-term consumption is compressed. Given the perception of widespread dissatisfaction with economic growth, the additional consumption would be intrinsically important to households and might increase the latitude of governments to pursue politically risky reforms. Finally, as shown in chapter 4, given the need to absorb substantial growth in the labor force in most countries, TFP growth could partly offset the negative effect on real income growth as large amounts of new investment are devoted to equipping new labor force members with sufficient capital so they can be productively absorbed.

Conclusion

The disillusionment in parts of the Arab world partly stems from the perception of stagnating prospects, rooted in a modest decline in *relative* prosperity though absolute living standards have been rising. Falling behind was not preordained as demonstrated by the disparate experiences of other nations. The acceleration of India's economic growth since the early 1980s, for example, demonstrates that countries are not doomed by either nature or irreversible policies to low income growth rates in perpetuity. On the other hand, Argentina, which in 1940 had an income per capita that was 63 percent of the US level, has fallen behind steadily since, despite being very well endowed with natural resources and possessing a highly educated population (Maddison 2003). Argentina's politically derived dysfunctional economy illustrates that the constraints imposed by the latent threat of political upheaval often used to explain the absence of thoroughgoing reform in many Arab countries may not be all that different from political pressures faced elsewhere.

The success and failure of these and other countries can shed light on the problems of a country like Egypt and perhaps lead to insights about whether Egypt or another Arab country's problems reflect their Islamic legacy or standard interest group politics. Too often analysts conclude, without sufficient attention to detail and with a paucity of international perspective, that in Arab countries it is solely the former, and nothing can be done. If, on the contrary, Egypt's problems are not all that different from those posed by the popularity of dirigiste policies during India's three decades after independence, a more optimistic scenario for the future can be envisioned. The same holds for the state-dominated economy of Algeria. India's remarkable turnaround that began under Prime Minister Rajiv Gandhi in the 1980s and accelerated in the early 1990s suggests that concluding that all is hopeless is premature. Similarly, some of the experience of the transition economies of Eastern Europe is germane, though their experience offers some caution as discussed in chapter 7. But before that we examine how changes in incomes in the Arab countries have actually translated into changes in living standards in the region.

3

Welfare, Happiness, and Discontent

Many observers caution that the economic growth measures presented in the previous chapter do not provide a sufficiently informed picture of the welfare of the population. Increases in real per capita income may not diffuse to all members of the population. Income inequality could be large or growing, and health and education levels may deteriorate or improve slowly, leading to growing dissatisfaction despite the improving aggregate economic data. Thus, in this chapter we examine many social indicators. We find that most of the measures of welfare show a sustained improvement in the Arab countries. While it is possible to parse the indicators and find shortcomings in achievement in one area or another, the same is true for all nations—the overall picture indicates considerable improvement over time in social performance of the Arab countries and in their levels relative to other nations.

Yet these social improvements have not assuaged the unusually high levels of dissatisfaction among Arab populations. For example, in the very influential *Arab Human Development Report 2002* (UNDP 2002), written by a group of well-known Arab intellectuals, an early subsection is titled "Bridled Minds, Shackled Potential," a phrase that aptly summarizes the main message of the report. This typical expression of widespread disappointment at the lack of political and cultural progress may well have spilled over and adversely affected the perception and evaluation of the actual economic and social performance documented in this and the preceding chapters. Indeed, one of the dilemmas facing any analysis of the Arab economies is the considerable improvement in both material consumption and social indicators over the last three decades and the current expression of deep discontent that is so widespread.[1] Rapid urbanization, by diminishing the social networks and fabric of life in rural areas, may have inevitably led to a depth of unhappiness that cannot by its nature be ameliorated by the improved conditions reported in this chapter. Such phenomena are widely reported for Europe during various periods of rapid social change (Hill 1967). Obviously other multiple potential sources of discontent exist, and we argue in the succeeding chapters that they are relevant to the region's economic development. Popular discontent may reinforce the reluctance of authoritarian governments to liberalize, fearing unmanageable social and political mobilization if repression is eased. This observation may be particularly true where much of the political opposition has religious color, as is the case in the Middle East. From an economic standpoint, such deep political uncertainty heightens risk and deters both local and foreign investors. In the extreme, such dissatisfaction may manifest itself in terrorism directed at local or foreign targets.

Social Indicators

Income and productivity discussed in chapter 2 involve conceptual abstractions. One cannot eat dollars or dinars. Although income establishes the potential of the economy to enhance well-being, consideration of more basic indicators of the quality of life may be revealing if one wants to assess the economy's performance. Indeed, over the past half century it appears that for some of the things that one cares most about—life expectancy, infant mortality, literacy, and gender equality—both improvements and cross-country convergence have been considerably more robust than for income (Kenney 2005). The Middle East appears to be a particularly striking example of this phenomenon.

On many measures, the gains in social indicators are astonishing. Life expectancy has risen by more than 20 years in most countries of the region (figure 3.1), with life expectancy in Kuwait (77), for example, exceeding that achieved in comparators such as Venezuela (74) and virtually equaling that exhibited in the United States (UNDP 2004a). Life expectancy of females in Saudi Arabia increased by 12 years over the period 1980–2000 and by 11 years for males. In both historic and international perspectives, such increases are extraordinary. In the 19th and early 20th centuries, similar increases in life expectancy took a half century or more. Life expectancy in the typically endowed Arab countries (70 years in 2004) is in the same league as other normally endowed comparators and has surpassed that achieved in the developing countries of East and South Asia (66 years) by

---

1. Farrukh Iqbal (2006) documents the Middle East and North Africa's (MENA) very good performance in many social dimensions compared with other regions but doesn't address the dissonance between these achievements and the widespread malaise.

Figure 3.1   Life expectancy, 1960–2004

years

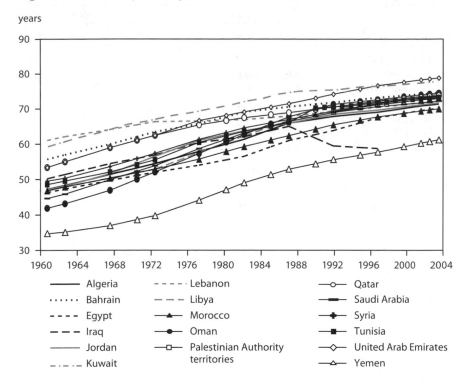

Note: Life expectancy at birth. Actual data availability varies. Data between tick marks linearly interpolated.

Source: World Bank, *World Development Indicators*, May 2006.

a noticeable margin (table 3.1). This improvement has been accompanied by increases in the female-male differential, suggesting that women are benefiting fully from development (figure 3.2).

One reason for the increase in life expectancy is that the children of the Middle East are getting an increasingly good start in life: Infant mortality is down dramatically in most countries (figure 3.3), with performance in Kuwait (9 per 1,000) and some of the smaller oil-producing states approaching that of the United States (7) and that in Saudi Arabia (23) exceeding by a large margin performance in comparators Botswana (80) and Nigeria (110) and approximating Venezuela (19).[2] Similarly, the results on this measure for the region's non–oil based economies generally equal or exceed the relevant comparators from outside the region. Infant mortality while still greater in 2000 than in Latin America or East Asia fell more than

_____

2. Declines in infant mortality translate into increased life expectancy, but the former does not completely explain the growth in the latter.

Table 3.1   Life expectancy at birth, 1982 and 2004 (years)

	1982			2004		
Region	Total	Female	Male	Total	Female	Male
Normally endowed Middle East	61	62	59	70	72	69
East Asia and Pacific	60	62	59	66	68	64
Latin America and Caribbean	66	68	63	71	74	69
South Asia	53	54	53	66	67	65
Sub-Saharan Africa	50	52	48	48	49	48
OECD	75	78	71	79	82	76

OECD = Organization for Economic Cooperation and Development

Source: World Bank, *World Development Indicators,* May 10, 2006.

Figure 3.2   Difference between female and male life expectancy, 1960–2004

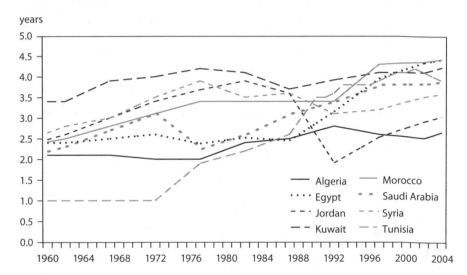

Note: Calculated as excess of female over male life expectancy.

Source: World Bank, *World Development Indicators,* 2004, April 2006.

in any other region, from 73 to 38 for all of the Middle Eastern countries. In poorer countries such as Egypt, this improvement was even greater. Infant mortality in Egypt fell by two-thirds in the two decades, and its level was comparable to that of Indonesia, a considerably richer nation, by the end of the period. Saudi infant mortality was, however, above that in Latin American nations despite its considerably higher income per capita

Figure 3.3 Infant mortality rate, 1960–2004

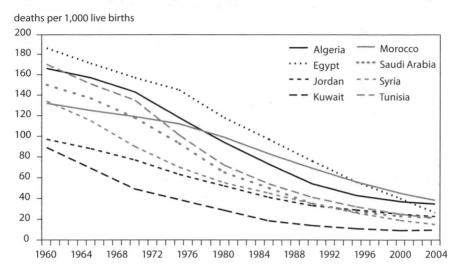

deaths per 1,000 live births

Source: World Bank, *World Development Indicators*, 2004, April 2006.

in terms of purchasing power parity. In most countries the fall in infant mortality has been accompanied by a decline in maternal mortality as well, with the achievements in 2000 in Kuwait (5 per 100,000) and some of the smaller oil producers actually exceeding that in the United States (8), while Saudi Arabia (23) surpassed Venezuela (60) and the other resource-rich comparators by a large margin (table 3.2). The performance of countries such as Tunisia and Morocco is in the same league as most other similarly endowed comparators, the better-performing Egypt (84) exceeds all other comparators with the exception of socialist China (53), and Jordan (41) exhibits the best performance of all.[3]

---

3. Iraq is an exception in this regard. According to the UN Development Program (UNDP), the rate of infant mortality rose steadily from approximately 22 per 1,000 in 1988 (the first year that they could construct direct, as opposed to indirect, estimates), to 33 in 2003—well below speculative pre–second Gulf War estimates in excess of 100. The infant mortality figure was highly politically sensitive, since a high figure, ascribed to the economic sanctions regime that was imposed after the first Gulf War, could be used as an argument for sanctions removal (i.e., sanctions had "killed one million Iraqi babies"). Indeed, in addition to doing secondary checks to reaffirm the accuracy of the survey estimate, the survey's authors express surprise that the infant mortality rate did not spike after the imposition of sanctions but instead continued its steady climb, which had begun at least as early as 1988. The 2004 UNDP survey debunks the estimates of extraordinarily high levels of infant mortality in sanctions-era Iraq (see UNDP 2004c for secondary literature citations) and by showing that the trend was rising prior to the first Gulf War also supports the notion that the Iraqi decline began with the Iran war, if not earlier.

Table 3.2   Maternal mortality, 1990, 1995, and 2000
(per 100,000 live births)

Country	1990	1995	2000
Bahrain	n.a.	n.a.	28[a]
Egypt	170[b]	170[b]	84[b]
Jordan	n.a.	41[b]	41[b]
Kuwait	n.a.	25[c]	5[a]
Morocco	610[d]	390[d]	220[d]
Qatar	n.a.	41[c]	7[a]
Saudi Arabia	n.a.	23[b]	23[b]
Syria	180[b]	n.a.	n.a.
Tunisia	n.a.	70[b]	120[c]
Yemen	n.a.	850[d]	570[d]

n.a. = not available

a. Data derived from vital registration: countries with good death registration and good attribution of cause of death.

b. Data derived from the Reproductive Age Mortality Study (RAMOS). This method involves identifying and investigating the causes of all deaths of women of reproductive age.

c. Data derived from vital registration: countries with good death registration but uncertain attribution of cause of death.

d. Data derived from the direct sisterhood method adjusted estimates. The direct sisterhood method is a variant of the sisterhood method— a survey-based technique that obtains information by interviewing respondents on the survival of all their adult sisters.

Source: United Nations Statistical Division, 2003.

These trends continue into childhood. There has been an astonishing rise in childhood immunization, which is now virtually universal (figures 3.4a and 3.4b). The data are fragmentary, but childhood nutritional status appears to have improved in most countries though the rate of improvement perhaps slackened in the 1990s, possibly reflecting the lack of robust economic growth during this period (table 3.3). In most Arab countries access to improved water supplies also increased modestly during the 1990s. As a result of these improvements, the death rate among children five years and younger is down considerably, mirroring the decline in infant mortality.

A major issue in developing countries is the extent to which aggregate economic growth is accompanied by large inequality of income limiting the gains from such growth to lower income groups. As reported in table 3.4, setting aside the oil producers, contemporary income inequality in the Middle East as measured by Gini coefficients is comparable to other developing countries; if one looks at the ratio of the top fifth to the bottom fifth, the region (6) is comparable to East Asia (8) and South Asia (5) and well below Africa (15) and Latin America (18). Income equality measured by

Figure 3.4a   Childhood immunization, normally endowed countries, 1980–2004

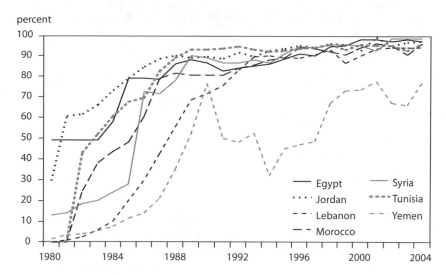

Note: Average of percent of children aged 12 to 23 months immunized against DPT and measles.

Source: World Bank, *World Development Indicators*, 2004, April 2006.

Figure 3.4b   Childhood immunization, resource-rich countries, 1980–2004

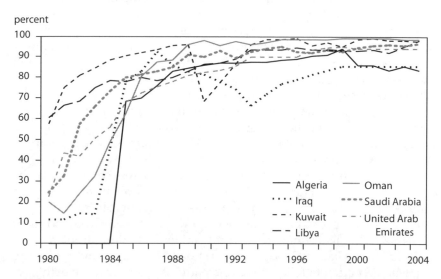

Note: Average of percent of children aged 12 to 23 months immunized against DPT and measles.

Source: World Bank, *World Development Indicators*, 2004.

Table 3.3   Childhood nutritional status
(percent share of underweight and stunted children)

Country	1975–79	1980–84	1985–89	1990–94	1995–99	2000–2003
Algeria	n.a.	n.a.	11	14	16	13
Egypt	27	n.a.	22	19	19	12
Jordan	n.a.	n.a.	n.a.	11	6	n.a.
Morocco	n.a.	n.a.	19	17	16	n.a.
Tunisia	30	n.a.	n.a.	n.a.	11	8
Yemen	57	32	n.a.	38	45	n.a.

n.a. = not available

Note: Average of data available for period.

Source: World Bank, World Development Indicators, 2004.

Gini coefficients is much better in the Middle East than the Latin American and African countries and similar to many of the Asian countries, except Taiwan. The Asian benchmark is notable as many analysts have argued that one source of strength in the East Asian countries was their relatively equal distribution, which gave the governments greater legitimacy. Policymakers were thus enabled to respond flexibly to crises as citizens felt that both growth and the occasional belt tightening necessary in the face of external shocks such as the oil price increase of the 1970s were shared equitably (World Bank 1993, chapter 5). The relatively good distribution of income is even more striking when comparing the income ratio of the top to bottom fifths—the Middle Eastern ratios are, for example, roughly a quarter of those in Latin America.

Concentrating on absolute poverty—the percentage of population below either $1 or $2 per day of income (measured at purchasing power parity)—rather than relative inequality within each country, the Arab countries are among the best in the developing world, comparable to some of the supersuccessful Asian countries (table 3.5). Using $2 per day as the poverty line, Morocco has roughly a quarter the poverty rate of Indonesia, which has been one of the fastest growing economies in the developing world and whose per capita income in 2000 was almost that of Morocco (table 2.6). Only Yemen exhibits typical levels of Third World poverty.

One aspect of the evolution of income inequality across countries may be of particular interest, namely the effect of land reform in resource-poor countries. After the expulsion of Japanese colonialists, neither the Taiwanese government of Chiang Kai-shek nor the South Korean government of Syngman Rhee had strong ties to rural landlords. Both confronted Communist rivals that had initiated land reforms, and both were under pressure from their US patron to follow the same path. As a consequence both governments undertook comprehensive land reforms that boosted agricultural productivity and contributed to reducing income and wealth (land) in-

Table 3.4   Gini coefficients measuring income inequality

Country	1960 Income	1960 Land	1970	1980	1990	2000
Middle East						
Algeria	n.a.	n.a.	n.a.	n.a.	39	35
Egypt	42	67	40	38	32	29
Jordan	n.a.	n.a.	n.a.	41	41	36
Lebanon	n.a.	n.a.	n.a.	55	n.a.	n.a.
Morocco	n.a.	n.a.	n.a.	39	39	40
Tunisia	n.a.	n.a.	42	43	40	42
Yemen	n.a.	n.a.	n.a.	n.a.	n.a.	33
High-performing comparators						
South Korea	32	39	33	39	34	32
Taiwan	32	n.a.	29	28	31	32
Large comparators						
India	33	52	32	32	30	38
China	n.a.	n.a.	n.a.	32	35	40
Normally endowed comparators						
Bangladesh	38	n.a.	36	39	29	32
Brazil	53	85	58	58	60	61
Turkey	56	68	51	n.a.	44	40
Resource-rich comparators						
Botswana	n.a.	n.a.	n.a.	n.a.	63	n.a.
Indonesia	33	n.a.	31	36	33	30
Nigeria	n.a.	n.a.	n.a.	37	41	51
Venezuela	n.a.	n.a.	48	39	54	49

n.a. = not available

Sources: Land: Rodrik (1994); Income, 1960–90: Deininger and Squire (1996); World Bank, *World Development Indicators,* 2000.

equality (table 3.4).[4] For small labor-surplus economies, especially those taking advantage of access to international markets for manufactured exports, the long-run growth implications of boosting productivity in agriculture and facilitating the redeployment of labor to higher-productivity activities in the industrial sector can be profound (Kuznets 1966; Gollin, Parente, and Rogerson 2004).

---

4. Due to Taiwan's unusual political status, it is often omitted from standard data sources. Careful comparisons based on Taiwan's national sources indicate that broadly speaking, South Korea can represent Taiwan's experiences.

Table 3.5 Population below income poverty line (percent)

Country	Year	$1 a day	$2 a day	National poverty line
Middle East				
Algeria	1995	2.0	15.1	22.6
Egypt	2000	3.1	43.9	16.7
Jordan	2003	2.0	7.0	11.7
Morocco	1999	2.0	14.3	19
Tunisia	2000	2.0	6.6	7.6
Yemen	1998	15.7	45.2	41.8
High-performing comparators				
South Korea	1998	2.0	2.0	n.a.
Large comparators				
China	2003	16.6	46.7	4.6
India	2000	34.7	79.9	28.6
Normally endowed comparators				
Bangladesh	2000	36.0	82.8	49.8
Brazil	2003	7.5	21.2	22
Pakistan	2002	17.0	73.6	32.6
Turkey	2003	3.4	18.7	27
Resource-rich comparators				
Botswana	1993	23.5	50.1	
Indonesia	2002	7.5	52.4	27.1
Nigeria	2003	70.8	92.4	34.1
Venezuela	2000	8.3	27.6	n.a.
Memoranda:				
Middle East	2002	1.6	19.8	n.a.
East Asia	2002	11.6	40.7	n.a.
Latin America	2002	8.9	23.4	n.a.
South Asia	2002	31.1	77.8	n.a.
Sub-Saharan Africa	2002	44.0	74.9	n.a.

n.a. = not available

Note: Data are most recent available for the period 1990–2004. Regional averages correspond to World Bank definitions and refer to 2002.

Source: World Bank, *World Development Indicators*, May 2006.

Again, in this regard South Korea and Taiwan appear unique. Egypt is in the middle—more egalitarian than Brazil, in the same ballpark as India and Turkey, and probably more unequal than Indonesia. (On many indicators of interest, long historical time-series data are available only for Egypt, which may be interpreted as representative of at least some subset of the Arab countries.)

In the subsequent evolution of the income inequality measure, neither Egypt nor the other Arab countries for which data exist appear distinct

Figure 3.5 Gender gap in literacy, 1970–2004

percentage point

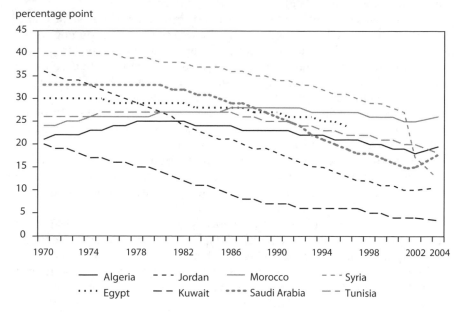

Note: Calculated as excess of male over female adult literacy rate.

Source: World Bank, *World Development Indicators*, 2004, May 2006.

(though admittedly the large oil producers would presumably display considerable inequality). Indeed, in the most recent period Egypt is the most egalitarian of the comparators identified, though probably not by a statistically significant margin. Farrukh Iqbal (2006) argues that the region experienced reductions in income inequality through the mid-1980s but that both the narrowing of inequality as well as the reduction of absolute poverty slowed after the decline in oil prices following the second oil shock.

Once they reach school age, most Arab children enter school, though the intake rates vary, with some countries such as Algeria having achieved universal education while others such as Saudi Arabia lag. Figure 3.5 shows a consistent decline in the gender literacy gap, with the difference in some countries falling more rapidly than that in others, underscoring the notion that both boys and girls share the fruits of economic development. Across the region, 9 girls entered primary school for every 10 boys, and at the secondary level the gap is even narrower, with 74 and 77 percent of girls and boys enrolled respectively. For the female population as a whole, women's average years of schooling increased from 0.5 in 1960 to 4.5 in 2000, and the average literacy rate rose from 17 to 53 percent over the same period (World Bank 2004a). However, there is evidence that conditional on the level of development and other factors, majority-Muslim countries continue to exhibit unusually large divergences in male-female education attainment ratios (Pryor 2006).

The increases in intake and educational duration have been steady, and improvements in educational attainment together with a demographic structure that implies a growing cohort of new entrants to the labor market means that the average number of years of education embodied in the labor force has been rising steadily (figures 2.3a and 2.3b). The share of Arab youth enrolled in tertiary education has risen steadily and now approximates that of its comparators, as does the share of these students graduating as scientists and engineers—a key to mastering technology (table 2.5). In some Middle Eastern countries the number of women at local universities exceeds the number of men, though this does not necessarily mean that more women are entering tertiary education—in some cases, this result may be explained by the men enrolling in universities abroad and not being captured in local enrollment data.[5]

It is important to understand the sources and durability of these gains and not simply to enumerate them. The question immediately arises as to what explains this apparent divergence between performance on income and social indicators, with the former varying and growing slowly and the latter on a continuous upward path.[6] Part of the story, documented by Charles Kenney (2005), is that there may be large payoffs to expenditures on basic health and education at low levels of income and attainment (i.e., these expenditures have a declining marginal product).[7] But this is not the whole story, as Kenney admits.

---

5. Again, Iraq is exceptional: For males, literacy peaked among the cohort born in the 1960s (in excess of 80 percent) and fell thereafter (UNDP 2004b, 2004c). The pattern is slightly different for females: Literacy trends upward from a lower base, peaking for the cohort born in 1980 and declining afterward. These declines accelerated after 1980: With the state's failure to rebuild schools destroyed in the Iran and Kuwait wars, or build new schools to reflect population growth and shifts, public schools were forced to operate triple shifts to accommodate excess demand. By 2003, when Saddam Hussein was removed from power, Iraq, which had once been the most literate of Arab societies, had the highest rate of illiteracy among the 15 to 24 age group of any Arab country. Educational attainment was actually higher among middle-aged Iraqis, who had completed their schooling before the 1979–80 turning point, than it was in the cohort entering the labor force.

6. The conundrum implicitly assumes that both income and social indicators are measured correctly. It is sometimes alleged that because of the existence of a large underground or informal economy, incomes in the Arab countries are underestimated, providing a possible explanation of the divergence between measured income growth and social indicators. But there is no reason to believe this phenomenon is quantitatively more significant than in other regions or that the relative size of the informal sector grew systematically over time or that the sector's per capita output grew more rapidly.

7. In the case of the Middle East, starting points were sufficiently low that it is plausible that these investments had high initial payoffs. We argue in chapter 5 that additional accumulation of educational capital is unlikely to have a high rate of return in the absence of new technology—education is complementary to new knowledge whether it is embodied in hardware or in intangible knowledge. The Arab countries have been conspicuously low recipients of such knowledge.

Given that the social indicators continued to improve even when growth rates slowed considerably after the peaking of oil prices in the early 1980s, it is possible that conscious tax-transfer-expenditure policies were undertaken, perhaps generating negative incentive effects and sacrificing growth, to improve social services and greater equality. But the careful documentation by Iqbal (2006) of the sources of social improvement generally does not identify such causal mechanisms, though targeted public expenditures, such as subsidized prices for staple foods, may have played a role, and there is some evidence of improved efficiency in the delivery of services (Page and van Gelder 2002, Iqbal 2006).

John M. Page (2003) and Richard Adams and Page (2003) posit two sources of the relative equality of incomes, namely the provision of public-sector employment and the impact of repatriated earnings, the former described as "a kind of blunt policy instrument for providing welfare employment to an ever-increasing proportion of the labor force." Page (2003) notes that the share of the central governments' wages in GDP was about 10 percent for all Middle East and North Africa (MENA) countries in contrast to 4.3 percent in Asia and 4.9 percent in Latin America and that it is the only region where the average public-sector wage exceeds that in the private sector. Whether public-sector employment limits inequality depends of course on where those employed in the public sector stand in the income distribution. If the typical employee is a high school or university graduate, the combination of employment and high (relative) wage may increase inequality and do little for those at the lower end of the distribution. Yet it is likely that at least some of those on the public payroll are lower-skilled and/or uneducated workers, and thus public employment will raise the income of at least some at the bottom.

Adams and Page (2003) conclude from cross-country regressions that the significant repatriated earnings that have flowed to MENA from the Gulf (reflecting the oil boom from 1973 through the mid-1980s) and the flow of emigrants to Western Europe from the Maghreb have had a significant effect on the poverty headcount. In the absence of actual household data on sources of income, this conclusion while plausible is suggestive but not dispositive.[8]

Yet even if further research using household data confirms that public employment and remittances were important in limiting poverty, looking forward is problematic with respect to both sustainability and possible negative effects in other dimensions.

The public sector is by all accounts quite inefficient and simultaneously receives a substantial percentage of investment funds. Thus, a given investment in it may lead to a lower growth rate of output than would have

---

8. Iqbal (2006) casts doubt on the impact of public employment on income distribution, noting that much of it accrues to the more highly educated, but no systematic assessment exists on the net effects of employment and taxes necessary to support it.

resulted from a better allocation of investment funds. Moreover, the cost is not only the more efficient allocations of investment that have been forgone but also the impact of any distortions caused by the taxes necessary to raise the funds. Assuming that the poor would have benefited from more rapid growth, their absolute incomes are lower than they could have been. Counterfactually, it is quite possible that still faster growth, with maintenance of initial inequality, would have more rapidly reduced absolute poverty, as it did in South Korea and Taiwan in the 1960s and 1970s (World Bank 1993). As Iqbal (2006) points out, the absolute number of poor in some of the Arab countries increased over this period, and several measures of poverty indicate a greater percentage of the population is at risk of falling into poverty.

The issue of sustainability arises in two ways: one actuarial, the other political. Given the stagnation of productivity and the demographic pressures of rising populations, the question arises as to whether growing public welfare expenditures can be maintained given political constraints on taxation and spending and financial-market curbs on borrowing. Such pressures are likely to intensify as the reduction of deaths from communicable diseases means that future improvements in health and life expectancy will increasingly revolve around addressing noncommunicable diseases, which are more expensive on average to treat (Iqbal 2006).

Nevertheless, even if such effects could be measured precisely and demonstrated, proponents of a public expenditure–based strategy might well argue that the tradeoff was worthwhile given the intrinsic value of the benefits to the poor in the short term and the greater political stability. Yet even if the pattern of public expenditure is financially sustainable in a technical sense, a deeper issue is whether in the context of stagnating productivity and job opportunities they contribute to a milieu of unfulfilled expectations, potentially raising the critical issue of political instability. Ironically, the expansion of educational opportunities and attainment documented earlier in the chapter and the heightened expectations that they bring may exacerbate such problems.

Reliance on remittances to attenuate poverty raises a similar set of concerns. Remittances may have the same effect as natural resources, causing "Dutch disease" exchange rate appreciation, thereby discouraging the expansion of potentially competitive labor-intensive tradable sectors, which might have generated jobs for the poor. Moreover, remittances depend at least in part on oil prices, and while a sustained price of $75 per barrel cannot be completely ruled out, it would be imprudent for resource-poor countries such as Egypt and Jordan to rely on it as an antipoverty strategy.

In sum, both public employment and remittances may have had a short-term positive impact on poverty but may have yielded lower long-run growth in income for the poor relative to alternative scenarios. This observation is particularly important given Iqbal's (2006) finding that absolute poverty in some Arab countries has increased. Going forward, the sustainability of such drivers is not obvious. As shown in chapter 4, two sources of financing, namely aid flows reflecting the geopolitical situation and diffusion of oil rents to nonoil producers, are less likely to provide the cushion that they have in the past. Public employment in the nonresource-rich countries is likely to stagnate, perhaps even decline. This will place more of a burden on private-sector employment growth.

Happiness

Given both improving social indicators, whatever their source, and growing real income per capita in many countries, purely material explanations of growing discontent are not sufficient. A large and growing literature on the determinants of "happiness" relies on correlations between subjective measures of happiness and measurable characteristics either at the household or national level.[9] While the studies can only establish correlation, not causality, a number of relatively robust findings in most of the reported results also accord with intuition.

As might be expected, happiness is correlated with health status and income at both the household and national levels. A higher level of household income or GDP per capita at the national level is associated with greater life satisfaction, but there are diminishing returns, with developing countries below the threshold at which diminishing returns set in. More rapid growth in GDP per capita, holding constant the level of per capita income, is also a source of greater happiness. Income inequality in Europe (but not the United States) diminishes satisfaction. Presumably the same result would be replicated in most less developed countries (where household survey evidence does not exist) because of the absence of the extensive European-style social welfare system on the one hand and the absence of the immigrant experience–derived American optimism of social mobility on the other. It is exceedingly difficult to get a handle on how these achievements translate into introspective notions of satisfaction that have been studied in the "happiness" literature. The World Values Survey, which conducts global opinion polls on a wide range of attitudes and publishes an index of subjective well-being derived from responses to two questions, one asking respondents to assess their personal happiness and another to score their life satisfaction (table 3.6). Across the 84-country sample, there is a correlation between national scores on subjective assessments of well-being and per capita income, but it is far from perfect. Controlling for income, Latin Americans appear to be unusually happy, the morose Argentine tango being offset by the happiness of the Brazilian samba. Puerto Ricans express the greatest sense of personal well-being in the sample, followed by Mexi-

---

9. See Layard (2005) for a nontechnical introduction. Donovan, Halpern, and Sargeant (2003) is a good survey of the academic literature. See also Helliwell (2005).

Table 3.6   Subjective self-assessment of well-being, 2004 (percentile rank)

Country	Rank
Middle East	
Algeria	68
Egypt	71
Jordan	74
Kuwait	n.a.
Morocco	66
Saudi Arabia	28
Syria	n.a.
Tunisia	n.a.
High-performing comparators	
South Korea	60
Taiwan	39
Large comparators	
China	59
India	82
Normally endowed comparators	
Bangladesh	70
Brazil	41
Pakistan	85
Turkey	63
Resource-rich comparators	
Botswana	n.a.
Indonesia	100
Nigeria	23
Venezuela	16

n.a. = not available

Note: Larger number indicates lower subjective well-being.
Sample: n = 84.

Source: World Values Survey, 2004.

cans. Residents of former Communist countries (especially parts of the former Soviet Union) are unusually dissatisfied, which is easily explained by declines in real income and some social indices such as health. There is some evidence that Muslims are unusually happy, after controlling for their countries' levels of development and other factors (Pryor 2006). Nevertheless, in absolute terms, the rank of several Muslim-majority countries such as Indonesia and Pakistan included in table 3.6 is typically low.

In these subjective well-being rankings, most of the Arab countries surveyed fall into the category labeled "medium-low," bunching around the 70th percentile in the ranking. The one exception is Saudi Arabia (28th percentile), falling into the category "medium-high." The Saudi score, together with those of Venezuela (16th percentile) and Nigeria (23rd percentile), might lead one to conclude that having oil may contribute to a sense of personal well-being—rentiers are the happiest of campers. A more likely explanation is that oil contributes to income, which in turn underpins a subjective sense of well-being. However, the happiness studies find that even more than income, unemployment is a major determinant of unhappiness. Besides the obvious characteristic that it enables individuals to support themselves and their families, employment provides a source of self-respect and for many an important network of supportive social relations. Though the happiness studies find that those who are unemployed but living in a milieu in which unemployment is widespread are not particularly dissatisfied, such studies have largely been carried out in the welfare-oriented societies in Western Europe that guarantee substantial income and other benefits for the unemployed, conditions that do not hold in the Middle East. Thus, a reasonable but not proven conjecture is that unemployment is a potent source of dissatisfaction even when it is a widespread economic characteristic.

Although systematic unemployment data are not available, the data that do exist suggest Arab unemployment rates are greater than in regions other than sub-Saharan Africa (table 3.7), and some alternative sources yield much higher estimates (Richards 2001, table 1). It is necessary to be cautious about such data as it has long been noted that open unemployment in societies that do not provide social insurance may reflect search for unemployment by those with higher family incomes or greater education who will not settle for low-income or low-status jobs that they could easily obtain. (Indeed, Richards [2001, 28] asserts that unemployment in Jordan is a "monotonically rising function of education.") These data are consistent with the observations of regional specialists who argue that awareness obtained through immigrant networks of European labor markets creates expectations about wages and working conditions relative to productivity that prices Middle Eastern workers out of the world market (Henry and Springborg 2001).

Data on real wages reinforce this impression of relatively unfavorable labor-market outcomes (table 3.8). Again the data are not ideal: They are limited to the manufacturing sector, which is small in most Middle Eastern countries, yet may be indicative of trends in urban labor markets more broadly. The data show that real wages have at best stagnated since 1980, mirroring the performance of aggregate productivity.

A second contributor to happiness, which may be more important than income, is "good government," encompassing notions of competence in the delivery of services as well as accountability (Helliwell and Huang 2006). At lower levels of income, subjective assessment of satisfaction is more highly correlated with governmental effectiveness, regulatory quality, rule of law, and control of corruption, and as income rises, voice and

Table 3.7   Unemployment (percent)

Country	1980–90	1990–2000	2000–2004
Middle East			
Algeria	18.4	24.4	28.5
Egypt	6.3	9.4	9.9
Jordan	n.a.	14.4	13.2
Kuwait	n.a.	n.a.	n.a.
Lebanon	n.a.	8.6	n.a.
Morocco	15.2	17.0	12.1
Saudi Arabia	n.a.	4.5	4.8
Syria	n.a.	n.a.	11.5
Tunisia	15.3	15.7	15.0
Yemen	n.a.	11.5	n.a.
High-performing comparators			
South Korea	3.7	3.4	3.6
Taiwan	2.0	2.4	4.4
Large comparators			
China	2.6	2.8	3.6
India	n.a.	3.1	4.3
Normally endowed comparators			
Bangladesh	0.9	2.9	3.3
Brazil	3.7	6.9	9.4
Pakistan	3.5	5.4	7.6
Turkey	10.2	7.7	9.2
Resource-rich comparators			
Botswana	25.3	18.6	17.2
Indonesia	3.0	6.1	8.6
Nigeria	n.a.	16.9	n.a.
Venezuela	9.4	10.6	14.9
Memoranda:			
Middle East	14.3	15.4	13.9
OECD	7.7	8.1	6.6
East Asia and Pacific	4.4	4.2	5.0
Latin America and Caribbean	10.4	10.2	9.8
South Asia	6.4	7.1	6.9
Sub-Saharan Africa	10.8	12.5	14.9

Note: Table shows average of available data. Taiwan is not included in regional averages.

Sources: World Bank, *World Development Indicators*, May 2006; Taiwan: *Taiwan Statistical Databook*, 2005.

stability come to the fore. It may well be that in these statistical correlations with happiness, the governance indicators are acting as proxies for a broader set of societal institutions and speak to broader and more diffuse notions of belonging and inclusion than the simple functioning government per se. Thus, unhappiness might be associated with rapid transi-

Table 3.8   Compound growth rate of real manufacturing-sector wages
(percent)

Country	1970–80	1980–90	1990–98
Middle East			
Algeria	1.9	−5.8	−10.9
Egypt	1.0	1.1	−2.7
Jordan	9.5	−8.8	−1.2
Kuwait	7.3	−1.9	2.9
Lebanon	n.a.	n.a.	n.a.
Morocco	n.a.	−7.4	−0.2
Saudi Arabia	n.a.	−2.1	n.a.
Syria	4.0	3.8	6.5
Tunisia	n.a.	n.a.	n.a.
Yemen	n.a.	n.a.	n.a.
Memoranda:[a]			
Middle East	4.8	−3.0	−0.9
OECD	6.6	1.4	−0.6
East Asia	5.9	2.1	4.9
Latin America	3.6	−6.4	2.3
South Asia	0.8	−1.9	−2.4
Sub-Saharan Africa	3.9	−7.7	−3.1

n.a. = not available

a. Samples vary across decadal growth rates due to data availability.

Source: Albuquerque, Loayza, and Servén (2005).

tions from agrarian to urban residence and the attenuation of the social anchor provided by rural life, and weakness of urban institutions in low-income countries in coping with this phenomenon. This conjecture is consistent with developments within the Middle East, but one cannot definitely say so on the basis of the evidence.

In this connection Eli Berman and Laurence R. Iannaccone (2005) argue that the social networks created by religious sects may facilitate economic life in a variety of ways and can be interpreted as a rational collective response to a situation in which the government fails to provide public goods. This reasoning goes back to Adam Smith, who observed that membership in a religious sect may act as a reputational signaling device in regard to prospective employers, creditors, or trading counterparties and that the ability of sects to sanction miscreants could facilitate lending and other forms of exchange in environments where legal enforcement of contracts was prohibitively costly or unavailable. Unfortunately, the same characteristics such as intragroup cohesion that make religious sects efficient organs of social welfare can make them highly effective perpetrators of violence as well.

Whether the statistical correlations are interpreted broadly or narrowly, the political regimes of the Middle East as a group are distinctively authoritarian (figure 1.4), and as discussed in chapter 6 they do not score particularly well, at least in an absolute sense, on indicators of government effectiveness either. This suggests that discontent in the Middle East is comprehensible in terms of motives and norms observable elsewhere in the world. But it does not explain away the possibility that these may be unusually discontented populations.

In sum, money cannot buy happiness, though it helps. Employment, which is tightly bound to notions of worth and respect in one's own eyes and those of others, is even more important. And the quality of government, which may be a proxy for a broader set of social institutions, counts as well. The data presented at the beginning of this chapter and the previous chapter suggest that the Middle East as a whole has not done terribly with respect to income growth and has made impressive strides with respect to a broad set of social indicators. However, the data we have on employment and governance suggest that the region has not performed well in these dimensions, which are critically related to self-assessments of well-being and such subjective views may be understood by governments and limit their perceived potential flexibility in economic policymaking.

The unhappiness expressed by the term "bridled minds, shackled potential" may reflect a subjective sense of isolation, at least among the intellectuals despite the measurable gains in both income and the indicators discussed in this section. In all of the *Arab Human Development Reports*, there is an emphasis, perhaps exaggerated by intellectuals who travel extensively and are at home with the vast array of media and Internet access in the rich countries, on the paucity of Internet connections, nongovernment-controlled newspapers and broadcast media, and perhaps the absence of translations into Arabic of Western books and media. The *Arab Human Development Report 2002* notes, almost with anger, that more books are translated into Spanish in one year than have been translated into Arabic in a century. It is difficult to know whether such concerns of very well educated, and it must be said, relatively well-to-do individuals by local standards, are also shared by a broader segment of the population with much more immediate needs—better employment prospects, greater access to clean water, and quality education for their children. But even if the disillusion is not representative of those with limited voice, such views are inevitably of concern to reigning governments, as they establish the climate of discourse for the entire society and have the potential to foment considerable political unrest.

Discontent

In the extreme, discontent may manifest itself in terrorism. Beyond the obvious toll on human life, we argue that terrorism may have significant economic effects as well, largely by increasing risk and deterring investment. Yet some commentators seeking to explain the origins of terrorism reverse this causality, alleging that terrorism is the weapon of the dispossessed and that poverty causes terrorism. For example, James D. Wolfensohn, former president of the World Bank, argued that "it is necessary for rich countries to acknowledge that poverty is a serious issue, which is close to us, especially after the September 11 events . . . and poverty is related to terrorism. . . . One of the causes of terrorism is poverty in the sense that it creates an environment in which terrorism can flourish. And so one of the things that we hope for is that we can give people hope by reducing poverty" (*La Republica*, May 24, 2003). And the then-chairman of the US Senate's Foreign Relations Committee, Richard Lugar, recommended a special fund to improve economic conditions in the Middle East. "By so doing, it [the fund] can become a catalyst for positive change throughout the region, where millions of people suffer from grinding poverty and hopelessness. This has led some young people to terrorism and to express their despair by lashing out at others more fortunate. At the extreme, some have chosen suicidal missions" (Lugar 2004).

If one interprets terrorism, rooted in discontent, as an asymmetric tactical response by challengers to the political order, then economic performance including growth, income distribution, and employment should all play a role as should the quality of government and other factors. The link between poverty and terrorism is not simple (Krueger and Maleckova 2002, Laquer 2003, Abadie 2006). If it were, Kenya and Tanzania would have many homegrown terrorists rather than imported ones; India, with 400 million people living on less than $1 per day, would be exporting terrorism rather than software; and Haitian suicide bombers would make the evening news nightly.

If there is any systematic explanation for large-scale, sustained terrorist campaigns, it appears to be a tactical response by political challengers associated with the stresses of transition from rural traditional societies to urban industrial societies in the presence of weak economic and political institutions. Perhaps the best historical precedent for the current situation in the Middle East is the experience of Eastern and Southern Europe with the anarchists from their rise following the largely failed liberal revolutions of 1848 until their effective liquidation roughly a century later in the Second World War and its antecedent conflict in Spain. As in the case of Islamist radicals today, the earlier European anarchists rejected the contemporary world as irredeemably corrupt, harkened back to an earlier utopia, and adopted nihilistic violence as a tactic to puncture the dominant system, which they regarded as poised for collapse (Bremer and Kasarda 2002).[10]

---

10. Not all Islamist political parties and movements are alike. Abdeslam Maghraoui (2006, 4), for example, provides the following typology: "Islamist" political parties and movements seek to legitimate or overturn a political order on the basis of their interpretation of Islamic principles. "Extremist" groups eschew nonviolence in the name of the principles of the pious ancestors (*al-salaf al-salih*) and literal interpretation of the Koran. "Moderate" parties and

Contemporary Arab countries, which arguably are laboring through this transition encumbered by weak institutions, are disproportionately afflicted by terrorism, both as a location of terrorist attacks and as a producer of terrorists (Richards and Waterbury 1996). Yet these communities appear to be in deep denial, at least with respect to *international* terrorist activities: A 2006 poll by the Pew Center found that majorities in Egypt and Jordan (and indeed majorities of Muslims worldwide) did not believe that Arabs carried out the 9/11 attacks (The Pew Global Attitudes Project 2006a).

Admittedly the oil-dependent economies experienced considerable declines in per capita income between the mid-1970s and 2000 (roughly 40 percent from its peak in the case of Saudi Arabia), and this decline in fortunes is correlated with (but may not entirely explain) feelings of disaffection and pessimism about the future in many Arab countries. It is not surprising that 15 of the 19 9/11 hijackers were Saudis. If this interpretation is correct, then the two-decade-long decline in the price of oil, and hence income, could have been accompanied by rising frustration and discontent over evaporating prospects. There is some evidence that this is indeed the case with respect to young men in Saudi Arabia, who at the time the poll was conducted (i.e., before the recent rise in oil prices), expressed discouragement not only with their own prospects relative to their parents' generation but also with their children's prospects relative to their own (Zogby 2002). That is, they foresaw a multigenerational period of decline. This pessimism and dissatisfaction was greatest among young, educated males and positively correlated with Internet usage. Of course, if real income growth is the principal driver behind these results, then a secular increase in the price of oil might assuage some of this discontent, and Middle Eastern–generated terrorism might attenuate.

Yet simple economic determinism cannot explain terrorism. The authoritarian nature of these societies and absence of effective political voice in governance, which are known to be important determinants of satisfaction, are key. The 20th century's first violent Islamist group grew out of Egypt's Muslim Brothers in the 1970s following repression by the government. Similarly in Algeria violent splinter groups, including the al Qaeda–affiliated Salafist Group for Preaching and Combat (Groupe Salafiste pour la Prédication et le Combat, or GSPC), emerged following the banning of

---

movements accept and apply human reason to Islamic principles, law, or precedents. They see no incompatibility between participation in the modern political process and Islamic values. Within these camps, theological variations and differing degrees of "extremism" and "moderation" are the products of local power relations. Amr Hamzawy (2005) provides a similar nomenclature using "militant" instead of "extremist." Many Muslims object to the description of "extremists," "militants, " or "radicals" as "fundamentalists"—from the perspective that adherence to fundamentals of Islam should be regarded as praiseworthy, not a term of opprobrium. Where the term "fundamentalist" appears in this book, it is meant to signal rigorous adherence to religious doctrine, not support for political violence.

the Islamic Salvation Front (Front Islamique du Salut, or FIS) after it had won elections in 1990 and 1991. A similar pattern of blockage followed by the formation of violent Islamist groups occurred in Morocco in the 1990s (Maghraoui 2006). Most obviously, the US-led involvement in Iraq may prove to be the training ground of a new generation of terrorists, much like the war against the Soviets in Afghanistan did a generation earlier, even if other underlying drivers show improvement.

Poor economic performance may well contribute to pessimism about the future, and perceptions of relative deprivation and social marginalization may generate feelings of alienation and anomie. But in most cases disaffection does not find its expression in political violence directed at targets, foreign or local. Conversely, neither is prosperity a fool-proof antidote. The Baader-Meinhof gang in Germany and the Red Guard in Italy were the products of rapidly growing Western Europe, not grinding Third World poverty. Even among less developed countries, one would not expect Sri Lanka to rank high on the list of countries with unusual levels of terrorism, its per capita income and social indicators having been relatively high at the onset of domestic terrorism in the 1980s, yet it was its Tamil Tigers who pioneered suicide bombing.

Even casual observation of the income or education of individual terrorists demonstrates the tenuous link between poverty and violence, as does more systematic analysis (Krueger and Maleckova 2002, Pipes 2002, Bergen and Pandey 2006).[11] Poverty matters—not because the poor form a reserve army of terrorists but rather because poverty, or more precisely the state's inability to address poverty and inequality, fuels the outrage of the intelligentsia and delegitimates the incumbent order in their eyes (Richards 2001).

From Hezbollah to Hamas to the Tamil Tigers to the 9/11 pilots, most often the terrorist leadership is fairly well educated and drawn from middle-class backgrounds. No elasticity of definition would locate Osama bin Laden, the scion of Saudi millionaires, in a low position on an income-education spectrum. Often this education is of a technical nature—for example, the "engineer" Yehiya Ayash, who was responsible in the 1990s for devising and improving the explosive belts worn by Islamic Jihad and Hamas terrorists, or the American-trained engineer Khaled Sheik Mohammed, who is alleged to be the logistical mastermind behind al Qaeda's most notorious acts. September 11 pilot Mohammed Atta, who apparently aspired to be the Gavrilo Princip of this century, was trained as an urban planner. One analysis of Palestinian suicide bombers found that the bomber's level of education was positively correlated with the lethality of

---

11. Berman and Stepanyan (2004) argue that Jewish, Christian, and Islamic fundamentalist families—as distinct from terrorists—are characterized by a common pattern of high fertility, low educational attainment, and low returns to education and that this behavior is consistent with a nondenominational model of religious clubs or sects.

the attack, both through the selection of targets and the likelihood of mission success (Benmelech and Berrebi 2006).[12]

Martin Kramer, editor of the *Middle East Quarterly*, labels this group disaffected "counterelites," who despite wealth and education for some reason are unable to achieve their aspirations through conventional channels and turn to Islamism and the recruitment of disadvantaged foot soldiers to realize their ambitions (cited in Pipes 2002). This dynamic may be particularly important in the application of suicide bombing, which requires the principal to thoroughly dominate the agent. This insurgent quality may also create a dynamic in which essentially intra-Arab disputes are externalized by groups like al Qaeda, Hamas, and Hezbollah, particularly in regard to the United States and Israel, as a mechanism for raising the stakes and mobilizing support.[13]

As in the case of the European anarchists, the foot soldiers are drawn from the cities, not the countryside, and are led by educated, charismatic individuals not unlike Pierre-Joseph Proudhon, Mikhail Bakunin, and Peter Kropotkin from an earlier age. In the words of one scholar, "the basic profile for today's violent militant is a young person with some education, who may have recently moved to the city. Such young people are often unemployed or have jobs below their expectations" (Richards 2001, 12). In North Africa they are colorfully known by the hybrid *hetistes*, combining the Arabic word *heta* (wall) with the French morpheme *iste* (i.e., one who leans against a wall).

The terrorist phenomenon cannot be solely attributed to religious fanaticism, as the global ubiquity of avowedly secular terrorist groups demonstrates. Even the tactic of suicide bombing, often associated with radical Islamist groups, was developed by the Marxist-Leninist Tamil Tigers of Sri Lanka, who remain among its most enthusiastic practitioners (Pape 2005), and when the tactic was introduced to the Middle East in Lebanon in the 1980s, secular not religious groups primarily practiced it (Harrison 2003). And as Berman and Iannaccone (2005) point out, sectarian groups are remarkably adept at redefining their theology as circumstances warrant, and the militancy of sectarian groups is not constant and varies over time, citing Hamas as an example.

In short, while poor economic performance may be conducive to producing terrorism, it is neither a necessary nor sufficient condition. Im-

---

12. Walter Laquer (2003) observes that effective *international* terrorists have to possess sufficient education and familiarity with modern society to perform effectively. They need to be able to order airline tickets, make hotel reservations, or rent apartments without making themselves conspicuous, and they often speak an international language, usually English. Local operators obviously do not have to be so omnidimensionally skilled, however, and we argue that purely local events can have significant economic ramifications, even if they do not generate the headlines that incidents in the West do.

13. Mamoun Fandy, "Beware of 'Contagion' Spreading in the Middle East," *Financial Times*, August 10, 2006.

provement in economic performance may ameliorate terrorism, but it is not a cure-all. The converse argument, that terrorism impedes economic performance, can be made with greater confidence and will be taken up in chapter 9.

Conclusion

In sum, the life prospects of a typical Arab—either male or female—have improved substantially over the past generation or so. This improvement would be consistent with the generally positive if unspectacular performance of most economies in the region over this period. Yet while performance measured either in money or life expectancy has improved in absolute terms, economically the region as a whole has increasingly fallen behind the rich countries as well as comparable countries in the developing world.

Moreover, there is some evidence of unhappiness or grievance, at least in parts of the population, which may be linked to a perception that while past performance was praiseworthy, future opportunities may be dwindling. It may also be linked to deeper institutional characteristics of these countries. Either way, the existence of widespread discontent increases risk and may impede both investment, and, if not properly channeled, political reform, thereby establishing the possibility of a vicious downward spiral in both economic and political dimensions. Each of these possibilities is taken up in the subsequent chapters.

4

The Demographic Challenge and the Role of Globalization

Problems in the Arab economies are frequently cited in the post-9/11 world, often with an undertone of urgency. However, as previous chapters have shown, while performance deteriorated to some extent during the 1980s and 1990s, for the most part the Middle Eastern economies have performed comparably to other developing countries, East Asia excluded, and basic measures of well-being such as life expectancy and infant mortality have improved despite the slowdown in growth.

That said, these economies face a looming challenge. Across the region, labor force growth of 3 percent or more is expected for the next 15 years. Productively absorbing these new labor entrants will not be easy. Already, despite the growth in real income per capita, data suggest a low growth of real wages in urban areas (table 3.8). The frequent grumbling about economic issues may be the result of low wage growth combined with high unemployment rates in general and the poor prospects for many more educated workers.[1] Educated and inoculated, the issue is finding work.

Employment generation has been a major concern of development economists for half a century (Lewis 1954, Ranis 1973, Baer and Hervé 1966)—the issues are hardly sui generis to the Arab world. One component of the

---

1. See, for example, the *Arab Human Development Reports* (UNDP 2002, 2003); "Rapid Prescription Needed," Al Ahram Online, September 19–25, 2002; and "Arab Reform, or Arab Performance?" *The Economist*, July 17, 2003. In the Palestinian elections of January 2006, a frequent complaint of those who voted for Hamas was the absence of employment and the need to bribe Fatah officials to obtain a government job. Simultaneously, members of Fatah held violent demonstrations after the elections, partly motivated by a fear of losing government employment.

solution to this looming employment problem would be more labor-intensive production, often channeled into exports, the engine that allowed some of the Asian economies to dramatically increase labor absorption in the 1960s and early 1970s.[2] Yet this Asian strategy may be more difficult to replicate than in the past because the world is now increasingly competitive, and many countries—China, India, some nations in Latin America, and the Eastern European transition economies—have moved into commanding positions in the production and export of low-cost, high-quality labor-intensive as well as technologically sophisticated commodities.

In this chapter we first present projections of the huge prospective increase in the region's labor force. We then calculate the combinations of investment and productivity growth rates needed to provide the necessary jobs. If jobs were created and output increased, then exports would facilitate the sale of the additional supply. We assess international trade performance in the next section and show how the internal policy environment in many Arab countries poses significant obstacles to trade, preventing these countries from globalizing as rapidly as the non-Arab comparators. This failure to globalize manifests itself in a variety of ways, among them the unimpressive manufacturing export performance of many of the Arab countries. This attenuated globalization is both a cause and an effect of the local policy environment, and we consider if national level soft budget constraints underwritten by a combination of aid, remittances, and energy-derived rents have enabled the Arab countries to temporize while others, less fortunate, initiated policy reforms.

To meet investment targets for employment generation, financial inflows to Arab economies will have to rise significantly and be sustained. The next section therefore looks at the current levels of and obstacles to such inflows—foreign direct and portfolio investment, which can constitute an important supplement to domestic saving, and other inflows such as oil rents, external aid, and remittances by nationals employed abroad, which augment domestic saving in many Arab nations. If investment is forthcoming, it will have to be allocated efficiently through the financial sector, so the next section assesses the state of the financial sector in the Arab economies, including the development of Islamic finance.

Demographic Changes

As shown in table 4.1, the countries of the Middle East have exhibited rapid, though slowing, population growth. On a regionwide basis, total fertility rates (total births per woman over her reproductive life cycle), which were once the highest in the world, have now fallen below Africa, equaling South Asia, and converging on East Asia and Latin America

---

2. DeMelo (1985) and Chenery, Robinson, and Syrquin (1986) provide numerical detail.

Table 4.1 Population growth (percent)

Country	1960–70	1970–80	1980–90	1990–2000	2000–2004
Middle East					
Algeria	2.4	3.1	3.0	2.0	1.6
Egypt	2.5	2.1	2.5	2.0	1.8
Jordan	6.0	3.8	3.8	4.4	2.7
Kuwait	10.3	6.3	4.4	0.3	2.9
Morocco	2.8	2.4	2.2	1.8	1.6
Saudi Arabia	3.5	5.0	5.4	2.7	2.9
Syria	3.2	3.4	3.4	2.9	2.4
Tunisia	2.0	2.2	2.5	1.6	1.2
High-performing comparators					
South Korea	2.5	1.8	1.2	0.9	0.6
Taiwan	3.1	2.0	1.3	0.9	0.4
Large comparators					
China	2.1	1.8	1.5	1.1	0.7
India	2.3	2.3	2.1	1.8	1.5
Normally endowed comparators					
Bangladesh	2.6	2.5	2.6	1.8	1.8
Brazil	2.8	2.4	2.0	1.4	1.2
Pakistan	2.8	3.2	2.7	2.5	2.4
Turkey	2.5	2.3	2.4	1.8	1.6
Resource-rich comparators					
Botswana	2.9	3.6	3.5	2.8	0.8
Indonesia	2.3	2.4	1.9	1.5	1.3
Nigeria	2.7	2.9	3.1	2.8	2.5
Venezuela	3.5	3.5	2.7	2.1	1.8

Note: Compound annual growth rates.

Source: World Bank, *World Development Indicators*, April 2006; *Taiwan Statistical Databook*, 2005.

(World Bank 2004a, figure 3.3). Infant mortality rates have fallen well below Africa and South Asia and now approach those in Latin America and East Asia (World Bank 2004a, figure 3.2). Table 4.1 shows that through the 1980s a number of Arab countries—Algeria, Jordan, Kuwait, Saudi Arabia, and Syria—had higher rates of population growth than most other countries with the exception of some in Africa.

These high rates of population growth are the product of multiple drivers: an initially high crude fertility rate, a rapid decline in infant mortality, and a general rise in life expectancy as documented in the previous chapter. Beginning with Tunisia in the early 1960s, the fertility rate peaked and began falling across the region at an accelerated rate in some countries (figures 4.1a and 4.1b). The movement from one steady state charac-

Figure 4.1a Initiation of fertility declines, normally endowed countries, 1960–2004

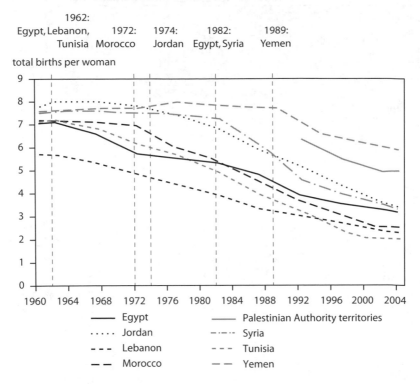

1962:
Egypt, Lebanon, Tunisia | 1972: Morocco | 1974: Jordan | 1982: Egypt, Syria | 1989: Yemen

total births per woman

Legend:
- ——— Egypt
- · · · · · Jordan
- – – – Lebanon
- — — Morocco
- ——— Palestinian Authority territories
- –·—·· Syria
- – – – Tunisia
- — — Yemen

Source: World Bank, *World Development Indicators*, 2004, April 2006.

terized by high rates of births and deaths to a new steady state character-ized by low rates of both births and deaths is known as demographic tran-sition. Adjustment does not occur instantaneously however, and the in-terim period in which fertility rates have not fully adjusted to the new environment gives rise to an unusually large cohort bulge. The Middle East is in the midst of this adjustment, and the cohort bulge is now enter-ing the labor force. One implication of this bulge is that the region has been characterized by extremely high, though declining, dependency ra-tios, the ratio of nonworkers to total population (figures 4.2a and 4.2b).

As noted earlier, authoritarian governments may have a particularly difficult time establishing credible policy precommitments. An example would be the provision of social security. Przeworski et al. (2000) make the interesting observation that one of the sources of differences in per capita income growth across democracies and authoritarian regimes is that, ce-teris paribus, population growth is systematically higher under authori-tarian regimes due to higher fertility rates, which could be due to much

Figure 4.1b   Initiation of fertility declines, resource-rich countries, 1960–2004

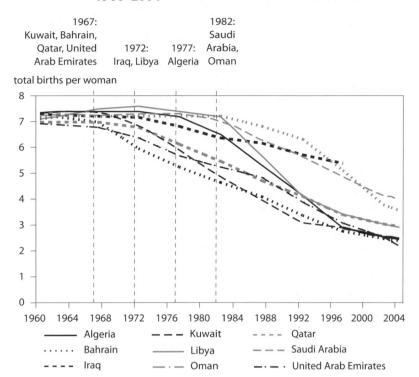

1967:
Kuwait, Bahrain,
Qatar, United
Arab Emirates

1972:
Iraq, Libya

1977:
Algeria

1982:
Saudi
Arabia,
Oman

total births per woman

————— Algeria   — — — Kuwait   - - - - Qatar
· · · · · · Bahrain   ————— Libya   — — — Saudi Arabia
- - - - Iraq   —·— Oman   —·—· United Arab Emirates

Source: World Bank, *World Development Indicators*, 2004, April 2006.

higher rates of contraceptive use in democracies. While contraception is far from universal, there is no Koranic injunction against birth control, and a majority of married women in most Arab countries use it (table 4.2). High fertility rates are more likely related to the demand for old-age support and the inability of authoritarian political regimes to make credible social security commitments. (The region indeed appears to be characterized by unsustainably large pension commitments [Robalino and Bogomolova 2006].) As a consequence people invest in the least risky asset capable of supplying that service—children.

In the Middle East, the absence of credibility in government commitments, together with a variety of subsidies aimed at buying off urban discontent, has created incentives for large families—children (preferably sons) are needed for old age support, while housing and other subsidies reduce the private costs of having children. While a large number of children may make sense as an insurance mechanism at the level of individual households, collectively it depresses saving and investment, slows productivity

Figure 4.2a Age dependency ratio, normally endowed countries, 1960–2004

dependents/working-age population

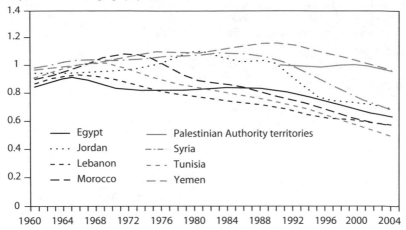

Notes: Ratio of dependents to working-age population.

Source: World Bank, *World Development Indicators,* May 2006.

Figure 4.2b Age dependency ratio, resource-rich countries, 1960–2004

dependents/working-age population

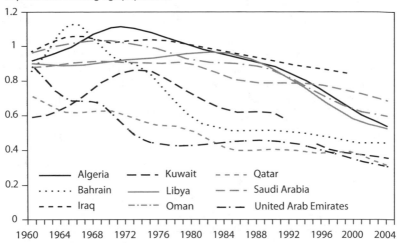

Notes: Ratio of dependents to working-age population.

Source: World Bank, *World Development Indicators,* May 2006.

Table 4.2 Contraceptive prevalence rates among married women, 2002 (percent)

Country	Rate
Algeria	64
Bahrain	62
Egypt	56
Jordan	53
Kuwait	52
Lebanon	61
Libya	45
Morocco	58
Oman	24
Qatar	43
Saudi Arabia	32
Syria	40
Tunisia	60
United Arab Emirates	28
Yemen	21

Source: World Bank (2004a, table A.8(d)).

and income growth as it requires a higher percentage of investment to be devoted to social overhead capital, and contributes to underemployment and associated social maladies. This effect may well have been reinforced historically by low rates of female educational attainment (greater female education is associated with lower fertility) though, as shown in the previous chapter, female educational attainment has been rising rapidly in most countries in the region. When thinking about changes in per capita income, one tends to focus on income—the numerator in that expression—which indeed exhibits more short-run volatility than population. But one should not ignore population: In the long run, variations in population growth rates can have an appreciable impact on the secular trend in per capita income through their effect on the level of saving and the composition of investment.

Fortunately, compared with most economic variables, population changes are relatively predictable. Table 4.3 reports two sets of demographic projections adapted from the *Arab Human Development Report 2002*: Scenario one represents a relatively conservative set of assumptions about fertility changes, and scenario two embodies greater behavioral changes. In the first scenario, between 2000 and 2020, the region's population increases by 150 million or the equivalent of two additional Egypts. Even under the more optimistic assumptions incorporated in the second scenario, the region's population increases by 45 percent in 20 years.

Table 4.3 Population projections

Country	Total population (millions) Scenario 1			Scenario 2			Dependency ratio (percent, based on scenario 2)			Median age (years, based on scenario 2)		
	2000	2010	2020	2000	2010	2020	2000	2010	2020	2000	2010	2020
Algeria	30	36	43	30	35	41	0.76	0.52	0.44	20	24	29
Bahrain	1	1	1	1	1	1	0.50	0.41	0.36	26	31	33
Djibouti	1	1	1	1	1	1	1.01	0.86	0.57	18	19	22
Egypt	68	84	102	68	79	91	0.73	0.53	0.46	20	24	29
Iraq	23	31	41	23	30	35	0.92	0.75	0.51	17	20	24
Jordan	5	7	9	5	6	7	0.78	0.68	0.50	19	21	25
Kuwait	2	2	3	2	2	2	0.45	0.39	0.37	27	32	34
Lebanon	4	4	5	4	4	5	0.88	0.51	0.47	18	23	28
Libya	5	7	8	5	6	8	1.09	0.64	0.45	15	20	25
Morocco	30	36	43	30	35	41	0.69	0.55	0.45	21	25	29
Oman	3	4	5	3	4	4	0.51	0.73	0.51	26	22	24
Qatar	1	1	1	1	1	1	0.41	0.38	0.33	27	33	36
Saudi Arabia	20	29	39	20	28	33	0.51	0.72	0.49	26	23	25
Syria	16	21	27	16	20	24	0.91	0.61	0.50	17	21	26
Tunisia	9	11	12	9	11	12	0.67	0.49	0.46	22	26	30
United Arab Emirates	3	3	3	3	3	3	0.29	0.33	0.38	30	36	41
Yemen	18	29	43	18	28	37	0.99	1.11	0.79	16	15	18
Arab region[a]	238	305	388	238	294	346				20	22.6	26.7

a. Excludes Comoros, Mauritania, Somalia, and Sudan. Median age figures are population-weighted averages.

Source: UNDP (2002, 144).

Table 4.4   Net migration (thousands)

Country	1980	1985	1990	1995	2000
Algeria	6.2	83.3	–70.0	–58.1	–184.9
Egypt	–750.0	–350.0	–550.0	–600.0	–500.0
Jordan	–79.8	69.3	75.2	494.6	35.0
Kuwait	154.6	102.1	174.1	–625.8	347.0
Morocco	–209.0	–50.0	–175.0	–300.0	–300.0
Saudi Arabia	870.1	1,400.0	1,120.0	–325.0	75.0
Syria	–125.0	–75.0	–45.0	–30.0	–30.0
Tunisia	–16.7	–12.4	–23.0	–22.3	–20.0
Total	–149.6	1,167.3	506.3	–1,466.6	–577.9

Source: World Bank, *World Development Indicators*, 2004.

Median population ages are projected to rise for the region as a whole from 20 years in 2000 to nearly 27 in 2020. The median age remains under 30 for most countries in both scenarios. This presents the region with both an opportunity and a challenge. One implication of the region's population structure is that the dependency ratio, which has been declining, should continue to fall. The youthful labor force entrants are, on the whole, better educated than their forebears. If these individuals are gainfully employed, the region could experience a demographic dividend, particularly a higher domestic saving rate.

Relatively high levels of cross-border migration complicate the situation, with most of the more typically endowed economies being net exporters of labor and the oil producers of the Gulf being net importers and with the magnitude of these flows (and status of the region as a whole) responding to changes in the price of oil (table 4.4). Thus, in 1980 at the height of one oil boom Egypt had net emigration of three quarters of a million people, the number falling by half as lower prices set in during the mid-1980s. Saudi Arabian flows also mirrored this change in fortune. In principle this pattern affords the governments of the Gulf the safety valve of increasing job opportunities for citizens through indigenization programs and the expulsion of guest workers.

The possibility of constraining in-migration in the Gulf may be limited by the lack of interest or ability of local citizens to do jobs currently performed by foreigners. And even if this were a serious option, it would simply underscore the vulnerability of the more labor-abundant sender countries of the region.[3] Yet the importation of labor is not limited to the

_____

3. See Ibrahim (1982) for a sociological analysis of this pattern of intraregional migration from the perspectives of both the sender and receiver countries. The intra-Arab labor migration is mirrored by the remittances sent home by such workers. These have been, in different periods, a significant source of foreign exchange for Egypt and Jordan, whereas for Morocco and Tunisia remittances are largely from emigrants to Western Europe. See also Adams and Page (2003).

resource-rich economies of the Gulf. Even in Jordan, one of the "sender" countries in the intraregional labor market, considerable underemployment or unemployment among nationals has historically coexisted with the importation of labor from beyond the region. Workers from South Asia fill many of the jobs in the recently established qualified industrial zones (QIZs). Richard M. Auty (2001, 199), citing Ismail Serageldin, director of the Bibliotheca Alexandrina, writes "a generation has grown up within a dependency culture that is ill-suited to cope with the expected increasing exposure to market pressures. That generation lacks 'achievement motivation, vision of opportunities, sense of discipline, work ethic commitment, and self esteem' that one generation passes on to another in a motivation and progressive society."

Such phenomena raise deep issues about the nature of the employment challenge the region faces. They suggest that the region not only has to generate jobs but also has to generate jobs of a certain type, which local residents would be willing to fill, at least under prevailing conditions. If the region cannot generate sufficient employment opportunities, it will experience a sustained period of high youth unemployment and underemployment with all the attendant social and political disruption. This is the crux of the challenge facing the Middle East.

Employment Generation and Productivity Growth

Labor force data are very unreliable for most developing countries, including the Middle Eastern countries.[4] The size of the labor force itself is often unknown given weak or nonexistent household surveys. Both employment and unemployment data are problematic. While unemployment figures are often cited in news stories in the Western press, many appear to have been obtained from local taxi drivers and waiters. Few reliable country sources exist. The World Bank's *World Development Indicators*, which collates country sources, provides only a few figures for unemployment rates for the Arab countries as does the International Labor Organization's major database, laborsta.ilo.org. A more informative measure of the potential unemployment problem facing the Arab countries is to use the more reliable census of population data, which as seen in the previous section indicates a rapid increase of the working age population. This growth in the labor force will be augmented by the steady increase in female labor force participation rates (figures 4.3a and 4.3b) as well as projected future increases underpinned by rising female educational attainment and urbanization (Gardner 2003).

---

4. This is true for the United States as well. In late 2003 and early 2004, the increasing discrepancies between household and firm surveys of employment led to major policy dilemmas. The former suggested considerable employment growth whereas the latter indicated a much more muted response to economic expansion.

Figure 4.3a   Female labor force participation, normally endowed countries, 1950–2020

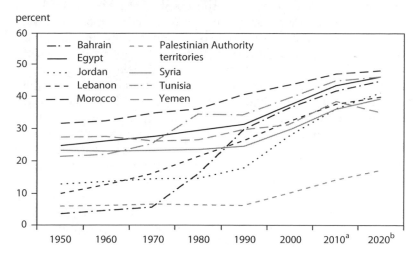

a. International Labor Organization estimates.
b. World Bank staff estimates.

Note: Ages 15 to 64.

Source: World Bank (2004b, table A3).

Figure 4.3b   Female labor force participation, resource-rich countries, 1950–2020

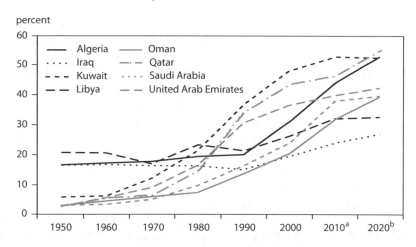

a. International Labor Organization estimates.
b. World Bank staff estimates.

Note: Ages 15 to 64.

Source: World Bank (2004b, table A3).

Given the push to increase the female labor force participation rate, and the need to reduce the unknown but presumed very high current rates of unemployment or underemployment, the number of jobs created likely will have to increase by more than 3 percent per year for most countries. A World Bank study argues this increase is 3.5 percent, and another by the International Monetary Fund (IMF) concludes that it is 4 percent, but the precise number depends on unknowable changes in labor force participation rates by sex and age and the current unknown unemployment rates (World Bank 2004a; Dhonte, Bhattacharya, and Yousef 2000). We use the World Bank's 3.5 percent as a benchmark to illustrate the implications of what may well be a low estimate of required job creation and proceed with a simple calculation that illustrates the magnitude key variables must reach if unemployment is not to increase. In considering the implications of the need to generate employment, we also assume that job creation should be accompanied by an increase in the real wage of 2 percent annually. One of the complaints often voiced is that real wages have fallen in recent years, and there is some corroborating evidence, at least for the manufacturing sector (table 3.8).

Appendix 4A shows that the rate of growth of employment varies positively with the rate of growth of total factor productivity (TFP) and capital and negatively with the real wage. The intuition is that the growth of TFP and capital with which each worker is endowed makes each one more productive and increases his or her value to the firm, leading to more employment. Noneconomists often view productivity growth as detrimental to employment growth, as a given amount of output can be produced with fewer workers. While this may be true if demand is constant, as output increases, whether it is sold to domestic or foreign purchasers, employment will grow.

There is a close connection between job growth, capital accumulation, and productivity growth. Insofar as an absence of interaction with the world economy reduces total factor productivity growth, it slows not only the rate of growth of aggregate supply but also the growth of employment. Some analyses do not make this crucial connection, assuming that globalization is just one measure of an economy's performance. But as will be discussed below, the influx of technology—whether in the form of improvements embodied in foreign equipment, technology licenses, foreign direct investment, free transfers from foreign buyers, foreign consultants—is an important source of the growth of total factor productivity (Pack 1992). Solving the employment problem as well as increasing per capita income are intrinsically intertwined with globalization, and the absence of it, documented below, has been a major constraint on the growth of the Arab economies. Similarly, high levels of technological absorptive capacity, facilitated by specific types of higher education, are also critical to increasing the growth rate of total factor productivity, A^*.

Table 4.5   Alternative scenarios for labor force absorption

Scenario	L*	K*	A*	Investment/ GDP	Implied growth of GDP
1	3.5	6.4	1.0	28.4	5.5
2	3.5	3.5	2.0	21.3	5.5
3	3.5	7.8	0.5	32.0	5.5
4	3.7	6.6	1.0	28.9	5.7

Assumptions: Capital share = 0.35; initial capital/output ratio = 2.5; depreciation rate = 5 percent; growth rate of real wages = 2 percent. See text for more information.

Source: Authors' calculations.

The assumption is that aggregate demand increases sufficiently rapidly to absorb the new output. On the other hand, the growth of real wages (given worker productivity) limits the additional profitable jobs that the firm can offer. This implies that the substitution of labor for capital, which would require lower real wages relative to the cost of capital, is precluded though in principle this substitution would be possible. Such substitution would also reduce the investment requirement, but we view a reduction in real wages as politically problematic for the countries in question given widespread discontent.

Table 4.5 shows a few combinations of variables that allow the realization of the desired rates of growth of 3.5 percent for employment, L^*, and 2 percent for real wages. K^* is the growth rate of the country's capital stock. It is assumed that the initial capital output ratio is 2.5 (reflecting the experiences of Algeria, Egypt, Jordan, Morocco, and Tunisia during 1995–2000), and the depreciation rate of the fixed capital stock is 5 percent per year. The calculations show that with TFP growth, A^*, equal to 1 percent per year, the required investment rate is 28 percent (row 1), dropping to 21 percent when $A^* = 2$ (row 2) and rising to 32 percent when $A^* = 0.5$. For employment to grow at 3.7 percent (to reflect the growing participation rate of women or the absorption of the existing but unknown pool of unemployed individuals, consistent with the IMF's higher labor force growth projection), an increase in the investment rate would be necessary.[5]

Many permutations of these simple calculations can be performed, but the basic point is that given the very high labor force growth rates, the hurdles for these economies to overcome are very substantial. These economies could raise their investment/GDP ratios, but it requires a very large

5. The required increase in the investment rate suggests one of the ambiguities of the often-asserted need to absorb more women in the labor force. While absorbing more women may be socially desirable, it must be accompanied by increasing saving and thus lower current consumption to allow them to be absorbed productively.

reduction in consumption in the short term. From this perspective the value of accelerated TFP growth resides not only in the "free" economic resource it offers, forestalling the need to suppress consumption, but also by extension it relieves some of the pressure on the political system to choose among competing demands for scarce resources.

TFP growth is thus critical and depends on many factors discussed more thoroughly in chapter 6. The economies considered here are not at the technological forefront of the sectors in which they are active. Productivity could be improved by intensive interaction with other nations including tapping of foreign knowledge through technology-licensing agreements, foreign direct investment (FDI), and use of foreign consultants. Greater competition, particularly from imports, would foster TFP growth as might privatization of large-scale, inefficient state-owned enterprises, which with the proper regulatory regime could be run more efficiently by the private sector without yielding excessive profits to the new owners. Similarly, greater flexibility in labor markets would be conducive to TFP growth. Many of the potential sources of improving productivity are inextricably linked to globalization—greater participation in the world economy. While many domestic actions can augment productivity, from improved infrastructure to reduction of arbitrary monopolies, some such as greater FDI are by definition a component of globalization. Behind the value-free and seemingly innocuous A^* in equation 4A.3 lies a set of activities that an economy needs to undertake to accelerate growth.

As shown in chapter 2, countries such as Jordan and Algeria had negative TFP growth in the 1990s, and one suspects the same is likely to have been true of countries such as Syria, Kuwait, and Saudi Arabia for which the requisite data are not available. In these nations, the investment requirements to absorb the rapidly growing labor force will be exceptionally high, as they had very high population growth in the 1980s, though some reductions in the 1990s. Even in the case of the oil exporters of the Gulf Cooperation Council (GCC), not considered here but often viewed as a model, simple job creation may not be enough—they have to be jobs that nationals are prepared to take.

Viewed through the prism of the arithmetic relations of income and employment growth, the focus on the necessary economic reforms in the Arab countries that are needed to improve efficiency and globalization can be viewed not solely as an argument about how to achieve greater efficiency. For governments concerned with legitimacy that might accrue from increased economic growth including improved consumption levels, reforms conducive to more effective economic performance offer an alternative to unpopular policies that compress current consumption. Alas, there is no truly free ride for policymakers. Liberalization of foreign trade or the privatization of state-owned enterprises, which might improve TFP growth relatively quickly, generate fierce opposition from groups that have a well-developed sense of their own risks, opposition that can be overcome only by extraordinary political consensus, sometimes born out of trauma (post-Soviet Central Europe or Latin America following its "lost decade") or faced down by authoritarian governments. Neither the political threats posed by threats to rents nor prospective reductions in consumption growth rates can be taken lightly, and indeed in chapter 6 we review survey evidence of widespread opposition to these policies in the Middle East.

In chapter 6 we also discuss the possibilities for realizing higher productivity growth. These are very complex and have long gestation periods. In contrast, it is technically possible to increase national saving rates—the Singaporean mandatory pension contribution scheme providing an interesting and successful example. But the suppression of consumption in a highly volatile political atmosphere is clearly problematic (Romania under Nicolae Ceauşescu, an example with which some Arab leaders are undoubtedly familiar given their extensive interactions with Eastern Europe before the collapse of Communism).

Thus there is a need for greater domestic saving to finance investment and/or greater productivity growth, neither of which will be easy to achieve given the deep political uncertainty characterizing many of the region's regimes, concerns over terrorism, and uncertainties about the future price of oil. If such saving and investment were to materialize, and both the capital stock and employment grew more quickly, one implication is that aggregate output would also increase more rapidly, its precise rate of growth being dependent on TFP as well. The last column of table 4.5 shows the implied rate of growth of aggregate supply under the various assumptions. The aggregate growth rates are 5.5 to 5.7 percent per year, reflecting increased capital accumulation and/or faster productivity growth. While it is possible to implement a monetary-fiscal policy that would permit sustained growth in aggregate demand of this magnitude, a domestically oriented economy will have greater difficulty doing so than one with growing exports. Increasing a small country's share of the huge world market by .1 percent per year can generate a rapid growth rate in exports over a long period. It is considerably more difficult to pursue a domestically oriented growth strategy that stimulates growth rates in demand of this magnitude without quickly encountering diminishing returns especially in the relatively small countries (other than Egypt) of the Middle East. Moreover, GDP growth of 5.5 percent or more per year will necessitate considerable amounts of imported intermediate and capital goods, and the commensurate growth in foreign exchange. These considerations imply the need to consider recent export performance in some detail.

International Trade Performance

In the Arab countries, production of labor-intensive manufacturing goods could provide some of the necessary employment growth. Yet countries cannot simply produce large quantities of these goods for a purely domestic market. They could try a "big push" strategy in which simultaneous expansion of output of many industries would provide sufficient growth of demand so that the complementary income elasticities would prevent diminishing returns. But such diffuse growth is technically difficult in many industries at once—certainly in nations with relatively little industrial experience. It is difficult to imagine a large economy like Egypt successfully pursuing this development strategy; it is virtually impossible to conceive of a smaller one like Syria or Tunisia doing so.

Exports permit economizing of relatively scarce industrial expertise as well as providing a vent for surplus for a rapidly growing labor force. If nations attempt a more domestically oriented growth strategy instead of export growth, they are likely to run into diminishing returns to capital, and the resulting decline in rates of return will discourage the continuation of high investment. In the "miracle" economies of Asia, perhaps the main miracle was the maintenance of a high rate of investment and its relatively efficient absorption, which may not have transpired with a domestically oriented big push. Even if a government possesses the considerable skills necessary to successfully follow a disciplined fiscal policy combined with a monetary policy that leads to low interest rates to encourage investment, the effort will founder due to the skill constraints encountered if a nation enters many industries simultaneously. Moreover, export growth is also needed to finance increased imported intermediates and capital goods.

Outside the petroleum sector, the Arab countries have, however, been largely inward looking since World War II and more importantly since 1970 in terms of manufacturing. Obviously oil and related exports have been increasing, but these have limited labor inputs and often form an enclave within the economy that has few production-side benefits though obviously incomes are higher.

Although nonoil trade exceeded the world average in the 1950s, it has fallen steadily since (World Bank 2004b). There is some evidence that Arab countries have "undertraded" both intra- and extraregionally relative to gravity model–derived norms and that this deterioration in performance has worsened over time (Al-Atrash and Yousef 2000, Nugent 2002, Miniesy and Nugent 2004, Bolbol and Fatheldin 2005). Figure 4.4 and table 4.6 show the level of manufacturing exports in current dollars for 1980 and 2003 or 2004 respectively for our benchmark countries.[6] Clearly this was an astoundingly open period for countries increasing their participation in the world economy. In the early 1960s the level of per capita income in Egypt, South Korea, and Taiwan was virtually identical, but the latter two quickly pulled ahead leaving Egypt a generation

---

6. Data for many individual countries are available for 2004, though regionwide data are not.

Figure 4.4   Manufacturing exports, 1980 and 2003

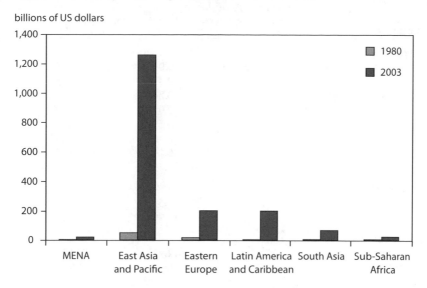

billions of US dollars

MENA = Middle East and North Africa

Source: UN Comtrade database, August 2005.

behind. In 1980 each of the Asian countries already achieved exports of manufactures more than eight times that of Egypt today. And although Egypt has a population greater than South Korea's and Taiwan's combined, the Asian countries export more manufactures in two days than Egypt does in an entire year. East Asia as a whole increased its exports of manufactured goods from $48 billion in 1980 to nearly $1.3 trillion in 2003, while Latin America and the Caribbean increased theirs from $3 billion to $198 billion over the same period (figure 4.4). The Eastern European transition economies increased their manufacturing exports from $16 billion to $198 billion between 1990 and 2003, while the traditionally inward-looking South Asian nations increased their manufactured exports by $63 billion during the same period.

In contrast, both the absolute size of Middle Eastern manufacturing exports and the growth after 1980 (that is, after the oil price increase) were very small, and today manufacturing exports from the region lag far behind Eastern Europe, South Asia, and Latin America, and indeed in 2003, the most recent year for which regionwide data are available, sub-Saharan Africa (figure 4.4). Some of this pattern is due to the pull into the extractive sector of capital and labor that might otherwise be deployed in manufacturing and the expansion of the nontraded-goods sector, underwritten by rents derived from the exploitation of natural resources, which would also draw productive factors away from manufacturing.

Table 4.6   Exports of manufactures, 1980 and 2004
(billions of current US dollars)

Country	1980	2004
Middle East		
Algeria	0.04	0.65
Egypt	0.33	2.35
Jordan	0.21	2.79
Kuwait	2.04	1.11[d]
Morocco	0.59	6.72
Saudi Arabia	0.70	8.88[e]
Syria	0.14	0.56
Tunisia	0.79	7.51
High-performing comparators		
South Korea	15.68	233.99
Taiwan	17.99	171.55
Large comparators		
China	12.46[b]	542.20
India	5.03	55.05
Normally endowed comparators		
Bangladesh	0.51	7.30
Brazil	7.49	52.19
Pakistan	1.28	11.42
Turkey	0.78	53.60
Resource-rich comparators		
Botswana	n.a.	2.22[d]
Indonesia	0.50	40.55
Nigeria	0.02[a]	0.47[c]
Venezuela	0.33	3.98

a. 1981
b. 1984
c. 2003
d. 2001
e. 2002

Sources: World Bank, *World Development Indicators*, April 2006; *Taiwan Statistical Databook,* 2005 (Exports of Industrial Products).

Yet manufacturing exports, in contrast to natural resources, are likely to generate productivity gains due to learning and be labor intensive. While it can be argued that comparative advantage in oil products and the foreign income including remittances that has accrued to these countries imply that manufactured exports should not be high, this exceptionally low level seems surprising. For example, Indonesia, which has a total population similar to the eight large Arab countries and has considerable natural resources in addition to oil and thus might have suffered from "Dutch disease," had a total of $40.5 billion of manufactured exports in 2004, up from $500 million in 1980 (table 4.6). By 2003 the Arab countries had fewer manufactured exports than the Philippines, though Egypt and the Philippines have a similar population. These comparisons also suggest one of the problems of the Middle East. Not only is it late relative to China, it is now faced with competition from a whole range of countries, some of which have similar wage levels but comparable or better education systems as noted in chapter 2.

The volume of trade not only has been unimpressive but also heavily concentrated in fuels. Even within nonfuel products, exports are relatively concentrated, though there is no real standard or norm for judging the optimal degree of concentration, and in some circumstances this concentration could be interpreted as efficient specialization according to comparative advantage. However in the case of the Middle East and North Africa (MENA), there appears to be some evidence that nonfuel exports are relatively concentrated in slow-growing products (World Bank 2004b).

The level of intraindustry trade (IIT), even among the resource-scarce economies, is also modest relative to comparators from outside the region (World Bank 2004b, table 2.7). One interpretation of this phenomenon, based on the traditional demand-preference–driven motivations, is that it reflects the relatively low levels of income in these countries and the lack of convergence in income levels as discussed in chapter 2 (IIT typically rises with income and partner income similarity). MENA countries have little IIT because their relatively poor populations have relatively low demands for sophisticated differentiated products.

But there is a more worrisome possibility based on more recent ideas about the supply-side drivers of IIT, namely that a significant component of IIT consists of cross-border movements of components associated with global production networks and intrafirm trade. Under this interpretation, the region's low level of IIT reflects its relative lack of participation in these trends. Some evidence on this can be adduced from table 4.7, which reports evidence on the breadth of linkages derived from the World Economic Forum's *Global Competitiveness Report 2005–2006*. This sort of evidence should not be regarded as dispositive, but suggestive. Across the sample, the Middle East is in the middle of the pack. Among the Arab economies, Tunisia consistently scores better than the others on these indicators. There is a tendency for the more resource-extractive economies (Algeria, Kuwait, Qatar, Botswana, Indonesia, Nigeria, and Venezuela) to score low on these indicators. Indeed the wording of the "value chain" question, which focuses on exporters' nonproduction activities (design, marketing, and after-sales services), makes it almost a tautology in the case of the natural resources exporters. Yet the scores could also be interpreted as documenting the United Arab Emirates' uniquely successful transition away from a purely extractive economy.

Setting these resource-abundant nations aside to concentrate on more typically endowed economies, the Arab economies consistently score

Table 4.7   Exporting and backward linkages (percentile)

Country	Value chain presence	Local supplier quantity	Local supplier quality	Local availability of process machinery	Local availability of specialized research and training services
Middle East					
Algeria	1	33	20	24	17
Bahrain	27	38	51	11	15
Egypt	61	37	28	56	46
Jordan	51	40	46	51	52
Kuwait	16	54	58	55	51
Morocco	50	57	33	54	44
Qatar	18	22	44	17	15
Tunisia	74	65	62	62	68
United Arab Emirates	67	66	73	40	27
High-performing comparators					
South Korea	85	82	80	97	84
Taiwan	85	89	87	86	85
Large comparators					
China	56	69	43	95	70
India	79	97	78	82	76
Normally endowed comparators					
Bangladesh	30	46	36	15	5
Brazil	53	78	70	85	80
Pakistan	52	67	47	53	37
Turkey	69	72	69	76	61
Resource-rich comparators					
Botswana	17	11	32	29	28
Indonesia	54	32	30	70	57
Nigeria	43	44	25	61	30
Venezuela	10	12	22	9	16

Note: Data are percentiles (higher number is better); sample: n = 117.

Source: World Economic Forum, *Global Competitiveness Report 2005–2006.*

worse than the high-performing economies of South Korea and Taiwan as well as the large economies of China, India, Brazil, and Turkey. Their scores are comparable to the remaining resource-scarce comparators, Bangladesh and Pakistan. One could argue that these scores are largely a function of economic size—smaller economies will have less capacity to generate supplier networks internally—but they just underscore the notion that agglomeration economies and the late start of the Arab countries on industrialization confer a considerable disadvantage on the Middle East with respect to many competitors.

Limited Globalization: A Symptom of Internal Environment

How does one explain the limited globalization (World Bank 2004a, 2004b; UNDP 2002, 2003) of the Arab economies, the definition of which includes, inter alia, low levels of exports and imports relative to GDP and low levels of FDI? This lack of deeper integration with world markets may be symptomatic of deeper problems within these societies reflecting suspicions at both the elite and popular levels about of the benefits of international economic integration, as will be discussed in greater detail in chapter 7. In this regard it is reminiscent of notions similar to those held by intellectual proponents of dependency theory (and its populist reincarnation in some of the less responsible criticism of globalization), who argue that integration inevitably does economic harm to the poorer countries. There is also a recurrent refrain that the absence of greater integration reflects a desire to avoid the cultural impact of broader globalization. Conversely it could also reflect lack of trust or assessments of risk by trade partners from outside the region as will be discussed in greater detail in chapter 8—after all, it takes two to tango. Whatever the "true" underlying source of limited globalization, the policy stance has typically been the encouragement of import substitution plus the accompanying overvaluation of exchange rates. Such policies inimical to trade have also been pursued in other regions but have, to a large extent, been abandoned.

Historically the Middle East—except the GCC countries, which maintain a uniform 5 percent tariff—has been characterized most notably by high tariff rates and significant quantitative restrictions (table 4.8). Tariff levels generally increase with the degree of processing, conveying to manufacturers high levels of effective protection.[7] Regulations applied in a discriminatory manner against foreign exporters or service providers act as nontariff barriers (Zarrouk 2000a).[8] Yet the maintenance of these policies, which act as an effective tax on exports, is not sufficient to explain shortfalls in trade expansion in the 1980–2004 period.[9] Historically implementation of export

---

7. See Hoekman and Messerlin (2002, table 4) for data on Egypt, Morocco, and Tunisia.

8. See Kheir-El-Din (2000) for an analysis of Egyptian use of product standards as a nontariff barrier.

9. See Angels-Oliva (2000) and Zarrouk (2000c) for comprehensive analyses of formal trade barriers in MENA countries. Cassing et al. (2000) provide a detailed analysis of Egypt. For a study of the adverse effects of Egypt's earlier import-substitution regimes, see Hansen and Marzouk (1965).

Table 4.8 Trade barriers

Country	Mean tariff rate			Nontariff barriers, 2001	Overall protection, 2001	Global Competitiveness Report (GCR) score		
	1990	1995	2000			Hidden trade barriers	Prevalence of trade barriers	Irregular payments in exports and imports
Middle East								
Algeria	24.6	22.9	24.2	29.1	22.0	29	33	38
Egypt	33.5	28.3	19.7	0.8	15.0	5	10	47
Jordan	n.a.	n.a.	14.4	36.7	28.3	68	42	73
Kuwait	n.a.	n.a.	n.a.	n.a.	n.a.	n.a.	70	56
Morocco	23.5	22.8	26.0	13.0	28.3	46	12	17
Saudi Arabia	n.a.	n.a.	n.a.	10.2	11.3	n.a.	n.a.	n.a.
Syria	20.4	14.8	n.a.	n.a.	n.a.	n.a.	n.a.	n.a.
Tunisia	27.5	27.5	29.9	21.1	30.0	48	45	59
High-performing comparators								
South Korea	13.3	11.5	9.4	0.6	8.0	49	64	56
Taiwan	9.7	8.0	9.7	n.a.	n.a.	72	74	83
Large comparators								
China	40.3	37.5	17.5	19.4	16.5	32	29	60
India	79.2	55.2	32.9	43.8	36.0	60	54	38
Normally endowed comparators								
Bangladesh	102.2	81.2	22.1	5.1	23.7	28	41	1
Brazil	30.0	12.0	14.6	14.2	16.9	21	25	50
Pakistan	58.8	61.1	n.a.	n.a.	n.a.	27	31	18
Turkey	22.7	9.0	13.5	13.4	10.1	40	61	31
Resource-rich comparators								
Botswana	11.0	19.7	7.2	n.a.	n.a.	62	69	55
Indonesia	20.3	17.0	11.9	9.1	6.6	38	50	9
Nigeria	34.3	32.8	n.a.	2.9	17.1	13	17	13
Venezuela	30.6	13.4	12.0	23.7	16.8	1	18	16

n.a. = not available

Notes: Nontariff barriers are ad valorem equivalent of nontariff barriers, import-weighted, if nontariff barriers exist. GCR figures are in percentiles (higher number is better); hidden trade barriers, n = 104; other GCR indicators, n = 117.

Sources: Tariff data: Park and Lippoldt (2003); Nontariff barriers: Kee, Nicita, and Olarreaga (2004a); Overall protection: Kee, Nicita, and Olarreaga (2004b); Hidden trade barriers: Global Competitiveness Report 2004–2005; Other GCR indicators: Global Competitiveness Report 2005–2006.

processing zones, which might serve as a geographically delimited testing ground for reform, has been desultory (Rao 2000), though governments in the region have been more receptive to qualified industrial zones (QIZs) and other measures, as discussed in chapter 8 and appendix 8B.

Beyond explicit border measures, however, a variety of evidence points to a nexus of issues involving logistics and customs management that may significantly deter exporting, particularly integration into cross-border supply networks, which requires the ability to move components across borders in a timely and reliable fashion. For example, Denise Konan (2003) estimates that in Egypt, the largest potential exporter of manufactured goods, border delays are equivalent to a 50 percent tariff. Other problems in Egypt include inadequate physical infrastructure and unreliable air cargo service. Hamstrung by inadequate capacity, airlines bump manu-factured exports for tourists and perishable goods—a deterrent to entering markets that require fast supply response or transborder supply chains. Sea freight may be more reliable, but lack of consolidation means many containers leave port empty, driving up costs to exporters. Similar coordi-nation problems afflict trucking. Poor communication and information systems mean that trucks are used inefficiently: Trucks finishing deliver-ies cannot find return loads, driving up costs. Moreover, a high tariff on trucks means that the fleet is aged, expensive to maintain, and unreliable. The picture is not uniformly dark, however: Over the past decade the port of Casablanca has reportedly reduced its container processing times from 18 to 20 days in 1996 to a few hours.[10]

These "physical" issues are related to the way the transportation sector is organized, specifically the prevalence of entrenched public-sector mo-nopolies. Dan Magder (2005) reports an extraordinary illustration of this from Egypt: The Cairo Airport Authority restricts the number of pieces of equipment that carriers are permitted, forcing exporters to rent equip-ment from Egypt Air at very high rates—in the case of container dollies, the rental fee per hour is reportedly almost equal to the purchase price of a new dolly.

Practices within the public sector itself reduce efficiency even further. According to a survey of 230 firms in eight Arab countries conducted be-tween July and December 2000, it took on average 2 to 5 days to clear im-ported airfreight through customs, 2 to 10 days to get a seaborne ship-ment released, and 1 to 3 days for road transit (Zarrouk 2003). Magder (2005) reports that in Egypt export customs clearance generally takes 1 to 3 days; however, import clearance can exceed 10 days. And while one might discount the importance of a delay in getting a consumer good into the country, holdups of this magnitude make it very difficult to get into cross-border supply chains if one cannot get imported components into

---

10. Alan Beattie, "Forget Tariff Cuts, the Poor Need Trade Facilitation," *Financial Times*, April 1, 2006.

the country in a consistent and timely manner. Nor do the trade impediments appear to be purely time-related: The survey respondents also reported capricious assessments of product standards.[11]

Jamel Zarrouk's survey found that in the region 10 to 20 signatures are needed on average to process an air or sea freight shipment. The average company in the survey spent 95 days of labor per year resolving problems with customs and other officials. Such extensive contact can, and apparently does, facilitate the solicitation of bribes, though the evidence on "hidden barriers" and irregular payments is mixed: In the *Global Competitiveness Report 2005–2006* the Arab countries do not look particularly bad relative to similarly situated countries with respect to survey perceptions of "hidden barriers" and irregular payments to customs officials (table 4.8). Zarrouk's survey paints a very different picture, however: Customs clearance costs and bribes were identified as adding significant costs, though the responses indicated that some countries, notably Egypt and Jordan, had made progress on this score in recent years, while others such as Lebanon, Saudi Arabia, and Syria had stagnated or regressed.[12]

Moreover, to take the case of Egypt, while there may have been improvements with respect to these issues in recent years (and more in process due to ongoing reforms of trade policy and customs administration), Rania Miniesy and Jeffrey B. Nugent (2004) report econometric evidence that suggests Egypt's competitiveness has declined over time. There is no necessary contradiction here: The improvements may have been too recent to be picked up in their statistical analysis. But this points to a deeper issue as well: While Arab countries may be making improvements in an absolute sense in a variety of areas, their relative competitiveness may be declining if their rivals are improving even more quickly.

Gains from Deeper Integration

The failure to expand international trade has several implications. Countries may forgo gains in productivity from reallocation of resources according to comparative advantage and from improved productivity. Although these benefits have not been definitely proved to everyone's satisfaction, there is a strong presumption that countries as closed as many of the Arab ones would gain in several ways. Greater export orientation, induced by

---

11. One, admittedly dated, assessment of the costs imposed by these practices concluded that in 1995, "public monopolies in ports and port services combined with poor infrastructure for loading and storing goods, make the costs for discharging a container 2 to 3 times higher in Alexandria than other Mediterranean ports" (Hoekman and Messerlin 2002, 13).

12. It should be noted that the survey was carried out prior to the implementation of the US-Jordan free trade agreement. The provisions on transparency in this agreement may have encouraged even further improvements in Jordan in recent years.

policy changes that would make exporting more profitable, could lead firms to invest more in improving their productivity and the quality of their products. Import liberalization would allow firms lower-cost access to a greater variety of inputs, some of which embody the fruits of research and development in trading partners.[13] And there is some evidence that importing firms exposed to foreign technology engage in more innovative activity than those that are not (MacGarvie 2006). More intensive competition from imports could force locally oriented firms to improve their productivity to stay competitive with now cheaper imported final goods. None of these benefits is guaranteed and the experience of countries with greater integration has not been uniformly beneficial. But in countries as diverse as China, India, Chile, and Thailand, the total effect has accelerated growth after liberalization. While some countries such as South Korea were protectionist during their period of accelerated growth, their exporting firms did not suffer from disabilities imposed by tariff restrictions, but rebates allowed exporters to face international prices for the inputs embodied in exports (Pack and Westphal 1986).

Given that exporting requires considerable investment by firms in establishing networks and meeting quality standards and delivery times, governments cannot simply command its growth (Clerides, Lach, and Tybout 1998). Exporting requires supportive public policies including a competitive real exchange rate and access to tradable inputs at world prices. Absence of either of these policy-determined variables militates against profitable exports by firms even if they incur the costs necessary to improve their competitiveness. Moreover, despite optimism in some analyses about the potential for increasing exports (World Bank 2004a), largely based on the low export-GDP ratio compared with other countries, it may now be much harder to export successfully than it was even two decades ago.[14]

China (and increasingly India) has become a major exporter of a vast array of labor-intensive products, the type most important for the Arab economies if exporting is to partly address their employment problem. A considerable array of industrial skills has been accumulated in the last two decades in these nations, to say nothing of other lower-middle-income Asian countries such as Indonesia, Thailand, and the Philippines. Moreover, industrial regions in each nation now benefit from agglomera-

---

13. On the importance of international technology spillovers, see Coe, Helpman, and Hoffmaister (1996).

14. Though assuredly the Arab countries are below their "expected" or "potential" level of exports given their per capita income, it is not clear how likely it is that these deviations from expectations can be closed. Increasing exports is not a matter of erasing half the gap in a statistical norm. Rather it requires both good national policies and firm-cost structures that allow them to meet international competition. But these costs may depend not only on individual firms' efforts but also on the context in which each firm is embedded to allow it to take advantage of agglomeration economies. These issues will be addressed in chapter 6.

tion economies due to a large complementary range of industrial prod-ucts, business services, and a large pool of workers with sufficient skills to be productive employees in a variety of businesses.[15] Anthony Venables and Diego Puga (1999) have argued that given agglomeration economies, existing industrial complexes can satisfy almost all demand for manufactured goods. Even if this view is exaggerated, today entry into the most labor-intensive product areas is daunting. Whatever the optimality of past performance, and it seems very likely that trade in manufactures was too small, exports are necessary to help increase productivity growth, to provide employment, and arguably to ease the complexity of macroeconomic policymaking.

As an alternative, Middle Eastern countries could develop labor-intensive service sectors, circumventing some of the problems that plague the industrial sector. Tourism is one such possibility—building on the region's geography in the form of its long Mediterranean and Red Sea coastlines and the abundance of antiquities reflecting the region's long multicultural history. (According to the World Bank, controlling for economic fundamentals, Egypt is an enormous "overachiever" in tourism—one supposes that it is hard to control for the Pyramids in a regression model [World Bank 2004b, figure 1.17].)

However, MENA has been losing world market share since at least the mid-1980s (World Bank 2004b), and attacks on tourists at Luxor, Sharm el-Sheik, and Cairo in Egypt and the intifada in the Palestinian Authority territories have created at least temporary and localized disruptions. Expanding the region's tourism industry, however, immediately raises issues of cultural acceptance and personal security, which are discussed in greater detail in chapter 9. Dubai, a UAE emirate, has established itself as a regional transportation hub and with sun, sand, and more relaxed mores than its neighbors has carved out a niche in the tourism industry, attracting 5.5 million visitors in 2004 and aiming for 15 million in 2010, which would rival Orlando as an international tourist destination.[16] But Dubai is an anomaly: Emiratis make up only about 10 percent of the labor force, and as a consequence unemployment is not such a pressing concern. In any event, workers imported from outside the region would fill most of the anticipated jobs. Nevertheless, Dubai's success could stimulate variants on the formula, such as Islamic-, eco-, or family-oriented tourism, as is being contemplated elsewhere in the region.

The region has also been losing ground in nontourism services. Another possibility for resurgence, and one requiring less of a physical presence by foreigners, lies in the potential for becoming back-office outsourcing locales,

---

15. For a recent discussion and extensive references to the literature on agglomeration economies, see Harrigan and Venables (2004).

16. Matthew Garrahan, "Kerzner Plans $1.2bn Dubai Palm Venture," *Financial Times*, October 27, 2005.

particularly for the former French colonies of the Maghreb.[17] The United Arab Emirates is trying to break into this market among the Anglophones, though in the latter's case, most of the employees are expected to be imported from outside the region. Education and health care are emerging industries in the Gulf. Bahrain aims to become a regional alternative provider for health care services currently sought abroad, primarily in Europe and Southeast Asia. Dubai has established a "knowledge village" hosting branches of 13 foreign universities, while Qatar has an "education city" with four.[18] Other similar plans are on the drawing board. These are all positive initiatives, no doubt, but at least in the case of education schemes, one wonders if they are just a proliferation of suboptimal scale institutions that will not survive the next decline in the oil price, at least without some consolidation. And, as in the case of the tourism and back-office industries, employees from outside the region are expected to fill many of the jobs.

In summary, the absence of globalization is both a symptom of the problems of some of the Arab countries and a source of some of their difficulties. Without greater participation in the world economy, the overriding political economy problem of providing additional employment will be difficult to resolve, as will be realizing the foreign exchange necessary to facilitate imports of investment goods and intermediates. In chapters 8 and 9 we consider the potential role of the world community in fostering additional exporting (and importing) through a variety of trade agreements and other measures.

Capital Flows

Foreign Investment

The extractive sector's prominence in some Arab economies complicates cross-national comparisons of FDI inflows. Generally speaking, FDI in the Middle Eastern economies has typically been quite low outside the natural resource–based sectors, particularly oil and gas (table 4.9).[19] The Arab countries are uniformly "underperformers" when it comes to attracting FDI, a point emphasized in the *Arab Human Development Report 2002* and

---

17. Even this has proved controversial with some French politicians floating proposals to force call center staff to tell callers their locations or their legal (Arabic) names.

18. "A Survey of Higher Education," *The Economist*, September 10, 2005.

19. Although Western firms initially developed the region's oil wealth, most of the oil industry was subsequently nationalized and foreign participation restricted. Kuwait is contemplating relaxing historic restrictions on inward FDI in the oil sector, however, as state firms have encountered difficulty meeting booming demand without access to the most advanced technology (Carola Hoyos, "Kuwait Says It Needs Foreign Oil Companies," *Financial Times*, December 13, 2005).

Table 4.9   Inward foreign direct investment

Country	Cumulative for period (billions of US dollars)				Share of GDP (percent)[a]			
	1970–79	1980–89	1990–99	2000–2004	1970–79	1980–89	1990–99	2000–2004
Middle East								
Algeria	1.0	0.3	1.6	4.2	0.5	0.1	0.3	1.5
Egypt	1.7	8.6	7.5	2.6	1.0	2.7	1.3	0.7
Jordan	0.1	0.5	0.9	1.3	0.6	0.9	1.2	3.6
Kuwait[b]	0.0	0.0	0.5	-0.2	0.0	0.0	0.2	-0.1
Morocco	0.1	0.7	5.6	6.0	0.2	0.4	1.7	4.0
Saudi Arabia[c]	-2.9	23.5	7.2	-5.0	-1.1	1.6	0.5	-0.5
Syria	0.0	0.3	1.1	0.6	0.0	0.3	0.9	0.8
Tunisia	0.5	1.6	3.6	2.5	1.4	1.8	2.1	3.0
High-performing comparators								
South Korea[d]	0.3	3.8	25.8	26.6	0.2	0.3	0.6	0.9
Taiwan	n.a.	4.6	14.6	12.8	n.a.	0.5	0.6	0.9
Large comparators								
China	0.0	15.1	283.1	240.4	0.0	0.5	3.9	3.2
India	0.4	1.0	15.1	24.6	0.0	0.0	0.4	0.9
Normally endowed comparators								
Bangladesh	0.0	0.0	0.6	1.1	0.0	0.0	0.1	0.4
Brazil	13.4	17.4	104.7	100.1	1.1	0.7	1.6	3.7
Pakistan	0.2	1.1	5.0	3.2	0.1	0.3	0.9	0.8
Turkey	0.5	1.7	7.7	9.8	0.2	0.2	0.5	1.0
Resource-rich comparators								
Botswana	0.2	0.6	0.2	0.9	1.7	4.6	0.3	3.0
Indonesia	2.0	3.3	21.6	-7.0	0.8	0.4	1.1	-0.9
Nigeria	3.1	4.3	11.8	8.1	1.6	1.7	4.1	3.0
Venezuela	-1.0	1.0	21.4	13.3	-0.4	0.2	2.8	2.5

a. Simple average of available data; b. Data not available for 1970–74; c. Data not available for 1970; d. Data not available for 1970–75.

Sources: World Bank, *World Development Indicators,* May 2006; Taiwan: Central Bank of China, Republic of China (Taiwan), and *Taiwan Statistical Databook,* 2005; Saudi Arabia: World Bank, *World Development Indicators,* April 2006.

Eid and Paua (2003).[20] In all but a few countries, the absolute size of inflows has been very small, and it has accounted for less than 1 percent of GDP and a very small percentage of fixed capital formation. In the last several years FDI has noticeably increased in a number of countries such as Egypt, which experienced 50 percent increases in 2003 and 2004 fueled in part by the surge in oil prices and one-off privatizations.

Much of the investment has been concentrated in real estate and/or tourism (i.e., there has been a boom in hotel and resort construction). Only time will tell whether these projects are sustainable and generate tourism revenues (hence might be considered at least partly in the "tradable" sector and contribute to the balance of payments), though the multiplicity and grandiosity of these projects certainly give one pause. Likewise, whether these increases can be sustained and extended to greenfield investments outside tourism or the extractive sector is an open question and would appear to depend, at least in significant part, on whether the oil boom is sustained—that is, in aggregate terms will the future look more like the previous three years or the previous 25? Increased FDI could potentially also contribute to technological and marketing skills in the recipient countries as will be discussed in chapter 9.

Another potential source of investment financing is the repatriation of capital owned by Arab nationals (further discussed below). A. T. Sadik and Ali A. Bolbol (2003) provide a lower-bound estimate of capital outflow from the Arab countries for the 1975–2000 period of $212 billion and an upper-bound figure of $318 billion, which if repatriated could provide a large source of investment financing. Such a development would be desirable for supplementing national saving, suggesting the potential payoffs to the region of both better economic performance and a more stable environment including a reduction in both terrorism and extremist rhetoric.

A notable development in the banking sector has been the growth of Islamic banks, one institutional manifestation of Islamic finance more broadly, which seeks to accumulate or channel capital through distinctively Islamic institutions. (Islamic finance should not be confused with terrorist finance [box 4.2]). The Koran contains an injunction against *riba*, interpreted by some as usury, though under a more strict reading it could be regarded as a complete prohibition on the charging of interest.[21] Other Ko-

---

20. It is worth noting that the figures for most Arab countries are higher than those for South Korea and Taiwan, which did quite well despite their relatively inhospitable stance toward FDI, but far below that for China, which succeeded while adopting a more open approach. From a macroeconomic standpoint, South Korea and Taiwan did well partly because they maintained very high domestic saving rates. The technology transfer aspect of FDI is discussed in chapter 6.

21. See Siddiqi (1981), Khan and Mirakhor (1987), Kuran (1992), Henry and Wilson (2004), Iqbal and Molyneux (2005), and El-Gamal (2006) for surveys of Islamic economic institutions and thought. Rodinson (1973), Kuran (1993, 2003b), and Pryor (2006) argue that in reality, uniquely Islamic economic practices and institutions have minimal impact on resource allocation.

ranic teachings may restrict or deny the use of other financial instruments such as options, futures, and insurance contracts (Al-Suwailen 2006). In place of interest on deposits, Islamic financial institutions use a variety of *sharia*-compliant instruments to generate returns to savers. The Islamic Development Bank in Jeddah, Saudi Arabia, has supported the development of Islamic finance, and in recent years a number of transnational official or semiofficial institutions have been set up to provide regulatory and religious guidance, including the Islamic Financial Services Board established in 2002 by the central banks of a number of Islamic countries (El-Hawary, Grais, and Iqbal 2004). Such institutions are needed because rulings on sharia compliance are not uniform across different schools of thought, different regulatory frameworks are applied in different locales, and compliance has become an issue with some investment funds.[22] Ironically, much of the financial innovation in creating sharia-compliant instruments has been undertaken by the Islamic finance arms of Western institutions such as ABM Amro, Citibank, Deutsche Bank, HSBC, and Merrill Lynch. Often these products are "white-labeled" through local, Islamic institutions.

Contemporary Islamic banking started in Egypt in the 1960s under the leadership of Ahmed al-Najjar, who had worked in a West German credit association, receiving the official imprimatur of the Egyptian government in 1971. Al-Najjar sought to extend access to formal financial institutions to less advantaged Egyptians, many of whom had never before had bank accounts, by establishing a network of retail Islamic banks and adopting marketing innovations such as operating them on Islamic hours and having bank employees dress in Islamic clothes to reassure customers. His less idealistic successors have largely targeted high net worth individuals in the Gulf. The first Islamic commercial bank, the Dubai Islamic Bank, was established in 1975. After 1979 a number of governments including Iran, Pakistan, and the Sudan attempted to "Islamicize" their national financial systems. Islamic banks now number in the hundreds. The first independent sharia-compliant investment bank announced plans to go public in 2006.

One recent estimate of deposits at Islamic banks puts the figure at $300 billion, though Munawar Iqbal and Philip Molyneux (2005) caution that if they do not improve their performance relative to conventional banks, their deposits will inevitably erode. In May 2005 the International Monetary Fund (IMF) estimated that Islamic financial institutions as a whole controlled perhaps $400 billion, a figure that had been rising at a rate of 10 to 15 percent.[23] There is some anecdotal evidence that this trend, especially in the mutual funds sector, has accelerated in recent years. Moody's

---

22. Charles Batchelor, "Investment Funds 'Not Complying with Sharia Law'," *Financial Times*, May 12, 2004.

23. "Arab Banks, Investors Frown on World Bank Bonds," Reuters, September 20, 2005; El-Hawary, Grais, and Iqbal (2004); Henry and Wilson (2004).

estimates that 250 Islamic mutual funds manage $300 billion in assets.[24] The proequity bias of Islamic finance could make it a vehicle for venture-type financing and relieve the capital constraints on small and medium-sized enterprises. In the insurance area, institutions organized as *takaful,* a kind of mutual insurance scheme, are making inroads (El-Gamal 2006).

From the standpoint of cross-border investment, the role of Islamic financial institutions is ambiguous. The Koranic prohibition on riba, and the consequent unease about portfolio investment in bank loans and bonds, has encouraged a strong equity orientation in the investment portfolios of Islamic financial institutions. However, local stock markets have limited absorptive capacity, while those in the United States are large, deep, and transparent. So while one might expect Islamic institutions, given their religious orientation, to exhibit home- or at least Islamic-bias, Rodney Wilson (2004) concludes that their propensity to channel capital into the markets of non-Islamic countries is as big as, if not bigger than, that of conventional financial institutions.

The increasing popularity of *sukuks,* or sharia-compliant Islamic bonds, is also likely to influence regional debt markets. Sukuks, introduced in 2001, pay dividends from cash flows from tangible assets rather than interest. Issuers have included the governments of Saudi Arabia, the United Arab Emirates, Qatar, the Sudan, Pakistan, and Malaysia, as well as the Islamic Development Bank, the World Bank, the German state of Saxony-Anhalt, and private firms in the Gulf region. In 2005 the volume of corporate sukuks more than doubled to $11.4 billion (El-Gamal 2006). In January 2006 Dubai Ports World raised $3.5 billion in the largest sukuk issuance to date. Relative to conventional bond issuance the size of the Islamic bond market is minuscule but is growing exponentially. Ratings agencies have begun to rate sukuks as they would any other bond, and in 2006 Citigroup introduced a sukuk index.

While this is an interesting institutional development, it is not clear how if at all the increasing use of this instrument will affect either aggregate capital accumulation or its sectoral allocation and hence growth performance. However, as these examples demonstrate, issuers of sukuks are not limited to the Middle East, or even Islamic entities, so in principle the impact of the development of this asset class on cross-regional financial flows is indeterminate. Nevertheless, it is not implausible to expect that as this asset class develops, the net effect will be to increase the degree of home-bias in Middle Eastern portfolio investments.

Ultimately whether this scenario is realized comes down to how large and sustained the post-9/11 increase in home-bias is. One could argue that in light of the quality and depth of Western financial markets in comparison to the casino-like atmosphere of the region's bourses, this effect is

---

24. Gillian Tett, "Banks Create Muslim 'Windows' as Islamic Banking Expands Its Niche," *Financial Times,* June 2, 2006.

likely to be small and/or transitory, and there is some evidence of inertia in portfolio allocation behavior: European and Asian private investors throughout the 1990s and early 2000s continued to purchase American real and financial assets despite a significant equity correction and what some feel are overvalued American asset markets. Looking forward, Middle Eastern markets may be subject to relatively high political risk associated with political instability—even if it were not an issue in the past. Investors seeking high returns for a given degree of safety and under current relatively turbulent conditions may not make large portfolio adjustments.

Conversely, post-9/11 developments may have led to an increase in outsiders' subjective assessment of the riskiness of investment in the Middle East as will be discussed in succeeding chapters. It may well be the case that the greater knowledge and cultural sensitivity of investors from within the region may yield more nuanced risk assessments. If this is the case, such differences in risk assessments across investors may actually increase the incentives for intraregional investment, since in essence the investors from outside the region have been scared off.

Beyond the region, Arab investors have indeed become more prominent, particularly in real estate and regulated services such as telecommunications.[25] Many are public or quasi-public entities—the Abu Dhabi Investment Authority is estimated to manage $300 billion.[26] (See box 4.1 on the Dubai Ports World controversy.) Yet it is unclear from where their competitive advantage derives, beyond liquidity-driven portfolio diversification, and keeping with the relative paucity of investment in traded-goods sectors, Bolbol and Ayten M. Fatheldin (2005) found little complementarity between intraregional FDI and exports.

Nevertheless, heightened political tensions, perhaps arising from future terrorist attacks in the West, could intensify home-bias, as might strengthening local financial sectors (see box 4.2 on terrorist finance). The latter, at least, are amenable to policy intervention. Dubai has established a financial center with its own commercial laws, regulators, and courts. The Dubai International Financial Exchange opened in September 2005 is intended to be a more transparent, better-regulated market aimed at international

---

25. Recent examples include the takeover by Saudi Oger of the Turkish telecom provider Turk Telekomunikasyon (July 2005, $6.6 billion); a minority stake investment by the United Arab Emirates' International Petroleum Investment in Taiwan's Chinese Petroleum (October 2005, $5 billion); Kuwait's Mobile Telecommunications' takeover of Dutch-registered sub-Saharan African cellular phone service provider CelTel (March 2005, $2.8 billion); Emirates Telecommunications' purchase of a 26 percent share of Pakistan Telecommunications (June 2005, $2.6 billion); and the June 2006 stated intention of Dubai's Emaar and Dubai World to invest more than $30 billion in a variety of projects in Pakistan (Farhan Bokhari, "Dubai in Huge Pakistan Investment," *Financial Times*, June 3, 2006).

26. As a point of comparison, the United States' largest pension fund, the California Public Employees Retirement System (CALPERS), runs $200 billion (Leslie P. Norton, "The Gulf's Other Gusher," *Barron's*, April 24, 2006).

Box 4.1   The Dubai Ports World (non)deal

In October 2005 Dubai Ports World (DPW) bid to acquire the Peninsular and Oriental Steam Navigation Company (P&O), a UK-registered private entity operating ports in 18 countries, including the United States. DPW is owned by the government of Dubai.

The takeover was subject to regulatory approval in the United Kingdom as it would give DPW control over a British firm. In the United States, although the proposed deal amounted to one foreign firm taking over another, it would involve the transfer of P&O's US subsidiary that operated the ports of six US cities and was subject to approval by the interagency Committee on Foreign Investment in the United States (CFIUS).

By January 2006 the deal was cleared by the authorities in both countries, which considered the potential impact on security, and in the case of the United States, extracted a side letter committing DPW to additional security-related requirements.

However, in February controversy exploded, apparently sparked by a small US firm seeking to increase its leverage over P&O in an unrelated dispute. CFIUS, apparently for the first time since its creation in 1975, backtracked and requested that the case be reopened.

Congressional demagogues were not to be assuaged however, introducing legislation to block the deal. In March the congressional leadership informed the White House that there were insufficient votes to sustain a presidential veto. DPW announced that it would divest the US assets, but the House nevertheless voted overwhelmingly against the deal, with one headline reading "House Puts a Bullet in Port Deal's Corpse." The fiasco, along with an imbroglio over the takeover of Unocal by the China National Offshore Oil Corporation, spurred proposals to reform the regulatory process (Graham and Marchick 2006).

Yet as long as the United States runs current account deficits, it will require counterpart capital inflows from abroad, and one way of attenuating investment disputes would be to reduce US reliance on foreign finance. These deficits are mirrored by oil-fueled surpluses in the Gulf, and quite naturally Arabs will be prominent among investors in US assets. Indeed, the affair is reminiscent of past episodes involving Japanese investors in the 1980s. As before, the DPW controversy appears to have been driven as much by xenophobia as finance.

The affair damaged the United States' already tattered reputation in the Middle East, where, against a backdrop of American calls for greater openness, US behavior was interpreted as hypocritical, if not racist. This outcome was doubly unfortunate because the United States had been painstakingly painting the United Arab Emirates as an ally—indeed the leading foreign host of US Navy ships.

Box 4.2 Terrorist finance

Terrorist finance, which should not be confused with Islamic finance, generally involves relatively small and irregular transactions of funds often derived from legitimate activities but put to severely destructive ends. al Qaeda, for example, has used a variety of channels to transfer funds for its operations, including smuggling cash, gold, and diamonds; *hawala*, a traditional money transfer system; the inadequately regulated Islamic financial system; and wire transfers and other instruments used by modern Western financial systems.

In the Middle East, the main, though not exclusive, focus has been on Saudi Arabia, believed to be the primary source of al Qaeda financing and front businesses. Historically al Qaeda exploited the regulatory inadequacies of the Islamic financial system and the reluctance of financial-sector regulatory authorities in the Gulf to implement effective anti–money laundering systems. Bahrain, Lebanon, the United Arab Emirates, and Egypt all strengthened their anti–money laundering laws during 2000–2001. Saudi Arabia followed suit after the advent of al Qaeda terrorism within the kingdom in May 2003, though the adequacy of the Saudi response has been questioned (Council on Foreign Relations 2002, 2004).

Much of the focus has been on hawala and the activities of lightly regulated charities (El Qorchi, Maimbo, and Wilson 2003). The role of charities is particularly problematic because it sets up a potential conflict between the Islamic obligation of *zakat* (or charitable giving) and law enforcement.

The spotlight on hawala is ironic insofar as of the 45 cases of terrorist financing between 1998 and 2004, 18 involved wire transfer and only 4 involved alternative remittance systems (Reuter and Truman 2004, table 3.1). Hawala thrives in environments where the formal financial system is inadequate or prohibitively costly. While regulation may play a role, technical assistance to develop the formal financial system may be a useful accompaniment to law enforcement.

There have been debates about how best to tackle terrorist finance. In the United States, the regulatory regime introduced as part of the USA Patriot Act has been criticized as being burdensome and inefficient. European countries complain, in turn, that requests by the US Treasury's Office of Foreign Asset Control to freeze the assets of particular individuals or entities are not accompanied by sufficient evidence to defend these actions in local courts. Existing anti–money laundering laws may be useful in disrupting terrorist finance. But the differences between say al Qaeda transferring $100,000 or less and the Medellin Cartel trying to launder millions of dollars on an ongoing basis can make this effort "like looking for a needle in the haystack" (Reuter and Truman 2004).

investors. Among the assets envisioned for trading on the exchange are the stocks of the Dow Jones Arabia Titans index of 50 leading Arab stocks as well as Islamic bonds packaged for Western investors. It is off to a slow start, however, with a limited number of traded listings. Long a center for gold trade, Dubai launched gold futures trading in 2005 and trading in currency futures in 2006. An oil futures contract based on Omani crude is envisioned, and the government of Oman has taken a 30 percent stake in the commodities exchange. Arguably none of these instruments are sharia-compliant.

Saudi Arabia is attempting to strengthen regulatory quality to improve the attractiveness of its financial markets, including permitting a greater role for foreign institutions. It has announced plans to build a $6 billion financial district in Riyadh. Kuwait is also exploring the possibility of developing itself as a center of financial intermediation and, like Saudi Arabia, is permitting greater participation by foreigners. Qatar has established a similar financial free zone, and Bahrain is attempting to position itself as the center for Islamic finance. Yet as in the case of the forays into the market for higher education, the economics of agglomeration suggest that not all of these initiatives are likely to bear fruit, and indeed, one response to the decline in stock prices beginning in late 2005 may be retrenchment and possibly a reversal of these liberalizing trends.

However, if some of these projects prove successful and financial-sector modernization is extended more broadly, it would not be difficult to imagine more of the region's investable capital staying home. Increased preference for sharia-compliant or Islamic finance could also lead to an effective increase in home-bias.

Oil Rents, Aid, and Remittances

If the demonstration effect of contemporary globalizers was a "pull" that the Middle East resisted, the region also escaped the "push" of crisis, which has forced policymakers in some regions, most notably Eastern Europe, to undertake radical reforms. Instead, most of the Middle Eastern nations have been the beneficiaries of three features of the post–World War II geopolitical landscape: rapidly rising demand for energy given the unprecedented boom in the countries of the Organization for Economic Cooperation and Development (OECD), the Cold War, and the declining fertility rate in advanced countries, particularly those in Western Europe.

The rapid economic growth in the postwar period and the heavy reliance on fossil fuel helped to maintain steady growth of demand for oil. The oil price increase in 1973 and then in 1979 provided the major oil exporters with a huge increase in foreign exchange earnings, partly used to finance high levels of fixed investment. The rents were enormous for most countries as the price far exceeded the marginal cost of even the high-cost producers. In a sense the members of the Organization of Petroleum Exporting Countries (OPEC) were the de facto beneficiaries of a foreign aid program whose size was unprecedented, insofar as the countries received additional income from the rest of the world with little commitment of additional national inputs. Given the declines in real per capita income beginning in the early 1980s in Kuwait, Oman, and Saudi Arabia, this experiment in foreign aid was hardly a resounding success. The recipient nations, like most of the other OPEC members, were not able to transform their additional resources into investments that increase long-term growth. As noted in chapter 2, their experience tracked that of Nigeria rather than that of Indonesia, not a very encouraging parallel as Nigeria is widely acknowledged to have had a singularly inept policy environment (Bevan, Collier, and Gunning 1999). Whether the spike in oil prices beginning in 2003 is likely to be sustained is unknowable. While there are indications that lessons have been learned from the earlier experience, another view is that the greater revenues have reduced any sense of urgency about the need for reforms, a pattern exhibited in the past (Richards 2001).

In addition to the direct recipients of revenue, there were indirect beneficiaries, particularly nonnationals from other Arab countries who were employed in these countries and whose remittances constituted an important source of foreign exchange and investment finance in their countries of origin, which may have generated a "Dutch disease" pattern, as a disproportionate share of remittances was invested in the nontradable sector, particularly housing (Page 1998). Egypt and Jordan were particularly large beneficiaries of these remittances, as shown in table 4.10. However, in the 1980s and 1990s, with the decline in the real price of oil and the prospective dwindling of reserves, this cushion both for the oil producers and indirect beneficiaries was limited.

Finally, during the Cold War the Middle East benefited from considerable aid inflows (table 4.10). In relative terms, the amounts reported for Jordan, Egypt, and Syria are equivalent to or surpass the magnitude of peak aid levels provided to South Korea and Taiwan during the 1950s, which declined rapidly during the 1960s as their economies expanded. Egypt and Syria particularly benefited from Soviet aid until the Camp David agreement with Israel in 1979, and then Egypt received large amounts of US aid in the ensuing period. After the Gulf War period, there were significant economic benefits in the form of debt write-offs for Egypt (not reflected in table 4.10) and Saudi aid to a number of Arab participants in the coalition, particularly Syria after its participation in the Gulf War in 1991.[27] In this regard the most apt (though in the opposite direction) comparators may be the Eastern European nations that abruptly encountered hard budget

---

27. There is also evidence that Egypt received lenient treatment from the IMF in the 1991 negotiations as a result of its participation in the Gulf War (Momani 2004).

Table 4.10 Aid, workers' remittances, and fuel exports (percent of GDP)

Country	Aid				Remittances				Fuel exports			
	1975–79	1980–89	1990–99	2000–2004	1975–79	1980–89	1990–99	2000–2004	1975–79	1980–89	1990–99	2000–2004
Middle East												
Algeria	0.7	0.3	0.5	0.4	1.5^p	0.8	n.a.	n.a	26.8	21.6	23.0^b	35.7
Egypt	14.9	5.0	5.8	1.4	10.2^p	10.1	7.7	3.4	2.9	6.3	2.6^e	2.6
Jordan	27.0	14.4	9.6	6.8	19.8	19.5	17.7	19.5	0.1	0.0	0.0	0.1
Kuwait	0.0	0.0	0.0^t	0.0	0.0	0.0	0.0	0.0	64.9	26.9^f	34.8	46.6^c
Morocco	3.3	3.7	2.5	1.4	5.7	6.7	6.4	8.2	0.2	0.5	0.4	0.6
Saudi Arabia	0.0	0.0	0.0	0.0	0.0^p	0.0	0.0	0.0	57.7	42.4^k	30.4^l	34.7^m
Syria	10.7	5.5	2.8	0.7	0.0^p	0.0	0.0	1.3	9.2	8.5^n	16.3^o	19.1
Tunisia	4.4	2.6	1.5	1.3	3.5^q	4.2	3.7	4.8	8.6	8.8	3.1	3.2
High-performing comparators												
South Korea	0.6	0.1	0.0	0.0	0.0^q	0.2	0.1	0.0	0.3	0.5	0.7	1.5
Taiwan^a	0.0	0.0	0.0	0.0	n.a.	n.a.	n.a.	0.2	n.a.	n.a.	n.a.	n.a.
Large comparators												
China	n.a.	0.4	0.5	0.1	n.a.	0.1^r	0.1	0.1	n.a.	1.7^d	0.9	0.7
India	1.1	0.8	0.6	0.2	0.7	1.1	1.7	3.1^i	0.0	0.3	0.1	0.6
Normally endowed comparators												
Bangladesh	6.7	6.5	4.2	2.4	0.7^q	2.7	3.2	5.4	n.a.	0.1	0.1	0.0
Brazil	0.1	0.1	0.0	0.1	0.0	0.0	0.3	0.3	0.0	0.4	0.1	0.5
Pakistan	4.9	3.1	2.0	1.9	6.0^q	7.5	2.9	3.5	0.3	0.3	0.1^j	0.3
Turkey	0.3	0.6	0.3	0.1	1.9	2.7	2.1	1.2	0.0	0.3	0.2	0.3
Resource-rich comparators												
Botswana	12.3	8.1	2.4	0.5	0.0	0.0	0.0	0.0^i	n.a.	n.a.	n.a.	0.0^c
Indonesia	1.5	1.2	1.1	0.7	n.a.	0.1^s	0.4	0.7	16.0	14.9	7.6	7.6
Nigeria	0.1	0.3	0.8	0.6	0.0^p	0.0	2.6	2.7	28.7	32.2^g	38.2^h	38.0^i
Venezuela	0.0	0.0	0.1	0.1	0.0	0.0	0.0	0.0	22.8	20.8	21.1	22.6

n.a. = not available

Note: Table shows simple average of available data.

a. Aid to Taiwan assumed zero; b. 1990–98; c. 2000–2001; d. 1984–89; e. 1990–95, 1997–99; f. 1980–2005, 1987–99; g. 1981, 1983–87; h. 1991, 1996–99; i. 2000–2003; j. 1990–93, 1995–99; k. 1980–82, 1985, 1988–89; l. 1990–96, 1998–99; m. 2000–2002; n. 1980–87, 1989; o. 1990, 1992, 1995–99; p. 1977–79; q. 1976–79; r. 1982–89; s. 1981–89; t. 1990–91, 1995–99.

Sources: World Bank, *World Development Indicators*, May 2006; Central Bank of China; *Taiwan Statistical Databook*, 2005.

constraints as the Eastern Bloc collapsed and were forced to reform. We shall return to this theme in chapter 7.

Financial-Market Development

If domestic and foreign saving are to materialize, a major issue is the state of financial-market development and the ability to mobilize and efficiently allocate domestic and foreign savings, a process that was underappreciated until the financial crises of the 1990s forced economists to reconsider the "real side" implications of financial distress.[28] This renewed interest has generated a second wave of theoretical and empirical research that has documented the relationship between financial-sector development and economic growth as well as the channels through which it works and possible influence of alternative forms of financial-sector organization.[29] This research has identified multiple functions that the financial sector plays in facilitating growth including identifying projects, monitoring management, pooling risk, and secondary-market transactions that relieve the dependence of project finance on the liquidity constraints of individual investors. Moreover, financial-sector development may contribute to growth if liquidity-constrained small and medium-sized enterprises are disproportionately innovative (Rajan and Zingales 1998) or if relaxation of financial constraints increases technological absorptive capacity (Aghion, Howitt, and Mayer-Foulkes 2005). Conversely, given the financial system's role as a "lubricant," financial crises can cascade through the real side of the economy by impeding interfirm transactions.

In the context of the Middle East, the efficacy of the financial sector in fostering capital accumulation depends on the ability of the financial system to not only mobilize local saving but also attract external inflows. Reductions in the rate of growth of consumption could be avoided if foreign saving could provide more of the financing through portfolio investment and FDI or if Arab nationals repatriated large foreign asset holdings. However, analysis of long-term impacts is clouded by the current worldwide liquidity glut generated in significant part by easy US monetary policy since the Asian financial crisis, the Long-Term Capital Management failure, and the 9/11 terrorist attacks, as well as the close to zero nominal interest rate policy of the Japanese central bank. In the Middle East, global conditions are compounded by the run-up in oil prices starting in 2003, explicit calls for the repatriation of capital invested in the West, and a heightened reluctance among some Arab investors to invest outside the region in the wake of the 9/11 attacks and associated increase in interna-

---

28. For the older tradition, see Gurley and Shaw (1960), MacKinnon (1973), and Shaw (1973).

29. See, for example, King and Levine (1993), Levine (1997), and Levine and Zervos (1998). Aghion (2006) provides a useful survey of this literature.

tional tensions (Warde 2004).[30] After experiencing explosive growth for several years, asset prices in the Middle East began falling in late 2005. This reversal simply underscores the difficulty of disentangling permanent change from transitory factors.

In an overview of the region's financial markets, IMF economists attempted to devise a broad set of quantitative and qualitative indicators of financial-sector development (Creane et al. 2003). They concluded that in comparative terms, MENA financial-sector development unsurprisingly trails the OECD but is above most other developing-country regions. The trends in financial-market development are consistent with those observed with respect to other aspects of economic life: Although MENA was more advanced than Asia in the 1960s, it fell behind in the 1970s and 1980s. Financial-sector development is now accelerating, with Egypt, Jordan, Morocco, and Tunisia exhibiting the greatest improvements, though these countries still lag the Gulf Cooperation Council (GCC) countries— Bahrain, Kuwait, Oman, Qatar, Saudi Arabia, and the United Arab Emirates—in terms of current level of sophistication. The latter may provide templates that countries of interest could replicate. However, for some countries replication would require a relaxation of controls to improve the quality and availability of information that financial markets need to function efficiently. Among the nonoil exporters, financial-sector development is greatest in Lebanon and Jordan, followed by Egypt and Morocco, with Syria bringing up the rear—an ordering, perhaps not coincidentally, corresponding to their relative degree of media openness.

The IMF overall assessment is consistent with time-series data on the development of direct and indirect (bank) finance within MENA indicating that with the exception of Algeria and Syria, financial depth, measured as the ratio of private credit to GDP, has increased over the past decade in all of the Arab countries for which data are available, with increases of 50 percent in some of the normally endowed countries (figures 4.5a and 4.5b). The results in table 4.11 derived from the *Global Competitiveness Report 2005–2006* also place Jordan, Morocco, and Tunisia in the middle of its ranking. This report presents country scores based on surveys of approximately 8,000 business executives in more than 100 countries and could be interpreted as providing an indication of reputation, if not reality.[31]

The IMF economists gave the region generally good marks for basic issues of monetary policy—rates of return are freely determined, govern-

30. One analysis indicates that assets were in fact repatriated; in 2002 net foreign assets for GCC countries fell $18 billion despite a current account surplus of $24 billion (IIF 2005).

31. The survey asks respondents to judge local conditions relative to a global best practices benchmark on a scale of 1 to 7. The World Economic Forum and its network of local affiliates attempt to get a cross-section of respondents from firms of differing sizes across a range of economic activities. The potential weakness of this approach is that the respondents may not know enough about the best practices standard to meaningfully compare with local circumstances. Methodological details of the survey are reported in Blanke and Loades (2005).

Figure 4.5a   Financial depth, normally endowed countries, 1980–99

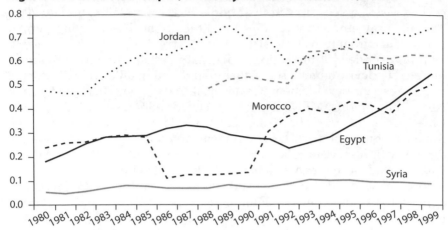

Note: Ratio of private credit by banks and other financial institutions to GDP.

Source: Albuquerque, Loayza, and Servén (2005).

Figure 4.5b   Financial depth, resource-rich countries, 1980–99

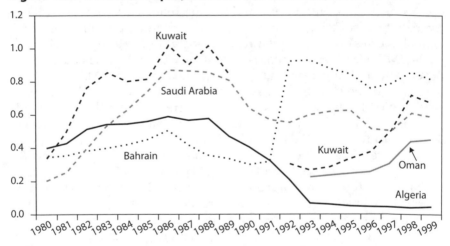

Note: Ratio of private credit by banks and other financial institutions to GDP.

Source: Albuquerque, Loayza, and Servén (2005).

ment securities exist, and monetary authorities can use indirect tools to control the money supply, though unsurprisingly there is some intraregional variation in achievement. The banking sector is reasonably well developed in the GCC countries, but elsewhere it tends to be dominated by public-sector banks, highly concentrated, and subject to considerable

Table 4.11 Financial-market development indicators (percentile)

Country	Financial-market sophistication	Ease of access to loans	Access to credit	Venture capital availability	Local equity market access	Number of listed companies as a percent of market capitalization, 2004
Middle East						
Algeria	3	16	13	18	10	n.a.
Bahrain	84	68	77	62	74	63
Egypt	34	39	20	39	48	26
Jordan	60	47	73	50	71	43
Kuwait	75	79	84	79	80	n.a.
Morocco	32	22	15	26	40	73
Qatar	50	78	65	61	59	n.a.
Tunisia	39	49	32	66	50	30
United Arab Emirates	61	84	87	79	66	83[a]
High-performing comparators						
South Korea	70	62	60	74	60	58
Taiwan	74	88	98	91	91	n.a.
Large comparators						
China	26	25	11	42	28	71
India	74	79	100	76	99	36
Normally endowed comparators						
Bangladesh	25	29	56	21	68	11
Brazil	78	40	42	23	50	81
Pakistan	40	74	94	63	75	25
Turkey	57	30	89	28	79	66
Resource-rich comparators						
Botswana	43	62	48	75	61	48
Indonesia	41	45	41	52	57	56
Nigeria	46	15	2	47	56	32
Venezuela	49	33	22	15	21	44

n.a. = not available

a. 2003 data.

Notes: Higher percentiles correspond to greater development. Sample size = 117 developed and emerging-market economies; 108 for "number of listed companies."

Sources: First five columns: *Global Competitiveness Report 2005–2006*; Number of listed companies as percent of market capitalization: World Bank, *World Development Indicators, 2006*.

barriers to entry, conclusions with which economists affiliated with the Islamic Development Bank generally concur (Hussein and Omran 2005).[32]

Historically, state-owned banks have controlled a large share of total assets, and even where banks were nominally privately owned, regulation tended to be heavy and direct. These conditions affected both the lending culture and the composition of lending. Specifically, the lending function was heavily bureaucratized, "manifested in a lack of qualified credit officers capable of assessing risk" (World Bank 2006a, 57). Tax provisions in countries such as Egypt encourage holding government debt over other instruments. One unintended consequence has been to limit capital available for relatively efficient small and medium-sized enterprises. Some support for this notion can be inferred from the relatively weak scores of Jordan and Morocco on the "ease of access to loans" and "access to credit" rankings in table 4.11. Instead, lending to the public sector constitutes an unusually large share of bank portfolios (World Bank 2006a).

The state banks have been used to channel capital to preferred borrowers or projects and as a consequence have been shielded from foreign competition and rigorous regulatory oversight, though Saudi Arabia, Kuwait, and Iraq have all recently eased restrictions on foreign banks. If the local banks effectively assess risk and allocate credit, their development is encouraging—they can serve as intermediaries for lending by foreign banks, subject to successfully managing currency and term matches. Lending by OECD banks to local banks was an important form of capital inflow in South Korea, for example, so at least in some circumstances this inflow can usefully supplement domestic saving. However, if what is actually occurring is simply on-lending to state-supported projects where the risk is socialized, then taxpayers will eventually bear the bill.

Creane et al. (2003) estimate that the share of nonperforming loans (NPLs) varies between 10 and 20 percent across the region, though it varies with macroeconomic conditions: Relatively robust growth in some countries in recent years has probably allowed some existing NPLs to resume some repayments, while lax lending standards under current boom conditions in the oil exporters have probably meant the extension of loans that will never be repaid, storing up problems for the future.[33] The Institute of International Finance (IIF 2005) estimates that GCC bank credit to the private sector increased $42 billion in 2004, more than double the increase in

---

32. A recent potential source of knowledge transfer has been the recruitment to return home by countries such as Egypt of nationals who have gained experience in more sophisticated GCC banks.

33. More recent estimates for the GCC countries put NPLs at around 5 percent in Saudi Arabia, Kuwait, and Qatar and around 13 percent in Oman and the United Arab Emirates (IIF 2005). The World Bank (2006a) reports even lower estimates of NPLs for the Gulf oil exporters. However, NPLs for the region's nonoil exporters appear to have risen—whether this is intrinsic reflecting deteriorating economic conditions or a statistical artifact of improved regulatory oversight is unclear.

the previous year and five times the average rate in 1991–2001. There is some concern that with the decline in stock market values in 2006, NPLs will increase—bank loans for stock purchases are often collateralized with securities.

Trends in capital-market development are obscured in part by the correlation between commodity prices and stock valuations, especially in the markets in the oil-producing countries (figures 4.6a and 4.6b). Currently, of the Arab countries, only Egypt, Jordan, and Morocco are constituents of the widely used MSCI Emerging Markets equity index, each with minuscule (0.3 percent or less) benchmark weights, and at least one attempt to assess capital-market development on a comparative basis concluded that the region trailed other countries at similar income levels (Hoekman and Messerlin 2002). Another pair of researchers found that in 2001, prior to the current run-up in stock prices, market capitalization and turnover ratios in Egypt, Jordan, Morocco, Saudi Arabia, and Tunisia averaged 26 and 6 percent respectively, compared with 33 and 20 percent for developing countries as a whole (Bolbol and Omran 2005). They described Arab stock markets as a "sideshow" characterized by opaque family ownership, weak prudential regulation, few listings, and ubiquitous restrictions on investment.[34] In the words of the World Bank (2006a, 67), bond markets are "almost nonexistent outside the GCC."

Nevertheless between 2001 and 2005, asset prices rose by dot-com proportions, driven by the worldwide liquidity glut, rising oil prices, and an increased reluctance to invest outside the region in the wake of the 9/11 terrorist attacks, which could be interpreted as an increase in home-bias. The market capitalization of the six stock exchanges of the main oil exporters tripled to $875 billion, and July 2005 price-earnings ratios on the stock exchanges of Saudi Arabia (38), the United Arab Emirates (38), and Jordan (40) stood at more than double that in other emerging markets. Saudi Arabia's market capitalization reached three times its national income, despite the fact that the "tradable" share of the economy is relatively small due to the prominence of nontraded public corporations in the Saudi economy. A boom in initial public offerings (IPOs) accompanied the run-up in asset prices.[35] These IPOs have been routinely oversubscribed, and

---

34. See also the papers contained in Hussein and Omran (2005) for analyses of the efficiency of Arab country stock markets.

35. The IIF (2005) estimates that in the GCC countries, $1.8 billion was raised through IPOs in 2004, with a further $4 billion raised through this channel in the first half of 2005. Observers have predicted considerable future increases; one locally based investment banker anticipates $5 billion to $10 billion in additional IPOs in the Gulf over the three years running through mid-2008. See Roula Khalaf, William Watts, and Gillian Tett, "Sky-High: Arab Economies Are Booming Amid Strong Liquidity and Patchy Reforms," *Financial Times*, July 6, 2005; and Stephen Negus and Christopher Brown-Humes, "Markets in Gulf See Big Falls as Bull Run Falters," *Financial Times*, March 15, 2006. How much of this projected activity survives the 2006 downturn remains to be seen.

Figure 4.6a Market capitalization, normally endowed countries, 1988–2004

percent of GDP

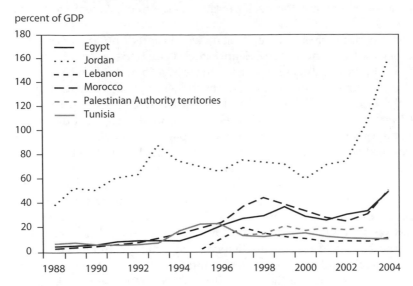

Source: World Bank, *World Development Indicators*, May 2006.

Figure 4.6b Market capitalization, resource-rich countries, 1988–2004

percent of GDP

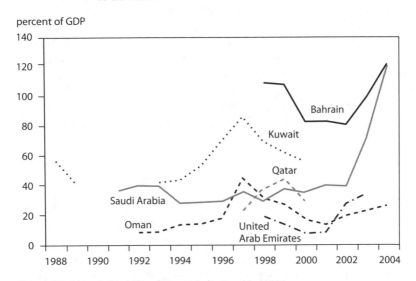

Source: World Bank, *World Development Indicators*, May 2006.

some observers argue that this underpricing was by design, effectively creating rents that could be allocated to insiders.[36] This allegation, if true, is particularly pernicious in the case of privatizations, where public assets were in effect transferred to insiders through the IPO process, a development that might have been precluded with some attention to Eastern European privatization efforts. Three cabinet ministers in Qatar were sacked after one such episode.

Financial-sector activity in the oil-rich states has had significant spillover effects in other Arab countries. The Shuaa Capital Arab Composite index, which tracks 254 companies in 12 Arab countries, was up 63 percent in the first half of 2005, on top of 60 percent gains in 2003 and 2004. In the well-worn tradition of using hydraulic metaphors for financial-market activity, one commentator observed "the oil money pouring in is akin to pushing Niagara Falls through a kitchen faucet."[37] This observation suggests a strong element of "contagion" from the oil-rich to other nations.

The danger, of course, is that any collapse in the former will have serious real side effects due to the same contagion as has occurred several times in the last decades in emerging markets, and indeed, asset prices began to fall in late 2005. The decline accelerated in early 2006, and on "Black Tuesday," March 14, 2006, markets throughout the region declined, with the Dubai market falling 12 percent following a regulatory change that encouraged Saudi investors to sell on margin calls.[38] As of December 2006, the Saudi and Dubai markets are down roughly 60 percent from their peaks (figure 4.7).

Whether this decline is simply a "pause" or "correction" in the context of a long-run bull market or whether it amounts to something more sustained remains to be seen. In the past, when financial markets in the region have collapsed, sometimes associated with scandals, local governments have tended to intervene to protect investors, attempt to restore confidence, and perhaps unintentionally create moral hazard, extending

---

36. Illustrative of the hothouse atmosphere was the May 2005 IPO of the UAE-based Aabar Petroleum Investments. The company had sought to raise $135 million in capital, but its offering was more than 800 times oversubscribed, with investors submitting pledges totaling $107 billion! The UAE central bank subsequently found that four local banks had excessively leveraged subscribers but did not divulge the names of the firms. Four months later, police had to be called to quell a riot that broke out when crowds of retail investors descended on local brokerages to invest in an IPO that was 139 times oversubscribed (Steve Negus, "After the Growth, Dubai Exchange Aims to Fill Trading Void," *Financial Times*, February 22, 2006).

37. Vito Racanelli, "European Trader," *Barron's*, May 23, 2005. See also John Dizard, "The Middle East Offers Fertile Soil for Value Hunters," *Financial Times*, March 14, 2006.

38. The Saudi bourse regulator was dismissed in May 2006, and the market rose 17 percent (equivalent to roughly 8.5 percent of GDP) in the two days following the appointment of his successor. Somehow it is hard to believe that one individual could single-handedly impede the economy on this scale.

**Figure 4.7   Saudi stock market (TASI) closing price,
May 2001–January 2007**

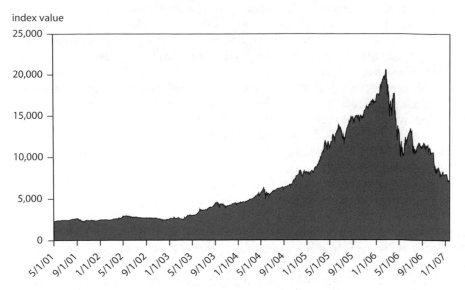

Source: Tadawul Stock Market Performance, www.tadawul.com (accessed June 13, 2006).

and even exacerbating the crisis. For example, in 1977 the government of
Kuwait responded to a relatively small stock market crash by bailing out
investors and introducing stricter regulations. These actions had the unintended effect of encouraging the development among less risk-averse
investors of an unofficial market in postdated checks, which in turn experienced a much larger crash in 1982. During the March 2006 episode,
the Kuwait state investment authority injected funds into the market. To
be clear, Kuwait is not alone in this regard: The Saudi government also announced in May 2006 a plan to establish a "risk-free fund," in effect creating a one-way bet, for lower-income first-time investors, generously defined.[39] It also relaxed restrictions on foreign investors.

The possible bubble is not limited to stocks, either: Under construction
in Dubai is what is to be the world's tallest building, as well as the world's
largest shopping mall, to go along with the world's only 7-star hotel, Burj
Al Arab (shown on the cover of this book). A land reclamation project, al-
legedly the only man-made structure visible from the moon, is whimsi-

---

39. The Saudi action hints at the possible social repercussions of the downturn. Trading on
the Saudi exchange was reportedly dominated by retail investors, despite the existence of little Arabic-language research on these stocks. Day trading had reached epidemic proportions
prompting the minister of education to rebuke public-school teachers for neglecting their official responsibilities in favor of punting.

cally creating new parcels in the shape of existing continents, allowing investors to "buy Australia" or "live in South America" without ever leaving home. Similar, if less grandiose, projects are under way throughout the Gulf. Despite large volumes of additional commercial and residential stock coming to market as a result of this building activity, real estate prices have risen sharply, with some investors in Dubai reportedly realizing returns of 20 percent per month.

Such developments pose obvious risks: One is the distortion of investment decisions or simple resource misallocation. One view (Bolbol and Omran 2005) that Arab stock markets exert little influence on resource allocation suggests limited real side potential damage of a stock market bubble. However, local banks are heavily invested in local real estate and have permitted borrowers to use their loans for stock market investments. In the case of IPOs, the IIF estimates that some banks were lending up to 20 times the cash contribution of the subscriber. Real estate and stocks, in particular, lend themselves to sharia-compliant instruments and hence are a natural component of the portfolios of Islamic financial institutions. A fall in the price of oil could not only pull down local stock and real estate prices but also bring down the banking sector with it (Texas in the 1980s or Japan in the 1990s), contributing to subpar growth while the financial sector is rehabilitated and transmitting real-side shocks to the neighbors through financial-market linkages. Recognizing these growing risks, in 2005 the UAE central bank set a limit on commercial bank lending for IPOs at five times the cash contribution of the subscriber.[40]

A subtle and important issue in this regard is the extent to which the increase in post-9/11 home-bias in investor preferences has translated into an increased demand for local assets as distinct from regional assets more broadly. While many of the region's bourses are up strongly, this is not uniformly the case: The market in Morocco, geographically and culturally furthest from the Gulf, was actually down, partly due to issuance for the first time in the local market of a dirham-denominated bond by the International Finance Corporation, the World Bank group's private-sector arm. This bond at least temporarily reduced demand for other local assets including stocks. The point is that the impact of rising oil prices, positive or negative, on asset-market returns is unlikely to be felt uniformly across the region.

As a consequence, the role of foreign investors from outside the region could be potentially important. These investors may differ from local investors in their capacity to evaluate risks and returns, and they may be subject to a different set of liquidity shocks. Their participation could re-

---

40. This parallels the preemptive action of the Philippine central bank prior to the Asian financial crisis that enabled the Philippines to fare better than some of its neighbors (Noland 2000).

duce market volatility. Not surprisingly the run-up in oil prices and ample liquidity have attracted Western financial-service providers to the Gulf.[41]

In this regard the financial markets of the region differ considerably, in size, sophistication, and restrictions on foreign investors or service providers. Foreigners, for example, accounted for more than 40 percent of ownership on the Amman Stock Exchange (with foreign Arabs accounting for more than 60 percent of this total), while in Saudi Arabia foreigners are forced to invest through a limited number of locally controlled funds, and even other Gulf investors reportedly account for less than 5 percent of ownership. Historically, the weak financial sector and the only average growth of the real economy account for the relatively meager inward portfolio investment, and in relative terms the Arab countries lag their comparators, by large margins in some cases (table 4.12). However, the reported figures undoubtedly understate current investment flows, at least in absolute terms, for countries like Egypt and Jordan that benefit from proximity to the Gulf and Tunisia and Morocco, which have encountered at least modest success in tapping the growing market for emerging-market debt. (Egypt, Lebanon, Morocco, and Tunisia are constituents of the commonly followed JPMorgan Emerging Bond Index Global, each with small weights; so for example, the PIMCO Emerging Market Fund, one of the largest US-based mutual funds, allocates about 4 percent of its portfolio to these countries.)

Conclusion

The Middle East is under multiple stresses. It is imperative that it rapidly generate employment to absorb new labor force entrants. One of the demonstrably effective ways of quickly creating employment is through expansion of labor-intensive manufacturing and service exports. But the region is lagging in its effort to globalize, trailing a diverse set of competitors that have already established strong footholds in global production and trade networks.

Until recently the Middle East's traditional safety net of financial flows generated by strategic location and mineral rents had been eroding, making it more difficult to finance capital accumulation and to pay for social overhead capital necessitated by the rapid population increase. In this regard the rise in oil prices since 2003 has ambiguous effects: On the one hand it potentially increases investable capital for the region as a whole, on the other it is likely to dampen the urgency of reform, leaving these economies even more vulnerable if the oil price trend reverses. In the next chapters we explore some of the determinants of the Middle East's

---

41. The 2005 IPO for Dana Gas in Abu Dhabi reportedly earned the 10 receiving banks $270 million in fees and profits off margin loans to investors (Will McSheehy and Lina Saigol, "Petro-Dollars Lure a Wave of Foreign Bankers to Gulf State," *Financial Times*, December 6, 2006).

Table 4.12 Cumulative portfolio investment (billions of current US dollars)

Country	Total 1980–89	Total 1990–99	Total 2000–2004	Bonds 1980–89	Bonds 1990–99	Bonds 2000–2004	Equities 1980–89	Equities 1990–99	Equities 2000–2004
Middle East									
Algeria	0.0	n.a.	n.a.	0.9	-1.5	0.0	0.0	0.0	0.0
Egypt	0.0	1.4	1.2	-0.1	0.1	1.4	0.0	1.0	0.2
Jordan	0.0	0.0	-1.6	0.0	-0.1	-0.6	0.0	0.0	-0.4
Kuwait	-2.1	-18.4	-50.3	n.a.	n.a.	n.a.	n.a.	n.a.	n.a.
Morocco	0.0	0.5	0.6	-0.2	0.3	0.3	0.0	0.5	0.6
Saudi Arabia	-26.1	9.0	-50.0	n.a.	n.a.	n.a.	n.a.	n.a.	n.a.
Syria	0.0	0.0	0.0	0.0	0.0	0.0	0.0	0.0	0.0
Tunisia	0.4	0.4	0.0	0.0	1.5	1.6	0.0	0.3	0.0
High-performing comparators									
South Korea	0.8	74.7	46.7	2.0	38.3	n.a.	0.0	41.9	n.a.
Taiwan	-0.2	0.0	0.0	0.2	4.3	11.6	-0.4	23.4	62.7
Large comparators									
China	4.1[a]	1.0	-2.6	4.7[b]	10.3	4.9	0.0	7.0	28.7
India	0.0	14.7[c]	14.4[e]	2.3	6.7	5.9	0.4	17.0	23.3
Normally endowed comparators									
Bangladesh	0.0	0.0	0.0	0.0	0.0	0.0	0.0	0.0	0.0
Brazil	-1.6	145.1	2.5	-2.0	26.8	9.7	0.2	30.7	12.6
Pakistan	0.5	2.9[d]	-0.8[g]	0.0	0.7	-0.1	0.0	2.4	0.0
Turkey	3.0	7.8	6.4	4.2	15.6	8.9	0.0	2.4	2.7
Resource-rich comparators									
Botswana	0.0	-0.1	-1.0[e]	0.0	0.0	0.0	0.0	0.0	0.0
Indonesia	0.6[b]	8.3	-0.9[f]	0.5	8.6	-1.7	0.4	-3.1	3.6
Nigeria	2.8	1.3	2.0	0.0	0.0	-0.5	0.0	0.0	0.0
Venezuela	2.6	20.3	-7.2	-0.1	3.4	0.1	0.0	4.4	-0.6

n.a. = not available

Notes: Total figures exclude liabilities constituting foreign authorities' reserves except South Korea and Taiwan. Figures for these are taken from different sources and are not completely comparable to the others. All figures are in current dollars and thus only approximate cumulative investment.

a. 1982–89; b. 1981–89; c. 1990–98; d. 1990–97; e. 2000–2003; f. 2000–2002; g. 2002–04.

Sources: South Korea bonds and equities: Bank of Korea Economics Statistics System; Taiwan: Central Bank of China, Republic of China (Taiwan), Balance of Payments Statistics, www.cbc.gov.tw; Others: World Bank, *World Development Indicators*, May 2006.

performance and the inability of some countries to transform a favorable set of economic parameters into better growth.

Current countervailing trends such as oil price increases and their spillover dampen the need for immediate economic reform while the absence of future aid inflows and greater competition militate in favor of it. Moreover, the growing popular discontent in many of the Arab countries makes further reform urgent, particularly to create more jobs, while at the same time it makes reform more risky as some of the reforms will have adverse short-term consequences such as a reduction in the number of jobs.

Appendix 4A
Labor Force Absorption

Assume a national production function that is Cobb-Douglas,

$$Q = AK^{\alpha}L^{1-\alpha} \tag{4A.1}$$

The equilibrium condition in the labor market is

$$F_L = A(K/L)^{\alpha} = w/p \tag{4A.2}$$

where F_L is the marginal product of labor, w/p the real wage, and A an index of total factor productivity (TFP). The rate of growth of employment is then

$$L^* = [A^* + \alpha K^* - (w/p)^*]/\alpha \tag{4A.3}$$

where L^* is the rate of growth of employment, A^* is the rate of growth of TFP, K^* the rate of growth of the capital stock, which depends largely on the national investment rate, and $(w/p)^*$ is the rate of growth of the real wage. The rate of job creation is increased by additional investment with which labor is complementary and decreased by any growth in the real wage firms pay. Greater growth in TFP also increases job creation as it increases the marginal product of labor.

5

Religion, Institutions, and Growth

In the evolving understanding of development, economists have identified proximate and more fundamental sources of economic development. The former include the investment to GDP ratio, level and growth of education, economic policies, and characteristics of the economy such as corruption. These determinants may in turn be endogenous, reflecting "deeper" characteristics of nations that can potentially explain diverse outcomes: in increasing order of amenability to intentional alteration, geography and the dependence of institutions on history, social groups, and religious affiliation.

Geography is obviously important in myriad ways, but economists tend to focus on two issues thought to have particular salience for development: whether a country is landlocked and as a consequence unable to exploit sea transportation or is dependent on its neighbors to do so and whether a country has a tropical climate and as a consequence its population is subject to deadly and debilitating tropical diseases.

Geography in this sense does not appear to pose a major constraint for the Middle East: Most of the countries have access to the Mediterranean Sea or other navigable bodies of water. And given the arid conditions of the region, tropical disease is generally not an issue, though malaria is a limited risk in some rural areas and Egypt experienced bilharzia as a result of the flooding of the Nile. Lack of fresh water, and the misallocation of this scarce resource, poses a challenge for most countries in the region, however (box 5.1).

At the level of political geography, it has been argued that the fragmentation of the region that accompanied the decline and eventual collapse of the Ottoman Empire, the partial colonization by England and

Box 5.1   Water

The Middle East may be drowning in oil but is one of the world's most naturally water-scarce regions. This challenge is exacerbated by the odd fact that in some of the Arab countries this scarcest of resources is allocated badly. Analyses using optimizing models suggest that the shortage can be remedied using better pricing policies, although these may be politically difficult and require coordination across countries (Fisher et al. 2002).

The region faces both quantity and quality issues with respect to water: In Jordan, Saudi Arabia, Yemen, Tunisia, and Algeria, renewable supplies account for less than half of the demand, while quantity problems are compounded by quality problems as governments implement programs to reuse water (Richards 2001, Shetty 2006). Water management is further complicated by the fact that major rivers and aquifers span national boundaries.

Much of the region's fresh water is used in agriculture, reflecting both incentive policies such as generous support prices, which encourage agricultural production generally, and water pricing policies, which encourage the overuse of this specific input. For example, both Saudi Arabia and Syria subsidize wheat production, with Saudi Arabia even emerging as a significant exporter in the early 1990s, though budgetary pressures associated with the 1990s collapse of oil prices subsequently forced a scaling back of incentives. According to Shobha Shetty (2006), in some countries water prices do not even cover private costs. In the case of Syria, "most farmers tend to over-irrigate with water use reported at three times the optimal rate as defined by research trials" (Shetty 2006, 24).

Adjustment in agriculture is politically problematic, however. Not only do the rural beneficiaries of these distortions lobby for their continuance but also a squeeze on agriculture could accelerate potentially politically destabilizing rural-urban migration.

The ubiquity of such distortions also poses problems for trade policy both in the Doha Round of negotiations in the World Trade Organization and intraregional economic integration initiatives discussed in chapter 8. All of the Arab countries except Morocco are net importers of food, and agricultural reforms that would reduce export subsidies by major exporters such as the European Union would have the effect of increasing world prices to the detriment of the Middle Eastern importers. Agricultural products are also covered in the intraregional proposals, but the prevalence of distortions both with respect to agriculture generally and the use of water specifically presents politically challenging adjustment issues for would-be reformers.

France, and the establishment of the state of Israel disrupted traditional patterns of commerce and social interaction, contributing to a stultifying parochialism (Said 1978, Fromkin 1989, Karsh and Karsh 1999). There is surely something to the notion that fragmentation and arbitrary borders have been a drag on development, though the magnitude of the impact is difficult to assess. As for the presence of Israel, given the existence of the Mediterranean and other sea routes, air transportation, and telecommunications, for most countries of the region Israel would seem to be less of a geographic obstacle to integration than a handy foil for governments seeking to deflect responsibility for local problems.[1]

The invocation of these political geography considerations, as distinct from the more narrow way that economists normally think of geography, leads quite naturally to a discussion of local institutions and their possible historical, religious, or cultural bases.

Religious Affiliation and Growth Across Countries

A large literature argues that the institutional environment—the man-made constraints that structure political, economic, and social interaction, consisting of both informal constraints (taboos, customs, and codes of conduct) and formal rules (constitutions and laws)—may have an important impact on development. Policies can be thought of as the content-specific rules or decisions implemented through the institutional framework. Despite some assertions, Islam has not been inconsistent with growth in the Middle East nor in other areas—witness the spectacular performance of Indonesia and Malaysia between 1970 and the onset of the East Asian crisis in 1997 and the recent acceleration of growth in Bangladesh.

On a worldwide basis, Muslims largely reside in countries categorized as "lower middle income" in standard international classifications. In chapter 2 we showed that the heavily Muslim countries of the Middle East exhibited slow to average growth during the 1980s and 1990s, although we did not go into the fundamental determinants of the slower growth. Few in the region would consider Islam, the Middle East's dominant religion, an obstacle to development; indeed they would find this line of inquiry odd, but it appears that many from outside the region disagree. Luigi Guiso, Paola Sapienza, and Luigi Zingales (2003, 228, 280)

---

1. A particularly apt account is given in a long article in the *New York Times* by Michael Slackman ("Beneath the Rage in the Middle East," February 12, 2006) in discussing the government-led efforts to shift attention from their shortcomings in 2005 and 2006 by focusing on Danish cartoons depicting the Prophet Mohammed. These problems included the slow response of the Egyptian government to a major boat catastrophe and the need for Syria to deflect attention from its role in the assassination of Rafik Hariri, the prominent Lebanese politician.

characterize Islam as being negatively associated "with attitudes that are conducive to growth" and among adherents to the world's major religions, Muslims as being the most "antimarket." Stefan Voigt (2005, 66) is blunt, stating, "Islamic values are a central cause of the poor economic performance of Muslim countries."

Islam prescribes some unique economic institutions such as the prohibition on *riba*, commonly believed to be equivalent to the charging of interest, or the injunction to observe *zakat*, narrowly construed as the paying of alms, which could serve as the causal links between theological belief and economic performance at the aggregate level. The issue is whether these institutions can be shown to be the reason that countries still are "only" lower middle income or have experienced slow growth rates. There is some reason to be skeptical on this count: As reported by Frederic Pryor (2006), the share of zakat contributions in income or in conventional tax receipts, or the share of Islamic financial institutions in the financial sector as a whole is small, and the largest Muslim country in the world, Indonesia, is one of the few developing countries that did converge on the Organization for Economic Cooperation and Development (OECD) over the past half century. More generally economic growth tends to be fairly variable over both the short and long runs (Easterly and Levine 2001), so it is difficult to see how something as slowly evolving as religious practices or adherence could be the primary driver of economic performance. The relatively fast growth in 1960 to 1980 in the Middle Eastern nations considered in this book and the slowdown in the succeeding two decades can hardly be associated with a change in religion.[2]

The conventional wisdom is that the level of development in the Islamic world was higher than in Western Europe in the 10th century but that the West had caught up by the 17th or 18th century. The simplest interpretation would be that Islam is consistent with long periods of relatively rapid and slow growth and is not dispositive in any deep way. The other possible interpretation is that something fundamentally changed within either Islam or Christianity during this period that reordered the compatibility of these religions with economic development.

There are those who make the latter argument, from theological, sociological, and institutional perspectives. With respect to the first, what is needed is a theological break similar to the Protestant Reformation, which could alter behavior and provide the turning point between long periods of relatively successful and unsuccessful development. Bernard Lewis (1982) argues that somewhere between the 9th and 11th centuries, "the gate of *ijtihad*" (independent reasoning) was closed—meaning that all answers were

---

2. Consistency of course is not required in casual explanations of economic growth. Many analysts confidently ascribed the bad performance of South Korea and Taiwan in the 1950s and early 1960s to the inimical effects of "Confucianism" and with similar omniscience attributed their rapid growth in the following three decades to the same factor.

already available, hence there was no need for inquiry, just follow and obey. Lewis (1993a) expands upon this critique of "the authoritarian character of traditional pedagogy" and its emphasis on rote memorization. Of course, authoritarian pedagogy and rote memorization are not unique to the schools of Islamic countries, as any Japanese or South Korean schoolchild could attest. Traditional Muslim education systems taught a set of accepted propositions rather than how to "use their own judgment, exercise their critical faculties, and decide things for themselves" (Lewis 1993a, 354; UNDP 2002). Neither Sufism nor Shi'ism, the most prominent departures from the orthodoxy, could provide the basis for a rigorous critique of the dominant practices à la Protestant Christianity.[3] Not surprisingly, this interpretation is highly controversial; Nazih Ayubi (1993) accepts Lewis's interpretation of the closing of the gate of ijtihad but argues that it was reopened in the 19th century by the emergence of Jamal al-Din al-Afghani and his disciples. Wael Hallaq (1984, 1997) dismisses the whole proposition as "entirely baseless and inaccurate" (1984, 4).

With regard to the sociological origins of Islamic performance, Max Weber, following the writings of 14th century Islamic writer Ibn Khaldun, argued that Muslim societies were founded by nomadic warriors whose bands were characterized by intense group loyalty; once they settled down, however, their descendents succumbed to the vices of the cities and were replaced by another wave of tribesmen of greater social cohesion. Neither the warrior tradition with its plunder ethic nor the sedentary dynastic bureaucracy could provide the cultural rationale for development through intensive means.

Timur Kuran (2003a) provides an interpretation of how Islamic practices, for example inheritance rules, inhibited the development of commercial institutions comparable to those developed in the West during the Renaissance and as a consequence weakened Islamic merchants in competition with their Western counterparts.[4] Indeed, Kuran argues that these institutional constraints explain why commerce and finance within the Middle East came to be increasingly dominated by non-Muslim religious minorities until the widespread adoption of Western institutions and practices in the 19th century (Kuran 2003a, 2004).[5]

---

3. See Turner (1974), Metcalf (1999), and Peters (1999) for discussions of the superficial similarities between the 19th century Islamic reform movements and the Protestant Reformation.

4. See also Greif (1994) and Lal (1998) for a complementary interpretation of institutional change in Western Christendom.

5. Lewis (1993b, 24–25) provides a fascinating illustration of this phenomenon: "In 1912, forty private bankers were listed in Istanbul. Not one of them was a Turkish Muslim. Those who can be identified by their names included twelve Greeks, twelve Armenians, eight Jews, and five Levantines or Europeans. A list of thirty-four stock brokers in Istanbul included eighteen Greeks, six Jews, five Armenians, and not a single Turk." Kuran provides similar examples from Turkish and Arab commercial centers: "In 1826 individuals with names identifiable as

In sum, it could be that these negative interpretations of Islam's historical legacy are correct but that enough convergence in institutions, policies, and behavior has occurred so that the effects have been attenuated in the contemporary world or that other positive characteristics in Islamic societies overwhelm the negative influence of Islam, or that this received wisdom is simply wrong. After exhaustively analyzing a large number of indicators of institutions, practices, and outcomes, Pryor (2006) in fact concludes that today's majority-Muslim countries do not constitute a distinct group or define a distinct economic "institutional complex."

Ultimately, whatever the validity of these arguments, the question is, Does the empirical evidence provide any confirmation of the positive or negative effects of Islam during the last four decades? One way of getting at this is through the now ubiquitous cross-country regression approach. The earliest cross-country regressions attempted to account for growth rates using a production theoretic approach, explaining growth in output per worker by initial per capita income, a proxy for investment rates, and a measure of human capital in an effort to discriminate between endogenous growth models and the standard neoclassical growth model (Barro 1991; Mankiw, Romer, and Weil 1991). However, this early set of empirical estimates was soon supplemented by models that added measures of policy outcomes such as inflation rates, fiscal deficits, openness to foreign trade, quality of institutions, and size of government consumption. As Robert Solow (2001) and others have pointed out, this marked a change from a production theoretic basis—production functions do not conventionally include a measure of inflation as an explanatory variable. As noted above, other researchers have sought still more fundamental sources of growth such as colonial legacy, geography, and institutions. All of these studies have now departed substantially from the initial testing of the empirical evaluation of endogenous growth models versus the implications of the Solow-Swan model, which motivated considerable empirical research. Recent research is better interpreted as a search for empirical regularities without an agreed upon theoretical framework for interpreting correlations uncovered. But the correlations may prove to be of some interest.

The evidence on the impact of Islam on income and productivity growth derived from cross-country growth models is mixed, possibly due

---

Muslims constituted only 6 of the 34 traders included in lists of local Beiruti merchants in business with Europe; by 1848 this number had fallen to 3; and for the next three-quarters of a century the city's foreign trade remained almost entirely in the hands of Christian families. In Aleppo, Muslims maintained a major presence in commerce, but all the wealthiest merchants were Christians. Meanwhile, Baghdad's foreign trade fell largely under the control of local Jews, who benefited from their ties with Jewish merchant communities abroad. Alexandria, another major trading center, had 72 merchant houses in 1837; 43 belonged to Europeans, 27 to local minorities, two to Muslims, one a Tunisian, and the other a Turk" (Kuran 2004, 81). He goes on to observe that the official statistics document the same phenomenon with respect to trade within the Ottoman Empire and provides similar documentation of non-Muslim minority dominance of finance in these Arab commercial centers.

to the use of different samples, different economic fundamentals on which the religious adherence results are conditioned, and perhaps more importantly different excluded categories against which the estimated coefficients in the included religion categories are judged.[6]

Marcus Noland (2005a) extends the literature in several directions. Three sorts of evidence are brought to bear: first, a large sample of 78 countries over 1970–90 (most similar to Barro and McCleary 2003); second, a sample of 34 countries over the extended period 1913–98; and finally subnational data within three multiethnic, multireligious countries (India, Malaysia, and Ghana) with sizable Muslim populations from three different parts of the world. The last dimension of the analysis is particularly important—influences such as differences in trade policies or legal institutions that are difficult to control for in cross-country analysis disappear when examining subnational data for a single country. Moreover, Noland considers both per capita income growth and total factor productivity growth, while Barro and McCleary (2003) and Sala-i-Martin, Doppelhofer, and Miller (2004) examine only per capita income growth.

The results indicate that in both cross-country and within-country regressions, the null hypothesis that religious affiliation is uncorrelated with performance can frequently be rejected (i.e., religion matters), though the regressions do not yield a consistent and robust pattern of coefficients with respect to particular religions.[7] The correlations with respect to Islam do not support the notion that it is inimical to growth. As might have been expected on the basis of the analysis in chapter 2, predominantly Muslim countries are seldom outliers (either positively or negatively) in the cross-country regressions. In most cases, the coefficient on the Muslim popula-

---

6. Robert J. Barro and Rachel M. McCleary (2003) examine the impact of religious affiliation and intensity of belief in an unbalanced panel of 59 countries (maximum of 37 cross-sectional observations for any given time observation) over 1960–70. Their sample is mostly developed countries and includes only four predominantly Muslim countries. They find that Islam (as well as Hinduism, Orthodox Christianity, and Protestantism) inhibits economic performance relative to Catholicism. The difficulty of relying on such regressions can be seen when economic performance of the 1980s is considered—the overwhelmingly Catholic countries of Latin America experienced no growth in per capita income for that decade as a result of policies adopted to redress the debt default that occurred in the early part of the decade. It would be difficult to set out a causal role for Catholicism as opposed to the impersonal effects of capital markets as a determinant of growth.

In a paper by Xavier Sala-i-Martin, Gernot Doppelhofer, and Ronald I. Miller (2004), religious affiliation is but one of many variables affecting per capita income growth. They find that Buddhism and Islam have a positive impact on growth (though the magnitude of the coefficient on the share of the population professing Buddhism is nearly twice as large as for the Muslim population share) relative to an "other religions" catch-all.

7. In Sala-i-Martin, Doppelhofer, and Miller (2004), "other religions" is the excluded category against which the impact of the included religious affiliation variables are assessed, but while they include Confucianism as a religion and put Judaism in the "other category," Noland does the reverse.

tion share is statistically insignificant, with one exception—where it is significant, it is always positive. (The only case of a statistically significant negative coefficient is in a subnational regression for Malaysia.) Islam does not appear to be a drag on growth, as sometimes alleged. Even though the results are basically correlations without a strong theoretical foundation, they suggest that Islam has not been a notable correlate of growth retardation. The generally weak performance of most countries in the half century since World War II leaves a lot to be explained, both for Islamic and other countries.

At the same time, while Islam may not be strongly correlated with economic outcomes, it still could be the case that the Islamic religious tradition or other cultural or historical experiences may have affected the development of local institutions or conditioned local attitudes on a wide range of issues that could indirectly affect economic performance. Surveys and case studies indicate that Arab businessmen face a particularly unsupportive institutional environment (Nugent 2000). In this chapter we discuss economic institutions; in chapter 7 we discuss the possible constraints that elite and popular attitudes pose for internal reform; and in chapter 9 we discuss how local conditions may affect subjective assessment of risk that foreigners put on economic transactions with Middle Eastern countries.

Daron Acemoglu, Simon Johnson, and James A. Robinson (2001) in an influential paper argued that the quality of contemporary political institutions is highly correlated with colonial settler death rates between the 17th and 19th centuries. Societies where settlers had low death rates more successfully transplanted political institutions from Western Europe than those where disease impeded the establishment of significant settler populations with a stake in local governance. It might also be the case that differing colonial powers established political institutions of differing strengths in their colonies, though previous research does not appear to bear out this hypothesis (Przeworski et al. 2000). Most of the contemporary Arab countries were under Ottoman rule until the 19th century, when the British and French began expanding their influence at the expense of the Ottomans. With the possible exception of Algeria, the transplantation of large European settler populations was not widespread, however. From the standpoint of Acemoglu, Johnson, and Robinson, the absence of a core of colonists would not bode well for subsequent performance, since the European powers would have less of an incentive to match their diplomatic influence with investment in local institutions.

Legal Systems and Growth

A related argument is that a country's legal system may affect the quality of governance, economic performance, and/or political stability, and Middle Eastern businessmen in fact cite problematic "enforcement of the legal system" as the single biggest obstacle to doing business in their countries (Zarrouk 2003, table 4-8), supporting the theoretical prediction.

With respect to economic performance, this argument revolves around the national origin of the commercial legal system, specifically whether its origins are in the British common law system or the civil law system of continental Europe, whether it originated in the country or was transplanted, and if transplanted the receptivity of the local population to the introduction of this legal system.[8] The typical result is that common law systems dominate civil law systems and that effectiveness is related to the directness of and receptivity to the institutional transfer. So, for example, the transfer of British common law to Australia would be expected to be successful, since the British colonial administrators were transferring it directly and the local population predominantly consisted of migrants familiar with the concepts of the common law system.[9] In contrast, a country like Guatemala would be expected to perform poorly—its legal system was imposed by a country, Spain, that itself was not the originator of the legal system it was transferring, and the system was being transferred to a local indigenous population for whom the basic precepts of the civil law system were alien.

For the most part the Arab countries would appear to be an intermediate case: Their modern commercial legal systems come directly from their British or French originators but were introduced to populations more familiar with traditional *sharia* law practices. In this regard it is worth noting that in a poll conducted in Egypt, Jordan, Lebanon, Morocco, Saudi Arabia, and the United Arab Emirates, majorities in four of the six countries supported governing business by sharia law, with pluralities in all six countries indicating that it required further interpretation to enable businesses in the Muslim world to integrate into the global economy (Zogby International 2005). Such attitudes are not of mere theoretical interest: Perceived inconsistencies between World Trade Organization (WTO) rules and local interpretation of sharia played an important role in delaying Saudi Arabia's accession to that organization. Robert Jordan, the US ambassador to Riyadh at the time Saudi Arabia joined the WTO, has warned that sharia may continue to trump international arbitration decisions, and Charles Kestenbaum, a US Commerce Department official, has similarly expressed skepticism that in resolving commercial disputes, Saudi courts would challenge *fatwas* issued by the religious authorities (Clatanoff et al. 2006).

---

8. See LaPorta et al. (1999); Mahoney (2001); Berkowitz, Pistor, and Richard (2003); and Djankov et al. (2003).

9. Of course, many may have been familiar with criminal law from the wrong side of the bench as Robert Hughes (1986) has shown that a high percentage of Australia's initial colonizers were former criminals.

Table 5.1 summarizes data on the origins and perceived effectiveness of the commercial legal systems of our comparator countries. As it turns out, all of these countries are classified as "unreceptive"—the local populations had little familiarity with these legal systems at the time of their introduction, and in this sense the Arab countries are hardly unique. Most of these comparator countries received their legal systems directly via British or French imperialism, though there are exceptions—the origins of the commercial legal codes of South Korea and Taiwan lie in Japanese colonial occupation; the Japanese in turn adapted the German or more precisely the Prussian legal code of the late 19th century before imposing it on South Korea and Taiwan. China has a socialist legal system based on the Soviet model. Brazil, Indonesia, and Venezuela have commercial legal codes based on French law, which were transmitted indirectly via other European colonial powers.

The final five columns of table 5.1 report rankings of legal system effectiveness derived from survey data obtained from three sources. Data from the World Economic Forum's *Global Competitiveness Report 2005–2006*, as indicated in previous chapters, are based on a survey of roughly 8,000 business executives in more than 100 countries during the first five months of 2005. The World Bank governance indicators are constructed by aggregating data from 37 data sources originating in 31 public and private organizations (Kaufmann, Kraay, and Mastruzzi 2005). The Opacity index originally was derived by surveying PricewaterhouseCoopers executives; its most recent incarnation, like the World Bank governance indicators, is constructed by amalgamating multiple original data sources (Kurtzman, Yago, and Phumiwasana 2004). The fact that the World Bank and Opacity indices share some underlying data sources, including the Transparency International and *International Country Risk Guide* rankings, means that their apparent consistency may be partly illusory. Conversely, divergences might point to fragility in these indices.

The scoring methods and country samples used by the three surveys differ so the data must be normalized in some way. In table 5.1 the scores are reported as percentile ranks (a larger number is better) derived from a common sample of 48 countries.[10] Given the previously acknowledged difficulties in interpreting such cross-country survey data, it is hoped that the use of multiple surveys will increase the reader's confidence in the salience of these scores.

"Efficacy of the legal system" is the percentile rank of the assessment of how effectively the legal system resolves business disputes based on interviews with the corporate chief financial officers, equity analysts,

---

10. The responses have to be normalized to a common sample because the sample sizes typically expand by increasing the number of small, poor, low-scoring countries. Unless one controls for this expansion, the addition to the sample of the Togos of the world spuriously improves the apparent performance of the larger, richer, higher-scoring sample incumbents.

Table 5.1 Legal origins and effectiveness (percentile)

			Global Competitiveness Report (GCR) score				
Country	Family	Receptivity	Efficacy of legal system	Rule of law	Judicial independence	Efficiency of legal framework	Property rights
Middle East							
Algeria	French	Direct	n.a.	19	15	28	11
Egypt	French	Direct	35	33	n.a.	37	33
Jordan	French	Direct	n.a.	38	52	52	43
Kuwait	French	Direct	n.a.	50	61	61	35
Lebanon	French	Direct	15	23	n.a.	n.a.	n.a.
Morocco	French	Direct	n.a.	33	20	33	17
Saudi Arabia	English	Direct	48	40	n.a.	n.a.	n.a.
Syria	French	Direct	n.a.	19	n.a.	n.a.	n.a.
Tunisia	French	Direct	n.a.	38	54	63	43
High-performing comparators							
South Korea	German	Indirect	44	52	43	48	43
Taiwan	German	Indirect	52	56	46	57	52
Large comparators							
China	Socialist	n.a.	33	25	24	33	17
India	English	Direct	29	31	65	59	48

(table continues next page)

147

Table 5.1 Legal origins and effectiveness (percentile) *(continued)*

Country	Family	Receptivity	Efficacy of legal system	Rule of law	Judicial independence	Efficiency of legal framework	Property rights
						Global Competitiveness Report (GCR) score	
Normally endowed comparators							
Bangladesh	English	Direct	n.a.	8	15	13	11
Brazil	French	Indirect	23	21	17	20	26
Pakistan	English	Direct	21	15	13	7	13
Turkey	French/German	Direct	31	29	33	26	30
Resource-rich comparators							
Botswana	English	Direct	n.a.	46	65	63	46
Indonesia	French	Indirect	19	6	20	22	11
Nigeria	English	Direct	4	2	37	17	15
Venezuela	French	Indirect	2	4	7	2	2

n.a. = not available

Notes: Transplants are classified as "unreceptive" in all cases. Data are in percentiles (higher number is better); GCR sample: n = 46; All others: n = 48.

Sources: Origin and receptivity: Berkowitz, Pistor, and Richard (2003); Efficacy of legal system: Kurtzman, Yago, and Phumiwasana (2004); Rule of law: Kaufmann, Kraay, and Mastruzzi (2003); GCR score: *Global Competitiveness Report 2005–2006.*

businessmen, and PricewaterhouseCoopers employees residing in-country. Data are available for only three Arab countries: Egypt (35th percentile), Lebanon (15th percentile), and Saudi Arabia (48th percentile). On this measure Saudi Arabia fares noticeably better than its resource-laden comparators, Indonesia (19th percentile), Nigeria (4th percentile), and Venezuela (2nd percentile). Egypt does not look distinct from other resource-scarce comparators on this dimension, while Lebanon is obviously a laggard.

"Rule of law" is a broader index from the World Bank, combining indicators of confidence and acceptance of legal rules, effectiveness and predictability of the judiciary, incidence of crime, and enforceability of contracts (Kaufmann, Kraay, and Mastruzzi 2003). In absolute terms the region does poorly: Only Kuwait (barely) makes the top half of the sample. Yet the results are broadly consistent with the previous indicator: Saudi Arabia scores noticeably better than the other oil producers, and high-performing South Korea and Taiwan aside, Egypt and Lebanon are similar to other comparators. Robert Z. Lawrence (2006) analyzes the same data, normalizing it for per capita income levels, and finds that Morocco, Jordan, Egypt, and Tunisia all score at or above their expected levels, though adjusting for per capita income, and Lebanon lags. The 2005 accession to the WTO of Saudi Arabia (as well as prospective accession by Algeria, Iraq, Libya, and Yemen—all are observers in the process of negotiating membership) could be expected to contribute to the further strengthening and modernization of the legal system, at least in the commercial sphere, as it commits countries to an internationally enforceable set of global norms and procedures.

The next three columns in table 5.1 report data from the *Global Competitiveness Report 2005–2006* on judicial independence, the efficiency of the legal framework with respect to commercial issues, and the existence of clearly delineated and protected property rights. There is a very high degree of intragroup variation in these scores. Among the natural resource–based economies, Kuwait and Botswana stand out with high scores, while the remaining oil exporters score poorly. Focusing on the more typically endowed economies, the smaller and modestly more economically liberal Tunisia and Jordan are in the middle of the pack overall, placing them in the same league as South Korea, Taiwan, and India in these dimensions, while the larger and less politically open countries of Egypt and Morocco lag, more like China, Turkey, and some of the low-income comparators.

The same three sources report indices of regulatory quality, but there is far less consensus across these measures, possibly reflecting the less precise comparability in the information solicited (table 5.2). The PricewaterhouseCoopers index for regulatory structures is again a relatively narrow index comparing the financial or investment regulatory structure and the ability to settle disputes arising out of the investment process with those existing in the United States and the United Kingdom. The World Bank index attempts to proxy the regulatory burden imposed by "market-unfriendly policies such as price controls or inadequate bank supervision, as well as

Table 5.2   Regulation (percentile)

Country	Regulatory structures	Regulatory quality	Burden of regulation
Middle East			
Algeria	n.a.	13	11
Egypt	4	17	43
Jordan	n.a.	31	87
Kuwait	n.a.	35	30
Lebanon	15	15	n.a.
Morocco	n.a.	27	41
Saudi Arabia	2	29	n.a.
Syria	n.a.	4	n.a.
Tunisia	n.a.	25	87
High-performing comparators			
South Korea	17	25	83
Taiwan	42	52	93
Large comparators			
China	13	19	65
India	10	21	28
Normally endowed comparators			
Bangladesh	n.a.	2	17
Brazil	25	33	2
Pakistan	65	6	22
Turkey	21	27	39
Resource-rich comparators			
Botswana	n.a.	46	72
Indonesia	8	8	54
Nigeria	6	2	59
Venezuela	38	13	7

n.a. = not available

Note: Data are in percentiles (higher number is better); Burden of regulation sample: n = 46; All others: n = 48.

Sources: Structures: Kurtzman, Yago, and Phumiwasana (2004); Quality: Kaufmann, Kraay, and Mastruzzi (2003); Burden: *Global Competitiveness Report 2005–2006*.

perceptions of the regulatory burden imposed by excessive regulation in areas such as foreign trade and business development" (Kaufmann, Kraay, and Mastruzzi 2003, 3). The *Global Competitiveness Report* asks questions about whether regulations are "burdensome."

On the first criterion (regulatory structures), the listed countries generally score poorly on this measure with the Arab countries appearing distinctively bad. Pakistan scores the highest, and given the strong historical performance of at least some of these countries, one wonders what the PricewaterhouseCoopers index is capturing. A similar comment could be made with respect to the World Bank's regulatory quality measure: Most of the countries in table 5.2 score poorly, though some have done quite well, leading one to query the salience of this measure. Kuwait and Saudi Arabia, though lagging Botswana, outrank the other oil exporters by a considerable margin; Algeria appears to be more typical along this dimension. Among the more typically endowed economies, normalizing for income levels, only Jordan and Morocco reach their expected scores (Lawrence 2006). Oddly, on this measure, Pakistan, which scored strongly on regulatory structures, ranks quite badly on regulatory quality. Again, it gives one pause in interpreting these results.

The final column reports the "burden of regulation" rankings from the *Global Competitiveness Report*. As with the legal effectiveness criteria, Jordan and Tunisia score very highly with respect to lack of burdensome regulations, Algeria on the other end of the spectrum, with Egypt, Kuwait, and Morocco in the middle. The resource-scarce Arab countries generally do better than their resource-poor comparators on this criterion.

Whatever the "true" information provided by the various measures of legal structure, the Arab countries do not appear conspicuously weak relative to comparable countries. Moreover there is considerable intragroup variation among the Arab countries. Kuwait and Saudi Arabia generally score better than other oil exporters, while Algeria lags, comparable to Indonesia, Nigeria, and Venezuela. Among the nonoil-based economies, the existing legal institutions appear to be no more of a hindrance to development than those in comparable countries—they are far from distinctively bad.

Corruption and Growth

Microeconomic distortions (hence policy) and weak governance can generate opportunities for corruption. A small cottage industry now scores countries on this criterion. Table 5.3 reports corruption rankings from four sources (Transparency International is the additional source), again normalized for a common underlying sample. A wide range of behavior could be considered corrupt, and hence considerable scope exists for disagreement over what corruption is or how different forms of corruption should be weighted in forming an overall score, but the data in table 5.3 are relatively consistent across sources. This consistency may be in part due to the fact that the World Bank, Opacity, and Transparency International indices are based on some common components. Morocco is an exception in this regard, exhibiting significant variance across the four sources, ranging from the 35th percentile (World Bank) to the 4th percentile (*Global Competitiveness Report*).

Table 5.3   Corruption (percentile)

Country	Corruption	Control of corruption	Corruption perceptions index	GCR business costs of corruption index
Middle East				
Algeria	n.a.	15	17	15
Egypt	23	27	25	26
Jordan	n.a.	35	54	52
Kuwait	n.a.	58	46	30
Lebanon	2	25	17	n.a.
Morocco	n.a.	35	25	4
Saudi Arabia	40	48	29	n.a.
Syria	n.a.	27	29	n.a.
Tunisia	n.a.	40	54	46
High-performing comparators				
South Korea	40	38	46	41
Taiwan	56	56	56	61
Large comparators				
China	19	21	29	33
India	19	29	21	30
Normally endowed comparators				
Bangladesh	n.a.	4	2	2
Brazil	56	35	40	17
Pakistan	15	15	6	11
Turkey	25	23	25	22
Resource-rich comparators				
Botswana	n.a.	54	58	48
Indonesia	4	4	4	20
Nigeria	6	2	2	15
Venezuela	15	8	8	4

n.a. = not available

Notes: Data are in percentiles (higher number is better); GCR sample: n = 46; All others: n = 48.

Sources: Corruption: Kurtzman, Yago, and Phumiwasana (2004); Control of corruption: Kaufmann, Kraay, and Mastruzzi (2003); Corruption perceptions index: Transparency International (2004); GCR index: *Global Competititveness Report 2005–2006.*

The results are quite interesting. In an absolute sense the Arab countries do not look particularly good, mostly falling into the bottom half of the sample. In relative terms, the resource-scarce countries do not look all that different from their comparators though, in some cases, notably the smaller countries of Jordan and Tunisia, they rank markedly higher. (Along the same lines, Lawrence [2006] finds that Morocco, Jordan, and Tunisia surpass their income-adjusted expected scores by noticeable margins.) Saudi Arabia outranks the other oil producers but lags Botswana, which again scores distinctively high among the natural resource–based economies.

A real-life experiment on government officials' willingness to abuse diplomatic immunity for private gain confirms the tenor of these survey results. Raymond Fisman and Edward Miguel (2006) examine parking tickets received by diplomats posted in the United Nations in New York and find a strong correlation between violations per diplomat and the corruption indices reported in table 5.3, suggesting that there may indeed be "cultures of corruption." Two Arab countries, Kuwait (246.2 tickets per diplomat) and Egypt (139.6 tickets per diplomat), top the list of scofflaws, and Middle Eastern countries receive an unusually large volume of tickets even when other attributes such as per capita income are taken into account. All is not bleak, however: The United Arab Emirates and Oman are among the group of countries whose diplomats received no parking tickets during the sample period.

Not all corruption, whether it be bid rigging or double parking, has the same implications for economic performance, however. "Cascading corruption" in which interaction with the government is pervasive and transaction costs are imposed at all levels of the bureaucracy may be more debilitating than corruption that is concentrated at the top of the political system; the monetary costs to business may be the same, but the transaction costs are much lower (Shleifer and Vishny 1993). One might think of the Indian "license raj" as representing the former and South Korea as representing the latter—nontrivial levels of corruption but relatively effective administration of policy once decisions were made at the top.

Some indirect indicators of this distinction, taken from the *Global Competitiveness Report*, are reported in table 5.4. The first column reports the extent of bureaucratic red tape. There is considerable intraregional variation, with Tunisia scoring well, and Egypt and Jordan falling into the bottom decile along with socialist China, which did not preclude rapid Chinese growth. Recall from chapter 4 that in Jamel Zarrouk's survey, Middle East businessmen identified having to spend excessive amounts of time with customs and other officials and the opportunities that this contact created for the solicitation of bribes as being a serious nontariff barrier to international trade, though this problem appeared to be easing in Egypt and Jordan while worsening in some other countries.

The Arab countries do much better on the favoritism by government officials and organized crime criteria, however, with Jordan and Tunisia surpassing South Korea and Taiwan and Egypt not far behind. Even the normally laggard Algeria does not look bad on these criteria. On the bottom-line question of the magnitude of the business costs, Jordan and Tunisia actually outrank South Korea and Taiwan, with the others in the middle of the league.

Table 5.4   Indirect indicators of corruption typologies (percentile)

Country	Extent of bureaucratic red tape	Favoritism in decisions of government officials	Organized crime
Middle East			
Algeria	49	71	50
Bahrain	14	67	85
Egypt	7	51	65
Jordan	8	91	97
Kuwait	12	70	87
Morocco	38	47	48
Qatar	5	97	98
Tunisia	72	92	72
United Arab Emirates	48	80	94
High-performing comparators			
South Korea	64	89	54
Taiwan	74	97	66
Large comparators			
China	2	75	45
India	50	36	64
Normally endowed comparators			
Bangladesh	6	17	11
Brazil	43	3	16
Pakistan	32	21	24
Turkey	34	45	43
Resource-rich comparators			
Botswana	28	79	67
Indonesia	60	62	33
Nigeria	3	71	18
Venezuela	3	6	12

Note: Data are approximate percentiles (higher number is better); sample: n = 117.

Source: World Economic Forum, *Global Competitiveness Report 2005–2006.*

One does not want to push this sort of survey evidence too far: There are all kinds of problems with respect to interpretation of responses and comparability across regions. Nevertheless, by examining a variety of indicators generated from several sources, we have tried to derive the broad outlines of a portrait: Arab countries as a group are bureaucratic states with a lot of regulation and red tape but implemented through legal and administrative systems that are not dysfunctional.[11] Nor have they been captured by organized crime: As governments, they look more like pre-collapse Soviet Union than postcollapse Russia—i.e., they are not mafia states. As a group they might be compared with prereform India of the "license raj." There is noticeable within-group variation: Algeria appears to be the most bureaucratic, not surprising for a country that took the Soviet Union as a model, while Jordan and Tunisia appear the most liberal. Saudi Arabia actually compares favorably with some of its resource-abundant comparators, as does Kuwait on a more limited sample of indicators.

Concluding Remarks

To return to the original question, there is nothing here to suggest that the Islamic tradition has bequeathed these countries unusually weak institutions. If anything it could be the opposite. As a consequence, it could be that the negative interpretations of Islam's historical legacy reviewed earlier are correct but that enough convergence in institutions, policies, and behavior has occurred that the effects have been attenuated in the contemporary world. It could also be that other positive characteristics in Islamic societies overwhelm the negative influence of Islam, or it could be that this received wisdom is simply wrong.

In any event the evidence suggests that these are reasonably functioning states, embodying a modicum of state capability, at least with respect to their existing practices, which appear to impose considerable deadweight losses. It could well be the case, for example, that authorities competent to regulate highly repressed financial systems will prove inadequate to administer a more open sophisticated system. We now turn to the content of traditional economic policies, both macro- and microeconomic.

---

11. See Zarrouk (2003) for examples of bureaucratic red tape and Nugent (2000) for proposals for legal reform, judicial reform, and implementation of alternative dispute resolution mechanisms.

6

Economic Policies
and Their Effects

In the early post–World War II period, there was little understanding of the minimal requirements for sustained economic growth in the former colonial countries. Much of the analysis that existed was based on limited familiarity with poor countries and theories that ignored important realities such as the potential role of international trade. Often analysts drew sweeping conclusions from brief visits, and the generalizations had more than a touch of arrogance or worse: South Korea was hopeless in some descriptions because Confucianism was inimical to growth, and Taiwan would not succeed because the Chinese are interested only in trading and not production—notions that today's buyers of cellular telephones, laptop computers, and flat panel television sets would find bizarre. After the success of South Korea and Taiwan, many of the same "experts" concluded, without any hesitation, that this success was due to the traits inculcated by the discipline stemming from Confucian tradition.

Often better analysis reflected an increasing understanding of the success or failure of national economic policies rather than improved theoretical insights. The remarkable performance of a small group of Asian countries—Hong Kong, Japan, South Korea, Singapore, and Taiwan—led to a concerted effort to understand the foundations of their success. A second generation of success stories in Indonesia, Malaysia, and Thailand reinforced some of the principles derived from the first group.[1] And the still more recent success of China and India confirms some of the earlier insights, adding a few new twists.

---

1. For a comprehensive retrospective of their development, see World Bank (1993) and a follow-up study, Stiglitz and Yusuf (2001).

The experience of Latin American countries provided an interesting contrast to the Far East. The growth in per capita income in many of these countries between 1950 and 1980 was based on a strategy of import-substituting industrialization, which sheltered domestic manufacturing from international competition. Given the larger size of the domestic market in some of the Latin American countries, particularly Argentina, Brazil, Colombia, and Mexico, compared with the early industrializers in Asia, the strategy was feasible. Though it produced slower growth in income per capita than the Asian high performers' norm of 5 percent, it was sustained. However, the oil price increase imposed by the Organization of Petroleum Exporting Countries (OPEC) in the 1970s tested the long-term robustness of the strategy and exposed critical weaknesses. While the Asian countries were able to tighten their belts and encourage exports by restricting aggregate demand and changing the real exchange rate, the Latin American countries typically did neither and accumulated large deficits financed (largely) by commercial borrowing. This eventually led to the debt crisis of the early 1980s in which country after country defaulted on some of their foreign exchange obligations. Austerity was imposed, and the 1980s are often referred to as the lost decade, as per capita income stagnated.

The contrasting experience of the Asian newly industrialized countries and Latin American countries led to a growing agreement among economists in universities, international financial institutions, think tanks, and the private sector about a set of dos and don'ts, which was crystallized in John Williamson's famous (or villainous in some quarters) Washington Consensus, not all of which Williamson himself believed in (Williamson 1990). This set comprised fiscal and monetary discipline, secure property rights, sectorally neutral tax and expenditure policies, financial liberalization, unified and competitive exchange rates, openness to foreign trade and investment, privatization, and deregulation. However, disappointing results in Latin America, lackluster performance in the transitional economies of Eastern Europe after the collapse of Communism, and the Asian financial crisis of the late 1990s all contributed to significant doubts about the validity of many of the elements of the Washington Consensus. One response has been to augment the consensus with so-called second-generation reforms such as strengthening prudential supervision of financial markets or competition policy.

Some planks of the Washington Consensus, circa 1990, were articles of faith rather than a distillation of the sources of success in the Asian and Latin American countries. South Korea and Taiwan had, in fact, been protectionist for quite long periods though progressively reducing the extent of protection (Pack and Westphal 1986); they invested in some state-owned enterprises though many were privatized relatively quickly; financial liberalization was undertaken very late and arguably was one source of the crisis of the late 1990s in Indonesia, South Korea, Malaysia, and Thailand (World Bank 1998, Radelet and Sachs 1998, Noland and Pack

2003). Other deviations from the consensus can be set out. countries that achieved rapid growth did exhibit relativel macroeconomic policies, including low deficits and moder the money supply, and emphasized achieving rapid grow Their real exchange rates were set appropriately and exhibi bility (World Bank 1993). There is a lively and probably never-ending de bate on the precise role of exports and efforts to facilitate them through industrial policy on the growth of these countries (Noland and Pack 2003, World Bank 1993).

The issues raised by the Washington Consensus have formed the backdrop of much of the discussion over the past 15 years about the policies required to initiate and sustain economic growth. Any familiarity with the actual experience of successful economies suggests that some of the principles are almost surely prerequisites to growth, namely, those that lead to macroeconomic stability and an appropriate real exchange rate. Others may deviate with the circumstances and preferences of individual countries—Japan and South Korea were not receptive to foreign direct investment (FDI) while a linchpin of Singapore's effort was a mobilization of the country to attract FDI, a path emulated to a lesser extent in the "latecomers," Indonesia, Malaysia, and Thailand. In other regions as well debates about fine-tuning the nonfundamental policies have continued.

Policies in Arab Economies

But analysts and governments in the Arab countries, at least most of them, had not participated in the discussion of the policies until very recently.[2] Some of the countries have, in fact, had relatively good "fundamentals" in terms of fiscal and monetary policy, and there have been improvements in the last decade (Dasgupta, Keller, and Srinivasan 2002). On the other hand, they have, in many cases, deviated in major ways from the consensus, for example, in being slow to privatize the huge and inefficient state-owned sector. While state-owned enterprises can occasionally be efficient, for example the POSCO steel complex in South Korea, there is a general consensus that they have not been so in most of the Arab countries but have been utilized to provide employment to win political support. While this can be justified in the larger calculation of political and social stability, it has a long-term cost in terms of slowing the growth of productivity. Despite some efforts to initiate the discussion by international financial institutions such as the World Bank (1995, 2003a), there has been relatively limited follow-up.

---

2. In the early 1990s the World Bank funded the Middle East Economic Research Forum, and the research engendered has been an important source of knowledge.

.he absence of a focus on economic growth in many countries, the Arab ones being far from unique, may be contrasted to that of the Asian countries, ranging from Japan to South Korea to Taiwan. For reasons that differed in each case, these governments had little legitimacy following World War II. Japan had suffered a traumatic defeat after initiating the Second World War in the Pacific. South Korea had gained independence from Japan but had then been partitioned, and a devastating three-year war from 1950 to 1952 destroyed much of the capital stock and caused enormous casualties. Taiwan was the base of the defeated Kuomintang government, which hastily left the mainland in 1949. In each case, the government decided to establish its legitimacy by emphasizing economic growth—in the 1950s in Japan and in the early 1960s in South Korea and Taiwan.[3] In all three a land reform overcame one set of opponents to policies that were conducive to growth with equity; in turn this sharing in rapid growth led to a perception that government policies benefited the general population.[4] The combination of political trauma that disrupted existing structures of influence and the need to provide increased living standards to generate legitimacy may have weakened the political obstacles to development, but this never materialized in the wake of what some would describe as cataclysmic events in the Arab world.

Analysts often point to political and military shocks as a reason for the absence of a concerted effort to improve living standards in the countries of the Middle East but do not ask why these shocks did not have the benefits just alluded to in the Far East.[5] Each of the shocks might have provided the basis for an effort to further establish legitimacy through improved living standards. The argument that these countries were authoritarian is not wholly convincing—South Korea and Taiwan were hardly models of democracy when they began their rapid ascent. The violence of the Algerian war against the French and intra-Algerian convulsions that resulted in up to a million dead in the aftermath of the war never resulted in a program to generate growth nor did the government-Islamist fighting of the 1990s (Horne 1978, Quandt 1998). The Iran-Iraq war of the 1980s and its huge casualties did not lead to improved economic policy despite the absence of any effective internal opposition in Iraq. The 1952 coup against the monarchy, the Egyptian-Saudi war in Yemen in the 1960s, a number of

---

3. For an insider's account on Taiwan, see K. T. Li (1988).

4. This is part of what the World Bank (1993) describes as a virtuous circle, the diffusion of benefits increasing the political feasibility of further policy reform. See also Campos and Root (1996).

5. Mancur Olson (1982) suggested that postwar growth in a number of countries, particularly Germany and Japan, had been facilitated by the destruction of earlier institutions and also briefly argued this for some of the Asian countries. He omitted, perhaps presciently, the Middle East.

wars with Israel, the Iraqi invasion of Kuwait in 1990 and the ensuing Gulf War, and the US-Iraq war of 2003 have not led to notable reform in the affected or contiguous countries.

Often the dilatory tactics of governments are attributed to the ongoing problems between Israelis and Palestinians, and indeed the need to solve this dilemma was invoked to justify the disregard of American proposals in 2004 and 2005 for democratic and economic reform in Middle Eastern countries. Quite apart from the specifics of the plan and its American origins, the rejection is symptomatic of the diligent quest for excuses to justify delay of reforms. All of these traumatic events could have provided a compelling case for reformers. Instead, these political and military shocks are viewed as having deflected attention from the pursuit of systematic policies to improve living standards.

Paradoxically, favorable developments are also often invoked to explain the failure to concentrate on economic growth. The oil price increase of the 1970s and early 1980s provided oil exporters with a cushion on which to recline comfortably without undue attention to assuring future growth. The nonoil Arab countries participated in the bounty as the OPEC members had a high demand for labor, much of it supplied by other Arab countries, whose citizens repatriated considerable earnings to their country of origin. Even the frequent conflicts were a source of a benefit, namely, large aid inflows to insure allegiance during the Cold War or to reward countries for specific behavior, most notably Egypt after the signing of the Camp David agreement in 1979. Moreover, Egypt received a huge remission of its external debt after its participation in the Gulf War of 1991. Oil, repatriated earnings, and aid, three seemingly favorable developments, are combined with the adverse geopolitical shocks of the previous paragraph to explain the absence of attention to the details of economic policy. Even the relatively low level of absolute poverty is noted as a problem—the national governments are viewed as having to pay less attention to populist pressures.

In these views, both the bad and the good have adverse consequences for economic growth. Contrary to Dr. Pangloss, this is the worst of all possible worlds. Yet, to take the bad first, Japan and South Korea suffered huge physical damage compared with any Arab country, in any war, with the possible exception of Kuwait in the aftermath of the 1990 Iraqi invasion. South Korea and Taiwan both faced more than credible threats from heavily armed enemies whose intentions were not benevolent. Vietnam, a recently rapidly growing economy, suffered much more physical damage from US bombing than any of the Arab economies. And the psychological consequences of the Vietnam War on its leadership could not have been small—yet, perhaps because of a neighborhood effect and the presence of nearby successful Asian examples, Vietnam has taken economic growth as an important objective. Some of the previously stagnant nations of

Eastern Europe that experienced the presence of the Soviet army for more than 40 years also changed their focus.[6] While it would be facile to dismiss the deleterious consequences of external shocks, these and other examples suggest they are not a sufficient explanation of bad policymaking—too often countries in other regions have turned them to an advantage.

Similarly, unearned riches, whether in the form of natural resources or repatriated earnings, are not uniformly a source of decline. Botswana, a major diamond producer, has been an important success story, as has Indonesia, a significant oil producer. Sierra Leone and Liberia have been traumatized by civil wars, attributed by some to the same diamonds, albeit produced under different geological conditions using different extractive techniques from those in Botswana (Noland and Spector 2006). Nigeria, like Saudi Arabia, suffered a major collapse after the growth in the price of oil. While one strand of analysis, the literature on "Dutch disease," would attribute this to market-induced shifts from traded to nontraded goods, and the concomitant overvaluation of the real exchange rate that made production of conventional tradable goods unprofitable, a complementary view is that a huge waste of investment occurred in both the tradable and nontradable sectors due to corruption.

Measuring Policy Effects

In recent studies of the Middle East many variables measuring policy reform and institutions have been examined and the region is found lagging on many of them such as tariff liberalization, real exchange rates, receipts from sales of state-owned enterprises, and the business environment (World Bank 2003a, Page 2003). Low initial levels relative to other regions and slow improvement are often adduced as an explanation of weaker growth performance than occurred in other regions. But there is little evidence that the specific policy deficiencies cited in fact have had a serious quantitative impact—the connection between policy stances and growth may be more tenuous than many discussions imply.

For example, the Asian countries that provided the template for the components of the Washington Consensus did not have policies in place that were uniformly good in the 1960s, the period of their growth acceleration. They had high tariff rates, significant investment in state-owned enterprises, subsidies to sectors that were deemed to be national champions, a poor to nonexistent regulatory environment, no serious corporate governance laws, a lack of transparency in both the public and private sector, and so on (Pack and Westphal 1986, Wade 1990, World Bank 1993). What they did have was considerable macroeconomic stability and relatively constant and realistic real exchange rates. Moreover, exporters had access

---

6. In chapter 7 we attempt to explain the different response in Eastern Europe.

to traded inputs at international prices. China is a more recent instance of a similar historical trajectory, with good macro policies combined with a protected domestic market, a large (though declining) state sector, corruption, and other deficiencies in the "investment climate." While its special economic zones operate at world prices, the rest of the economy has been characterized by relatively high tariffs that are decreasing with China's accession to the World Trade Organization (WTO). Its major early reform, property rights in the rural area, has not been an issue discussed in the Arab economies. Similarly, a considerable part of the growth acceleration in India since the 1980s occurred without any deep nonmacro reform, though the International Monetary Fund–imposed policy changes of the early 1990s were one among many contributors to maintaining growth that had begun earlier.

A number of studies have measured the changes in the performance of the Middle East and North Africa (MENA) on various policy indicators (Page 2003; Dasgupta, Keller, and Srinivasan 2002). The indicators employed have typically been MENA-wide averages that show there has been limited reform, for example, average tariffs have been reduced by less than in other regions. But aside from measuring the smaller degree of reform, no connection has been demonstrated between this and low growth performance in individual countries. Policy reforms (or their absence) are described, but no quantitative estimate is provided of the size of the likely reduction in growth that can be attributed to dilatory policies.

Recently there has been a focus on the "investment climate" as a source of poor performance (World Bank 2005, 2006b). Much of the evidence of the deleterious effect of a bad investment climate consists of international comparisons that simply show the differences, for example, in the time it takes to open a new business. It is obviously difficult to interpret such a "fact" because of endogeneity problems—as countries become richer a growing middle class with entrepreneurial instincts may lobby for less regulation. A cross-country comparison might then show richer countries with lower levels of regulation, but the historical sequence within a given country may have been a growth in income followed by a reduction in regulation. Though such cross-country tabulations are useful as benchmarks to indicate the range of experience, the endogeneity of some of the explanatory variables suggests caution in imputing causality. Our presentation in chapter 5 of some investment climate variables was intended to convey that, whatever the degree of endogeneity, the Arab countries were not conspicuously bad on these measures though the precise interpretation is moot.

Rather than focus on one or another deficiency in the policy environment, it is useful to consider the effect of specific policy shortcomings in a comparable and systematic framework that can provide some quantitative measure of the importance of insufficient reforms by focusing on their calculated statistical effect rather than on good intentions signaled by reform.

While there can be no definitive resolution of the importance of policy, the exercise provides a preliminary test of the claim that one or another reform is *the* key to accelerated growth. To make such calculations, we employ the results of Barry Bosworth and Susan M. Collins (2003), who attempt a synthesis of the huge amount of research on the correlates of growth by searching for robust correlated variables for growth in output per worker and separately, capital-labor ratios and total factor productivity (TFP) growth. They estimate TFP growth using growth accounting and then explain growth in output per worker, TFP, and the capital-labor ratio using variables that are frequently assumed to have important effects. Their analysis is appropriate for the question that we are posing as it does not try to estimate production parameters simultaneously with the effect of policy variables, which is the standard procedure in other growth regressions. While there are a number of studies from which to choose, calculations with their model provide illustrative numbers and demonstrate the possibly tenuous relation between policy stances and growth.[7]

Questions can be raised about their methodology.[8] For example, growth accounting requires very strong assumptions about the production function and the functioning of factor markets, and econometric estimation of TFP growth often generates very different results than growth accounting (Kim and Lau 1994, Nelson and Pack 1999). The Bosworth-Collins results are employed here to illustrate the type of approach that is necessary to establish that policy-induced problems such as inflation are in fact empirically harmful to growth rather than simply reflecting a theoretical view. Thus our use of their estimated coefficients for the impact of particular policies is not meant to be definitive but an organizing framework that could be used employing other econometric estimates as well to sort out whether policies in the Arab economies have lowered growth rates.

Among the huge number of indicators that have been employed in various studies, Bosworth and Collins find that only a few of the policy variables or still "deeper" measures turn out to be significant in explaining growth in labor productivity or TFP.[9] After testing many specifications their preferred equation for the 1980–2000 period is one in which the

---

7. Also see Sala-i-Martin, Doppelhofer, and Miller (2004) and the references cited there.

8. See the comments on the Bosworth-Collins paper by Jeffrey Frankel (2003) and Steven Durlauf (2003).

9. In addition to the variables that are shown in the following footnote, other variables tested but not found to be significant were the following: control of corruption, average log change of annual consumer price index, restrictions on current and capital account, type of economic organization, international country risk guide index, economic risk, index of ethnolinguistic fractionalization, index of political freedoms, government antidiversion policies, index of institutional quality, rule of law, political risk, internal conflict, external conflict, corruption, military in politics, religious tensions, law and order, ethnic tensions, democratic accountability, bureaucracy quality, regulatory quality, and European settlers' mortality rate.

growth of output per worker is explained by the initial level of income per capita in 1980 (YC20), life expectancy in 1980 (LE20), the log of population (GPOP), a variable that describes international trade patterns (GRAVITY), and a physical location variable (GEOG).[10] Three measures of the quality of macro policy outcomes, the annual rate of inflation (DLCPI20), the budget balance relative to GDP (BAL20), and the Sachs-Warner measure of openness (SW20), were added to the predetermined variables, along with a measure of institutional quality (ICRG82).[11] Thus, the significant policy and institutional variables include a possibly endogenous policy variable (the budget balance) and a possibly more fundamental institutional one.

Figures 6.1 to 6.4 show the budget balance, the rate of inflation, the Sachs-Warner index, and institutional quality for the five Arab countries for which Bosworth and Collins have data and for other regional groupings. The figures indicate that the Arab countries of the Maghreb and Jordan have not been conspicuously poor in policy performance as is often suggested in popular accounts and in studies that concentrate solely on these countries without examining other nations. Over 1980–2000 Jordan had a fiscal deficit rate only slightly larger than all developing countries but considerably less than the countries of Southeast Asia, while its inflation rate was at East Asian levels. It was more open, using the Sachs-Warner index, than East Asia, but its institutional quality was, by a slight margin, the lowest. An answer to the question of whether the policy and institutional environment was *the* source of Jordan's abysmal growth record in this period requires weighting the indicators by their coefficients in the estimated regression equation. Jordan is used as an example, though as noted earlier its poor performance may in fact have had more to do with the dislocations following the Gulf War than any policy defects. Similar questions arise in the other Middle Eastern countries—their pattern on these indicators is mixed and not obviously correlated with

---

10. The estimated equation (6.1) is

$$Q^*-L^* = 0.28 - 6.51YC20 + 0.07LE20 + 0.25GPOP + 3.46GRAVITY + 0.37GEOG - 0.01DLCPI20$$
$$\quad\ (0.2) \quad (-7.9)^a \quad\quad (3.7)^a \quad\quad (2.8)^a \quad\quad (2.0)^b \quad\quad (1.9)^c \quad\quad (-0.5)$$

$$\quad\quad + 0.14BAL20 + 0.32SW20 + 2.09ICRG82$$
$$\quad\quad\quad (3.2)^a \quad\quad (0.9) \quad\quad (2.2)^b$$

n=77, adjusted R^2=0.60, t-statistics in parentheses, "a" indicates significance at the 1 percent level, "b" at the 5 percent level, and "c" at the 10 percent level.

11. "An economy is deemed to be open to trade if it satisfies five tests: (1) average tariff rates below 40 percent; (2) average quota and licensing coverage of imports of less than 40 percent; (3) a black market exchange rate premium of less than 20 percent; (4) no extreme controls (taxes, quotas, and state monopolies) on exports; and (5) not considered a socialist country by the standard" defined by Janos Kornai (Sachs and Warner 1997). ICRG82, an index of institutional quality, is an average of five subindexes developed from data by Political Risk Services (Knack and Keefer 1995).

Figure 6.1   Fiscal balance, 1980–2000

percent of GDP

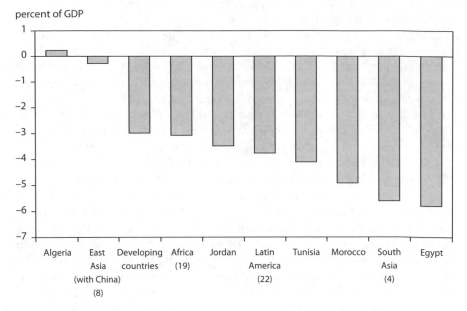

Source: Bosworth and Collins (2003).

Figure 6.2   Inflation, 1980–2000

average log change of annual consumer price index

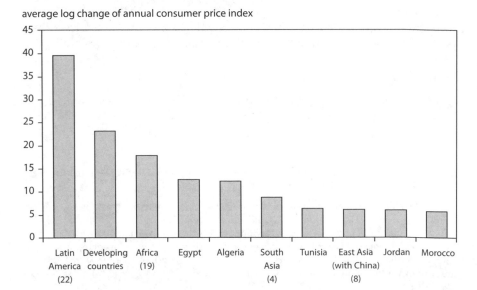

Source: Bosworth and Collins (2003).

Figure 6.3   Sachs-Warner openness index, 1980–2000

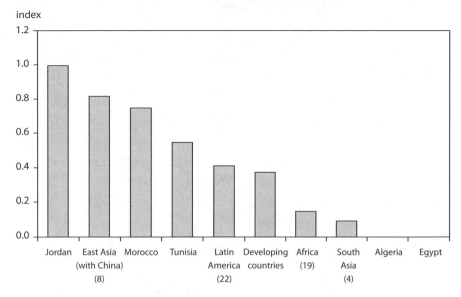

Source: Bosworth and Collins (2003).

Figure 6.4   Institutional quality, 1982

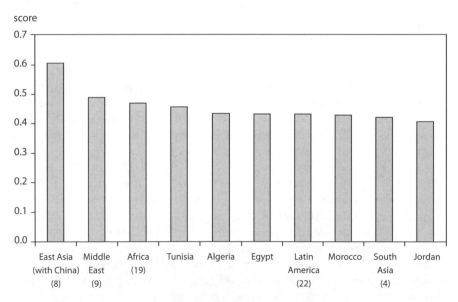

Note: Figure shows the *International Country Risk Guide* score in 1982.

Source: Bosworth and Collins (2003).

Table 6.1   Effects of policy variables and institutional quality on growth in income per worker, 1980–2000

Country	Annual rate of growth of output per worker	Effect of three macro policy variables	Effect of institutional quality	Total effect
Algeria	−1.52	−0.11	1.54	1.43
Egypt	2.18	−0.41	1.23	0.82
Jordan	−1.69	0.95	2.5	3.45
Morocco	0.51	0.59	2.22	2.81
Tunisia	1.33	0.39	1.09	1.48

Source: Calculated from Bosworth and Collins (2003), supporting data for 1980–2000.

economic growth. For example, Egypt had bad fiscal balance and fairly high inflation yet did relatively well.

Using the actual policy variables that characterized individual countries during the 1980–2000 period multiplied by the estimated coefficients in the regression, the calculated effects of policy on growth for the MENA countries in the sample are shown in table 6.1. The contribution of the policy variables does not account for the weak performance in Algeria and Jordan over the period. In all five countries institutional quality contributed positively to growth as did the three macro variables in Jordan, Morocco, and Tunisia. The sum of the effects of the policy variables shown in the last column exceeds the actual growth in the first column for Jordan, Morocco, and Tunisia suggesting that other forces constrained growth or that the cross-country regression used does not provide a good description of the structure of these countries. Again, the results depend on both the equation used and the specific measures of policy employed, but they underline that simple assertions that still greater policy reform in one dimension or another in the Middle East would bring accelerated growth are based on a priori views rather than demonstrated connection.

To repeat our earlier caution, these results are highly model specific: Other estimates would produce other results, and the continuing proliferation of cross-country regressions will undoubtedly generate still other empirical estimates that may or may not confirm these numbers (though these results generally coincide with those obtained in the massive econometric research exercise by Xavier Sala-i-Martin, Gernot Doppelhofer, and Ronald I. Miller [2004], who found a tighter correlation between growth and a variety of clearly predetermined fundamental factors, and possibly government consumption, than with other macroeconomic policy variables such as inflation or trade openness). The point here is that the assumed benefits of still greater reform may be correct but its importance in explaining slow growth in the past is not easily demonstrated. In pursuing a quest for changed policy stances and estimating their likely impact, it is likely to be more fruitful to derive the needed adjustments from detailed country analysis and historical episodes of policy change and response. Simply asserting that tariffs remain high or that it takes 120 days to open a business in Egypt is not sufficient to prove the likely payoff to still greater reforms that require spending considerable political capital. This is not to deny that policies matter, simply that we don't have even rough guidelines as to which matter a lot.

Indeed, a narrative history of the 1990s of laggards in growth, Algeria and Jordan, would not put policy measures in the foreground. In the case of Jordan, the political upheavals including the Gulf War in 1991 and the expulsion of large numbers of Palestinians from other Arab countries who returned to Jordan and the reduction in their remittances were important as was the decline in legal trade with Iraq as a result of UN sanctions. Throughout the period Algeria continued with an outmoded highly centralized state-dominated economy, never propitious for growth, a characteristic not caught in the particular measure of institutional quality, ICRG82. However, much of the reversal of growth in the 1990s undoubtedly reflected the chaotic conditions of a widespread conflict between the government and the Islamist opposition following the aborted election process in 1992. In this respect, Algeria had more in common with African countries that underwent civil wars than with its Maghreb neighbors. But similar calculations for other poorer countries suggest that the policy performance of the Arab economies for which Bosworth-Collins were able to obtain data is not that different from other countries.

Table 6.2 shows the predicted versus actual performance in our benchmark countries using the appropriate values of equation 6.1 for 1960–80 and 1980–2000 (see footnote 10). The growth in all of the MENA countries is faster than predicted in the earlier period whereas in the second period only Egypt and Tunisia have a positive value for the difference between actual and predicted. More generally, countries that have gotten their policies "right" by the Washington Consensus do not necessarily have superior performance—for example, Chile (not shown in the table) in the second period considerably lagged its predicted growth rate.

The big story, which could be told without the regressions, is that the East Asian counties do spectacularly well, and India turns around between the two periods. China, in particular, does very well among the East Asians. Countries that had many institutions "wrong" overcame such handicaps. For example, the extensive literature on the investment environment, governance, and corruption all imply that investment may be lower because of the high costs, especially to smaller firms, of obtaining funds for initiation or expansion, licenses, and clearances. It is alleged that small and medium-sized enterprises (SMEs) are discriminated against with the implication that they have greater rates of return than larger firms

Table 6.2 GDP per capita growth rates: Actual and predicted (percent)

Country	1960–80 Predicted	Actual	Actual minus predicted	1980–2000 Predicted	Actual	Actual minus predicted
Middle East						
Algeria	1.99	3.01	1.02	−0.38	−1.61	−1.24
Egypt	2.04	3.61	1.56	0.21	2.43	2.22
Jordan	1.68	1.68	0.00	1.76	−1.03	−2.79
Kuwait	n.a.	n.a.	n.a.	n.a.	n.a.	n.a.
Morocco	2.13	2.48	0.36	1.78	0.55	−1.22
Saudi Arabia	n.a.	n.a.	n.a.	n.a.	n.a.	n.a.
Syria	n.a.	n.a.	n.a.	n.a.	n.a.	n.a.
Tunisia	n.a.	3.82	n.a.	1.46	1.58	0.12
High-performing comparators						
South Korea	4.78	4.48	−0.30	4.39	4.52	0.13
Taiwan	5.62	6.27	0.66	3.92	4.99	1.07
Large comparators						
China	n.a.	2.17	n.a.	4.92	7.09	2.18
India	3.64	1.29	−2.35	2.43	3.50	1.07
Normally endowed comparators						
Bangladesh	n.a.	1.05	n.a.	1.27	1.95	0.68
Brazil	3.15	3.84	0.70	−0.49	−0.51	−0.02
Pakistan	2.93	3.28	0.35	2.02	2.33	0.31
Turkey	3.12	3.28	0.16	2.01	1.74	−0.28
Resource-rich comparators						
Botswana	n.a.	n.a.	n.a.	n.a.	n.a.	n.a.
Indonesia	2.26	3.49	1.23	1.79	2.70	0.91
Nigeria	2.11	2.70	0.59	−0.43	−0.47	−0.04
Venezuela	1.14	0.20	−0.94	0.03	−1.97	−2.00

n.a. = not available

Source: Bosworth and Collins (2003).

that are better able to cope with these obstacles whether through bribery, maintaining a larger staff to deal with these problems, or simply because the costs are not proportional to firm size. This has many similarities to an earlier literature that argued that large firms with substantial collateral were privileged recipients of loans from the banking system.

But the economic history of several successful nations suggests that these obstacles are not necessarily binding constraints on growth. Most countries in early stages of development have had small enterprises that succeeded in raising funds and improving productivity. For example, in Taiwan SMEs were begun on the basis of loans from relatives and acquaintances.[12] This diversity of experience may account for the failure of many of the measures of institutional quality to be significant in the Bosworth-Collins estimates. There are simply too many factors determining the success of firms, including the entrepreneurial ability of the population.

All else being equal, a badly functioning capital market, high levels of protection, and widespread corruption may reduce entrepreneurial activity and slow TFP growth. But a combination of offsetting policies might succeed. In South Korea in the 1960s and 1970s and China in the 1980s and 1990s there was considerable corruption, high protection, and an inefficient capital market, partly mitigated in South Korea by the better functioning internal capital market of the *chaebol*. Moreover, other features of the South Korean economy gave rise to productive investment. For example, South Korean firms typically imported considerable amounts of their equipment, which embodied new technology, and often hired consultants, particularly from Japan. Both of these activities were contingent on the availability of foreign exchange, which reflected the rapid growth of export earnings. The South Korean experience, which is one variant of the Asian experience, suggests a complex matrix of causation. No single deficiency establishes insuperable obstacles to growth. Other characteristics of the policy environment may impinge favorably on growth, and these policies are not captured by measures of investment climate or corruption or governance. A favorable real exchange rate or high protection (for a while) or low-interest loans accompanied by quid pro quo on the part of firms requiring them to export could generate greater and more efficient investment (World Bank 1993, Noland and Pack 2003).

Thus, the indicators by which the Arab economies fail to pass muster cannot be viewed in isolation. While it may be the case that if all of the measures of policy quality were at the best practice frontier a large industrial entrepreneurial class would unexpectedly emerge, various combinations of good and bad policies might also be successful and more politi-

---

12. That said, Taiwan subsequently intentionally and affirmatively attempted to regulate the curb market and boost the efficiency of financial intermediation for SMEs, for example by equipping banks with personal computers on which SME applicants could fill out common forms for loan approval, which could then be used to apply for loans at any bank.

cally feasible. This perspective assumes the latent existence of a capable entrepreneurial class that will respond to the net package of incentives. But in many of the Asian economies that have been successful, the entrepreneurial effort originated with foreigners, and the implications of this for the Middle East will be considered in chapter 9.

Technology and Productivity Growth

One of the problems highlighted in chapter 2 was the significant decrease in the rate of growth of TFP between the 1960–80 period and the succeeding two decades. Although it is well known that TFP growth may be attributable to many characteristics of any economy and is not solely a technological phenomenon, we believe that one "technological" interpretation helps to integrate the understanding of many of the characteristics of the Arab economies.

The specification in Bosworth and Collins, which is the conventional one, is that TFP growth is determined as a residual from growth accounting and then explained in terms of fundamental determinants.[13] But there are alternate views of the determinants of countries' growth. Some of the discussion of the success of the Asian countries notes their ability to improve their technological levels (Pack 1992), a process that was facilitated by the interaction between highly skilled labor and inflows of technology. The precise mechanism of this interaction is not captured in standard cross-country regressions.

Four decades ago, Richard Nelson and Edmund Phelps (1966) presented a model that provides a plausible alternative to growth accounting explanations that assume that growth is a function simply of factor accumulation that has no complex interactions among the factors.[14] The intuition of their model is that new technology is the major source of growth, and its successful assimilation into the economy depends on the presence of high skills. (See appendix 6A for an elucidation of the model.) Education will have its greatest impact when there is rapid technological change. If the basic technology (a loom used in weaving) is largely unchanged over time, the production process becomes routine, and the ability of more highly educated workers to deal with change is not germane—

---

13. An identical production function is assumed for all countries that employ the same elasticity of output with respect to capital and labor. While actual shares do differ across countries, this could be explained by differences in market power of labor and capital even where an identical production function does exist. For a discussion in the context of the East Asian countries, see Pack (2001).

14. The Nelson-Phelps model has recently obtained a second life in the endogenous growth literature, with financial sector development standing in for human capital. See, for example, Aghion and Howitt (1997) and Aghion, Howitt, and Mayer-Foulkes (2005).

growing education results in only limited productivity gains. In contrast, where technology is rapidly evolving, learning about the existence of new processes, learning to use them when they are deployed, and staying abreast of new developments require the adaptability provided by formal education. This view helps to explain the puzzling low apparent returns to education in some developing countries.[15]

To be clear, it is true that East Asia in general and South Korea in particular have accumulated human capital at a very rapid rate. Already in the 1950s, South Korea had a very high level of human capital relative to its level of per capita income compared with a broad range of both developed and developing countries (Noland and Pack 2003, table 2.1). From this relatively high base (at least relative to its contemporaneous level of income), South Korea increased its level of educational attainment rapidly, outstripping comparable countries (figure 2.3a in chapter 2).

At the same time education in South Korea had a more technical character, presumably more useful in the traded-goods sector, with the share of science and engineering graduates among university-level students ramping up quickly, exceeding all Arab countries save Algeria and nearly four times the level of Egypt (table 2.5). At least with respect to the contemporary period, the quality as well as quantity of this technical education also appears to be higher in Asia than in the Middle East: In the *Times of London* rankings of top 100 science universities, South Korea (2), Hong Kong (2), Taiwan (1), Singapore (1), China (1), and India (1) all have institutions within the top 100 while MENA has none; for the engineering and IT university rankings, the results are even more striking with universities from China (6), South Korea (2), Hong Kong (2), Singapore (2), Taiwan (1), and India (1) making the list but with no Arab institution making the grade.

To the extent that education is complementary to other imported inputs, investment in education while necessary may not be a sufficient condition for development. For poorer nations with low research and development (R&D), the primary vector of new technology is imports—new equipment, new intermediate inputs, and new disembodied knowledge (Enos and Park 1988, Hobday 1995, Coe and Helpman 1995). Absent such imports, TFP growth is likely to be low, though conventional sources of internal productivity growth such as R&D, organizational innovations, greater specialization, and better training could yield benefits as well, but the successful assimilation of these will also be contingent on high skills.

Much of the microeconomic and case study literature on the success of the Asian countries emphasizes the various modes of knowledge acquisition and absorption though the model is extremely difficult to test empirically. It might be argued that the openness variable in cross-country regressions captures this process to some extent, but the relation is very

---

15. See, for example, Pritchett (2001). For a more thorough analysis of the returns to education, see Hanushek (2005).

indirect. Yet another indirect way of substantiating this notion would be to point to the literature that establishes the complementarity between skills and capital in a variety of settings (Fallon and Layard 1975; Duffy, Papageorgiou, and Perez-Sebastian 2004) or that implies that skill-biased technical change is a pervasive phenomenon in both developed and developing countries (Berman, Bound, and Machin 1998).[16]

If one uses the Nelson-Phelps model as a departure point for thinking about growth, the TFP measures that have been calculated are not appropriate as they assume that TFP is a residual derived from an assumed standard multiplicative production function whereas the Nelson-Phelps model implies that newly available technology interacts with education to produce productivity growth. Growth accounting becomes a less reliable guide in explaining growth because of the interaction of factors that implies observed factor shares may not correspond to output elasticities with respect to individual factors. Econometric estimates of these interactions would be possible if adequate data on technology inflows were available—but as will be seen they are not. Measurable indicators of technology inflow (or generation within the domestic economy) could include domestic R&D, inflows of FDI, equipment imports, and more difficult, new intermediate inputs. All are best assimilated by those with high education, average years of education only indirectly reflecting this.

In contrast to this discussion, technology and education have usually been considered in isolation in discussions of the Middle East without noting their critical interdependence—for example, the *Arab Human Development Report 2002* identifies deficient education as one of a major critical obstacles to growth in Arab economies. The implication of the view taken here is different, namely, an increase in education (assuming it is of the right type) would have little payoff in the absence of a simultaneous increased inflow of international technology. The wider focus suggests looking at the level of R&D, FDI, technology licensing, use of consultants, imports of equipment, and other major vectors of imported technology. These are occasionally considered in some studies as one in a list of measures demonstrating the absence of globalization—but they are not typically incorporated into an effort to understand their importance as inputs in the productive efficiency of an economy rather than ends in themselves.

Any effort to implement this form of analysis immediately encounters serious analytic problems about causality. For example, countries may receive high FDI as foreign firms seek to sell in a country that has imposed tariffs to protect fledgling domestic firms. But such tariff-jumping FDI will occur only in nations with large markets as the tariff regime combined with overvalued exchange rates militates against the country as an export platform. Conversely, a country may experience FDI inflow in the context

---

16. De Ferranti et al. (2003, chapter 3) provides a comprehensive review of the evidence on the complementarity of education and technology.

of a preferential trade agreement that makes it a distinctively attractive export platform as will be discussed in chapter 8. Other factors may affect FDI inflows, and thus their size is a function of a complex process and is likely to have a large endogenous component. But whatever its source, FDI does not guarantee that the knowledge potentially provided to host country firms, through channels such as worker mobility, is fruitfully utilized by them. Potential knowledge recipients may not be sufficiently well educated. Local higher education may be driven by the need to offer alternatives to high school graduates and to delay their entry into the labor force. Little in the way of cognitive knowledge may be transmitted in the process. Thus, even if there are inflows, there is no guarantee that they will have a significant effect.

The available evidence provides a few largely suggestive measures of knowledge inflow—the pattern shown is fairly stark and provides part of the explanation why the rapid increase in education in the Middle East shown in chapter 2 has not necessarily translated into accelerated growth. Table 4.9 showed that the Arab countries have received little FDI as a share of GDP.[17] In some major countries with similarly low levels, such as India, there was a conscious effort to keep FDI out, following the regnant view in that nation until recently that FDI was a new form of imperialism. Other countries have also followed this cardinal tenet of dependency theory, whether or not explicitly articulated by policymakers. Not only is the level low in the Middle East, but unlike other regions, it has stayed low. Many countries, regardless of an initial perception that learning is best achieved by keeping FDI out, have reversed this policy—India, Japan, South Korea, and China are important examples. The increase in South Asia reflects the changing stance of India, but levels in Bangladesh and Pakistan remain low. Though as previously noted, dependency theory was never a particularly important part of the worldview of either intellectuals or policymakers in the Arab countries, until recently FDI has remained low and even in the recent surge appears to be largely oriented toward extraction. The possible reasons for this will be explored later. The point here is that one of the potential sources of improving productivity and generating employment in the manufacturing sectors has not been exploited.

The crude direct observation of FDI inflows can be supplemented with suggestive (but not definitive) survey data on technology transfer. Table 6.3 reports country rankings from the World Economic Forum's *Global Competitiveness Report* on technology importation via FDI. Algeria stands

---

17. There are difficult data problems, but the pattern shown would probably not differ much with still better measures. For many of the Arab countries of interest such as Syria, data are not available. While some of the oil countries receive substantial FDI inflows, much of it is directed to the petroleum sector whereas the role of FDI in improving TFP performance arises from the possibility of knowledge inflows that might accompany FDI and diffuse to the rest of the economy. In contrast, FDI into the petroleum sector is unlikely to provide technology transfers to the rest of the economy.

Table 6.3 Technology absorption (percentile)

Country	Foreign direct investment and technology transfer	Prevalence of foreign technology licensing	Intellectual property protection	Cost of importing foreign equipment	Brain drain	Technology innovation and diffusion: Firm-level technology absorption
Middle East						
Algeria	3	10	17	17	9	54
Bahrain	59	84	68	88	72	74
Egypt	82	67	54	18	22	58
Jordan	56	68	77	38	26	62
Kuwait	33	77	55	n.a.	97	74
Morocco	49	45	39	25	12	39
Qatar	94	74	73	n.a.	99	64
Tunisia	38	63	76	42	67	72
United Arab Emirates	63	88	74	97	98	88
High-performing comparators						
South Korea	53	72	78	63	79	94
Taiwan	79	100	79	83	90	97
Large comparators						
China	52	40	47	44	65	69
India	72	95	66	41	61	85
Normally endowed comparators						
Bangladesh	30	30	6	16	11	36
Brazil	74	69	45	6	68	62
Pakistan	67	26	26	46	23	61
Turkey	50	76	38	59	55	76
Resource-rich comparators						
Botswana	42	44	58	45	70	32
Indonesia	64	71	43	51	74	31
Nigeria	46	36	36	1	38	17
Venezuela	32	32	10	13	30	44

n.a. = not available

Note: Data are in percentiles (higher number is better); sample: n = 117; cost of importing foreign equipment sample: n = 104.

Source: World Economic Forum, Global Competitiveness Report 2005–2006; cost of importing foreign equipment: Global Competitiveness Report 2004–2005.

Figure 6.5 Royalties and fees for technology licensing, 1980–2004

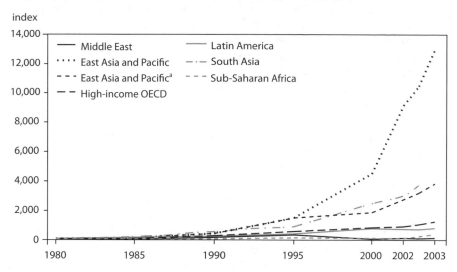

a. Excluding China.

Source: World Bank, *World Development Indicators*, June 2006.

out as one of the worst performers. The rest of the Arab countries range across the middle of the rankings.

There are alternatives to FDI for acquiring foreign knowledge, for example, technology licensing. While technology licensing may be more appropriate as countries shift to more technology-intensive sectors, it can be helpful even in the early stages of industrial development. Indeed, it was an important form of technology transfer in South Korea that eschewed FDI. Unfortunately, beyond the rich countries of the Organization for Economic Cooperation and Development (OECD), the data on this are highly fragmentary. Figure 6.5 displays regional indices constructed from a subset of countries for which consistent time-series data are available of royalties and fees for technology licensing in each region, with the initial level set to equal 100.[18] Because China did not begin reporting these data until 1997, yet is quantitatively important, two indices are reported for Asia, one including and the other excluding China. The index indicates that the Middle East has displayed the lowest growth in technology licensing of any region, with the level of technology licensing in the terminal year of

18. Country coverage for the OECD is complete. For the Middle East, the index is constructed from data for Morocco and Tunisia. Egypt is quantitatively important but reported the data only intermittently. East Asia is the Philippines, Thailand, and China. Latin America is Argentina, Brazil, Chile, Colombia, Costa Rica, Ecuador, El Salvador, Honduras, Jamaica, Mexico, Panama, and Peru. South Asia is India and Pakistan. Sub-Saharan Africa is South Africa.

2004 actually lower than at the start of the series in 1980 and completely dwarfed by the massive increases observed in East and South Asia. While the Middle East index consists only of Morocco and Tunisia (footnote 18), they are likely to have exhibited more licensing than other countries in the region because of their former colonial connection to France.

However, with policy reforms in recent years, including a number of countries joining the WTO and signing free trade agreements with the United States as will be discussed in chapter 8, intellectual property rights (IPR) protection has improved and with it technology licensing. Firms are less reluctant to do business with firms in countries with good IPRs. If they conform to the experience elsewhere (Branstetter, Fisman, and Foley 2005), as anecdotal evidence appears to confirm, with the passage of new IPR legislation and the signing of free trade agreements with the United States, which make enforcement credible, technology licensing arrangements may surge in countries like Morocco and Jordan (the latter scores well on the 2005–06 "prevalence of technology licensing indicator" in table 6.3), but one cannot as yet document this conjecture with actual data on financial flows. Others such as Algeria continue to lag on all indicators. Thus, during the period between 1960 and 2003 on which we are focusing, most Arab countries reported scant, if any, inward FDI or royalty payments, clearly not a stance for facilitating a move toward higher productivity levels. This situation has eased in recent years in some countries, though it remains difficult to document quantitatively.

Domestic knowledge generation can substitute for foreign technology. It is possible to construct many measures of potential effort, from R&D expenditures to enrollments in science and engineering programs in tertiary education institutions. The former are problematic—definitions of R&D vary widely across countries. In any case they are available in only a few instances for the countries in question—only Egypt among the Arab countries. While data on school enrollments are available, their interpretation is difficult without some benchmark of the quality of the instruction rather than numbers of students going through the education system. As noted in chapter 2, with respect to the Middle East there is reason for concern on this dimension.

Another tack would be to consider measures of the outcome rather than the input, such as the number of scientific and technical articles in journals and patent applications by residents. On both measures, the Arab countries have low levels. In journal articles they are comparable to Africa despite the latter's much lower levels of tertiary and science enrollments and other measures of education input. Of patent applications by residents, the data are highly fragmentary, but at least according to the reported data, for 2002, the latest year that data are available, Egypt was the only significant source, accounting for 86 percent of the region's patenting activity.[19] How-

---

19. World Bank, *World Development Indicators* (accessed August 4, 2005).

ever, only 15 percent of these patents went to Egyptian nationals (Council on Foreign Relations 2005). A similar story holds elsewhere in the region, for example in Algeria—of 111 patents granted in 2002, only 8 went to Algerians. In Saudi Arabia, where 25 patents were issued, only 2 went to Saudis. The Council on Foreign Relations report goes on to observe that Moldova, one of the poorest countries in Europe, granted more patents in 2002 than Algeria and Saudi Arabia combined.

Whatever the lacunae and imprecision in these indicators, the ineluctable image is one of nations in which little or no formal innovative activity is going on. It is possible, of course, that some effort at enhancing productivity is occurring but does not get reported in formal measures of effort. But if a major source of potential productivity growth stems from the productive absorption of foreign technology inflow, its absence implies absorptive capacity is low. Moreover, unlike South Korea, Taiwan, and many Latin American countries of the 1960s and 1970s, there are no case studies to suggest that this global picture is not valid.[20]

This absence of technology inflow is perhaps part of the general picture of limited industrialization and the restricted change in product or sectoral composition that would necessitate such inflows. It presumably is not due to the absence of foreign exchange. In particular, royalty and licensing payments are a tiny percentage of total foreign exchange earnings and could easily have been multiplied without any serious impact on the reserve position of the countries. New knowledge may have entered in the form of new intermediate goods or been embodied in new equipment. But these countries have typically not been major importers of either. That in part may be due to their cost—as shown in the fourth column of table 6.3, most of the Arab countries exhibit a high cost for imported equipment.

If the model of the interaction of new technology and education provides a useful adjunct (or alternative) to standard growth explanations, then much of the recent discussion, especially in the three editions of the *Arab Human Development Report*, needs considerable refinement. More and higher-quality education, the recommended panacea for the countries, absent new technology inflows or rapid change in product or industrial structure, will result in low social marginal productivity. If the output mix and the technology employed continue to be the same, there may be little need for additional skills, which have their payoff only when production in shifting rapidly. More education, absent "true" demand reflecting the productivity of education rather than politically dictated demand (stemming from the imperative to create jobs for the better educated), will create more of a problem with unemployed or underemployed graduates. Thus, a greater opening toward the international economy is a prerequisite for the success of improved education.

---

20. For an evaluation of this case study literature, see Pack (2006).

It might be argued that the inflow of technology is itself likely to respond to the presence of a highly educated labor force, a favorite argument of countries, states, and regions attempting to attract new investment from outside of the region. Without going into the determinants of FDI and licensing at this point, it is noteworthy that countries like South Korea and Taiwan experienced extensive emigration of the highly educated in the 1950s through the early 1970s as does the Philippines today. The same is true for India. While FDI was discouraged in South Korea, Taiwan was more open, but firms did not locate there until many policies were changed. The simple presence of an educated labor pool is no guarantee of the attractiveness to foreign firms absent other favorable conditions.

More generally, there is a serious coordination problem that no country has quite solved. Enrollments will not shift toward areas that may be useful in competitive industries until these sectors actually exist. Conversely, such industries may not develop absent a local skill base. A country could, as in the case of South Korea and Taiwan, choose an uncoordinated path—educate first, suffer underemployment and emigration, and hope to attract these workers home as new sectors begin. In the case of South Korea, and especially Taiwan, that brain drain was subsequently reversed and became a source of technological dynamism as will be discussed in greater detail in chapter 9. With the exception of Tunisia, the survey data from the *Global Competitiveness Report* suggest that the Arab countries face acute challenges retaining highly skilled people, with the phenomenon being particularly problematic for Algeria and Morocco, which have combined relatively weak economic performance with relatively strong historical ties to Western Europe as shown by the column on brain drain in table 6.3. Tunisia's relatively strong growth performance appears to be its saving grace.

Alternately, countries could industrialize first, use imported skilled labor initially, and then assume that current students observe the growing employment in specific sectors and occupations and change their enrollment. But such changes are difficult to mandate by a central government.[21] A government might give subsidies to change the enrollment patterns (as the United States did after the Russians launched Sputnik in 1957), but even this runs into severe monitoring problems. On the other hand the South Korea–Taiwan path (not that the strategy was planned) of emigration of the highly educated is impeded in the post-9/11 world nor, given the hostile climate, is the use of foreign nationals to staff new en-

---

21. Marwan Kardoosh and Riad al Khoury (2005) provide a concrete example of this coordination problem. As is discussed in appendix 8B in chapter 8, Jordan has established special zones to encourage foreign investment, much of which is in garment manufacture. To boost local employment it in essence has to create an industrial proletariat yet has encountered difficulty coordinating its vocational training programs with the needs of the garment producers. Developing the ability to work in a garment factory is presumably one of the easier coordination problems that prospective industrializers would encounter.

terprises, as in Singapore, an easy option. As in other areas, recent concern with terrorism precludes paths that have occurred in other countries.

It could also be the case that the existence of a substantial pool of highly educated workers with an internationally valuable skill could attract either FDI or outsourced business from OECD firms. The offshoring to other countries of US white-collar jobs, ranging from chip design to radiology, has become a serious policy concern in the United States. Yet journalistic accounts seldom mention Middle Eastern countries. China, India, Pakistan, Mexico, and the Philippines are among the major beneficiaries of still another source of potential technology transfer, though Tunisia, Egypt, and the United Arab Emirates are making inroads.

Taking the perspective offered here, the problems of the Middle Eastern countries discussed in chapter 4 become clearer. The absence of participation in the international economy, limited export growth in nonoil products, and the emphasis in imports on final consumer goods are all measures of the absence of technological stimulus from abroad. So are the relative paucity of FDI and technology licensing. Thus, education levels that are not bad by international standards, at least in years, can have only a limited payoff. However, the emphasis on education, a popular nostrum, absent the technological stimulus, is likely to have a limited effect on growth. And these deficiencies (along with the absence of internal competitive pressures) interact to limit the rate of productivity growth that might augment the growth of income per person for a given commitment of physical capital.

The limited domestic competitiveness given the still fairly high tariffs and the absence of substantial exporting activity that requires innovation undoubtedly contribute to the low demand for productivity-enhancing technology transfers. It is not necessary to invoke a millennial decline in attitudes toward innovation or the rote nature of much of education to explain the exceptionally low levels of R&D or patenting although these more fundamental forces may well contribute to the observed pattern.

Conclusion

The analysis thus far suggests that for the most part Arab economies such as Egypt or Morocco are comprehensible in terms of the experiences of other developing countries around the world. Their growth rates are not significantly different nor are their policy stances from those of a broad range of comparators. Within this group, Tunisia has done relatively well, while Syria has performed poorly. The major extractive economies, Algeria, Kuwait, and Saudi Arabia, understandably have exhibited a distinctive trajectory, strongly influenced by the price of their major export, oil. There have been many descriptions of the needed policy changes in these nations though they tend to be generic without any sense of the likely country-specific payoffs. Yet the payoffs are uncertain and may not be large—witness, for example, the recent controversies over the benefits to Mexico from the North American Free Trade Agreement (Lederman, Maloney, and Servén 2004).

The suggested policy changes typically are variants of the now familiar Washington Consensus combination of macroeconomic stability together with microeconomic sectoral neutrality, including such recommendations as liberalizing the trade regime including reduction of tariffs and quotas; decreasing the number of state-owned enterprises; improving the investment climate by cutting the number of licensing requirements, better enforcement of contracts, and lowering other "behind-the-border" limits on competition; eliminating obstacles to FDI and improving the transparency of the FDI regime; making labor markets more flexible by reducing minimum wage enforcement and allowing firms to fire workers without excessive difficulty; upgrading the education system so that students are more oriented to analysis than memorization as well as attempting to match more closely the generation of skills with their demand by potential employers; and providing a safety net including cash transfer and public works programs.

The cumulative effect of implementing these policies would be to create an environment conducive to private investment, provide a labor force that was responsive to shifting demands, and protect those who would suffer in the transformed environment resulting from privatization and liberalization. The last would be intrinsically desirable and reduce opposition to potentially wrenching changes. The time phasing, big bang or gradual, is usually omitted, perhaps intentionally.

There are few analysts of developing economies who would not advocate most or all of these policies, a large subset of the Washington Consensus discussed previously, though it is worth emphasizing that as demonstrated in this chapter, the effect of existing measures of many of these reforms is not statistically significant in explaining cross-country growth. The most successful economies, those in Asia, did not conform to all of these recommendations in their period of growth acceleration. Most had fairly high tariffs, significant levels of publicly owned enterprises, and corruption that was hardly at Nordic levels. Most did have macroeconomic basics in place including relatively low budget deficits, realistic and stable real exchange rates, and a variety of nonstandard policies designed to promote exports. South Korea and Taiwan pursued industrial policies that promoted individual sectors and firms by using the financial system to channel low-interest loans to particular firms in the sectors. In South Korea large conglomerates allocated funds among subsidiaries through an internal capital market that overcame some of the repression of the financial system though perhaps with later deleterious consequences (Noland and Pack 2003). South Korea and Taiwan also encouraged exports by a variety of means including drawbacks on tariffs on inputs necessary for the production of exports. There is a considerable empirical literature suggesting that industrial policies were, at most, a mild stimulus to growth (Noland and Pack 2003) though the relatively uniform industrywide export incentives may have been of some importance. While the Asian countries might have grown even more rapidly had they conformed to all of the points listed above, their experience does suggest that not all deviations from the Washington Consensus lead to absolute constraints on growth—some are almost surely critical (an appropriate real exchange rate level that exhibits limited variability) while some can be compensated for by countervailing policies (tariffs on imports combined with drawbacks on inputs entering into exports).

Although it obviously would be desirable to have only good policies, bad policies can be offset by a variety of countervailing stimuli if this is politically and socially feasible. The willingness and ability to exploit these opportunities is presumably a function of elite attitudes and interests set against internal and external policy constraints. The issue is whether Arab elites hold attitudes that would predispose them toward or against liberal economic policies and whether their polities face any unique internal or external constraints on (or enablers to) the implementation of an improved set of policies. The examples of the latter are not only the ideas or policy innovations that may arise from abroad but also the impact of demonstration effects of good (and bad) policies undertaken by regional neighbors and also the potential that commitments with other sovereigns, through free trade agreements for example, might have to leverage domestic reform or increase perceptions of its credibility and irreversibility.[22]

---

22. See Esfahani (2000) for a wide-ranging discussion of the issues of credibility and irreversibility from the perspective of MENA economies.

Appendix 6A
Interaction of Education and Technology

The discussion in this chapter of the interaction of domestic skills and in-flow of knowledge can be formalized following Nelson and Phelps (1966). Firms in less developed countries (LDCs) in the Middle East operate with a technology level equal to $A(t)$ in period t. Their peers in industrial countries operate technology $T(t)$. The rate at which developed-country technology in the form of licenses and consultants' knowledge is diffused into the LDC depends on the level of human capital, h, and is

$$A'(t) \mathbin{/} A(t) = \alpha(h) \left[\frac{T(t) - A(t)}{A(t)} \right]. \tag{6A.1}$$

The extent to which local LDC technology or total factor productivity improves depends on the amount of educated labor in the potential recipient—it is a positive function, $\alpha(h) > 0$, of the level of human capital and proportional to the difference between current and "best practice" technology. As the technology $T(t)$ does not have to be invented *de novo*, the potential productivity gain from the transfer of this technology can be rapid. It is one of the potential benefits of relative backwardness (Gerschenkron 1962) that has only rarely been capitalized upon in poorer countries except for a handful of Asian countries. Assume that the developed-country technology improves each year by φ percent so that

$$T(t) = T_0 e^{\varphi t} \tag{6A.2}$$

Given equations 6A.1 and 6A.2, the underlying differential equation implies that the path of technology of an LDC firm is

$$A(t) = [\alpha(h) / (\alpha(h) + \varphi)] \, T_0 e^{\varphi t}. \tag{6A.3}$$

This technology or productivity level will thus be higher: The greater a country's ability to absorb new technologies as a result of the presence of educated individuals on its staff, the greater the inflow of technology to firms in the form of new equipment, new material inputs, and new knowledge obtained from consultants, licensors, and foreign owners. The potential level of technology of the firm in the developing country is described by equation 6A.3 and depends solely on its own level of h and the rate of technical progress in the developed countries that becomes available to the LDC firm. If ideology, foreign exchange shortages, or arbitrary rules prohibiting some forms of technology imports reduce the inflow of new knowledge, the benefit conferred by having educated labor, h, is reduced.

There is a lower actual rate of technology inflow, $\gamma < \varphi$. In this case equation 6A.3 can be rewritten to reflect the lower rate of technology inflow:

$$A_\gamma (t) = [\alpha(h)/(\alpha(h) +\gamma)] T_0 e^{\gamma t} \qquad (6A.4)$$

and $A_\gamma < A$. If γ is close to zero as it appears to be in much of the Middle East, equation 6A.4 implies low productivity levels regardless of the extent of education. Indeed, equation 6A.4 implies that human capital will have no effect on the level of output obtained with conventional inputs unless $\gamma > 0$, which can only occur if new productivity-enhancing activities are constantly introduced. While education is indeed important, its payoff as noted in this chapter will be severely reduced unless there is a concomitant increase in the inflow of technology as part of the overall process of globalization of these economies.

7

Attitudes, Interest Groups, and Reform

In broad terms, policy reflects the accumulation of history, which conditions both elite and popular attitudes, and in all but exceptional circumstances those attitudes serve to constrain the scope of policy change in democratic and nondemocratic polities alike. Other regions abandoned inward-looking policies for several reasons. An extensive literature in the 1960s and 1970s documented the adverse effects of import-substituting industrialization. The initial success during the 1960s of several resource-poor Asian countries such as Hong Kong, Taiwan, South Korea, and Singapore, followed by a second wave of poorer Southeast Asian emulators in the 1970s, led to a reassessment of development strategies among many policymakers who were, one suspects, not devoted readers of the academic literature. In Latin America, the debt crisis of the early 1980s forced policymakers to attempt to earn more foreign exchange to enable nations to restore their international credit. In some countries, most importantly India, conditions imposed by the international financial institutions required greater openness (Krueger 2002, Joshi and Little 1996, Srinivasan and Tendulkar 2003). In the many instances of liberalization, the difficult objective conditions imposed by the hard facts of reserve positions were utilized by a substantial group of local analysts, often trained in American universities, who acted as local advocates of changes that were perceived to be long overdue. Export-oriented businesses also supported such moves. Few of the Arab economies faced the type of financial crisis encountered in Latin America in the 1980s or India in the early 1990s. Moreover, they were the beneficiaries of considerable inflows of foreign exchange that allowed a soft national budget constraint (see chapter 4).

Until now we have made little use of the former Eastern Bloc countries as comparators to the Arab countries. For most of the historical period under consideration, they operated as centrally planned economies with their own set of international institutions such as the Council for Mutual Economic Assistance and consequently were really not comparable to the Arab countries. But at least superficially they bear certain similarities—in both regions economic policy had a statist bent, accompanied by highly undemocratic and stable political regimes. However, the countries of Central Europe decisively reformed both economically and politically during the "third wave" of democratization of the late 1980s and early 1990s, while changes across the states of the former Soviet Union have been more uneven, with the Eastern European countries occupying a middle ground both geographically and politically. Comparing and contrasting the experiences of these countries with the contemporary experience of the Middle East may yield some insight into the constraints and opportunities that Arab policymakers face.

Czech novelist Milan Kundera begins an essay on Central European identity with a rumination on the following event: "In November 1956, the director of the Hungarian News Agency, shortly before his office was flattened by artillery fire, sent a telex to the entire world with a desperate message announcing that the Russian attack against Budapest had begun. The dispatch ended with these words: 'We are going to die for Hungary and for Europe'" (Kundera 1984, 33). Kundera observes that to express willingness to die for one's country is unremarkable; what is intriguing is the "*and* for Europe," a phrase that Kundera asserts "could not be thought in Moscow or Leningrad; it is precisely a phrase that could be thought in Budapest or Warsaw" (Kundera 1984, 33; emphasis in the original). The Hungarian émigré economist Béla Balassa similarly observed that Hungarians took their political and cultural cues from Paris, not Moscow (Balassa 1989). More salient is Balassa's passing mention that his first professional economics paper, written under Communist rule in Hungary, was on 19th century liberal John Stuart Mill.

These perceptions are rooted in the notion, recently popularized by Samuel P. Huntington (1996), that a civilization fault line runs through Europe, from the Finland-Russia border, south through Belarus, the Ukraine, and Romania, before turning west and separating Slovenia and Croatia from the rest of the former Yugoslavia. It is a border that separates Western Christianity circa 1500 from Eastern or Orthodox Christianity and Islam, with the relatively small Jewish population spread unevenly across it (figure 7.1). To the west, unintended consequences emanating from Roman Catholic theological innovations with respect to family law and legal institutions, followed later by the Protestant Reformation, contributed to the development of the basic institutions of modern capitalism (Kaufmann 1997, Lal 1998). To the east, the penetration of these social innovations occurred much more slowly, with equivalent local adaptations in areas such

Figure 7.1 Civilization fault line

as laws on partnerships and corporate entities not occurring until the 19th century in much of the Arab world (Kuran 2003a). If religious affiliation shares are any guide, this cultural division of Europe appears to be persistent, corresponding fairly cleanly with contemporary national borders if one simply aggregates the shares of the population professing Roman Catholicism and Protestantism (and perhaps Judaism) (table 7.1).

Despite the horrors of the 20th century, the political experience of Central Europe was modestly more liberal than the East. After lurching from monarchy to unstable populist democracies to Nazism, West Germany

Table 7.1   Religious affiliation shares, 1900 and 1990 (percent)

Region/country	1900					1990				
	Catholic	Protestant	Orthodox	Jewish	Muslim	Catholic	Protestant	Orthodox	Jewish	Muslim
Central Europe										
Czech Republic	86	6	n.a.	3	n.a.	40	3	1	n.a.	n.a.
Hungary	61	26	1	6	n.a.	62	25	1	1	1
Poland	77	3	8	9	n.a.	92	1	3	n.a.	n.a.
Slovakia	85	7	n.a.	3	n.a.	69	11	n.a.	n.a.	n.a.
Baltic Republics										
Estonia	1	54	43	1	n.a.	n.a.	15	16	n.a.	n.a.
Latvia	33	45	15	n.a.	n.a.	19	22	21	1	n.a.
Lithuania	90	1	3	n.a.	n.a.	83	1	3	n.a.	n.a.
Former Soviet Union										
Belarus	32	n.a.	61	n.a.	n.a.	12	1	46	1	n.a.
Russia	n.a.	1	77	6	9	1	1	55	1	8
Ukraine	18	2	71	3	n.a.	11	3	52	1	2
Former Yugoslavia										
Bosnia	17	n.a.	43	n.a.	40	22	n.a.	26	n.a.	46
Croatia	82	n.a.	10	n.a.	n.a.	85	1	8	n.a.	3
Macedonia	1	n.a.	86	1	8	3	n.a.	65	n.a.	22
Serbia and Montenegro	9	5	70	1	10	6	1	54	n.a.	16
Slovenia	95	n.a.	n.a.	n.a.	n.a.	83	2	1	n.a.	n.a.
Eastern Europe										
Albania	8	n.a.	20	n.a.	69	12	n.a.	11	n.a.	35
Bulgaria	1	n.a.	76	1	17	1	1	75	n.a.	12
Romania[a]	1	1	88	5	1	14	10	82	n.a.	1

n.a. = not available

a. 1990 figures for Romania reflect deliberate double counting of Catholics and Protestants claimed by the Romanian Orthodox Church.

Source: Barrett, Kurian, and Johnson (2001).

and Austria established stable liberal democracies post-1945, and East Germany adopted democracy and then merged into the larger democratic West German state once it had the opportunity in 1989. After the collapse of the Hapsburg monarchy, Czechoslovakia emerged as a liberal democracy only to be overwhelmed by Nazi Germany; democracy was briefly reestablished only to be once again subdued, this time by a Soviet-backed coup that installed a Communist regime. Poland and Hungary were less liberal, maintaining relatively soft authoritarian regimes during the interwar years.

Except West Germany and Austria, these Central European states were incorporated into the Soviet-led Eastern Bloc following World War II. And despite the prewar existence in these countries of indigenous Communist parties, significant parts of the population regarded the Soviet-installed regimes as alien transplants. The Soviet Union's status as a colonial power, paradoxically, gave statism a bad name, and the poor economic performance of these nations under Communism generated widespread sympathy for a more liberal economic order.

Ironically, Communism's success at creating literate urban populations contributed to its eventual downfall. In contrast to China with its vast reservoirs of politically docile peasants with whom to fill the ranks of the army, the militaries of Central Europe were unreliable politically as tools of internal coercion. Once it became apparent under Mikhail Gorbachev that the Soviets would not back their satellites militarily, the game was up.

As the Communist dominoes fell, the newly empowered democratic regimes of Central Europe looked west to the economic, political, and cultural pull of Western Europe and to European institutions such as the European Union and the North Atlantic Treaty Organization (NATO), which could serve as precommitment mechanisms and lock in the political and economic regime changes that had occurred. After some time the Central Europeans were followed by the newly freed Baltic nations and Eastern European states of Romania and Bulgaria, which also saw their future as part of an integrated Europe characterized by democratic politics and relatively liberal economic regimes. In the context of the multiethnic, multireligious, and arguably multicivilizational state of Yugoslavia, the moves by Slovenia and Croatia in essence to rejoin the West arguably set off the conflagration that subsequently swept the Balkans.

The Arab world, in contrast, has a very different cultural and political history. Apart from the direct impact of European imperialism, prewar European political influence mainly took the form of the illiberal corporatist fascism of Southern Europe manifested in local political organizations such as the Phalangist and Ba'athist parties. During World War II these illiberal tendencies were reinforced to an unknown degree by the Nazi attempts to recruit local Arab leaders into alliances of convenience against the British and their Western allies, particularly in the French-mandated region of Syria-Lebanon following the French surrender in 1940 and the establishment in the French colonies of North Africa of regimes sympathetic to the Vichy government in France.[1] Following the war, these illiberal tendencies were reinforced by the Soviets and in the Mahgreb by the French Communist Party.

The collapse of the Ottoman Empire at the end of World War I, and British and French imperialism following World War II, led to the emergence of weak states with arbitrary borders. In such conditions, political leaders will emphasize nation, or at least political regime, building. This means strengthening the state, and dirigiste economic policies are one way of generating rents through which political coalitions can be built. (In this respect the resource-rich countries have an advantage—one does not need to introduce distortions to generate the rents.)

Ideology reinforced these political incentives. Ironically while economically more liberal policies were eventually adopted in the Southern European fascist countries, assisted by US tutelage in the case of postwar Italy and through the process of EU integration in the case of post-Franco Spain and post-Salazar Portugal, in the Middle East the illiberal economic outlook of prewar corporatist-fascist ideas from Southern Europe was actually reinforced during the Cold War period through the influence of the Soviet Union. In both its political and ideological manifestations, a statist, bureaucratic approach to economic development would appear indigenous, nationalist, and politically legitimate.

This experience can be contrasted with that of Central Europe, where significant sections of the populace—in some sense more secure in their national identities—regarded the Soviet-installed governments as illegitimate, quasi-colonial regimes, something to revolt against rather than to support. In 1989, when the Eastern Bloc was pushed to the wall, it collapsed from the torque of the centrifugal push of the evidently failed statist policies of Communism meeting the centripetal pull of Western Europe with its liberal political institutions and economic policies. And while there were political liberalizations in the Arab world at this time, the Middle East did not make a decisive break.[2]

---

1. According to Ladan Boroumand and Roya Boroumand (2002, 7), "by the late 1930s, Nazi Germany had established contacts with revolutionary junior officers in the Egyptian army, including many who were close to the Muslim Brothers . . . whose slogan 'action, obedience, silence' echoed the 'believe, obey, fight' motto of the Italian Fascists." Bernard Lewis (2005) writes that although the Ba'ath Party was not officially founded until 1947, "memoirs of the time and other sources show that the Nazi interlude is where it began. From Syria, the Germans and the proto-Baathists also set up a pro-Nazi regime in Iraq." After the overthrow of this regime, its leader Rashid Ali al-Gailani spent the remainder of the war in Berlin with the mufti of Jerusalem, Haj Amin al-Husseini, as guests of Hitler. Also see Lee (2002).

2. Algeria and Jordan experienced modest political liberalizations at this time (Tunisia's had come a couple of years earlier). The constitutional changes in Algeria, which involved a reduction in the dominance of the National Liberation Front and the introduction of multiparty elections, were subsequently reversed. Another move toward more representative govern-

Popular Attitudes

Globalization

Polling data reveal the gulf in attitudes between the publics of the two regions. In 2002 the Pew Global Attitudes Project surveyed more than 38,000 respondents in 44 countries on their attitudes toward globalization (see appendix 7A for details on the Pew survey). A number of these survey questions, phrased in agreement/disagreement form, related directly to economic life, while other questions explored related aspects of globalization. For analytical purposes these questions could be thought of as falling into three categories: attitudes toward markets, economic manifestations of globalization, and broader social or cultural attitudes (Noland 2005b).[3]

There is considerable regional variation in the pattern of responses, with Western Europe generally exhibiting the most "proglobalization" attitudes, and the Middle East and South and West Asia harboring the greatest reservations. Among the primarily non-OECD regions the populations of East Asia tend to be the most enthusiastic; Africans tend to be supportive of globalization in its economic manifestations though they are more negative on the cultural issues, particularly homosexuality (table 7.2). The country-specific responses for the Middle East and Eastern European countries are reported in table 7.3.[4] On the first two questions relating to basic attitudes toward the market and efficiency, there is considerable variation within each region, with the Lebanese being the most liberal of the three Arab countries surveyed. On the whole, the responses of the Arab countries do not look much different from the Eastern Europeans.

The cultural tolerance indicator, acceptance of homosexuality, may provide an important economically relevant clue not to sexual mores per se but with respect to eliciting attitudes toward indifference or tolerance more generally. Richard Florida (2002) has found that the homosexual

---

ment began in 1995, following a period marked by extraconstitutional government and widespread political violence. In recent years there has been continued political liberalization, though the armed forces maintain a dominant role in politics. In Jordan the period 1989–92 witnessed the lifting of martial law restrictions on political activity, the integration of previously excluded groups into the political process, and the first national elections in 22 years in the context of monarchical rule.

3. One might question how accurately the Pew survey captured public attitudes. The wording of the questions on foreign multinational corporations and another question relating to trust in the United Nations are similar to questions posed by two GlobeScan surveys (GlobeScan 2003, 2004). The cross-country correlations between the Pew and GlobeScan responses are quite strong. A distinct issue is "preference falsification" or deliberately lying to pollsters, as will be discussed below.

4. Both positive and negative responses to questions are generally correlated with economic performance. In the interests of parsimony, only the more highly correlated response is reported.

Table 7.2 Regional Pew survey responses (percent deviations from global mean)

Question	Global average	North America	Western Europe	Eastern Europe	Latin America	Africa	East Asia	South and West Asia	Middle East
Markets									
Close factories	36.9	n.a.	n.a.	5.3	-8.8	5.2	9.9	-8.9	-2.6
Support free markets	59.1	7.4	7.7	-9.6	-10.1	8.2	10.1	-9.5	-0.8
Globalization									
Growing business ties, good for family	79.6	3.4	5.6	-4.4	0.0	3.0	5.6	-3.2	-16.6
Faster communication and travel, good	88.3	0.2	4.7	2.7	-2.9	4.6	3.7	-6.3	-16.6
Foreign media, good for family	74.7	15.8	14.8	6.6	1.7	1.5	12.5	-17.9	-12.0
Foreign products, good	79.0	8.0	8.3	-6.0	-3.7	7.3	3.9	-9.2	-11.6
Connected world, good	85.3	4.8	5.5	2.1	-0.4	1.3	5.4	-7.3	-16.6
Globalization, good	57.8	7.7	3.7	-11.3	-1.2	10.4	14.5	-15.6	-21.8
Multinational corporations, good	61.8	-9.3	-7.0	-7.3	-1.8	13.6	10.4	-13.8	-12.3
International organizations, good	59.9	2.1	4.4	-2.2	-5.6	11.8	6.6	-15.1	-21.9
Antiglobalization protesters, bad	34.4	15.1	16.6	3.3	-3.5	-1.7	-5.4	-14.8	14.1
Tolerance									
Superior culture, disagree	28.4	14.1	27.1	7.4	-2.6	-1.7	-11.4	-18.6	2.6
Do not protect against foreign influence	23.7	13.8	18.6	4.8	1.7	-6.7	-1.5	-14.7	1.0
Accept homosexuality	35.2	24.8	41.3	9.3	15.4	-24.5	-3.0	-24.2	-18.7

n.a. = not available

Source: Pew Global Attitudes Project (2003).

Table 7.3 Pew responses by country and regional average (percent)

Region/country	Markets			Globalization								Tolerance		
	Close large, inefficient factories	Support free markets	Growing business ties, good for family	Faster communication and travel, good	Foreign media, good for family	Foreign products, good	Connected world, good	Globalization, good	Multinationals, good	International organizations, good	Anti-globalization protesters, bad	Our culture is superior (disagree)	Foreign influence (do not protect)	Accept homosexuality
Middle East	34	58	63	72	63	67	69	36	50	38	49	31	25	17
Egypt	34	52	59	69	55	60	66	37	n.a.	n.a.	n.a.	18	11	n.p.
Jordan	27	47	53	54	50	60	57	27	42	32	57	54	43	12
Lebanon	42	76	77	92	83	82	83	44	57	44	40	21	20	21
Morocco	n.a.	n.a.	n.a.	n.a.	n.a.	n.a.	n.a.	63	n.a.	n.a.	n.a.	n.a.	n.a.	n.a.
Kuwait	n.a.	n.a.	n.a.	n.a.	n.a.	n.a.	n.a.	87	n.a.	n.a.	n.a.	n.a.	n.a.	n.a.
Eastern Europe	42	50	75	91	81	73	87	47	55	58	38	36	29	45
Bulgaria	38	31	67	90	83	81	79	33	55	48	15	13	23	37
Czech Republic	63	62	83	95	92	88	96	69	60	70	72	45	32	83
Poland	37	44	72	90	84	70	79	38	44	50	34	35	30	40
Russia	27	45	69	85	59	77	89	31	42	42	24	31	19	22
Slovakia	50	51	82	94	90	65	94	65	71	74	58	47	33	68
Ukraine	38	64	78	92	80	57	87	43	55	62	23	44	34	17
Memorandum: Central Europe	50	52	79	93	89	77	90	57	58	65	55	42	32	64

n.a. = not available

n.p. = question was not permitted

Note: Central Europe includes Czech Republic, Poland, and Slovakia.

Source: Pew Global Attitudes Project (2003).

population share is highly correlated with high-technology industry activity across US metropolitan areas. In turn, the highest demographic correlate with the gay population share was the foreign-born share, which could be interpreted as an indicator of acceptance of nontraditional cultural influences. Communities that accept social variety including foreign cultures may have low entry barriers to human capital, which is important to spurring creativity and prosperity (Florida 2002). Florida's conjecture is supported by other empirical evidence (Glaeser 2004, Glaeser and Saiz 2004, Berry and Glaeser 2005) about the role of tolerance, acceptance of foreign immigrants, and human capital formation in explaining the varied experiences of US cities in surmounting negative shocks. Presumably one aspect of this tolerance is relative freedom from discrimination, fear of harassment, or attack. There are many accounts of the critical role of immigrants from East Asia and India in Silicon Valley (Saxenian 2001, 2002), and accounts of expatriates returning to countries such as India and Taiwan who assume major roles in new sectors describe the need for the receiving country to be accepting of the cultural differences acquired after long residence abroad.

However, on the next nine questions relating to globalization in various manifestations, the average of the Arab countries is consistently lower than the average for Eastern Europe and well below the Central European average, sometimes by very large margins. Among the Arab countries, Lebanon is distinct, with its responses generally similar to those of the Eastern Europeans. Similarly, on the three "tolerance" questions, the Arab countries generally score lower than the Eastern European comparators.[5] This impression is reinforced by subsequent polling: Among the overwhelming majorities of Muslims who believe that their nations should be more prosperous, most identified Western policies as the primary impediment (including 59 percent of Egyptians and 66 percent of Jordanians), while government corruption was the second most widely cited response, topping other alternatives such as lack of education (Pew Global Attitudes Project 2006a). The same survey documented pervasive anti-Western attitudes among Muslims—largely unreciprocated by anti-Muslim attitudes among Westerners.

In sum, the polling data do not point to large differences in attitudes toward the market. However, it does reveal less support for globalization in parts of the Arab world and a higher incidence of chauvinism, xenophobia, or intolerance.

---

5. The difference is most stark for the question on homosexuality: The question was not permitted in Egypt, while the Czech Republic exhibited the most accepting attitudes of any country in the entire sample. The score for the most tolerant of the Arab countries, Lebanon (21), is roughly half the Eastern European average (45) and one-third that for the Central Europe subset (64). That said there is considerable variation within Eastern Europe: The scores of the Ukraine (17) and Russia (22) are in the MENA league.

Islam and Politics

What are the sources of this discomfiture? One early analysis located the sources in the effects of colonization on the individual psyche (Memmi 1965). This work is remarkably prescient, foreseeing a retreat into chauvinistic tribalism, nationalism, religion, and a rejection of science and other cultural innovations from abroad as at least a transitory outcome of the process of decolonization of the Arab world.[6] Yet, while offering undeniable insight, the level of broad generality in this psychological analysis militates against its applicability to specific situations today.

The 2003 Pew survey also examined attitudes toward Islam and political life in a number of predominantly Muslim countries around the world, as well as several such as Nigeria and Tanzania with large Muslim minorities. The poll revealed ubiquitous feelings of solidarity with coreligionists in the *umma* and widespread support among Muslims surveyed for the notion that Islam was under threat, though the perceived sources of threat were multiple and predominantly reflected local concerns. However, subsequent polling by the same organization revealed growing distrust of the West; for example, huge majorities of Muslims, including 87 percent in Egypt and 90 percent in Jordan, ascribed the Danish cartoon controversy to Western disrespect for Islam (Pew Global Attitudes Project 2006a).[7]

In this regard, concerns manifested through Islam may simply be one symptom of more complex social processes. Islam may matter—not in the simple sense that belief in Allah dooms one to a low personal saving rate or that Islamic banking systems handicap financial efficiency—but rather in a more subtle way. Today Muslim communities in the Middle East are relatively discomfited by aspects of ongoing social change. To the extent that adherence to Islam is a significant component of personal and communal identity, Islamic teachings will be one prism through which these developments are assessed. This pattern of apprehension may be reinforced if Islam itself is regarded as being part of this contested terrain.

Yet the centrality of religious belief in this formative process should not be overstated. As revealed in the Zogby poll, religious orientation is generally only a secondary or tertiary source of personal identity in most Arab countries in the Middle East—rather, Arab ethnicity is the primary identifier (Zogby 2002). It is almost surely the case that feelings toward

---

6. Albert Memmi's work was originally published in French in 1957. Similar analyses were produced by the Martinique-born psychiatrist Franz Fanon (1967, 1968, originally published in French in 1952 and 1961, respectively), who became politicized while treating mental disorders in colonial Algeria. Fanon's work partly inspired Gillo Pontecorvo's film *The Battle of Algiers*, which was revived in the wake of the US-led invasion of Iraq.

7. However, the same poll found that Europe's Muslims have significantly more positive views of the West and Westerners than their coreligionists in non-Western countries. We return to this issue in chapter 9.

"the other" are derived from some admixture of religious teachings and prevailing cultural norms. Religious beliefs are but one input in a complex reaction to globalization. And while secular liberals may be an important source of dissent in Arab polities, much of the popular dissatisfaction with governance is expressed in terms of Islam, and self-identified Islamic organizations are among the primary sources of internal concerns about political stability.

Elite Attitudes

If this is the situation at the grass roots, what about attitudes among the elite? What is striking in this regard is the relative absence of Arab voices in contemporary intellectual discourse on issues of development strategy. This absence of discussion parallels absence of earlier participation in either the standard mainstream literature on economic development or the highly charged polemics of "dependency theory" that offered a compelling (to some) account of the failure of postcolonial countries to benefit from sustained economic growth.[8] This analysis originated in Latin America but became an internationally articulated explanation of the adverse effects of the international economy on poorer countries, the periphery, much of it anticipating some of the current opposition to "globalization." Exporting and importing could only harm individual countries, foreign direct investment (FDI) had no benefits, and international commerce worsened poverty. Yet contributions from residents of the Arab countries to this literature were rare, a notable exception being Samir Amin, an Egyptian who for much of his life resided in Europe and subsequently dramatically altered his views and became a vehement proponent of the benefits of foreign investment. With some exceptions, Arab intellectuals focused on other issues, even though it might be assumed that they faced no repression or danger from participation in this discussion—after all, most of the dependency literature constituted a diatribe against the industrialized countries that were the former colonial masters and was thus presumably socially and politically acceptable.

More important than participation in polemics is the fact that throughout Latin America, India, and many parts of Africa there has been a major flowering of economic analysis and policymaking. Former devotees and major proponents of dependency theory such as Brazilian President Fernando Henrique Cardoso became adepts of some parts of the mainstream prescription, perhaps after noting the success of regional champions such as South Korea and Chile. Policymakers and analysts in the transition economies of Eastern Europe and China debated major issues such as "big

---

8. Lall (1975) contains a good account of its premises and factual validity. The canonical version for its adherents is Cardoso and Faletto (1979)—the first author went on to become the president of Brazil and once in office (or perhaps before) radically transformed his thinking.

bang" versus gradualism, as well as many questions of how best to privatize the huge state-owned enterprise system or communal farms. Arab analysts and policymakers have not been notably active in these discussions until very recently, and most have done so under the aegis of the Economic Research Forum for the Arab Countries, Iran, and Turkey—a network of researchers based in the Middle East, funded largely by the World Bank. This phenomenon is important as in most countries that have undergone significant economic reform, a relatively small group of local proponents has been instrumental in setting out the agenda and implementing it, albeit with considerable support from the international community.

While the increasing discussion of intrinsically complicated problems and the adoption of some of the policies of the Washington Consensus in other regions have by no means guaranteed success, good policymaking being the art of combining correct economic analysis within political constraints, the shift in discussion in both policy analysis and public policy has been notable. The publication by the United Nations Development Program of the *Arab Human Development Report 2002* (and its successor volumes) occasioned a burst of often breathless enthusiasm, at least among Western journalists, although the analysis presented was quite conventional to professional development analysts. Yet the mere fact that it was written by solely Arab academics in 2002 was viewed as a turning point. It is surprising to anyone versed in the more general literature on developing countries how little this document refers to the specific historical experience of other nations (rather than regional averages) and the potential transferability of some of the knowledge. Nor is there much awareness of the close parallels between the evolution of individual countries in the Arab world and those in other regions, as shown in chapter 2. Yet these other experiences suggest not only parallels but also, more importantly, the means of reversing the sometimes disappointing results of the last decades.

Many reasons can be adduced for the failure of either Arab intellectuals or policymakers to systematically address, until very recently, the problems of accelerating economic development. The first generation of post–World War II leaders, especially Gamal Abdel Nasser of Egypt, were more concerned with establishing their place in the nonaligned or third world movement. In this Nasser was not alone. Jawaharlal Nehru of India, Sukarno of Indonesia, Kwame Nkrumah of Ghana, and Jomo Kenyatta of Kenya, all major figures in their countries' move toward independence, or in the case of Nasser overthrowing King Farouk, did not bequeath to their citizens a legacy of sustained growth. The charismatic Nasser was not only dedicated to general "third world" issues but also was much taken with pan-Arabism, including an ill-fated union with Syria and an attempt to undermine the Saudi government through a war in Yemen in the 1960s (Lacoutre 1973). Like Nehru, his country followed many of the economic paths of his main ally, the Soviet Union—not an unmitigated blessing.

Because of the unusually long-standing stable nature of Arab political regimes (figure 1.5 in chapter 1), this legacy appears to have persisted considerably longer in the region than equivalent tendencies did in other regions. Today, Nehru's India, Sukarno's Indonesia, Nkrumah's Ghana, and Kenyatta's Kenya have all evolved into functioning democracies, while Nasser's Egypt remains mired in authoritarianism, still led by the National Democratic Party machine that Nasser helped create. Only in the late 1990s did a younger generation of more open technocrats begin assuming leadership in countries such as Egypt, Jordan, and Morocco, many of whom were educated in the West and/or have considerable professional experience working in the private sector, unusual for the machine politicians of earlier generations. In other countries such as Saudi Arabia and Kuwait, a certain degree of political opening is occurring, though it does not appear to be accompanied by the programmatic changes of the degree exhibited in some of the less resource-endowed countries. Other countries, notably Syria, continue to lag in both political opening and policy reform. And then there are special cases like Iraq and the Palestinian Authority territories.

Yet even where reformist technocrats have reached the cabinet, they face a number of profound internal obstacles. Elite opinion is split with the dominant voices opposing globalization, which is often equated with Americanization (Najjar 2005), and as the Pew survey results document, while popular attitudes in the Middle East do not appear to be "antimarket," they are not particularly supportive of globalization, at least on existing terms. As noted in chapter 5, poll data indicate widespread support for subjecting business to *sharia* law, tempered with the recognition that further interpretation is necessary to facilitate the entry of businesses from the Muslim into the global economy. Such views could be interpreted as forming a coherent basis for adapting the demands of globalization to local values. The construction of such practices and institutions would require some economic engineering and might encounter varying degrees of acceptance or resistance by non-Muslim counterparties. It would not be the Washington Consensus off-the-shelf and not what a newly appointed World Bank resident representative would be trained for or prepared to deal with, but it would not be impossible either.

Moreover, decades of state-centered development have created large educated and urban constituencies for its perpetuation. The government share of civilian employment in MENA is twice the world average, and relatively educated middle-class employees in make-work jobs would be disproportionate losers, at least initially, in any broad reform (Hoekman and Messerlin 2002).[9] One normally associates the rise of the middle class with increasing demands for democratization, and as will be discussed in greater detail in chapter 9, there is no reason to believe that this pattern

---

9. For example, the Libyan government's decision in January 2007 to fire 400,000 employees (Turkish Press, January 2007), roughly a fifth of the nation's total labor force.

will not hold in the Middle East. But while a rising middle class may demand greater political openness, ironically, this mass middle class in some sense owes its existence to Arab socialism and in programmatic terms may actually exert a conservative or reactionary stance with respect to economic policy, in contradistinction to its support for political opening.[10] There is a two-way relationship between individual attitudes or preferences and local policies and institutions (Alesina and Fuchs-Schuendeln 2005). Local practices influence individual's perceptions of the world, and individual beliefs condition the politically acceptable bounds of policy. Because of the self-reinforcing nature of this feedback loop, change tends to come only slowly. Once established, it can take generations for local beliefs to converge toward broader international norms.

Moreover, given the authoritarian nature of the local political regimes, people have an incentive to engage in what social scientists call "preference falsification," or colloquially "keeping one's head down" on a massive scale. Under these conditions, accurately gauging the collective psyche of the masses is difficult, if not impossible—a situation well understood by Middle Eastern leaders, hence their enormous investment in internal intelligence apparatus. The implication is that abrupt, unpredictable change is a constant possibility since people will only reveal their true preferences once the expectation of punishment falls below a particular threshold, which itself is a tipping-point function of how many others have "stuck their heads above the parapet" and signaled a decline in the likelihood that the regime will be able to punish dissenters (Kuran 1995). This simply means that under the current circumstances in the Middle East, it is very hard to predict the directions in which popular attitudes might push policy in more liberalized political systems.

Impediments to Reform

Two forces may obstruct reform. First, reforms may be regarded as potentially politically destabilizing. Beyond popular attitudes, specific groups may view their interests threatened by reform. When reforms have significant distributional implications, the potential losers will resist, further impeding the introduction of reform. Alberto Alesina and Allan Drazen (1991) model a "war of attrition" in which potential beneficiaries repeat-

---

10. This supposition would run counter to the experience of Central Europe documented by Jan Fidrmuc (2000a, 2000b), who found that in elections in the Czech Republic, Slovakia, Poland, and Hungary, support for reformist political parties was negatively affected by unemployment and the shares of retirees, blue-collar workers, and agricultural workers in the electorate but was positively affected by the existing size of the private sector, the shares of white-collar workers, and people with university education. In essence, the Central European urban middle class saw itself as constrained by the status quo. The issue with respect to the Middle East is whether the middle class regards itself as constrained by the existing system or its net beneficiary.

edly attempt to introduce reforms before finally overwhelming their opponents politically, who then bear a disproportionate burden of the costs.

For example, trade restrictions (at least of the formal sort) typically have implications for the distribution of income within a country, improving those in protected sectors while harming those who are implicitly taxed including persons employed in the nontraded-goods sector. The beneficiaries in large-scale manufacturing (often in the publicly owned sector) are loath to see their positions weakened by trade reform, and their political influence typically exceeds that of small farmers and those in the informal sector. The interests of state monopoly port service providers are equally straightforward. Privatization of state-owned enterprises, including ones in nontraded sectors such as electricity generation and telecommunications as well as those producing traded goods, is likely to run into severe opposition. The restructuring that often follows decreases employment while increasing the price of final goods to allow the firms to be self-sustaining. To cite another example, to improve the financial system many countries have loosened their restrictions on participation of foreign financial institutions in the domestic economy. This is often an unpopular move: The sector is viewed as the heart of the economy, occupying a "commanding height," and has been the subject of intense negotiations in the ongoing talks to expand the purview of the World Trade Organization (WTO). In addition to the problems encountered in other countries, the possibility of violating the strictures of Islamic banking is likely to give pause to governments considering this action. Governments already on the defensive, religiously and politically, are likely to be particularly cautious in pursuing policies that lead to these outcomes. Alan Richards (2001) identifies the principal losers from reforms attempted in Egypt in the 1990s as organized labor and managers of state-owned enterprises, government bureaucrats, holders of import licenses, and other rent seekers—all key constituencies of the incumbent regime.

Parsing the role of such policies as trade liberalization, privatization, or demilitarization on income inequality is difficult—the intensity of protection required to make local manufacturers competitive will depend in part on the natural resource base: Economies with more abundant natural resources will tend to have high wage rates and hence require more protection for the emerging manufacturing sector. As seen in table 3.4 in chapter 3, Egypt's land distribution was relatively equal in comparison to better-endowed countries such as Brazil and Argentina that also adopted import-substituting industrialization policies. In the absence of a fully specified general equilibrium model it is difficult to decompose the jointly determined impact of variations in endowments and policies applied and hazardous to make definitive statements on these policies' distributional effects.

Second, vested interests may hijack the reform process, ensuring a disproportionate share of the benefits at the expense of other social groups

(Hellman 1998). Richards (2001), for example, cites Jean François Seznec that in Saudi Arabia, King Fahd in essence divided the government into spheres run by the royal family (the security ministries) and the nonroyal civil service (the economic and petroleum ministries), with the latter effectively guarding the interests of the nonroyal citizenry. Liberalization could have the unintended consequence of opening the economy to the depredations of rapacious princes and in the end be politically destabilizing.

Another, less speculative example stems from the fact that the militaries of some Arab countries own, or are directly involved in the management and operation of, productive assets that would be controlled in the civilian sectors of most economies (Richards and Waterbury 1996, Kamrava 2004). In this light, the stance of the military and the defense industrial complex can have a fundamental bearing on the nature and prospects for successful reform. The case of China is notable in this regard. A key factor behind China's ability to undertake the rapid pace of economic reforms during the first 10 to 15 years of its Open Door policy was aggressive demilitarization of its economy. The key elements of the Chinese strategy included a concerted effort to shift the output of the military-industrial complex from military to civilian production, the large-scale transfer of military manpower, industrial facilities, and infrastructure for civilian use, and a significant downsizing of the armed forces. At the same time, the political clout of the military in the political process began to steadily decline though it is still far from negligible. Without this extensive and rapid demilitarization of the economy at the outset of reforms, the pace and scale of China's economic liberalization would likely have been much slower and more limited (Cheung 2001). In contrast, Richards (2001) argues that senior officers of the Egyptian military were direct beneficiaries of privatization. And given the prominence of the military in governance in many Arab countries, such concerns are by no means limited to Egypt. This approach, essentially allowing the military-industrial complex to maintain its perquisites, would be more akin to the experiences of the Soviet Union during the 1980s than to Chinese reforms.

The absence of reform can thus be interpreted in standard political economy terms of groups protecting their interests even when this conflicts with the requisites of improved national performance. There is no need to resort to explanations relying on cultural or religious fears that may exist but are difficult to demonstrate empirically. Many astute observers argue that the fear of loss of economic position and influence, including that of government bureaucrats, is quite important and arguably sufficient to explain the observed patterns.[11]

Of course, lurking in the background are fears of cultural or religious extremism, specifically that relaxation of political control would benefit

11. See Richards and Waterbury (1996), Henry and Springborg (2001), Richards (2001), and Kamrava (2004) for specific historical examples.

radical Islamists, who in a number of the Arab countries represent the only organized mass civil society alternative to the state. Having in essence foreclosed politics in the secular public sphere, these regimes have forced dissent into the mosque, the only institution to preserve a measure of autonomy from the state.[12] One can make an analogy, redolent in irony, to anticolonialist liberalization struggles of the past: Today the Islamists, proffering a pan-national form of identity politics, are playing the role of "nationalists" to the incumbent, undemocratic, "colonial" regimes.[13]

The configuration of political forces varies from country to country, but in general political Islam poses two challenges in terms of transition: one political, the other economic. The political challenge revolves around skepticism of the Islamists' ideological commitment to democracy, summarized in the witticism "one man, one vote, one time." Polling data from six Arab countries suggest that a plurality of Muslims believe that a popularly elected Islamist government would abide by the rules of democracy, though a significant minority expressed skepticism (Zogby International 2005). In Lebanon, only 20 percent of Christian respondents indicated that they believed that Islamists would follow the rules. One can point to various kinds of evidence to support both sides of this argument, and local historical idiosyncrasies and specific conditions will likely heavily influence specific outcomes.

From an economic policy standpoint, the fear is that newly empowered inexperienced groups would enact incompetent or populist economic policies. For the most part the Islamists have not evinced a great interest in economic, as opposed to cultural policies, and again one can invoke evidence to support both optimistic and pessimistic views. Few would hold up the most prominent example of an Islamic state, Iran, as a model of economic management. Indeed, the Iranian combination of theocratic governance with economic incompetence would appear to illustrate the worst-case scenario nicely.[14]

Yet such a result is not preordained: Clement M. Henry and Robert Springborg (2001), for example, suggest that in the early 1990s, the Islamic Salvation Front (Front Islamique du Salut) in Algeria may well have been more liberal economically than the government. Similarly, the Syrian Moslem Brotherhood counts among its supporters local Sunni capitalists

---

12. One should note in passing that this phenomenon is not unique to Islam or the Middle East. It can be observed in predominantly Christian areas such as Poland, El Salvador, Ghana, or the American South, where under repressive or authoritarian rule churches became a locus of political communication and organizing.

13. In "Beware of 'Contagion' Spreading in the Middle East," *Financial Times*, August 10, 2006, Mamoun Fandy argues that Iran deliberately supports insurgent groups as a means of weakening incumbent Arab governments and facilitating its attainment of regional hegemony.

14. See, for example, the detailed description in Michael Slackman, "Iran Chief Eclipses Clerics as He Consolidates Power," *New York Times*, May 28, 2006.

who are more favorably disposed to policy reform than the minority Alawite regime. Others argue that at least some factions of the Muslim Brotherhood of Egypt are bourgeois in their economic orientation and with greater democratic legitimacy might actually have an easier time implementing reforms than the incumbent authoritarian regimes.

This discussion points to a unique challenge facing reformers of any stripe in the Middle East. External commitments are a proven way of providing a policy anchor for internal reforms. Yet adopting such anchors and using them to leverage domestic reforms is difficult if the citizenry regards the international economic system as unjust and is fundamentally distrustful of foreigners and their institutions. As James Piscatori has observed, "The combined challenges of globalization and radical Islamism have clearly induced many Muslims to wonder how the encompassing liberal international economic order can ever respond to Muslim needs, or how a state system dominated by the US and the UN can ever be sympathetic to Muslim claims to justice" (quoted in Perkovich 2005, 86). This observation has been accompanied by numerous calls to reorganize international relations in ways that reject the norms and values implicit in the global order and replace them with ones explicitly derived from Islam. In the economics sphere, this might involve elevating locally issued *fatwas* above WTO commitments, for example. The salience of this perception may be underappreciated in the West, insofar as the grand mufti of Egypt has observed, "In authentic Islamic perceptions, justice structures all vital spheres of human existence. Justice is an absolute concept in Islamic teachings and precedes other central notions such as freedom and solidarity" (quoted in Perkovich 2005, 83).

In this context, the (non-Muslim) counterpart may sense this reluctance, born of the perception that the dominant institutions simply reflect the interests of the powerful and do not embody a just order, additionally complicating any sort of bargain. In the next chapter we consider the potential for external agreements to act as a spur to internal reform and a mechanism to promote credibility and irreversibility. In chapter 9 we return to these themes in the context of foreign private agents' subjective assessments of risk in the context of engendering supply response.

Appendix 7A
The Pew Survey

The complete set of questions, country sample sizes, fieldwork dates, modes of collection, and other details are provided in the annexes to the Pew Global Attitudes Project (2003). Egypt, Jordan, and Lebanon were included in the original survey; respondents in Morocco and Kuwait were surveyed in May 2003 in an addendum.

Questions were phrased in agreement/disagreement form, and respondents were asked to indicate whether they strongly agreed, somewhat agreed, somewhat disagreed, strongly disagreed, did not know, or had no response.[15]

Two questions fall into the first, market-oriented, category:

- The closing of large inefficient factories (enterprises) is a hardship but is necessary for economic improvement,[16] and

- Most people are better off in a free-market economy, even though some people are rich and some are poor.

Nine questions relate directly to the economic aspects of globalization:

- What do you think of growing business ties between [survey country] and other countries—do you think that it is a very good thing, somewhat good, neutral, somewhat bad, or very bad?

- And what about faster communication and greater travel between the people of [survey country] and people in other countries?

- What about the way movies, TV, and music from different parts of the world are now available in [survey country]?

---

15. There was a certain amount of repetition in the questions, generating highly collinear response patterns (for example, respondents were asked whether they regarded an expansion in cross-border exchange as good for both their family and their country), and for our purposes, some questions were poorly worded (for example, a question on immigration elicited a response toward national policy rather than the immigrants themselves), and in one set of questions it was not clear that the published results "added up." Communication with the Pew Center was not able to satisfactorily resolve these questions.

16. This question was not asked of respondents in North America and Western Europe, and in China the statement was phrased as which was closest to their opinion: Less inefficient large enterprises are helpful to economic improvement, or less inefficient large enterprises are not helpful to economic development. (This version of the question is sufficiently unlike the others that the responses were not included in the subsequent analysis.) Question 14 on attitude toward homosexuality was not permitted in China, Egypt, and Tanzania. The response to question 13 on foreign influence is not available for Vietnam. For Morocco and Kuwait, response data are only available for the globalization question, and it is phrased differently, "All in all, how do you feel about the world becoming more connected through greater economic trade and faster communication. . . ?"

- And what about different products that are now available from different parts of the world?

- All in all, how do you feel about the world becoming more connected through greater economic trade and faster communications?

- Do you think that globalization is a very good, somewhat good, neutral, somewhat bad, or very bad thing?

- Large companies from other countries have a very good, somewhat good, neutral, somewhat bad, or a very bad influence on the way things are going in our country,

- International organizations such as the World Bank, International Monetary Fund, and World Trade Organization have a very good, somewhat good, neutral, somewhat bad, or very bad influence on the way things are going in our country, and

- Antiglobalization protesters have a very good, somewhat good, neutral, somewhat bad, or very bad influence on the way things are going in our country.

Finally, a number of questions are potentially relevant to foreign entrants into the market inasmuch as they address local attitudes on social issues and may signal tolerance:

- Our people are not perfect, but our culture is superior to others,

- Our way of life needs to be protected from foreign influence,

- Homosexuality is a way of life that should be accepted by society, or homosexuality is a way of life that should not be accepted by society.

Noland (2005b) contains a complete analysis of the relevance of public attitudes as elicited in this survey to economic outcomes.

8

Global Engagement

Previous chapters have established that the Middle East and North Africa (MENA) region is a relative underachiever with respect to trade and investment. The issue is how to strengthen their performance in these dimensions to contribute to accelerated growth, labor absorption, and rising standards of living in the context of institutions and policies that are not particularly strong. One possibility would be to use external anchors such as the World Trade Organization (WTO) or preferential trade agreements to promote internal reforms, reinforce credibility, and lock in commitments. Such a strategy has clear attractions.

Yet historically Arab policymakers have hesitated in seizing these opportunities, and even today public opinion in the region exhibits ambivalence toward deeper integration with the outside world, exhibiting in the words of one observer, "widespread recognition of the need for change to more market-oriented economies without necessarily buying into the full logic of globalization" (AbiNader 2003, 2).

The comparison with Eastern Europe reinforces the notion that cultural orientation and historical experience matter and that political trauma may be a prerequisite for abrupt reform, a lesson undoubtedly not lost on the long-lived political regimes of the region. Moreover given the public's ambivalent attitudes toward external economic engagement, unlike the case of Eastern Europe, it is not at all clear that successor regimes would be liberal and not populist, whether Islamist or not.

Membership in Multilateral Institutions

We return to the comparison of MENA and Eastern Europe. Table 8.1 reports the accession dates and status of Arab and Eastern European countries

Table 8.1   GATT/WTO and Bretton Woods accession status, as of 2005

Country	GATT/WTO	World Bank	IMF Article VIII
Middle East			
Normally endowed			
Egypt	1970	1945	—
Jordan	2000	1952	1995
Lebanon	Observer	1947	1993
Morocco	1987	1958	1993
Syria	—	1947	—
Tunisia	1990	1958	1993
Yemen	Observer	1969	1996
Resource-abundant			
Algeria	Observer	1963	1997
Bahrain	1995	1972	1973
Iraq	Observer	1945	—
Kuwait	1963	1962	1963
Libya	Observer	1958	2003
Oman	2000	1971	1974
Qatar	1994	1972	1973
Saudi Arabia	2005	1957	1961
United Arab Emirates	1996	1972	1974
Central Europe			
Czech Republic	1948[b]	1945[c]	1995
Hungary	1973	1982	1996
Poland	1967	1946[d]	1995
Slovakia	1948[b]	1945[c]	1995
Baltic Republics			
Estonia	1999	1992	1994
Latvia	1999	1992	1994
Lithuania	2001	1992	1994
Former Soviet Union			
Belarus	Observer	1992	2001
Russia	Observer	1992	1996
Ukraine	Observer	1992	1996
Former Yugoslavia			
Bosnia	1966[a]	1945[a]	—
Croatia	1966[a]	1945[a]	1995
Macedonia	1966[a]	1945[a]	1998
Serbia and Montenegro	1966[a]	1945[a]	2002
Slovenia	1966[a]	1945[a]	1995

(table continues next page)

Table 8.1   GATT/WTO and Bretton Woods accession status, as of 2005
  (continued)

Country	GATT/WTO	World Bank	IMF Article VIII
Eastern Europe			
Albania	2000	1991	—
Bulgaria	1996	1990	1998
Romania	1971	1972	1998

GATT/WTO = General Agreement on Tariffs and Trade/World Trade Organization
IMF = International Monetary Fund

a. Joined as Yugoslavia.
b. Joined as Czechoslovakia.
c. Withdrew in 1954; rejoined in 1990.
d. Withdrew in 1950; rejoined in 1986.

Sources: IMF Annual Report, 2004; WTO and World Bank Web sites, www.wto.org and www.worldbank.org.

to the main global multilateral economic institutions—the General Agreement on Tariffs and Trade (GATT) and its successor the WTO, the World Bank, and the International Monetary Fund (IMF). (In the case of the Fund, the date listed is when the country acceded to Article VIII on currency convertibility, which originally indicated that the funds in that currency could be used for IMF lending activities but more broadly signaled an irreversible commitment to forgo capital controls on current account transactions.)

All of the Arab economies are members of the Bretton Woods institutions, and in some cases, involvement with the Bank began in the pre-independence period. The incentives for membership were straightforward: The Bank was a source of development finance and technical advice, and additionally it was distinct from the colonial power. Quite naturally, the more populous resource-scarce Arab countries tended to join these institutions earlier on, with the more financially stable resource-abundant countries accepting IMF Article VIII obligations more readily.

The real difference across the two regions is with respect to the GATT/WTO. While nonmembership is the exception in Eastern Europe, limited to some former members of the Soviet Union, almost half of the Arab countries are not members. It is notable that there is a correlation between the countries that are in the WTO (and have thus bound themselves to a globally recognized enforceable intellectual property rights protection regime) and the countries that ranked most highly on technology absorption measures in table 6.3.[1]

---

1. Bernard Hoekman and Jayanta Roy (2000) provide a MENA-centric introduction to the WTO.

For oil producers such as Algeria, Iraq, and Libya, their lack of interest in membership is not particularly surprising: Under the mercantilist logic that dominates trade negotiations, there is little incentive for them to join the WTO—no country imposes tariffs on oil. For these resource-abundant countries the advantages of membership are in leveraging internal institutional modernization and reform by committing themselves to internationally enforceable agreements. Militarily weaker oil producers have a second, strategic reason for joining international organizations: As relatively small countries they make potentially easy prey for their larger neighbors (for example, the Iraqi invasion of Kuwait), hence it is in their interests to embed themselves in the global institutions and to try and bind their fortunes with those of larger extraregional powers. In the case of Saudi Arabia, these considerations were reinforced by concerns that WTO rules would clash with local interpretations of *sharia* prohibiting the importation of pork, the establishment of cinemas, and the availability of certain financial instruments such as insurance deemed un-Islamic.

What is striking is that with the exception of Egypt, which has been active in a global coalition of developing countries within the WTO known as the Group of 20, the resource-scarce Arab countries such as Jordan, Morocco, and Tunisia have joined the WTO relatively recently or not at all. This is not to say that they have been entirely absent—after all, the agreement bringing the WTO into existence in 1993 was signed in Morocco, and the current round of negotiations was launched in Qatar. Yet even in the case of Egypt, its legally bound tariff rates are so far above the actual applied rates that its WTO commitments do not impose any real policy constraints in this dimension. This lack of enthusiasm for the binding trade commitment at least in part may reflect a fundamental political logic: In regimes where the creation, extraction, and channeling of policy-derived rents is a core component of regime maintenance, open borders and binding trade agreements actually undermine the political economy of regime survival. The general impression is that the Arab countries have embraced GATT/WTO late or not at all. From a historical standpoint, the contrast with the Central European countries, which despite membership in the Council of Mutual Economic Assistance and Soviet domination during the Cold War were members of the GATT, as were Yugoslavia and Romania, is remarkable. What is relevant is that the Central Europeans saw the international system as a mechanism for leveraging domestic reforms and reintegrating themselves into world markets, despite the constraints imposed by the Soviet Union. To cite but one example, Harold James (1996) provides an eye-opening account of formal and informal Central European contacts with the IMF beginning in the 1950s following de-Stalinization and running through the 1960s and 1970s. He quotes an internal IMF memorandum recounting a 1968 meeting between a representative of the Fund and a Polish representative to GATT in which the Pole explained, "There were some in authority in Poland who were aware that they were paying a high price in continuing to trade with Soviet Russia.... He thought that the Fund would do a good service if it produced a kind of critique of the economic policies of the socialist countries. Such an appraisal would be seriously studied and would serve to point out to those in power that their policies were out of date and not in the long-term interests of their countries" (James 1996, 559). He goes on to document the Fund's growing alarm at the political element in the Central Europeans' economic reform plans and the dawning recognition that their proponents were quite consciously aiming at the dissolution of the Soviet Union's European empire.[2]

The Central Europeans continually pushed the envelope of Soviet tolerance with Hungary joining the Bretton Woods institutions in 1982, and Poland rejoining after a 36-year interregnum in 1986. Romania and Yugoslavia had been in the institutions for some time. After the collapse of the Eastern Bloc in 1989, Czechoslovakia rejoined the institutions in 1990, accompanied in short order by Bulgaria (1990), Albania (1991), and the newly independent Baltic republics (1992).

In sum, a significant share of the Central European elite regarded themselves as part of the West and the period of Soviet domination as aberrant. Even during the Cold War they participated in the GATT and in some cases the Bretton Woods institutions. When the external constraints were removed, the Eastern Europeans moved with alacrity to join (or rejoin) these organizations to anchor liberal policy reforms. In contrast, it took Tunisia 30 years to join the WTO, beginning with provisional accession to the GATT in 1959, an application for full accession in 1980, and final approval of the entry accession protocol in 1990. Saudi Arabia began negotiations in 1990, joining only in December 2005.

Given differences in cultural orientation and historical experience the Middle East as a whole evinces greater ambivalence toward the West in general and these Western-dominated institutions in particular. Perhaps this hesitation reflects the underlying attitudes of the population. As reported in table 7.3, the average Arab response to the question of whether the international economic institutions are good is 38 percent, compared with 58 percent in Eastern Europe or 65 percent in Central Europe. A World Bank report speaks of a pervasive "deep pessimism about the region's trading potential" and a consequent "lack of commitment of leadership in governments of the region" to reform (World Bank 2003a, 38, 22). The issue is whether there has been sufficient convergence in values and interests such that the Arab countries can make better use of the opportunities afforded by the international system or whether there are al-

---

2. As further evidence of Poland's westward gaze, James later quotes Tadeusz Mazowiecki, the prime minister in Poland's first post-Communist government, as remarking without irony that "I am looking for my Ludwig Ehrhard!" referring to the architect of West Germany's postwar liberalization and revival (James 1996, 568).

ternative mechanisms more compatible with local interests and attitudes that can play a similar role of reinforcing internal reform.

Put in terms of interest group politics, the Eastern European countries made a conscious decision to destroy the economic practices that had underpinned the Communist political regimes. In contrast, the Arab countries as a group have not made such a decisive break with the constraints on rent channeling, which is part of the political survival strategy of a number of these regimes.

Role of Preferential Arrangements

In essence international trade agreements can benefit a country in two ways. One is through efficiency gains, in the form of either the traditional static efficiency improvements associated with resource reallocation according to comparative advantage and/or "dynamic" gains provided by greater scale economies, induced investment, and learning to become more efficient in order to meet international competition. The other source of potential gains is more subtle and difficult to document or evaluate, but these come from improvement in the business climate through direct improvements in commercial practices and dispute resolution plus reduced uncertainty associated with enhanced credibility and irreversibility achieved through binding national policies to enforce international agreements. In principle, countries can reap the benefits of direct efficiency gains and enhancements in business climate through both multilateral agreements such as the WTO and preferential arrangements such as free trade areas.

In any trade agreement, the magnitude of the conventional improvements in economic efficiency is determined by the size and economic complementarity of the agreement partners and the extent of reduction in existing barriers to trade. In this respect multilateral and preferential liberalization differ in one important way—in the case of preferential liberalization, under certain conditions the reallocation of trade away from efficient third-party trade partners and toward relatively inefficient preferred partners (called trade diversion) may be so large that a country could actually make itself worse off (as well as making third parties worse off). For this reason, economists generally regard multilateral agreements as superior to preferential agreements.

The problem with multilateral agreements is that the larger number of participants makes negotiating liberalization more complex and time consuming. As a consequence there is some tendency for these agreements to reflect a kind of lowest common denominator consensus, with respect to both the degree of liberalization and its scope across sectors and issue areas. In particular, while the WTO system has made considerable progress in removing border barriers to trade, especially tariffs that are particularly amenable to negotiated mathematical formulas for their reduction, the global organization has been less successful in addressing "behind the border" issues such as competition and tax policies, which are increasingly important in determining trade flows but are more difficult to negotiate and impinge directly on policies heretofore treated as purely internal matters.

One understandable response has been for countries to form the economic equivalents of "coalitions of the willing" and enter into preferential arrangements with like-minded countries that go beyond the global standards embodied in the WTO with respect to the elimination of border barriers as well as pursuit of transnational agreements on "new issues." Noneconomic political or diplomatic motivations often play prominently in the formation of these groups. The extent of conventional benefits under these agreements is driven by the size and complementarity of the partner country and the magnitude of the preexisting trade barriers; the nontraditional benefits are a function of the credibility derived from precommitting to liberal policies with a larger, more powerful partner and success in transforming trade commitments into broader reforms. For the Arab countries, two sets of potential partners are relevant: themselves and the United States and/or the European Union.

Intra-Arab Agreements

The Arab countries have a long history of entering into preferential arrangements among themselves, beginning with a 1953 treaty to organize transit trade among Arab economies, followed in 1964 by the establishment of the Arab Common Market, which failed.[3] Yet such initiatives, implying greater openness and competition, ran counter to the political imperatives of patronage, political control, and rent extraction on which a number of the region's political regimes relied, as manifested in the legacies of widespread industrial support policies, import substitution, and promotion of state enterprises.

Since then, the interest in preferential schemes within the Arab world has waxed and waned; the region is currently experiencing a renewal in interest in regional and subregional preferences, with the Arab Free Trade Area (AFTA), also known as the Pan-Arab Free Trade Area (PAFTA) or Greater Arab Free Trade Area (GAFTA), the most prominent. In 1998, 18 of the 22 members of the Arab League sanctioned the creation of a pan-Arab free trade area running from Iraq in the east to Morocco in the west (see appendix 8A). The original target for eliminating tariffs by 2008 was brought forward, and tariffs on intra-Arab trade were eliminated on January 1, 2005. The commitments cover only merchandise trade, not services or investment, and according to Robert Z. Lawrence (2006), nontariff barriers remain problematic.

---

3. See Zarrouk (2000b) for a history of these and other Middle Eastern integration initiatives.

Table 8.2   Middle East's total trade shares, 2004 (percent)

Country	United States	European Union	Middle East	Rest of the world	Exports to Middle East/GDP
Algeria	16	57	3	25	1
Egypt	12	38	8	41	2
Iraq	40	20	5	35	n.a.
Jordan	13	17	31	40	13
Kuwait	13	19	5	63	1
Lebanon	6	45	15	35	2
Libya	1	75	5	18	2
Morocco	4	65	6	25	1
Oman	4	13	4	79	2
Saudi Arabia	15	20	4	60	2
Syria	3	37	12	48	6
Tunisia	2	75	7	15	3
Yemen	3	13	13	71	3

n.a. = not available

Note: Middle East includes Algeria, Egypt, Iraq, Jordan, Kuwait, Lebanon, Libya, Morocco, Oman, Saudi Arabia, Syria, Tunisia, and Yemen.

Sources: International Monetary Fund, *Direction of Trade Statistics*, July 2005, and *World Economic Outlook* database, April 2005.

In 2004 foreign ministers of Egypt, Jordan, Morocco, and Tunisia signed an embryonic subregional free trade agreement, the Agadir Agreement, allowing for accession by any Arab country. The smaller number of members, the greater potential cohesiveness of interests, and the relatively reformist nature of the governments suggest that this subregional agreement may convey greater prospects for successful implementation and elaboration. A critical aspect of the agreement is the adoption of pan-European rules of origin, enabling cumulation of local content and perhaps facilitating the development of horizontal specialization and cross-border supply networks in industrial production that have facilitated development in East Asia.[4]

Even if implemented, given the low intensity of intraregional trade reported in the last column of table 8.2, there is little reason to expect that GAFTA would have a large impact, at least through the traditional resource reallocation channel, though admittedly, Ali A. Bolbol and Ayten M. Fatheldin (2005) find evidence of growing intraregional trade intensity that they attribute to the preferential agreement. Yet even if this is the case, there is some reason to believe that the agreement could reduce wel-

---

4. The Agadir Agreement is to establish the Mediterranean Arab Free Trade Area (MAFTA), not to be confused with the Bush administration proposal for a Middle East Free Trade Area (MEFTA). See Lawrence (2006) for further discussion of the Agadir Agreement.

fare for some of its members.[5] Trade with the United States and the European Union exceeds intraregional trade for every economy except Jordan, which imports oil from Saudi Arabia and where Iraq reconstruction-related exports have boomed in recent years. The only way that analysts have been able to generate large welfare gains is to posit substantial liberalization in the services sector through the elimination of implicit non-tariff barriers, even though these are not part of the agreement.

In any event, skepticism about implementation is warranted. Historically intra-Arab regional initiatives, long on ambition and short on implementation, have had a negligible impact on trade flows.[6] The reasons are multiple: With the aforementioned exception of Jordan and Syria with its pronounced, though perhaps eroding, ties to Lebanon, in no country do intraregional exports account for more than 3 percent of GDP—in strictly economic terms, there is little reason to take each other seriously (table 8.2).

Furthermore, it is unlikely that the major oil producers have any interest in committing themselves to preferential trade with their relatively inefficient neighbors, when they can import from the most efficient global producers. Rather than tie themselves to their poorer relations, their interest is in binding themselves politically to powerful oil-consuming nations, who can act as their security guarantors in relation to covetous neighbors (for example, Kuwait 1990). To this list of political impediments one can add personal rivalries among competing authoritarian leaders and questionable institutional capacity in some states. Egypt, for example, has already announced that it is delaying the implementation of its GAFTA commitments because of concerns that the rules of origin are too liberal and are not being properly enforced by other member states (Hoekman and Konan 2005). Lastly, the weakness of the global trade system in exerting policy discipline on preferential agreements paradoxically may have encouraged frivolous diplomatic schemes, which arguably crowded out the implementation of more modest though potentially constructive trade-facilitation initiatives.

As noted earlier, preferential agreements can potentially harm third parties through trade diversion, and as a consequence the WTO agreement contains a provision (Article XXIV of the GATT) that constrains the use of preferential trade arrangements. These requirements in essence discourage countries from entering into tailor-made partial liberalizations that would be most likely to harm third parties. In particular, Article XXIV

---

5. Hoekman and Konan (2005), using a computable general equilibrium model to assess alternative trade liberalization scenarios, find that Egypt would actually experience a slight decrease in welfare in a pan-Arab free trade area. Konan (2003) indicates that the same perverse result would apply to Tunisia as well.

6. A series of studies using gravity models to analyze trade flows have failed to uncover any positive impact of these schemes. See Al-Atrash and Yousef (2000); Nugent (2002); and Miniesy, Nugent, and Yousef (2004). One exception is Rock-Antoine Mehanna (n.d.), who finds that the Gulf Cooperation Council (GCC) has modestly boosted trade.

stipulates that the agreement must be comprehensive (i.e., it must cover "substantially all sectors"), must eliminate barriers within the preference area over a reasonable time horizon, cannot involve raising existing barriers to third parties, and specifies a procedure through which other signatories are notified of the agreement.

Article XXIV discipline is weak in general and even weaker with respect to the Middle East. It is weak in general because many of the key terms are vague, and there is no history for challenging or litigating preferential trade arrangements under Article XXIV. Just the opposite—the process of forming the European Economic Community in the 1950s and 1960s almost surely violated GATT strictures but for diplomatic reasons was never challenged. Furthermore, in the case of the Middle East as shown in table 8.1, most of the Arab countries have joined the WTO only relatively recently if at all. As a consequence, none of the multiple preferential trade arrangements among the Arab countries were ever registered with the GATT/WTO, and the organization has exerted no discipline on their formulation or implementation.

Looking forward, agreements among Arab countries are unlikely to constitute good precommitment mechanisms due to weak institutional capacity within the member states and a lack of ability to enforce noncompliance by signatories.

Against these doubts one could set the possibilities of unique benefits. In light of the skepticism about globalization expressed in public opinion polls, intra-Arab agreements may be more acceptable politically than agreements with countries outside the region, and in fact a poll of Middle Eastern firms found that intra-Arab agreements were perceived as the most beneficial (Zarrouk 2003). And it is at least arguable that for reasons of proximity and cultural affinity, Middle Eastern neighbors could exert policy surveillance more effectively than global institutions based elsewhere. Also to be considered is a sequencing argument that it may be preferable to expose one's firms to regional competition before developed-country competition.

One exception to these generally desultory results has been the Gulf Cooperation Council (GCC) comprising Bahrain, Kuwait, Oman, Qatar, Saudi Arabia, and the United Arab Emirates. With a greater commonality of interests and one dominant state to lead the way, the GCC formed a customs union in 2003 and established as a goal a currency union in 2011.[7] However the conclusion by Bahrain and Oman of bilateral free trade agreements with the United States has complicated the administration of the customs union, if not potentially undermining the project. Similarly, the currency union initiative has encountered rough sailing with member states unable to agree on the form of a centralized monetary authority, its location, or even the name of the currency. Now talk is of some looser form

---

7. See Lawrence (2006) for more details on the customs union aspect.

of monetary cooperation short of a full currency union. Some if not all of the members appear to be violating fiscal convergence criteria, as well.

This analysis suggests that while intra-Arab initiatives may not be a bad idea, one should have modest expectations about their ultimate impact. The same does not necessarily hold with respect to preferential agreements with the United States and European Union.

Club Med

From the perspective of the Middle East, Europe is a large, rich, complementary, and geographically proximate trade partner. For these reasons, most Arab countries trade intensively with the European Union, and only in the case of Iraq, for perhaps transitory reasons, does trade with the United States exceed that with Europe (table 8.2). Hence it is natural to begin any discussion of preferential trade with Europe, the Middle East's "natural" trade partner.

Preferential trade between Europe and the Arab Mediterranean states began in 1972 with the European Union's Global Mediterranean Policy to promote trade preferences, financial aid, and technical cooperation.[8] The European Union went on to conclude bilateral agreements with its Mediterranean partners between 1973 and 1980. The most recent agreement reached in Barcelona in 1995 initiated movement toward free trade in industrial products by 2012, as well as expanding cooperation in finance, technical assistance, education, and political and security issues. The Arab countries at that time had an incentive to update the agreements before the Eastern Europeans joined the European Union and the Western Europeans lost interest or were overwhelmed with their own adjustment issues. The European Union has subsequently encouraged regional integration through the Agadir process, for example by providing small amounts of funding and technical assistance, as well as an initiative to incorporate the Agadir rules of origin into the Euro-Med agreement.

However, the economic importance of these agreements is subject to dispute. As Bernard Hoekman and Patrick Messerlin (2002) observe, commitments under these agreements do not go much beyond existing WTO commitments. Eighty percent of the Mediterranean countries' agricultural exports to the European Union are granted tariff preferences, but they are still subject to nontariff barriers and other distortions associated with the Common Agricultural Policy (Péridy 2005). Existing Euro-Med agreements permit incorporation of services—however, none of the Mediterranean countries have followed up. At the same time that they are gain-

---

8. The Arab economies that have concluded preferential agreements with the European Union are Algeria, Morocco, Tunisia, Egypt, Lebanon, Jordan, Syria, and the Palestinian Authority territories. The European Union has a separate forum of negotiation for a free trade agreement with the GCC countries, but progress has been very limited.

ing preferential access of a sort in the European Union, the Mediterranean partners are obligated to a phased elimination of barriers on European industrial imports. Hoekman and Denise Konan (2005) estimate that the resulting trade diversion might actually reduce welfare in Egypt. Comparable estimates are not available for other Mediterranean countries.

Moreover, these preferences cannot be viewed in isolation: At the same time it extended preferences to the Middle East, the European Union was in the process of negotiating accession with Central and Eastern European countries, potentially eroding the Middle Eastern countries' effective preference margins. Conversely, as will be discussed below, some Arab countries have concluded preferential agreements with the United States—effectively reducing the preferences granted to European exporters.

Econometric modeling suggests that the Euro-Med preferences have had a positive impact on bilateral trade but that the effectiveness of the preference scheme is eroding. Nicolas Péridy (2005) estimates that at their peak, the agreements boosted bilateral trade by nearly 30 percent in the mid-1980s but that the effect steadily declined over the ensuing decade, and by the mid-1990s (the end of his sample period) the effect had declined to 12 percent and was falling. This decline could be ascribed to continued restrictions on agricultural trade, multilateral liberalization undertaken in the context of the Uruguay Round, including the phaseout of the Multi-Fiber Arrangement (a global network of product-specific bilateral textile and apparel import quotas), which eroded Mediterranean preference margins, and EU accession agreements with Eastern European countries starting in the early 1990s. This latter argument receives explicit support from the work of Anna Ferragina, Giorgia Giovannetti, and Francesco Pastore (2004), who compare the behavior of the Mediterranean and Eastern European countries to preferential trade opportunities in the EU market. They find Mediterranean-EU trade lower than expected on the basis of gravity models, and with the exception of Tunisia, this gap appears to have widened between 1995 and 2002. Bolbol and Fatheldin (2005) and Ludvig Söderling (2005) obtain similar results. Ferragina, Giovannetti, and Pastore obtain the opposite result with respect to Eastern Europe, which exhibited a marked narrowing of the gap between potential and actual trade over this period.

Arab textile and apparel exports to the European Union have been negatively affected, though not completely eliminated, by the complete phaseout of the Multi-Fiber Arrangement in 2005 (World Bank 2006c).[9] This is important insofar as textiles and apparel loom large in the export bundle of Tunisia and Morocco, the two Arab countries that have achieved the

---

9. A possible exception was exports from GCC countries, which were basically a product of the quota system and might disappear completely under a more liberal regime (Someya, Shunnar, and Srinivasan 2002). In any event, most of the employment in these operations went to workers from outside the region, mostly from South Asia.

greatest success penetrating European markets outside the petroleum sector. Though even in this case, the European Union's subsequent restrictions on Chinese exports effectively increased Arab preferences.

Given the seasonality and constantly changing nature of fashion, timely delivery is relatively important in textile and apparel trade, and there is some evidence that production is increasingly located near the countries of final demand (Evans and Harrigan 2005). As a consequence, the Middle East's geographical proximity to the European Union could potentially confer competitive advantage vis-à-vis rivals such as India and China in this important sector. Dan Magder (2005) explores this possibility using a formal supply chain model of apparel trade. His findings indicate that if logistical issues could be resolved, geographical proximity could be a source of competitive advantage for the Middle East as a production location, especially in niche markets such as summer fashion, where fast turnaround times have significant effects on retailer profitability.

Of course, the advantages of geographic proximity are not limited to textiles and apparel. Under improved circumstances one would hope that this advantage could be exploited across a whole range of light manufactures, with Middle East–based facilities, for example, becoming suppliers of parts in the global sourcing decisions of the large integrated automobile assemblers, as has occurred in Turkey. Allen Dennis (2006) uses a computable general equilibrium model to simulate alternative scenarios and concludes that in the context of EU-MENA agreements, the indirect reductions in transaction costs associated with improvements in trade facilitation would actually generate larger welfare improvements for the Middle Eastern countries than the elimination of border measures per se.

Preferential Trade Arrangements with the United States

From the perspective of the Middle East, the United States is similar to the European Union in that it represents a large, rich, complementary, though distant, potential trade partner. For most Arab countries, trade with the European Union is a multiple of trade with the United States. However, the United States is far more strategically important than trade figures alone would indicate.

Moreover the United States differs from the European Union in that "behind the border" issues—including environmental protection and labor rights—rank prominently on its negotiating agenda. Furthermore, unlike the Euro-Med agreements that tend to be couched in vague language, the template for American bilateral agreements is a highly specific and enforceable legal document. A crude indicator of this difference is that the texts of the US free trade agreements with Jordan and Morocco are more than four and ten times longer respectively than their equivalent Euro-Med accession agreements. For these reasons a preferential trade arrangement with the United States is likely to amount to a much more consequential commitment than the Euro-Med agreement.

The basic lesson coming out of the existing literature, which uses computable general equilibrium models to simulate alternative trade liberalization packages, is that the real gains from liberalization stem from liberalization of services trade and behind-the-border regulatory impediments to trade, at least for the typically endowed Arab economies.[10] As discussed earlier in this book, these problems appear to be pervasive in the non–oil based economies, particularly in Egypt, though there have been improvements of late. Recent research also suggests that US multinational corporations significantly increase technology transfer to countries strengthening their intellectual property rights regimes, a result that seems to find support in the case of Jordan, the Arab country with which the United States has its longest-standing preferential trade arrangement (Branstetter, Fisman, and Foley 2005). Similarly, Bolbol and Fatheldin (2005) find that the agreement has significantly boosted Jordan's trade with the United States in marked contrast to the Euro-Med agreement, which they find has had little if any impact on Jordan's trade.[11] The upshot is that for the Arab countries, the long-run payoffs to the deeper, more intrusive agreements with the United States may exceed the shallower, less demanding association agreements with the European Union. Of course, the potential risks are higher as well.[12]

Thus far the United States has concluded free trade agreements with Jordan (2001), Morocco (2004), Bahrain (2005), and Oman (2005); has begun negotiations with the United Arab Emirates; floated the possibility of additional agreements with others including Egypt and Tunisia; and announced the goal of creating a Middle East free trade agreement (MEFTA) by 2013.[13] In addition to the free trade agreements, the United States has

---

10. See Konan (2003), Galal and Lawrence (2004), and Hoekman and Konan (2005) and sources cited therein.

11. The rapid increase in exports to the United States has generated employment for not only Jordanians but also imported workers including Bangladeshis (Steven Greenhouse and Michael Barbaro, "An Ugly Side of Free Trade: Sweatshops in Jordan," *New York Times*, May 3, 2006, C1). If this is indeed the case, generating employment growth for local residents is much more difficult than the calculations carried out in chapter 4 indicate. In the Jordanian case, much of the investment in labor-intensive sectors was undertaken by multinational firms in order to benefit from the trade agreements. For unclear reasons, Jordanian nationals did not take up a considerable number of the jobs created.

12. From a pure negotiating standpoint, having accumulated considerable experience in negotiating free trade agreements, US negotiators are more seasoned. However, given the stakes, and the greater political centrality of these negotiations to the Arab governments, they are likely to commit more senior people.

13. See Lawrence (2006) for an analysis of this initiative. Tamara Cofman Wittes and Sarah E. Yerkes (2006) discuss its diplomatic context. Thomas Friedman ("New Signs on the Arab Street," *New York Times*, March 13, 2005) points out the domestic political difficulties in Egypt.

concluded qualified industrial zone agreements with the Palestinian Authority, Jordan, and Egypt.[14] (See appendix 8B for detailed discussions of individual agreements.)[15] These provide for preferential access to the US market for goods qualifying by meeting a local-content requirement specified in terms of US, Israeli, and the third-county's input content, even beyond what might be available through a free trade agreement, for example providing for accelerated tariff elimination or quota relaxation for products where the tariff phaseout may last up to 10 years.

"Deep integration" free trade agreements are a potentially useful mechanism for leveraging and locking in domestic reforms. As the discussion in chapter 4 made clear, informal barriers to trade such as monopoly public-sector service providers and problematic customs administration and attendant corruption significantly hamper cross-border integration, and US-style "deep integration" agreements may be useful in reforming these practices in a way that the "shallow integration" initiative of the Euro-Med almost surely cannot.

Yet they are not a panacea. Even proponents of this strategy admit that they require complementary changes in policies, institutions, and practices to be fully successful (Kardoosh and al Khoury 2005, Lawrence 2006). As Jean AbiNader (2003, 5) has observed, "preferential trade agreements cannot remake legal and educational systems, enhance work habits, protect environments, encourage human rights and respect for minorities, and all the other collateral benefits without shifts in how Arab governments perceive their leadership and management functions. But they can be helpful and maybe that's sufficient for defining a workable template for low-risk options that move Arab regimes with more confidence to face the severe challenges of the coming decades."

Conclusion

In the realm of trade policy, Arab countries have made progress, and it would be wrong to portray the region's stance as stagnant or unchanging. The countries are undertaking unilateral reforms and increasingly binding themselves with the strictures of the WTO. Moreover, in contrast to past quixotic efforts at regional integration, under competitive pressure from

---

14. See Kardoosh and al Khoury (2005) for an excellent overview of qualified industrial zones.

15. Among the Middle Eastern countries, the United States has also concluded trade and investment framework agreements (TIFAs) with Algeria, Egypt, Kuwait, Qatar, Saudi Arabia, Tunisia, and Yemen. It also has concluded a qualified industrial zone agreement with Turkey and has bilateral investment treaties with Bahrain, Egypt, Jordan, Morocco, and Tunisia. Libya and Syria are the only Arab countries with which the United States does not have some sort of bilateral economic agreement.

the world economy, some Arab countries are addressing regional integration with renewed seriousness, while others have been drawn into the preferential trade arrangement game with the European Union and/or the United States, powerful partners capable of demanding adherence to agreements. The issue is whether these efforts are sufficient given the demographic imperative the region faces.

In addition to their potential anchor for broader reforms, trade agreements have direct impacts, and this chapter has also reviewed evidence on the prospective effects of preferential agreements under consideration as well as those that have recently come into force. But the quantitative estimates of the payoffs assume a supply response, generated by either domestic firms or foreign investors. The issue is whether the assumption is correct that domestic and foreign firms will invest and increase production as an improving economic climate takes hold. But what happens if one throws a party and no one comes?

Appendix 8A
Select Regional Organizations

The Middle East has a long history of preferential trade arrangements and organizations. Among the more prominent are the following:

African Economic Community (AEC). Established in 1991, went into force in 1994, with the goal of creating an eventual continentwide economic and monetary union in 2028. This goal is to be accomplished through the gradual integration of five subregional groups of which one is the Arab Maghreb Union. Middle East and North Africa (MENA) members include Algeria, Djibouti, Egypt, Libya, and Tunisia.

Arab Maghreb Union (AMU). A Maghreb Customs Union was formed in the 1960s but for the most part was not implemented. In 1989 Algeria, Libya, Mauritania, Morocco, and Tunisia formed the AMU according to its founding treaty "to work gradually towards the realization of the freedom of movement of people, goods, services and capital," as a precursor to a free trade agreement in 1992; a common market, the North African Common Market in 2000; and eventually a monetary union known as the Maghreb Economic Space. Some progress was made on sectoral issues, but in 1993 members agreed to postpone further discussion of integration issues. Dormant, the AMU does not maintain formal relations with the AEC, despite being designated as one of the five pillars of that organization. See Brenton, Baroncelli, and Malouche (2006) for discussion of current preferential arrangements within the Maghreb.

Arab Common Market. Through the Arab League and its subgroup, the Council on Arab Economic Unity, the Arab Common Market was established in 1965 with Egypt, Iraq, Jordan, and Syria as founding members and Libya, Mauritania, and Yemen joining later. Needless to say the goal of establishing a common market was not reached, though preferential tariff cuts were undertaken. In 1989 a subset of its members, Egypt, Iraq, Jordan, and (then) North Yemen established the Arab Cooperation Council (ACC) with the goal of intensifying the pursuit of a common market.

Arab Free Trade Area (AFTA), also known as the Pan-Arab Free Trade Area (PAFTA) or Greater Arab Free Trade Area (GAFTA). In 1998 18 of the 22 members of the Arab League agreed to the creation of a Pan-Arab Free Trade Area running from Iraq in the east to Morocco in the west (see Zarrouk 2000b for an overview). Membership includes all six of the members of the Gulf Cooperation Council (GCC), three of the five members of the AMU, eight other countries, and the Palestinian Authority. This is the only preferential arrangement in which Yemen currently participates. Algeria is not a member. The original target for eliminating tariffs by 2008 was brought forward, and tariffs on intra-Arab trade were eliminated on January 1, 2005. The commitments cover only merchandise trade, not services or investment, and according to Robert Z. Lawrence (2006), nontariff barriers remain problematic. A similar Arab Common Market scheme was ratified by the Arab League in 1964 but failed.

Gulf Cooperation Council (GCC). Established in 1981, the GCC signed a preferential trade arrangement that led to the creation of a free trade agreement in agricultural and industrial products (though not petroleum products) and free movement of factors of production. The GCC originally envisioned forming a customs union by 1986, but progress on reducing internal barriers and establishing a common external tariff proceeded slowly. However, the customs union was eventually established in 2003, with a common external tariff set at 5 percent. Implementation of the customs union has been complicated by the conclusion of bilateral free trade agreements between Bahrain and Oman with the United States. The GCC also established as a goal a currency union by 2011, but is now backing away from this commitment, at least on this timetable. Members are Bahrain, Kuwait, Oman, Qatar, Saudi Arabia, and the United Arab Emirates. Yemen has been permitted to begin participating in some activities as an initial step toward eventual membership.

Common Market for Eastern and Southern Africa (Comesa). Another of the five pillars of the AEC, Comesa was established in 1993 as a successor to the Preferential Trade Area for Eastern and Southern Africa, and the Comesa Free Trade Area was launched in 2000. As its name implies, the organization's notional goals involve the establishment of a common market and eventual economic union. Among the MENA countries, Egypt and Djibouti are members.

Intergovernmental Authority on Development (IGAD). Established in 1996, IGAD is a Horn of Africa subset of Comesa. Djibouti is a member. It is not a pillar of the AEC.

Other Preferential Arrangements. Over the past 40 years, Arab governments have entered into a variety of preferential arrangements—for example, as part of the Non-Aligned Movement, Egypt (then the United Arab Republic) entered into the Trade Expansion and Cooperation Agreement with India and Yugoslavia, which came into force in 1968, and after several renewals expired in 1983. In June 2005 the Organization of the Islamic Conference, of which all the Arab countries are members, announced a preferential scheme among its members to go into effect at the end of 2005. Appendix table 8A.1 lists preferential trade arrangements currently in force or expected to enter into force soon.

Table 8A.1   Participation in preferential trade arrangements

Country	Name of agreement	Type of agreement	Year went into force	WTO notification status[a]
Algeria	African Economic Community	Customs union	1994	
	EC-Algeria	Association free trade agreement	1976	Report adopted
	EC-Algeria (updated)	Association free trade agreement		
Bahrain	Gulf Cooperation Council	Preferential arrangement		Notified 1984, no examination requested
	United States–Bahrain	Bilateral free trade agreement	2006	Examination not requested
	Arab Free Trade Area	Free trade agreement		
Djibouti	African Economic Community	Customs union	1994	
	Common Market for Eastern and Southern Africa	Preferential arrangement	1994	Examination not requested
Egypt	African Economic Community	Customs union	1994	
	Common Market for Eastern and Southern Africa	Preferential arrangement	1994	Examination not requested
	EC-Egypt	Association free trade agreement	1977	
	EC-Egypt (updated)	Association free trade agreement	2004	Factual examination not started
	Egypt-Jordan	Bilateral free trade agreement		
	Agadir Agreement			
	Arab Free Trade Area	Free trade agreement		
Jordan	EC-Jordan	Association free trade agreeement	2002	Under factual examination
	EFTA-Jordan	Association free trade agreement	2002	Under factual examination
	Egypt-Jordan	Bilateral free trade agreement		
	United States–Jordan	Bilateral free trade agreement	2001	Under factual examination
	Agadir Agreement			
	Arab Free Trade Area			

(table continues next page)

Table 8A.1 Participation in preferential trade arrangements *(continued)*

Country	Name of agreement	Type of agreement	Year went into force	WTO notification status[a]
Kuwait	Gulf Cooperation Council	Preferential arrangement		
	Arab Free Trade Area	Free trade agreement		
Lebanon	EC–Lebanon	Association free trade agreement	1977	
	EC–Lebanon (updated)	Association free trade agreement	2003	Factual examination not started
	Arab Free Trade Area	Free trade agreement		
Libya	African Economic Community	Customs union	1994	
	Arab Free Trade Area	Free trade agreement		
Morocco	EC–Morocco	Association free trade agreement	2000	Under factual examination
	EFTA–Morocco	Association free trade agreement	1999	Factual examination concluded
	United States–Morocco	Bilateral free trade agreement	2006	Factual examination concluded
	Agadir Agreement			
	Arab Free Trade Area	Free trade agreement		
	Turkey–Morocco	Free trade agreement	2006	Factual examination concluded
Oman	Gulf Cooperation Council	Preferential arrangement		
	Arab Free Trade Area	Free trade agreement		
	US–Oman	Free trade agreement	2006	
Palestinian Authority	EFTA–Palestinian Authority	Association free trade agreement	1999	Factual examination not started
	EC–Palestinian Authority	Association free trade agreement	1997	Factual examination not started
	Arab Free Trade Area	Free trade agreement		
	Turkey–Palestinian Authority	Free trade agreement	2005	Factual examination not started

Country	Agreement	Type	Year	Status
Qatar	Gulf Cooperation Council	Preferential arrangement		
	Arab Free Trade Area	Free trade agreement		
Saudi Arabia	Gulf Cooperation Council	Preferential arrangement		
	Arab Free Trade Area	Free trade agreement		
Syria	EC-Syria	Association free trade agreement	1977	Report adopted
	Arab Free Trade Area	Free trade agreement		
Tunisia	African Economic Community	Customs union	1994	
	EC-Tunisia	Association free trade agreement	1998	Factual examination concluded
	Agadir Agreement			
	Arab Free Trade Area	Free trade agreement		
	EFTA-Tunisia	Free trade agreement	2005	Factual examination not started
	Turkey-Tunisia	Free trade agreement	2005	Factual examination not started
United Arab Emirates	Gulf Cooperation Council	Preferential arrangement		
	Arab Free Trade Area	Free trade agreement		

EC = European Community
EFTA = European Free Trade Association

a. The WTO does not have a record on all agreements. Most trade deals, especially with respect to Arab countries, are never notified to the WTO.

Sources: World Trade Organization, Regional Trade Agreements Gateway, www.wto.org; Tuck School of Business at Dartmouth, Center for International Business, Trade Agreements Database and Archive; Office of the United States Trade Representative, www.ustr.gov.

Appendix 8B
US Preferential Trade Arrangements with Select Arab Countries

This appendix summarizes existing US preferential trade arrangements with Jordan and Morocco and the prospective one with Egypt.[16]

Jordan

From a US perspective, the free trade agreement (FTA) with Jordan was undertaken for a variety of motives. The Clinton administration wanted to reward Jordan for supporting reconciliation between the Palestinian Authority and Israel through the Oslo peace process and King Hussein's personal involvement in the failed Camp David negotiations. Furthermore, the US-Israel FTA had created trade discrimination against Jordan and the Palestinian Authority territories. The US-Jordan FTA could be regarded as a mechanism for redressing the adverse impact on Jordan of the US-Israel FTA, a repayment for diplomatic service, and a means of deepening the bonds between Jordan and the United States. From an American exporter's perspective, it could also be interpreted as leveling the playing field with respect to preferential access that EU competitors would receive through Jordan's Euro-Med agreement. At the time of the negotiation of the FTA, Jordan was unique among the Euro-Med partners in exporting more to the United States than to the European Union.

The FTA covers trade in goods and services, intellectual property rights (IPRs), environmental protection, labor standards, electronic commerce, safeguard measures, and dispute settlement and establishes a binational committee to supervise implementation. The FTA is in addition to the preexisting preferences that Jordan already received in the US market through the generalized system of preferences (GSP) and the qualified industrial zone (QIZ) program, which remain in place.

Unlike the Euro-Mediterranean Partnership agreement, which simply makes reference to existing World Trade Organization (WTO) commitments in services, the US FTA requires additional liberalization, on the basis of existing commitments under the General Agreement on Trade in Services. Under the FTA, Jordan committed to amending its laws and regulations on services trade over a three-year period. Most importantly it revised its basic investment law, which now grants US firms national treatment in most sectors, as well as laws and regulations on intellectual property. These changes encouraged a surge in foreign direct investment

---

16. The United States has also concluded FTAs with Bahrain and Oman. See Lawrence (2006) for discussion of these agreements.

(FDI), much of it going into manufacturing in the QIZs. However, the reforms also encouraged investment in the tourism, transportation, financial services, and health sectors among others. Improved IPR protection has contributed to the growth of the Jordanian pharmaceutical industry and retail trade of copyrighted products such as DVDs and supports Jordan's emerging software industry.[17]

Thirteen QIZs have been established in Jordan since 1998.[18] They are particularly important in the textile and apparel sector, where initial levels of US protection are high and the phaseout of protection under the FTA is slow, up to 10 years for some products. Exports to the United States are likely to exceed $1 billion in 2005, accounting for two-thirds or more of Jordanian exports to the United States. Employment in the QIZs is approximately 40,000, with Jordanians accounting for roughly 26,000. As noted earlier, many employees are from South Asia including Bangladesh. Seventy percent of the Jordanian employees are women, and a majority of these women were previously not in the labor force (World Bank 2004d). Investment in the QIZs has reached $85 million to $100 million, much of it by Asian textile and apparel firms. There have been widespread reports of labor abuse by these firms, particularly with regard to treatment of imported South Asian workers.[19] There is very little participation by non-Jordanian Arab investors (Kardoosh and al Khoury 2005).

However, Marwan Kardoosh and Riad al Khoury (2005) report that this investment has been associated with little technological transfer or backward linkages to the economy. They argue that this is due primarily to the lack of technological capacity on the part of indigenous firms, which for the most part are not capable of supplying inputs of sufficient quality, volume, and timeliness to the QIZ investors. Kardoosh and al Khoury also point to the difficulty of linking local vocational training programs to the needs of QIZ investors and thus encouraging the hiring of more local workers.[20]

From a regional perspective, Jeffrey B. Nugent and Fahyre De Alencar Loiola (2003) argue that the expansion of textile and apparel production

---

17. For further details, see Lord (2001); Rosen (2004); and Hale (2004).

18. In addition to the QIZs, Jordan has a special economic zone at the port of Aqaba. A trade facilitation agreement with Israel originally signed in 1995 was deepened in 2005 in the context of the two countries' Euro-Med agreements with the European Union.

19. Steven Greenhouse and Michael Barbaro, "An Ugly Side of Free Trade: Sweatshops in Jordan," *New York Times*, May 3, 2006, C1.

20. Kardoosh and al Khoury (2005) report other disincentives to hiring locals: They are perceived as less efficient than their foreign counterparts, regarded as possibly reluctant to accept some types of work as being below their social status, and in the case of women, less willing to accept overtime as well as subject to broader familial concerns about their activities outside the home.

in the Jordanian QIZs has amounted to the transfer of quota-constrained textile and apparel production from the United Arab Emirates to Jordan— i.e., a trade-diverting reallocation of regional production, not a net expansion. (This argument ignores the fact that UAE-based textile and apparel production is itself the product of the distortionary Multi-Fiber Arrangement regime and that the relocation of production to Jordan might actually be a move toward global free trade equilibrium but this is, of course, no consolation to UAE workers.) More worrisome is the claim by Kardoosh and al Khoury that the growth of the Jordanian QIZs has come at the expense of the Palestinian Authority territories, though given the existing political situation, it is unclear whether Israeli outsourcing to the West Bank would have continued even if the Jordanian QIZs had not existed. Similar trade diversion arguments have been made with respect to Egypt, but a careful analysis of the data suggests that significant diversion has not transpired (Magder 2005, box 1).

Despite the idiosyncratic connection to Israel and the peace process, one might argue that the US FTA with Jordan might have a demonstration effect with respect to other Arab countries. Some evidence indicates that this indeed has been the case.

Morocco

Following the conclusion of the Jordan FTA, the United States negotiated agreements with Morocco and Bahrain. In economic terms, Morocco would appear to be an even less likely partner for an FTA than Jordan. Again, US motivation would appear to be primarily political: to bind more closely to the United States another diplomatically moderate Arab regime.[21]

From the standpoint of Morocco, the benefits of the FTA as conventionally understood are likely to be small: Trade intensity with the United States is low (table 8.2), and roughly 60 percent of Moroccan exports already entered the United States duty free due to the absence of any normal trade relations (most-favored nation) tariff, GSP, or some other provision (USITC 2004). Presumably Morocco's motivation resides in the perception that the gains through the nontraditional channels of leveraging internal reform and locking in its credibility are relatively large.

The US-Morocco FTA covers merchandise trade, services (including specific provisions regarding financial services, telecommunications, electronic commerce, and intellectual property rights), investment, government procurement, safeguards, labor, environment, transparency, dispute

---

21. Ahmed Galal and Robert Z. Lawrence (2004) observe that the 1787 treaty of peace and friendship between Morocco and the United States, renegotiated in 1836, is the longest unbroken treaty relationship in the history of the United States.

settlement, and US technical assistance to Morocco with respect to customs administration.[22]

A number of studies using computable general equilibrium (CGE) models have attempted to assess the prospective impact of the agreement; these models focus on merchandise trade, and given the basic outlines of the pre-FTA status quo—low trade and a general absence of tariff barriers to Moroccan exports to the United States outside textiles and apparel and agriculture—the results that these models obtain are predictably small: The central estimate of the US International Trade Commission's analysis is a $119 million one-time increase in US welfare (USITC 2004). Other studies cited by the USITC reach similar modest results. The results for Morocco are similarly underwhelming. John Gilbert (2003) actually obtains the results that the agreement would be slightly welfare-reducing for Morocco: The loss of tariff revenue due to a diversion of imports from tariff-paying EU producers to duty-free American suppliers would outweigh the modest efficiency gains, though this result is misleading—under the Euro-Med agreement the tariffs on EU imports would have been eventually eliminated anyway.

Yet this class of models is notorious for greatly overestimating the impact of terms-of-trade effects (thus attributing too much impact to tariff changes) while ignoring issues that are not amenable to CGE modeling but may be quite important in reality. In the case of the US-Morocco FTA these concerns cut both ways. First, in all likelihood, the models do not capture well the impact of relaxations of quantitative barriers on Moroccan exports to the US market or the complicated rules of origin in textiles and apparel that encourage the sourcing of relatively high-cost textiles from the United States—and potentially negate the gains offered by US market opening. But more important than the inability to capture the impact of nontariff provisions on merchandise trade, the models ignore the services sector where much of the action is: Services account for 45 percent of the Moroccan economy and are arguably subject to greater policy-induced distortions than merchandise trade is. Finally there are process issues such as IPR, government procurement, and transparency, where improvements conceivably could have substantial impact on Moroccan welfare, if not US trade.

Moroccan welfare will also be affected by costs of implementation and, depending on one's welfare criterion, the distribution of benefits. Morocco may reap considerable long-run gains from progress on the less traditional "behind the border issues," but one estimate puts the one-time costs creating the necessary administrative capacity at $40 million to $48 million (Galal and Lawrence 2004). With respect to distribution there are concerns that liberalization of bulk grain imports may depress farm incomes and

---

22. The United States has also provided Morocco a small amount of aid to improve labor standards, including issues relating to child labor.

contribute to inequality. The fact of the matter is that no one has a good grasp of the ultimate impact of what are in reality complex agreements.

Egypt

If the agreement with Morocco is regarded as having a small impact, because of both the low level of US-Morocco economic integration and Morocco's peripheral place in the Arab world, the same cannot be said about a prospective US FTA with Egypt. Because of Egypt's economic size and centrality to any pan-Arab integration scheme, and Arab cultural and political life more generally, a US-Egypt agreement would probably represent a kind of tipping point with respect to economic integration between MENA and the United States.

Because such an agreement is prospective in nature, any evaluation is by definition provisional and speculative. But given the characteristics of other US FTAs one can be confident that this would be a "deep" agreement, addressing services, investment, and a range of behind-the-border issues in addition to the traditional elimination of border barriers. Bernard Hoekman and Denise Konan (2005) find that while elimination of border impediments would deliver modest gains to Egypt, the real opportunities are in the removal of nontariff barriers in the services sector, with the elimination of these impediments to trade yielding an improvement in welfare 10 times that of the abolition of tariffs alone.[23] Nevertheless, these estimated static welfare gains are small—less than 2 percent of GDP. The issue is how big the nontraditional welfare gains might be.

There are reasons to believe that Egypt could exploit a "deep integration" FTA as a mechanism to support its own internal reform efforts; a cabinet reshuffle in July 2004 increased the influence of a younger generation of more liberal technocrats. Under their leadership Egypt has pursued a number of economic reforms including a rationalization and liberalization of the trade regime and customs administration, an overhaul of the tax code, and a substantial effort to begin privatizing its extensive network of state-owned enterprises. Under these conditions the FTA could

---

23. The Hoekman and Konan model has some unusual characteristics that exaggerate the impact of services liberalization. The implied tariff on transportation is 50 percent, meaning that elimination of this nontariff barrier amounts to a large improvement in transportation efficiency, which in turn generates a roughly 50 percent expansion of the tourism sector (which is treated as pure exportable). The expansion of tourism accounts for the single largest increase in sectoral output and almost half of the increase in exports. While Dan Magder's (2005) case study of the Egyptian apparel sector suggests that it might not be an exaggeration to characterize the logistical problems in Egypt's transportation sector as amounting to a 50 percent tax on exports, a $1 billion increase in tourism revenues would seem to require a sweeping reorganization of the transportation and communications sectors—and absence of terrorism.

help lock in reforms that the Egyptian government is already undertaking unilaterally.[24] Presumably the reduction in uncertainty and risk would translate into increased private-sector investment from both local and foreign sources. The existing Euro-Med agreement, which covers neither services nor the right of establishment, cannot play this role.

At the same time it is unlikely that US negotiating demands would be limited solely to Egyptian reforms already in train. While there is no reason to believe that such US demands would necessarily be against Egyptian interests, there are risks in "deep integration" scenarios. These include harmonization to inappropriate standards or without proper time for adjustment or building complementary institutional capacity.

Recent US FTAs such as those concluded with Morocco, Australia, and Central America probably present the best guide to what US negotiating demands would be. These would include protracted phaseouts of protection in sensitive agricultural sectors, US content requirements in apparel, a "negative list" approach in services under which the right of establishment in any sector not specifically exempted is approved, enhanced regulatory transparency including anticorruption provisions particularly with respect to government procurement, enhanced IPR protection particularly with regard to pharmaceuticals, which in the past has been a point of contention between the United States and Egypt in other contexts, and finally labor and environmental considerations.

US demands with respect to agriculture and textile and apparel trade would presumably erode though not eliminate the conventional trade gains that Egypt might capture in these sectors. The IPR issue is a subtle one and depending on how the rules were written could benefit or harm Egypt or, more accurately, harm certain Egyptian interests while benefiting others. The nascent software sector and high-technology sector more generally, which could particularly gain from increased regional integration, including with Israel, would probably be beneficiaries. Pharmaceuticals are a different story, however, and the Egyptian negotiators would be well advised to proceed cautiously in this area.[25]

Given Egypt's low scores on some of the regulatory indicators discussed in chapter 4, the potential gains with respect to process issues such as the right of establishment, transparency, government procurement, and regulatory reform could be large. Reforms in these areas could be particularly important in leveling the playing field for private-sector entrants in competition with existing or newly privatized public-sector entities pos-

---

24. See Galal and Lawrence (2004) and Magder (2005) for details. The former argue that past Egyptian reforms have been more successful when anchored to external agreements through the World Bank, International Monetary Fund, or WTO.

25. The Egyptian negotiators probably did not win themselves any sympathy points when at the 2003 WTO ministerial meeting in Cancún they pushed the inclusion of Viagra on the WTO's list of "essential medicines."

sessing the advantages of incumbency and long-standing political ties to the government.

While the potential gains are speculative in nature, the potential drawbacks against which they should be weighed do not appear large. Egypt already risks exposing itself to welfare-reducing trade diversion through the Euro-Med agreement and the Greater Arab Free Trade Area, if implemented. Indeed, with the United States beginning to conclude FTAs with other Middle Eastern countries, Egypt risks being left behind. An FTA with the United States might actually represent a move toward a less distortionary free trade equilibrium.

The real downside risk is the flip side of the potential gain—the limitation on sovereignty represented by a binding agreement on a range of issues and practices not currently covered by external agreements. Here one has to trust the ability of the Egyptian negotiators to come back with an agreement that on net benefits Egyptian interests.

9

Risk, Credibility, and Supply Response

The Arab countries confront a number of microeconomic issues that appear to limit the growth of productivity. These involve local policies and practices and do not require international intervention to resolve, though external policy anchors as discussed in the previous chapter may be useful. The intraregional variation in their severity also implies that these policies and practices are not culturally or religiously predetermined, implicitly steering the analysis toward interest group politics as conventionally understood. The models reviewed in the previous chapter, which have calculated (modest) benefits from trade agreements, as well as much of the advice coming from multilateral institutions, assume that increased supply will be forthcoming in response to policy change. This chapter examines the validity of this critical assumption. For heuristic purposes we consider three potential sources of supply response: first, local firms and entrepreneurs; second, returnees from the large Arab emigrant community outside the Middle East; and third, foreign firms and investors. In reality the distinction is imperfect: Presumably one of the ways that domestic supply response would be manifested is through the integration of local firms into transborder supply networks. We then consider how perceptions are formed of local economic, political, and security risk by domestic entrepreneurs, foreign investors, and returnees and how high subjective risk might be reduced. This consideration inevitably involves discussion of the "enduring authoritarianism" of Middle Eastern political regimes, the likelihood of liberalizing change, and the obstacles domestic reformers face, which are taken up in the next chapter. We conclude this chapter by raising the possibility of a virtuous circle in which political reform could reduce risk, which would in turn lead to an expansion in cross-border economic integration and rising incomes, which facilitate more extensive economic and political reforms.

Domestic Entrepreneurship

The natural place to begin a discussion of supply response to policy change is with local firms and entrepreneurs. They presumably have the best information about "facts on the ground" and are best placed to seize opportunities that policy change presents.

Unfortunately, systematic evidence on the nature of entrepreneurship and the environment within which it acts in developing countries in general and the Middle East in particular is just beginning to emerge from large-scale surveys funded by the World Bank. As a consequence, our understanding, at least in a quantitative sense, of how the Middle East stacks up in terms of establishing an economic environment that fosters entrepreneurship is highly limited. Regulatory requirements appear to significantly raise the costs of forming new businesses (table 9.1), operating them once under way (table 9.2), as well as terminating failed ones (table 9.3). As discussed in chapter 4, the regulatory hurdles to business formation are reinforced by a financial system that tends to channel capital to investment in government bonds or loans to large, established, and possibly politically connected enterprises, rather than small and medium-sized enterprises (SMEs) and start-ups (table 4.12). Respondents in the survey conducted by Jamel Zarrouk (2003) cited the inability to enforce contracts as the single biggest problem in doing business within the region once a business is started. Barriers to exit may actually exacerbate the financing problems for SMEs: If creditors cannot be assured of being able to seize the assets of bankrupt enterprises in a timely manner, they will not lend in the first place. According to the World Bank (2006b), in Syria and Morocco, collateral averages more than twice the value of the loan. In Egypt, court approval for seizure of immovable collateral can take seven to eight years. That said, a comparison of the most recent indicators with those derived from earlier surveys done in the 1990s suggests that there have been improvements of late.

The relatively high cost of both entry and exit presumably deters business formation, dampens competition, and reduces efficiency. Among the Arab countries, Egypt scores particularly poorly on these measures while Tunisia rates the best, with Morocco and Jordan taking intermediate positions. This evidence is consistent with the fact that over the past generation Tunisia is the only Arab country to exhibit unconditional convergence in per capita income with the Organization for Economic Cooperation and Development (OECD) as documented in chapter 2. Indeed, this suggests that these indicators may be endogenous—Tunisia may score better because it

Table 9.1   Starting a business

Country	Number of procedures	Time (days)	Cost (percent of income per capita)	Minimum capital (percent of income per capita)	Domestic competition: Administrative burden for start-ups (percentile[a])
Middle East					
Algeria	14	24	25.3	55.1	18
Bahrain	n.a.	n.a.	n.a.	n.a.	83
Egypt	10	34	104.9	739.8	35
Jordan	11	36	45.9	1,011.6	72
Kuwait	13	35	2.2	133.8	n.a.
Lebanon	6	46	110.6	68.5	n.a.
Morocco	5	11	12.0	700.3	53
Oman	9	34	4.8	97.3	n.a.
Palestinian Authority territories	11	106	275.4	1,409.8	n.a.
Saudi Arabia	13	64	68.5	1,236.9	n.a.
Syria	12	47	34.5	5,111.9	n.a.
Tunisia	9	14	10.0	29.8	89
United Arab Emirates	12	54	44.3	416.9	92
Yemen	12	63	240.2	2,703.2	n.a.
High-performing comparators					
South Korea	12	22	15.2	308.8	59
Taiwan	8	48	6	216.3	88

(table continues next page)

Table 9.1   Starting a business   *(continued)*

Country	Number of procedures	Time (days)	Cost (percent of income per capita)	Minimum capital (percent of income per capita)	Domestic competition: Administrative burden for start-ups (percentile[a])
Large comparators					
China	13	48	13.6	946.7	70
India	11	71	61.7	0	55
Normally endowed comparators					
Bangladesh	8	35	81.4	0	24
Brazil	17	152	10.1	0	9
Pakistan	11	24	24.4	0	13
Turkey	8	9	27.7	20.9	60
Resource-rich comparators					
Botswana	11	108	10.9	0	49
Indonesia	12	151	101.7	97.8	69
Nigeria	9	43	73.8	43.3	25
Venezuela	13	116	15.7	0	4

n.a. = not available

a. Larger percentile indicates less administrative burden.

Sources: World Bank, *Doing Business 2006* database (accessed, June 12, 2006); Administrative burden for start-ups: *Global Competitiveness Report 2004–2005.*

Table 9.2   Enforcing contracts

Country	Number of procedures	Time (days)	Cost of enforcing contracts (percent of debt)
Middle East			
Algeria	49	407	28.7
Egypt	55	410	18.4
Jordan	43	342	8.8
Kuwait	52	390	13.3
Lebanon	39	721	26.7
Morocco	17	240	17.7
Oman	41	455	10.0
Palestinian Authority territories	26	465	21.4
Saudi Arabia	44	360	20.0
Syria	47	672	34.3
Tunisia	14	27	12.0
United Arab Emirates	53	614	16.0
Yemen	37	360	10.5
High-performing comparators			
South Korea	29	75	5.4
Taiwan	28	210	7.7
Large comparators			
China	25	241	25.5
India	40	425	43.1
Normally endowed comparators			
Bangladesh	29	365	21.3
Brazil	24	546	15.5
Pakistan	46	395	35.2
Turkey	22	330	12.5
Resource-rich comparators			
Botswana	26	154	24.8
Indonesia	34	570	126.5
Nigeria	23	730	37.2
Venezuela	40	445	28.7

Source: World Bank, *Doing Business 2006* database (accessed June 12, 2006).

has a vibrant business sector, which has successfully influenced the government to maintain a relatively efficient environment. Successful economic performance also contributes to higher tax revenues, which may enable the government to recruit more highly paid, capable, and less corruption-prone individuals and implement administrative systems that offer fewer opportunities for corruption.

Table 9.3   Closing a business

Country	Time (years)	Cost (percent of estate)	Recovery rate (cents on the dollar)
Middle East			
Algeria	3.5	4	37.5
Egypt	4.2	22	16.2
Jordan	4.3	9	27.9
Kuwait	4.2	1	38.4
Lebanon	4.0	22	18.6
Morocco	1.8	18	35.1
Oman	7.0	4	25.0
Saudi Arabia	2.8	22	28.4
Syria	4.1	9	28.6
Tunisia	1.3	7	51.6
United Arab Emirates	5.1	30	5.5
Yemen	3.0	8	28.3
High-performing comparators			
South Korea	1.5	4	81.7
Taiwan	0.8	4	89.5
Large comparators			
China	2.4	22	31.5
India	10.0	9	12.8
Normally endowed comparators			
Bangladesh	4.0	8	24.3
Brazil	10.0	9	0.5
Pakistan	2.8	4	44.3
Turkey	5.9	7	7.2
Resource-rich comparators			
Botswana	2.2	14	54.4
Indonesia	5.5	18	13.1
Nigeria	1.5	22	31.2
Venezuela	4.0	38	6.1

Source: World Bank, *Doing Business 2006* database (accessed June 12, 2006).

Yet even accepting the provisional nature of these indicators, compared with the countries outside the region, the Arab countries as a whole do not look so bad. Setting aside the oil producers, in terms of procedural complexity, administrative burden, and time in establishing a business, enforcing contracts, and dissolving a business, Morocco and Tunisia are superior to most of the comparators, with only South Korea, Taiwan, and Turkey generally comparable on these dimensions. However, Egypt and Syria, at the other extreme, do not fare well. Starting a formal business in these countries is complicated and costly, comparable only to India. Operating one is not much easier: The number of procedures required to enforce a contract is higher in Egypt than anywhere else, and in Syria enforcement takes nearly two years. And if a business fails, the recovery rate is among the lowest in the sample, among the more typically endowed countries comparable only to India.

Comparing Saudi Arabia and Algeria with the other resource-abundant comparators, there is a fair amount of dispersion in the scores from indicator to indicator, but taken in totality it is hard to argue that the Arab countries are significantly worse than the relevant comparators and indeed generally score better than the others.

In sum, there is considerable variation within the Middle East, with Morocco and Tunisia comparable to the better-performing middle-income countries of the past generation, Egypt and Syria comparable to the worst, and the highly resource-endowed economies not noticeably distinct from other natural resource–based economies elsewhere. Two points are worth noting in this connection: First the institutions and practices under discussion are amenable to reform at the national level—these are internal matters and do not require the involvement of the international community, though external policy anchors may be useful. Second, the degree of intraregional variation in these indicators belies the notion that these institutions and practices are culturally or religiously determined. If it takes on average less than a month to enforce a contract in Tunisia, there is no obvious reason why it should take well over a year in Egypt.[1] Indeed, the Egyptian government of Prime Minister Ahmed Nazif has made the elimination of red tape a priority.

These are indicators of the environments in which entrepreneurs operate. One large-scale survey has attempted to track entrepreneurial activity directly across a large number of countries. The Global Entrepreneurship Monitor (GEM) project reports data on "total entrepreneurial activity" (TEA), defined as the prevalence rate among individuals aged 18 to 64 active in either the start-up phase or managing a new business. There is no information on competence, success, or survival. The study also distinguishes a TEA-necessity index defined by those who pursue start-ups because they have "no better choices for work" (in contrast to those motivated by opportunity).[2] Necessity can be interpreted as the absence of

---

1. We do not know the equivalent delay in enforcing a contract in Tunisia when it was at Egypt's current per capita income. Thus some of the difference between the countries may reflect the growing clout of businesses as the economy grew—the endogeneity problem. Nevertheless, we doubt that this is entirely the source of the difference between the two nations.

2. "Opportunity motive" businesses amounted to 52 percent of the start-ups while "necessity motive" constituted 33 percent, and "mixed motives" accounted for the remainder. For the young business "entrepreneurial firms," 72 percent were "opportunity" businesses, 19 percent were "necessity" businesses, and the remainder reflected mixed motives (Reynolds et al. 2004, table 15).

formal-sector employment and the imperative to initiate some income-generating activity in the "informal" sector. Considerable literature documents the importance of "informal-sector" activities in developing countries that result from the inadequate growth of jobs in the formal sector. Although definitions differ, the informal sector is characterized by small firms with low capital-labor ratios, few employees, failure to register with the government, and relatively free entry. The necessity index may capture this phenomenon, however imperfectly. It is obvious that the necessity index may be a measure of desperation rather than ability-driven entrepreneurship. Nevertheless, the data can be utilized to obtain some tentative insights into the potential entrepreneurial supply in the Middle East.

These data were derived from more than 100,000 interviews conducted in 31 countries in 2003 (Reynolds et al. 2004).[3] Compared with the entire universe of firms, the associated businesses tend to be the transformative (construction, manufacturing, transportation, and wholesale) and business services sectors. The indices measure the extent of business formation—only implicitly do they shed any light on survival rates, and again the raw numbers may reflect other environmental characteristics as discussed below.

The entrepreneurship indices are correlated with a number of country characteristics (Reynolds et al. 2004, tables 17 and 18). Entrepreneurial activity is associated with populations with large shares of young adults, and men are twice as likely as women to be involved in start-ups, though women are relatively more active in developing countries. A supportive cultural context in which entrepreneurship is valued and regarded positively (as measured by survey responses and local media coverage) is associated with greater entrepreneurship, but personal networks and contacts have an even larger impact—people who know entrepreneurs are significantly more likely to become entrepreneurs themselves. Educational attainment and socioeconomic status affect the form that entrepreneurship takes—the poor are more likely to be entrepreneurs out of necessity.

The entrepreneurship indices are correlated with both past and future income growth rates, though the persistence of the indices from year to year suggests that the cross-country incidence of entrepreneurship is not driven purely by the pattern of macroeconomic shocks (Reynolds et al. 2004, tables 1 and 16). Indeed, there is also a set of structural or institutional correlates that would appear to represent implicit and explicit opportunity costs associated with involvement in a new business, including the level of public-sector employment (possibly representing the availability of low-risk employment), collected tax revenue, employer contributions to social security, and total social security costs. All of the size of

---

3. Interviews were conducted in 41 countries over 2000–2003.

government or government burden indicators are negatively associated with entrepreneurship, with the employer social security costs having the largest negative impact on "opportunity" start-ups. These correlations suggest that there is an economic calculus as well as a pure demographic component to the TEA indices.

Lastly, there is a set of variables that could be interpreted as implicit entry barriers to new firms including the cost of registering a new firm and an index of "economic freedom." Interestingly, these tend to be positively correlated with entrepreneurship, especially "necessity" entrepreneurship. The impression one gets is that institutional weaknesses as reported in tables 9.1 to 9.3 manifest themselves in weak economic performance, thereby encouraging small-scale, badly financed informal entrepreneurial activity by people unable to secure acceptable employment in larger-scale established enterprises. Similarly, there are strong negative correlations between performance on the sorts of indicators of innovative activity discussed in the previous chapters, such as the number of scientific publications, Internet usage, and the quality of intellectual property rights (IPRs) protection, and entrepreneurship by necessity. Again, weak local technological performance is associated with poor performance (whatever the specific direction of causality) contributing to necessity-driven entrepreneurship. This description would appear to be a reasonably good capsule description of the economic environment of the more distorted Arab economies.

Unfortunately, there are no Arab countries in the GEM sample so one cannot test this mental mapping directly. However, one can exploit the systematic correlation between the prevalence of entrepreneurship and economic and demographic variables to estimate how the Arab countries might rank under the assumption that entrepreneurship in the region adhered to the same statistical relationship. Ideally one would want to construct a model of demand and supply of entrepreneurship, distinguishing between total entrepreneurship and entrepreneurship resulting from the absence of formal sector jobs. Instead, given the limitations of the data, we will report a simple, reduced form relationship between the TEA prevalence rate and a handful of the most robust correlates.

Across countries, the TEA prevalence rate is inversely correlated with the level of per capita GDP, the growth rate of per capita income over the previous five years, and the unemployment rate over the previous three years. All of this implies that poor economic performance drives much of the activity. Indeed, all of these variables are likely to be associated with the generation of formal-sector jobs but the correlation is weak—for example, recent rapid growth in India has been accompanied by little growth in formal sector employment, a pattern similar to that noticed four decades ago in Latin America (Baer and Hervé 1966). It is also highly positively (negatively) correlated with the share of younger (older) male or female adults in the population.[4] A cross-country regression of these variables against the TEA index explains a bit less than two-thirds of the sample variation.[5]

Under the possibly heroic assumption that the pattern of potential entrepreneurship in the Middle East conforms to the cross-country statistical norm, one can use the estimated regression to project what the Arab countries' TEA scores would have been if they had been included in the sample. These are reported, along with the actual values of the sample countries, in table 9.4. The Arab countries tend to clump toward the upper end of the distribution, partly a function of their relatively young populations. Setting aside the oil exporters, the projected values for Syria and Jordan approximate Thailand; Egypt and Morocco fall into an interval defined by India and Argentina on the upper bound and Chile and South Korea on the lower bound. Tunisia is between Mexico and China, while Algeria scores the lowest, in the range of Australia and Ireland.

Obviously these are very rough indicators, and one should not lean too heavily on either the original index or the associated projections. The main message though of these results is that in quantitative terms there is no reason why the Arab world should be expected to exhibit uniquely low entrepreneurship. This is mixed news as some of the result is driven by bad economic performance, but conditional on this, the demographic and economic characteristics of the countries suggest there is a pool of potential responders , purely in terms of numbers without any information on probable quality. In sum, assuming that entrepreneurial instincts and responses to economic opportunity are reasonably similar across nations, in similar environments the demographic features of the Arab countries are conducive to the emergence of local firms.

This exercise raises three related issues. First, is the entrepreneurship actually there, and importantly, is it competent or simply a measure of the failure of the economies to afford stable employment growth? We can observe the predicted values based on a statistical model, but we cannot observe whether in fact reality conforms to this prediction. The results cited in earlier chapters on the quality of institutions of higher learning are not particularly encouraging with respect to technical ability. Second, suppose that entrepreneurship is not observed—is it due to something intrinsic or is it reflective of other problems in the business environment or

---

4. There is a very high degree of collinearity among these variables. Of these four variants, the younger adult female share was slightly more correlated, and this regression specification is used to construct table 9.4. The choice among these four variants made no material difference to the results.

5. The regression is TEA = 25.78 (1.27) − 3.24 ln GDP per capita (2.44) − 0.93 GDP per capita growth 1998–2002 (2.72) + 0.80 share of young women (2.52) − 0.42 rate of unemployment (2.64); $R^2 = 0.65$; n = 40. All of the explanatory variables were statistically different from zero at the 5 percent confidence level.

Table 9.4 Total entrepreneurial activity values and projections

Country	Value	Country	Value
Uganda	29	Norway	8
Venezuela	27	Switzerland	7
Saudi Arabia	26p	Israel	7
Kuwait	25p	Greece	7
Yemen	23p	Hungary	7
Syria	22p	Spain	6
Jordan	20p	Denmark	6
Thailand	19	United Kingdom	6
India	18	Finland	6
Argentina	17	South Africa	6
Egypt	17p	Singapore	5
Morocco	17p	Germany	5
Chile	16	Italy	5
Korea	15	Poland	4
New Zealand	14	Slovenia	4
Brazil	13	Taiwan	4
Mexico	12	Sweden	4
Tunisia	12p	Netherlands	4
China	12	Belgium	3
Iceland	11	Hong Kong, China	3
United States	11	Croatia	3
Australia	10	Russia	3
Algeria	10p	France	2
Ireland	9	Japan	2
Canada	9		

p = projections (using authors' calculations)

Note: Higher value is better.

Source: Reynolds et al. (2004).

deeper hostility to entrepreneurship in the political system? Put differently, if the Syrian financial system were not so repressed, would we observe a much higher level of activity among young energetic entrepreneurs who are currently capital-starved, or would it serve to undermine the symbiotic relation between the Alawite-based security services and the Sunni-dominated business interests?

Obviously, the extent of local entrepreneurial response and the policy environment are related. Reform of the previously documented microeconomic impediments combined with the maintenance of macroeconomic stability should, in principle, stimulate growth provided that there is a responsive entrepreneurial class. The analysis in chapter 6 showed that few of the conventional measures of policy have had a significant effect on capital accumulation or total factor productivity (TFP) growth. Three measures of the impact of general "macroeconomic" quality, namely inflation, the budget balance, and the Sachs-Warner measure of openness, are significant. Of the "second-generation" reform measures, that of "institutional quality" taken from the international country risk guide index is the only statistically significant one of 15 measures.

As noted in chapter 6 most of the Arab countries have done reasonably well on macro reforms, while micro reforms have been weaker, and the statistically significant effect of institutional quality is on TFP growth rather than capital accumulation. If this is the case, then the weaker Arab performance in this dimension could be the source of the limited supply response to improved macro policies. And the lower institutional quality, assuming it is even worse in the countries not included in the sample, might be of greater importance. From this perspective, poor entrepreneurship could be a response to an inhospitable environment rather than an exogenous factor determined by cultural or social factors.

Alternatively, good entrepreneurs could have prevailed over many of the hurdles imposed by weak institutions. A long literature in the 1950s described in detail the obstacles to growth faced by newly industrializing countries including South Korea and Taiwan.[6] Yet these were overcome, though gradually government policies became more supportive, at least for exporters. Arguably the explicit support merely compensated for government-created obstacles, resulting in a roughly neutral regime in terms of the prices of inputs and outputs. Some of the components of institutional quality have never been particularly high in the fast-growing economies in Asia including China, India, South Korea, and Taiwan. In other countries, particularly Indonesia and Thailand, these deficiencies may have contributed to the crisis of the late 1990s, but there had been two decades of rapid growth, and retrospective analyses of the sources of the crisis assign a much greater role to other factors, particularly premature opening of the capital account and the role of short-term international flows (Furman and Stiglitz 1998, Radelet and Sachs 1998, World Bank 1998). The role of institutional quality, viewed in terms of the historical experience of individual countries, is moot, though the cross-country evidence of the association between institutional quality and growth is clear. However, the causation could of course go from growth rates to institutional quality.

To some extent, the weak business climate appears to be designed to channel rents to politically connected local residents. The Egyptian intellectual Saad Eddin Ibrahim once described Saudi entrepreneurs as "lumpen capitalists"—products of the oil boom, neither traditional Arab merchants nor Western entrepreneurs taking risks with their capital but rather rentiers,

---

6. For a particularly thorough document that became a standard for much of the 1950s and 1960s, see United Nations (1955).

either portfolio investors or "sponsors" of nonnative entrepreneurs unable to legally operate without a Saudi partner (Ibrahim 1982).[7]

But what if the problem is deeper, reflecting a fundamental antipathy to sources of power and prestige beyond direct state control? A commonly heard complaint throughout the region is that decades of Arab socialism have dampened traditional Arab entrepreneurial instincts. Yet Clement M. Henry and Robert Springborg (2001) go further, documenting the hostility of the Algerian and Syrian regimes, for example, to the existence of an autonomous private business community—suggesting not just a dulling of entrepreneurial instincts but an active attempt to emasculate them. Such tendencies perhaps reached their apotheosis (or nadir depending on one's perspective) in Libya, where private property and employer-employee relations were banned under the revolutionary *Jamahiriyah* ideology of strongman Muammar Gadhafi following his seizure of power in 1969. These proscriptions were relaxed in the late 1980s for anyone brave enough to try, but this legacy and associated uncertainty about property rights and criminal liability continue to impede development of a vibrant private sector in Libya.

This relates to a potentially fundamental issue, namely the absence of a private entrepreneurial class with technological and marketing skills in manufacturing that would enable them to participate in the international economy.

The region has a large number of individuals with considerable business acumen, though often in wholesaling and retailing rather than in manufacturing or advanced services. One interpretation is that the Arabs appear to have gotten the worst of all worlds: the deadened entrepreneurial instincts of socialism but without the accompanying rigorous Soviet bloc technical education.[8] The latter had high quality and levels of formal education including in engineering and science but little entrepreneurial activity for 40 (Eastern Europe) to 75 years (the former Soviet Union). In contrast, some of the Middle Eastern economies display considerable trading acumen but quite low levels of technical skill, a combi-

---

7. Stephen Glain (2004) documents a similar "sponsor" phenomenon in financially repressed Syria, where the politically connected extract rents from entrepreneurs for enabling them to access the state-owned banking system. The description by Henry and Springborg (2001, 126) is worth quoting at length: "The bargain consists of deals between individual Alawi patrons and Sunni capitalist clients whereby the former provide protection, contacts, and permissions for services rendered. That bargain underpins the political economy of Syria, thereby preserving Alawi rule, but at the cost of more rapid economic growth, as rent seeking, requiring as it does an absence of transparency and accountability and militating as it also does against export-led growth, has devoured the country's resources."

8. Dan Magder (2005) provides the example of Egyptian textile and apparel managers— who were socialized in the Nasserist era, reflecting the impact of Egypt's Soviet patron— lacking marketing skills or even the sense of a need for marketing of big orders and placing little emphasis on product quality or the need to respond to customer preferences.

nation that has considerable implications for understanding past and potentially future performance.

However, another interpretation is that the emphasis on trading and other businesses amenable to "mobile capital" is not necessarily due to technical weakness but rather is a rational adaptation to a predatory environment that discourages investment in large fixed facilities that could be subject to seizure.[9] The good news is that under different governance, one might see a resurgence in technically competent entrepreneurship. The bad news is that if the political inhibitors are this deep, substantial investment in technology, education, or other precursors are unlikely to manifest themselves in economic dynamism.

Ironically, this underlying political logic establishes a dynamic in which foreign entrepreneurs are actually preferred, posing less of an implicit threat to the political regime. The complementary economic logic is that larger foreign multinational firms have diversified portfolios and may fear predation less than local capitalists and hence are more willing to make irreversible industrial investments. A development strategy based on foreign investors can work as the experience of Southeast Asia in particular demonstrates.[10] The Asians were accommodating to these investors, however.

Apart from the extractive sector, where geology determines the location of production, the problem for the Arab countries is actually attracting that investment in a competitive world. The issue for the Middle East is how to transform the local economy through internal and external drivers in a way that would enable the capture of latent opportunities presented by globalization. Is there any way of using foreign connections to strengthen local capacity or circumvent its weakness? In the next section we take up the possibility of attracting returnees from abroad and then follow with an analysis of the perceived risks in investing in the Middle East from the standpoint of foreign investors.

---

9. See Henry and Springborg (2001), particularly with respect to Syria.

10. The starkest case is Singapore, whose industrial growth was largely dependent on foreign direct investment intensively encouraged by the government. But Indonesia and Malaysia also were heavily dependent on such investment, some sourced from the ethnic Chinese diaspora around the Pacific Rim (Cheong 2003). In Hong Kong and Taiwan, both of which followed a path of encouraging small and medium-scale enterprises, many of the entrepreneurs had been industrialists in pre-Communist China and had fled to these countries. Although it may be assumed that the technical and marketing skills of the mainland of the 1930s were not the same as those required in the 1960s and 1970s, neither were they different in kind but in quality and could be learned fairly rapidly. Even here, in the new rapidly growing sectors, foreign skills were important such as those transmitted by the buying offices established by large wholesalers and retailers based in the OECD countries that provided design and quality control knowledge to local firms (Lall and Keesing 1992; Rhee, Ross-Larson, and Pursell 1984).

Reversing the Brain Drain

Returnees who received training or work experience in more advanced institutions abroad might provide a potential synaptic link between local economies and the opportunities presented by the global economy. These returnees played an important role in the industrial development of South Korea and Taiwan, encouraged by the cultural pull of the homeland (particularly in relation to raising children) and sometimes supported by public policy that consciously targeted emigrant engineers and scientists. For example, in the case of Taiwan, the government established a science park and provided tax and financial inducements for Taiwanese abroad to return to Taiwan and establish high-technology firms. Much of today's booming high-technology sector in Taiwan can trace its origins to firms established by returnee scientists and engineers under these programs. Similarly, as discussed in box 9.1, nonresident Indians and returnees have played a significant catalytic role in the rise of the Indian computer software industry.

Even if returnees do not establish new high-technology firms, simply reversing the brain drain, as has occurred in Ireland over the past generation, would amount to raising the social rate of return on educational investment, conceivably by a significant margin. More systematic econometric studies have documented the impact of cultural affinity in general and diaspora communities in particular on trade and investment flows.[11] The issue is whether Arab communities in North America and Europe can play a similar role in revitalizing the Middle East.

Arabs in North America

The North American Arab community is relatively small: The 2000 US census identifies 850,000 people of exclusively Arab ancestry and a larger group of 1.2 million people if those of mixed ancestry are included (Brittingham and de la Cruz 2005). In addition there are roughly 195,000 Arabs in Canada, with another 40,000 having mixed Arab and European ancestry, according to Canadian government statistics.[12] The composition of the North American Arab community does not mirror the population profile of the Middle East: In the United States, Lebanese (29 percent) are the single largest group, followed by Egyptians (15 percent). Twenty percent

---

11. On the role of cultural affinity, see Guiso, Sapienza, and Zingales (2004) and Noland (2005b). On the impact of diaspora communities, see Rauch (2001), Rauch and Trindade (2002), Choi (2003), Combes, Lafourcade, and Mayer (2005), and Hernander and Saavedra (2005).

12. See Statistics Canada, 2001 Census of Canada: Data and Analysis, available at www.statcan.ca.

Box 9.1 Asian experience with diaspora entrepreneurs

The potential beneficial role of returnees and foreign entrepreneurs of domestic origin can be gleaned from the Asian experience. In China, for example, "overseas" Chinese were early investors in China's special economic zones and provided marketing and production skills to the many township and village enterprises, which were an important source of growth.

In India, as in China, foreign skills provided an important adjunct to local skills. Many of the new firms in the higher-technology sectors, especially software, were aided substantially by expatriates, who provided critical advice and in some cases infrastructure, such as a satellite. These inputs were complemented by a large flow of graduates from the Indian Institutes of Technology and other institutions (Saxenian 2002). Bangalore, the center of the industry, has an abundant supply of IT graduates from 3 universities, 14 engineering colleges, and 47 polytechnic schools.

A catalytic factor has been the transfer of skills by foreign firms. Forty-eight percent of Indian software firms are foreign owned, joint ventures, or owned by Indian nationals with intensive participation by foreigners. Although foreign wholly owned firms make up only a small fraction of the software firms in India, they account for a disproportionately large share of the investment made by the software industry and have facilitated software exports, the largest part of current sales.

Foreign firms, often staffed by Indian expatriates, also invested in India, started new Indian firms, helped raise US venture capital, organized conferences in the United States to heighten awareness of the potential of India's software industry, and facilitated networking between Indian technology entrepreneurs and their counterparts in the United States.

Even a fairly advanced education system and a robust private sector have their greatest impact if they are part of an international network. But with some notable exceptions such as the Taiwanese experience with the Hsinchu Science Park and the Institute for Technological Research and Innovation (ITRI), most Asian research institutions have not been well connected to the international innovation system (Hou and Gee 1993). Education of more researchers without efforts to embed them in productive networks is likely to have low returns.

Moreover, the role of foreigners inevitably changes the dynamics of local power—the Indian software sector is largely unbeholden to government (and some would argue that is part of the source of its success). It has its own satellites, partly or totally financed by cooperating foreign firms, and is not taxed on its inputs, and its very success allows it a seat in discussions on India's economic evolution.

of the respondents identified their ancestry as generic "Arab." In Canada, where Lebanese also account for a majority of the Canadian-Arab community, the disparities are even more pronounced with generic "Arab" (25 percent) and Egyptians (16 percent) making up the next largest components. The North American Arab community, like many immigrant communities, is disproportionately male, 57 percent in the United States and 54 percent in Canada.

In 2000 the median age of the Arab-American community was 33 years, though there was variation within the group, with Syrians and Lebanese being the oldest (39 years) and the generic Arabs being the youngest (27 years). Almost half of the members of the broad Arab ancestry group were born in the United States (well over half in the case of the Lebanese and Syrians), while nearly half of foreign-born Arabs arrived during the 1990s. Again there is variation across national origin: The Lebanese, Syrians, and Palestinians have the oldest or most established communities and are least likely to have arrived in the 1990s, while a majority of Iraqi and Moroccan immigrants arrived during the last decade. The home ownership rate among the Lebanese (70 percent) is double that of the Moroccans (35 percent). Similar patterns apply with respect to the Arab-Canadian community: The Lebanese are the oldest community, while Moroccan, Iraqi, and Algerian communities are composed almost entirely of immigrants.

The Arab-American community is on average both richer and better-educated than the US population as a whole. Median Arab-American household income is roughly $52,000 compared with a national average of $50,000, with the median Lebanese, Syrian, and Egyptian households earning around $60,000. In Canada, average and median household incomes are generally a bit lower than the national average, except in the case of Egyptians.

Presumably this earning power is related to educational attainment: The proportion of adult Arab-Americans with a bachelor's degree (41 percent) was more than half again as large as for the nation as a whole (24 percent). In Canada the share of Arabs with a bachelor's degree (30 percent) is more than twice the national rate (12 percent). Indeed, in Canada the share of Arab females with a bachelor's degree (24 percent) is double the national standard—in noticeable contrast to the Arab-European data discussed below.

In the United States there was considerable variation across national origin groups with the Egyptians exhibiting the highest rate of college graduation (64 percent) and the Moroccans the lowest (31 percent)—though even the Moroccans exceed the US national average. These differences are less pronounced in Canada, though again, the Egyptians display the highest rate of educational attainment with more than half holding a bachelor's degree.

In the United States, Arabs are more likely to be in management or professional work (42 percent) than the national average (34 percent). Again, the rate is highest for the Egyptians (51 percent) and lowest for the Moroccans (31 percent). In Canada, the shares in management (14 percent) and business or finance (13 percent) are comparable to the national profile, while the percentage employed in natural and applied sciences (11 percent) is more than double the national average.

The US census does not ask respondents about religious affiliation, but anecdotally it would appear that the Arab-American community is also disproportionately Christian, at least relative to the religious makeup of the countries of emigration. The Canadian government does collect religious affiliation data, however. About two-thirds of the Arab-Canadian population is Muslim and about one-third is Christian. The latter make up the majority of the Lebanese, Egyptian, Syrian, and Iraqi communities, while large majorities of the generic "Arab," Moroccan, and Algerian communities are Muslim.

One gets the impression that the North American Arab community comprises both an older, more settled, perhaps more Christian segment primarily of Lebanese, Syrians, Palestinians, and Egyptians and a younger more recent immigrant community from other regions such as Morocco with Egyptians being disproportionately in professional fields and the Lebanese in business.

Momentarily setting aside reservations about conditions in their countries of origin, is it plausible that this community could drive economic revitalization in the Middle East? It is not obvious that the answer is "yes." The national origins of the North American Arab community do not mirror that of the region; parts of the community are sufficiently old and established to augur against return; and casual observation and inference drawn from the Canadian data suggest that the community is disproportionately Christian—and these communities are declining in much of the Middle East (Sennott 2002). In short, while these parts of the community may be valuable potential sources of capital, technology transfer, and marketing links, they are unlikely to supply large numbers of returning entrepreneurs.

However, there is a younger, less established component of the community for whom return might be an option under sufficiently attractive conditions. As a first cut, we assume that anyone born in the United States or Canada is sufficiently acculturated that "return" to the Middle East is not probable. That is to say we limit our analysis to "foreign-born" North American Arabs. (We do not exclude citizens of the United States or Canada per se, however: Possession of a foreign passport reduces the irreversibility of the decision to return and as a consequence could actually facilitate repatriation.) We further exclude anyone from a major oil producer on the theory that they are unlikely to engage in the sort of industrial-sector entrepreneurship in which we are most interested. This leaves 445,000 adult Middle Easterners of whom 165,000 are Lebanese and 123,000 are Egyptians.

Of these 445,000 foreign-born adults, roughly 60,000 have graduate degrees, with Egyptians (40 percent) and Lebanese (30 percent) accounting for approximately two-thirds of the total. Roughly 120,000 are in management or professional jobs, with Egyptians and Lebanese again accounting for roughly two-thirds of such employment. In the United States, employment in the manufacturing and information technology sectors is 22,200 and 5,700 respectively, with Egyptians and Lebanese accounting for approximately 60 percent in both cases. (Canada does not report comparable sectoral employment data.) Unfortunately the census data do not allow us to cross-tabulate characteristics, so, for example, we cannot say what share of the 22,200 employed have advanced degrees. Nevertheless this discussion suggests that from the standpoint of targeting potential returnees, the numbers are relatively small and are concentrated on two countries, Lebanon and Egypt.[13] It is also likely given historic intracommunal conflict that a disproportionate share of both the Lebanese and Egyptians are Christians though data on these affiliations are unavailable.

Of the more normally endowed Arab countries, Egypt typically scores badly on institutional and process indicators such as those in tables 9.1 to 9.3 and those reviewed in chapters 4, 5, and 6. The pessimistic interpretation is that Egypt chases away a lot of homegrown talent. The more optimistic scenario is that with sufficient reform, perhaps spurred by a "deep integration" agreement with the United States, it might be able to lure some expatriates back.

By point of comparison, Egypt today is less politically repressive than Taiwan or South Korea were in the 1970s, though income relative to the OECD is noticeably lower today in Egypt than it was in the 1970s in the two Asian countries, implying that a returnee to Egypt would be making a greater leap than his or her Taiwanese or Korean counterpart had made a generation earlier and could anticipate slower growth in real income. At the same time improvements in telecommunications have vastly improved access to information, so in some ways the degree of self-imposed isolation from one's former life would be less decisive than in the case of the Taiwanese or Koreans in the 1970s. This could be both a blessing and a curse: One would feel less removed from life elsewhere, yet this greater awareness could contribute to feelings of regret. Again, as in the case of our earlier gross estimates of the potential pool of local entrepreneurs, the quantitative analysis can establish the putative existence of a pool of entrepreneurs. What the data cannot document at this level of aggregation is personal characteristics and network connections within North America.

---

13. Although how small is "too small" is an interesting question. Presumably one would not need too many returnees if one were Bill Gates.

Arabs in Europe

The data on Arab-Europeans are less informative. Differing country historical experiences have shaped the development of national legal and administrative frameworks for dealing with immigration; as observed by the International Centre for Migration Policy Development (ICMPD 2003, 12), "Not only do the fundamental concepts of immigrants, migrants, and minorities used in each national context connote considerable differences in definitions and meanings but the poor quality, erratic availability or even absence of data effectively prevents meaningful comparisons of most indicators across countries." The conditions underlying this observation are unfortunate since due to both numbers and proximity, one might expect the European returnee channel to be a more propitious one.

Appendix table 9A.1 reports estimates of the number of Arab immigrants and their descendants in Europe derived from European government census data. It should be emphasized that for several reasons these figures understate the actual number of European Arabs and should be regarded as a lower bound: Some countries (e.g., the United Kingdom) do not report the relevant data; in many other cases only a single nationality (usually Moroccan) and not all Arabs are identified; in most cases only foreign-born residents are counted and not their children; and all of the figures pertain only to legally documented migrants and their descendents, so illegal immigrants, who are likely to be more important in the European than in the North American context, are not counted. Some attempts to take these considerations into account have yielded much larger estimates of the Arab-European population than can be derived on the basis of official census data alone.

Even on these fragmentary data, the total figure, nearly 5 million, appears to be roughly four times as large as for North America, with Moroccans alone in Western Europe double that of all Arabs in North America. Unfortunately the fragmentary nature of the data prevents the same sort of systematic demographic analysis as for the United States and Canada. Existing data, however, paint a pointillist portrait very different from the generally successful assimilation of the small North American Arab population: While on average Arab-Americans are richer and better educated than the typical American, educational attainment among European Arabs is disproportionately low, and unemployment is unusually high.

In contrast to North American Arabs, 39 percent of whom have a bachelor's degree or better, the median educational attainment of Moroccans in the Netherlands, both male and female, is primary school; only 1 percent of Moroccan men and 2 percent of Moroccan women in the Netherlands have a college education (Schreimer 2004, table 4). Nor are their children's rates of educational attainment auspicious: At the high school level, Moroccans in the Netherlands exhibit disproportionately high dropout rates, though the rate of attendance has been rising over time.

The situation with regard to educational attainment while better elsewhere in Europe is still low: In Denmark more than half of Moroccan immigrant young people drop out of high school; less than 3 percent make it to university. The figures for the more broadly defined "Moroccan descended" category are better, though still sobering: More than one-third drop out of high school, and less than 6 percent make it to university (Documentary and Advisory Center on Racial Discrimination 2004, annex 3, tables 4 and 5). In Italy the failure rate among children of Moroccan descent was 0.7, 19.6, and 24.7 percent at the primary, middle, and high school levels, respectively (Luciak 2004).

In France, home to the largest and most settled Arab population, performance is better but still lags the general population: The rates of university attendance for Moroccans (16.4 percent) and Algerians (8.5 percent) are lower than their shares in high schools (Moroccans, 26.2 percent; and Algerians, 10.6 percent) implying that their rate of matriculation to university is lower than the rest of the population's (Luciak 2004). These outcomes may in part be related to discriminatory attitudes among the native French: A survey conducted by The Pew Global Attitudes Project (2003) found that a bare majority (51 percent) of French respondents indicated that North African immigrants have a bad influence on the nation.

Once at university, the evidence is mixed: In Denmark the Lebanese exhibit among the highest dropout rates, and among immigrants and foreigners attending university in Finland, Arabs (along with Estonians) have the highest rate of graduation. But the raw numbers in these Nordic countries are small.

In France, which alone accounts for almost half of the European Arabs, among those attending university the female share is noticeably low (35 percent for Moroccans, 42 percent for Algerians). In the case of Germany the difference is even more stark: Only about one of eight Arab students in German universities is a permanent resident of Germany, but of these, the children of parents who never obtained German citizenship, 80 percent of university attendees are male. From the standpoint of gender equity this difference is regrettable, but given that males have a higher propensity to immigrate, they represent a pool of university-educated potential returnees. Two-thirds of these Arab and Arab permanent resident students in German universities study mathematics, engineering, or natural sciences (Will and Rühl 2004, tables 20, 21, and 23), one of the few optimistic results in terms of potential technology transfers.

Outside the classroom, labor-market participation is low, and rates of unemployment are multiples of the national populations as a whole. For example, in 2000–2001, unemployment among Moroccans averaged 10 percent (8 percent for men, 15 percent for women) compared with 3 percent for the Dutch population as a whole (2 percent for men, 4 percent for women). But beyond the rate of unemployment, the Moroccans exhibit very low rates of labor participation with almost two-thirds of Moroccan adults classified as "inactive" (Houtzager and Rodrigues 2002, tables 4 and 6). Mohammed Bouyeri, who killed Dutch filmmaker Theo van Gogh, reportedly had been living on unemployment compensation for more than two years at the time of the murder.

Similar patterns can be seen in the Finnish data: Rates of unemployment are multiples of the rest of the population, and there is marked disparity between male and female performance. Statistics from the Ministry of Labor indicate that in 2000 more than three-quarters of Iraqis and more than half of Moroccans were unemployed in comparison to one-third of foreigners as a group and one-eighth of the population as a whole. For the Moroccans in particular the average masks very different rates of employment among men and women. For their part, the Arabs report considerable discrimination in employment practices (Finnish League for Human Rights 2002, tables 2 and 4).

Across Europe, those who were recruited during the period of high demand for unskilled labor in the 1970s tend to have "the lowest level of education and are predominantly employed in occupations requiring only low qualifications" and tend to be overrepresented in service-sector jobs such as cleaning and restaurant work (ICMPD 2003, 41). This pattern is not universal: In the Netherlands, Moroccans have a noticeable presence in blue-collar manufacturing jobs. Potential returnees from this community have undoubtedly acquired transferable skills on the job that under the right circumstances could prove valuable in developing or staffing manufacturing establishments linked to global supply networks. However, this group is aging and is unlikely to be the source of entrepreneurial talent that could break into these networks. The issue is whether it is plausible for the relatively limited numbers of technically trained university graduates to do so.

The European Muslims have significantly more positive views of Westerners and the West than their coreligionists (The Pew Global Attitudes Project 2006a). The French Arabs come mostly from Algeria and Morocco. Today those countries have better democracy scores than Taiwan or South Korea did in 1973 or 1980, the years that the Institute for Technological Research and Innovation (ITRI) and the Hsinchu Science Park, respectively, were established. Admittedly there is more to life than Polity IV ratings, but at least on this indicator of democracy, the degree of local political repression would not appear to be an insurmountable barrier to attracting returnees.

How about income? The data in table 2.6 indicate that between 1970 and 1980, per capita incomes in Taiwan and South Korea were 22 to 37 percent of the OECD average in terms of purchasing power parity. In comparison, the 2000 figures for Algeria and Morocco are 20 and 15 percent, respectively. So an Algerian or Moroccan returning home today would be returning to a society that in relative terms was about as poor as or poorer than what Taiwanese or Korean returnees faced a generation ago when there was in fact little return migration, this phenomenon beginning in the 1980s when both nations had further closed the relative income gap and afforded opportunities in higher-technology sectors.[14] Parenthetically, among the non–oil based Arab economies, Tunisia stands out with an income level 28 percent of the OECD average—almost precisely the mid-point defined by the Taiwanese and South Korean data from the 1970s, indicating that it is approaching the relative income position that the Asians had attained when they began attracting large numbers of returnees.

A final, and critical, issue is public policy. Taiwan actively recruited returnees. Would Algeria or Morocco (or any of the Arab countries for that matter) welcome an influx of educated risk takers? The role for returnees as a link between the local economies of the Middle East and developed economies may be limited. The number of potential returnees is large; the issue relative to the examples of other countries such as India or Korea is the extent of high-level industrial experience—the Taiwanese were able to recruit émigrés who had jobs at major high-technology firms, and Indians who contributed to the rise of that country's software industry may not have returned but helped from California. The above calculations establish a large potential reservoir of unknown capability.

Potential Role of Reverse Migration

The potential channels of human capital technology transfer would appear to be the greatest between North America and the Eastern Mediterranean on the one hand and Western Europe and the Maghreb on the other. But for this transfer to be effective, the countries of return will have to make themselves more attractive destinations, including by improving security of property rights and social stability. The brain drain will not be reversed unless returnees are confident that they will not be subject to economic predation and that their families will be safe. It may also be necessary to develop specific policy supports to lure back entrepreneurs, as was done in the case of Taiwan. Generic improvements in the protection of property rights and physical stability would also make the local environment more attractive to foreign counterparts and investors more broadly.

The benefits of externally provided skills may be understood in terms of the Nelson-Phelps framework used in chapter 6. These skills provide the education base that can fruitfully absorb foreign technology inflows whether of equipment or production and marketing knowledge, thus substituting for absent local competence. But such imported skills cannot fill all local gaps—a literate-numerate labor force must be present (see Noland and Pack [2003] on the skills present in Japan, South Korea, and Taiwan in the 1950s), and public infrastructure ranging from roads, ports,

---

14. Between 1971 and 1993, the rate of return of Taiwanese students ranged between 16 and 22 percent. The rate of return for Koreans with science or engineering PhDs was less than 10 percent (Smith 2000).

and telecommunications needs to be present, though as the Indian case demonstrates, the private sector can provide some of it.

Given the limited extent of existing manufacturing activity in the Middle East, and the absence of local equivalents to the Indian Institutes of Technology, it is possible that the spurt of labor-intensive exports necessary for employment growth would not materialize, even if accompanied by additional reform. China, the earlier Asian exporters, and now increasingly India have established positions in major product lines. Free trade agreements might provide preferential access to the European and US markets but are unlikely to completely offset existing cost differentials relative to incumbent Asian producers. Outsourcing of white-collar jobs from Francophone Europe is a possibility for the Maghreb, but none of the Arab countries can compete with India, the Philippines, or even China in terms of the number of well-educated English speakers.

It might be tempting for governments to introduce industrial policy—picking niche sector winners—but evidence on the success of such programs is not encouraging (Noland and Pack 2003), and earlier attempts to do precisely this, especially in Egypt, were demonstrated failures (Hansen and Marzouk 1965). While Egypt, a fairly large country, could follow a domestically oriented strategy that did not rely on exports, it would probably entail slower growth than is required to absorb the rapidly growing labor force. To expand rapidly based largely on domestic skills will take considerable time—mastery of production technology and marketing are slow processes. Thus some utilization of foreign skills whether through FDI, joint ventures, consultants, or intensive technology licensing will be necessary for rapid growth. Although a template exists from East Asia, its implementation in the Arab economies may face significant social and political obstacles, an issue discussed below.

Role of Foreign Investment

Direct investment is the fastest-growing segment of cross-border capital flows. Although the theoretical impact of foreign investment on economic performance is ambiguous, most research suggests that it is positively correlated with growth, at least conditional on education, financial-market development, and trade policy openness, though the causality relationships among these variables are subject to dispute (Gao 2005).[15] As ob-

---

15. Recent empirical work suggests that FDI inflows are growth-promoting conditional on outward orientation (Balasubramanyam, Salisu, and Sapsford 1996), education (Borensztein, De Gregorio, and Lee 1999), and financial-sector development (Alfaro et al. 2003). The impact of FDI in the presence of a distorted trade regime is more controversial, however. It is theoretically possible that capital inflows that are FDI induced into a protected capital-intensive import-competing sector could actually be immiserating (Bhagwati and Srinivasan 1983), though the likelihood of this extreme result is subject to dispute.

served in chapter 4, traditionally Arab countries have attracted relatively little foreign direct investment (FDI), especially outside the extractive sector (table 4.9). In recent years there has been a surge in FDI, but it is unclear how much of that is a product of a possibly unsustainable rise in oil prices and in some countries one-off privatizations that can temporarily boost the FDI figures. Most analyses conclude that the Middle East and North Africa (MENA) has "underperformed" with respect to attracting FDI (Nugent 2001, Nugent and De Alencar Loiola 2003, World Bank 2003a). Likewise, portfolio investment has been low (table 4.12), though recently it has surged, driven by rising oil prices, attempts to improve the quality of local financial markets, and a post–September 11 increase in regional home-bias.

There are a variety of reasons why the region has attracted little inward investment, just as there are multiple motives on the part of investors. In the case of the oil exporters, natural resource–derived rents have provided plenty of investable capital, and nationalization of the oil sector has meant little opportunity for foreign investment in the economy's dominant sector. Foreign firms play important roles in this sector, though generally not as investors.

For the nonoil economies where the likely sectors of investment have been manufacturing or services, local conditions have not been particularly propitious. One can think of direct investment occurring both "horizontally" across countries, as multinational firms reproduce similar activities across countries with similar incomes and endowments, and "vertically" across countries of differing incomes and endowments as these firms disaggregate the production process and geographically site activities to minimize costs.[16] David L. Carr, James R. Markusen, and Keith E. Maskus (2001) produce an elegant synthesis of these approaches, but their model is highly stylized, and its implications are rejected by the data (Blonigen and Wang 2005).

One is left with an empirical literature that for the most part attempts to explain the bilateral volume of FDI flows using gravity-type models in which investment flows are functions of income and transaction costs (often proxied by physical distance—hence the "gravity" moniker), augmented by specific considerations, such as the role of trade barriers (e.g., Park and Lippoldt 2003), taxes (e.g., Park and Lippoldt 2003, Grubert and Mutti 2000, Mutti and Grubert 2004), corruption (e.g., Wei 2000), intellectual property rights protection (e.g., Park and Lippoldt 2003), financial-sector development (e.g., Albuquerque, Loayza, and Servén 2005), market potential (e.g., Carstensen and Toubal 2004, Cieślik and Ryan 2004), and local population health status (e.g., Alsan, Bloom, and Canning 2004). Moreover, these determinants likely interact—e.g., FDI inflows are positively associated with high incomes together with large host markets (FDI

---

16. Caves (1996) contains a survey of this literature.

to serve the local market—for example Honda in the United States) or low wage rates together with trade openness (think consumer electronics assembly for export in China).

The sheer multiplicity of motivations and models covered by the common rubric of "foreign direct investment" raises deep specification issues; there is no meta-model template, and there will probably never be one. That said some correlates appear to be robust. Corporate tax rates are almost always negatively associated with FDI. Trade openness is generally associated with FDI (with the caveat that the "jumping the tariff wall" effect works in the opposite direction). As alluded to previously, privatizations are generally associated with at least temporarily increased FDI inflows. If one runs through these kinds of considerations—taxes, trade openness, and privatization—plus intellectual property rights protection, corruption, financial-sector development, and local market size, among others, the Arab countries would not be expected to score particularly well or attract large volumes of inward investment.

But the studies that have examined this issue from a MENA perspective generally go further and conclude that inward flows are not only low as might be expected on the basis of the fundamentals but also below the norm. What could explain this differentially substandard performance?

One possible explanation for this relative dearth of inward capital flows is that foreign investors attach a relatively high subjective assessment of risk to investment in the region. Terrorists have a long history of targeting foreign investments, and in a world of mobile capital where investors can choose across alternative locations, terrorist risk can significantly deter FDI inflows (Abadie and Gardeazabal 2005, Lutz and Lutz 2006). Table 9.5 reports percentile ranking of the Arab and comparator countries on the perceived business costs of terrorism. To be clear, these perceptions may not coincide with actual costs or risks, but they do reveal how 7,000 business executives—presumably the class that is making investment decisions over alternative locations—interviewed in the first five months of 2005 viewed the world. And in fact the rating is highly correlated with FDI inflows.[17]

From the standpoint of the Middle East, the results are not good. Jordan is the region's best scoring country, placing it at the global sample median, followed closely by Tunisia (58th percentile). The remaining three Arab countries—Morocco, Algeria, and Egypt—fall into the worst quintile of the distribution. While this intra-MENA ranking might coincide with one's prior expectations about the relative costs, the scores for the other comparators raise questions about what is being captured in this ranking. The United States scores poorly on this measure; Taiwan, which has mili-

---

17. The simple correlation coefficient is 0.34 for a sample of 94 countries, significantly different from zero at the 1 percent level.

Table 9.5   Macroeconomic environment: Business costs of terrorism

Country	Percentile rank[a]
Middle East	
Algeria	87
Egypt	90
Jordan	50
Morocco	83
Tunisia	58
High-performing comparators	
South Korea	38
Taiwan	57
Large comparators	
China	43
India	68
Normally endowed comparators	
Bangladesh	96
Brazil	2
Pakistan	80
Turkey	72
Resource-rich comparators	
Botswana	40
Indonesia	85
Nigeria	63
Venezuela	77

a. Larger value indicates a higher business cost of terrorism.

Source: World Economic Forum, *Global Competitiveness Report 2004–2005.*

tary tensions with China, but no internal terrorist threat to speak of, lags Jordan and is well behind China, which does occasionally experience terrorist incidents. This may simply be indicative of the difficulty of people with local knowledge to relate their circumstances to a broader set of comparators beyond their immediate region. Nevertheless, at a minimum the results underscore that some Arab countries are perceived to be highly risky or costly places in which to do business.

The economic impact of such perceptions does not appear trivial, even if the precise implications are uncertain or speculative. As an illustration, according to a regression model of FDI, if Egypt, Algeria, and Morocco were to achieve the plausible goal of reducing the perceived business cost of terrorism in their economies to the level achieved in Tunisia or Jordan, the best among the regional countries surveyed, and roughly at the median of the global rankings, the projected increases in FDI inflows would be 31, 25, and 17 percent, respectively.[18] Conversely, Alberto Abadie and Javier Gardeazabal (2005) estimate that a one standard deviation increase in the terrorist risk induces a fall in the net FDI position of roughly 5 percent of GDP.

Moreover, economic risks are not limited to terrorism. The responses revealed in the 2002 Pew Global Attitudes Project discussed in chapter 7 revealed a considerable degree of cross-country variation in attitudes toward globalization in both its economic and noneconomic dimensions, with the citizenries of the Arab countries surveyed evincing decidedly ambivalent attitudes toward globalization and the expansion of cross-border economic exchange. These attitudes in turn potentially raise red flags about the reception that foreign investors are likely to receive from government officials, their employees, suppliers, and customers. From the standpoint of public policy the risks include direct as well as indirect expropriation through the ex post imposition of policies such as new labor regulations, corporate taxes, or restrictions on the repatriation of capital. Popular attitudes may also signal the degree of security risk—the possibility that local staff or facilities could be subject to harassment or attack.

These observations coincide with a growing body of evidence that suggests that international exchange may be less frictionless and such concerns may play a bigger role in determining outcomes than economists might have once believed. Noland (2005b) integrates the previously discussed Pew survey data into a series of economic models that explain FDI, where the investor is foreign and has a physical presence; sovereign bond ratings and spreads, where the investor is foreign but has no physical presence in which local public opinion may constrain official policy; and local entrepreneurs, who have a physical presence but are indigenous. The results indicate that the cross-national responses to a number of Pew survey questions correlate with economic variables of interest and appear to convey information about risk beyond what can be explained by fundamentals such as corporate taxes or trade openness and, by extension, outcomes.

The general pattern that emerges—stronger correlation between the Pew survey responses and FDI that involves the physical presence of a for-

---

18. The following results were obtained for a regression of the FDI inflow share of GDP 1997–2002 on the corporate tax rate, the Transparency International indicator of the absence of corruption, a privatization indicator, OECD membership, and the business cost of terrorism score, all in logs:

$$\text{FDI} = 2.4 - 0.55\text{OECD} - 1.30\text{TAX} + 0.73\text{NOCORRUPTION} + 0.56\text{PRIVATIZATION}$$
$$(0.92) \quad (-1.77)^c \quad (-2.21)^b \quad (2.72)^a \quad (1.68)^c$$

$$+ \ 1.14\text{TERRORISM}$$
$$(1.70)^c$$

$n = 47$, $R^2 = 0.43$. T-statistics are in parentheses. The designation "a" indicates a coefficient significantly different from zero at the 1 percent level; "b" at the 5 percent level; and "c" at the 10 percent level.

eign entity as distinct from purely financial transactions or the presence of indigenous entrepreneurs—suggests that the pattern of cross-national responses may contain information about subjective assessments of security risk. Foreign direct investors may be particularly sensitive to antiglobalization sentiment inasmuch as they are subject to both political risk at the policy level and, to a much greater extent than portfolio investors, direct security risk to themselves, their employees, and their facilities.[19] Further, the Pew responses that are more highly correlated with cross-border economic outcomes tend to be ones relating to basic notions of tolerance and absence of chauvinism and xenophobia than to attitudes toward the more narrowly economic manifestations of globalization per se. The unsurprising exception to this pattern regards the prevalence of local entrepreneurship where it is fundamental attitudes toward markets, not globalization, that matter—and where the pattern of Arab responses relative to those obtained in other regions do not appear distinctive.

To get a sense of how quantitatively significant the public attitude variables are, the following calculation was performed. The exclusively OECD-member North America and Western Europe regions were excluded, and a "best practice" standard was formed by averaging the highest Pew survey score from each of the remaining predominantly non-OECD member regions. So, for example, for the "international economic organizations are good" question, this "non-OECD best practice" score is 75 (the simple average of Guatemala, 73; Slovakia, 74; Côte d'Ivoire, 87; Vietnam, 85; Uzbekistan, 85; and Jordan, 44). The estimated coefficients were then used to calculate the increase in FDI that would be associated with an increase in a country's actual score to the best practice score. Egypt, Jordan, and Lebanon were the only Arab countries covered in the Pew report, and even in these cases, missing data sometimes make calculating these kinds of counterfactuals impossible. Nevertheless, in cases where it is possible to perform such counterfactual calculations, the potential increases appear significant, implying a near doubling of FDI inflows in the cases of Jordan and Lebanon.[20]

These results suggest one impediment to cross-border integration, namely the role that popular attitudes may play in generating subjective assessments of risk. These attitudes toward globalization are most important with respect to FDI in which the investor is both foreign and physically present and relatively less important with respect to portfolio investment where there is no physical presence or entrepreneurship by in-

---

19. In contrast, Jonathan Eaton and Mark Gersovitz (1984) argue that foreign direct investors may actually be less subject to expropriation than portfolio investors since FDI often is associated with an intangible asset that is difficult to expropriate.

20. These effects are not limited to FDI. Noland (2005b) reports a similar analysis of sovereign ratings, another measure of risk, in this case the risk of default on a financial obligation. For Jordan and Lebanon, attainment of the non-OECD "best practice" would be associated with a single step-change upgrade implying a 65 basis point improvement in sovereign borrowing costs.

digenous residents. Moreover, among the Pew responses, those relating to general notions of tolerance, lack of chauvinism, and xenophobia are significant more frequently than those relating to more narrowly economic manifestations of globalization per se, and the magnitudes of the estimated coefficients are large in the sense that changes in public attitudes of plausible magnitudes imply economically meaningful changes in FDI and sovereign debt ratings. For many countries, reducing terrorism risks and/ or transforming public perceptions toward globalization could improve significantly the terms on which globalization occurs.

Affinity, Democracy, and Risk

The discussion thus far has proceeded from the standpoint of the potential of local attitudes to constrain the pace, depth, and modality of cross-border economic integration. Of course it takes two to tango, and while social opposition to integration may exist on the recipient side, the same sorts of issues may exist symmetrically on the sender side as well.

Again, we cannot observe these risk assessments directly, but recent research on trade flows provides some intriguing clues that presumably apply to other forms of economic exchange as well, including investment. There is evidence that terrorism, which disproportionately afflicts the Middle East, inhibits trade (Barth et al. 2006, Blomberg and Hess 2006). There is also some evidence that the degree of cross-national trust or affinity may have a significant impact on the volume of trade.[21]

Since 1978, the Chicago Council on Foreign Relations (CCFR) has sponsored quadrennial surveys of US public attitudes on foreign policy issues.[22] One aspect of these polls has been to survey American public opinion by asking respondents to rate their feelings toward other countries on a scale of 0 to 100, with higher figures indicating greater affinity. Table 9.6 reports the rankings from the initial survey in 1978 and the most recent survey conducted in 2002. The results are not enormously surprising: Canada and the United Kingdom, countries with which the United States has long historical and cultural ties, are at the top of the table in both the initial and terminal years of the sample. Some countries exhibit significant

---

21. Luigi Guiso, Paola Sapienza, and Luigi Zingales (2004) argue that cultural distance or trust is a robust explanatory variable of the volume of international trade in goods in the context of a conventional gravity model, with a one standard deviation increase in trust of the importer toward the exporter increasing exports by 32 percent. Similarly, Noland (2005b) finds that a one standard deviation increase in affinity, proxied by the Chicago Council on Foreign Relations "temperature" score, is associated with a 20 to 31 percent larger volume of bilateral trade between the United States and its trade partners when evaluating the sample means. Richard Portes and Helene Rey (2005) extend this kind of analysis to portfolio flows.

22. See Chicago Council on Foreign Relations (2004) for a description of the survey methodology.

**Table 9.6   Chicago Council on Foreign Relations
"temperature data," 1978 and 2002**

Country	1978	Country	2002
Canada	72	Canada	77
Great Britain	67	Great Britain	76
France	62	Italy	65
Israel	61	Germany	61
Mexico	58	Japan	60
Germany (West)	57	Mexico	60
Italy	56	Brazil	55
Japan	56	France	55
Brazil	52	Israel	55
Taiwan	51	Russia	55
Iran	50	Poland	50
Poland	50	South Africa	50
India	49	Taiwan	50
Saudi Arabia	48	China	48
South Korea	48	Argentina	47
South Africa	46	India	46
China	44	South Korea	46
Russia (Soviet Union)	34	Egypt	45
Cuba	32	Turkey	45
Afghanistan	n.a.	Nigeria	42
Argentina	n.a.	Colombia	36
Colombia	n.a.	Cuba	35
Egypt	n.a.	North Korea	34
Iraq	n.a.	Saudi Arabia	33
Nigeria	n.a.	Pakistan	31
North Korea	n.a.	Afghanistan	29
Pakistan	n.a.	Iran	28
Turkey	n.a.	Iraq	23

n.a. = not available

Note: Higher figure indicates greater affinity of US public toward country.

Sources: Chicago Council on Foreign Relations, WorldViews 2002, Topline Data from US Public Survey.

changes in "temperature" (CCFR's term) over the sample period, however. Iran, for example, falls 22 points, and the Soviet Union/Russia rises 21, presumably reflecting the major political changes within these two entities and in their diplomatic relations with the United States during the sample period.

Saudi Arabia was the only Arab country included in the initial survey in 1978; between 1978 and 1998 its temperature fluctuated in the intermediate range of 46–53, before falling dramatically to 33 in 2002, actually scoring lower than North Korea and Cuba. The precipitous decline in public esteem was presumably driven by the identification of Saudi Arabia with the September 11 terrorist attacks, in which a majority of the hijackers were Saudis. Iraq was added to the sample in 1990 and was the least liked country in that and each subsequent poll, with a temperature ranging from 20 to 25. If nothing else, this suggests that American antipathy toward Iraq, or more probably the political regime of Saddam Hussein, did not begin with the George W. Bush administration. Egypt was added to the most recent poll sample and scored 45, putting it in the same league of American affection as Turkey, India, and South Korea.[23]

Affinity between the United States and other countries is determined, in turn, by observable cultural and ideological markers: specifically, the extent of ethnic and religious similarity in the counterpart population, the degree of partner country democracy, and whether the other country has a Communist government, with the last being the most robust correlate with affinity or in this case the lack thereof. Americans mildly prefer countries that have populations ethnically and religiously like themselves, but they like other democracies, and they really dislike Communists (Noland 2005c). For Americans, it appears that ideology trumps race.

American anti-Communism is not an issue for the Middle East, but the lack of democracy harkens back to the observation in chapter 1, that as a region, the Middle East is the least democratic in the world (figure 1.4). And while it is difficult to alter ethnic or religious affinity through public policy, the link between trade and democracy, and the presumably easier time that a more democratic government would have concluding a preferential trade arrangement with the United States, hold out at least the possibility of a virtuous circle in which political liberalization would be reinforced by prosperity through successful globalization.

Conclusion

A major question facing the Arab countries is whether even if they reform their economic policies an adequate entrepreneurial response will be forthcoming from local firms, native born who have emigrated, or foreign in-

---

23. Comparable data on European attitudes does not appear to exist, but if the previously cited data on attitudes toward immigrants from different sender countries is interpreted as a proxy for more general attitudes toward the sender countries, it is unlikely that European attitudes toward Middle Eastern countries are markedly better than those reported here. At least one bit of evidence would appear to suggest that affinity between Europeans and Arabs is not particularly high: When asked their reaction to the prospect of increased immigration by various nationalities, Arabs came in next to last (beating out Somalis), with less than 40 percent of Finns receptive. Moroccans were distinguished as a separate group and fared somewhat better than Arabs, while still less than 40 percent were welcoming, but Moroccans were preferred to Russians, Kurds, and Turks (in addition to Arabs and Somalis) (Finnish League of Human Rights 2002, figure 2).

vestors. Under current conditions, for differing reasons in each case, it is not obvious that any one of the three groups—local firms and entrepreneurs, returnees, and foreign firms and investors—will exhibit a strong, positive response to policy. The main constraint on local entrepreneurs in the manufacturing sector would appear to be a lack of technical capacity, though admittedly a negative statement is difficult to prove, and we would welcome being proved wrong.

With respect to returnees, the problem is twofold, relating both to the sender communities and the host countries of return. The sender communities of the Arab diaspora are located primarily in Western Europe and secondarily in North America. The North American community appears to have the requisite skills but is strongly oriented toward two countries, Egypt and Lebanon, and for reasons of age and possibly religious affiliation, it is questionable whether this community could be a source of large numbers of returnee entrepreneurs. A younger, less settled segment of the North American community might ultimately have a larger impact.

The size of the Arab community in Europe is at least four times as large as in the United States, and has the further advantage of geographical proximity. However, unlike the highly accomplished Arab-American community, the issue with this community is whether it has the necessary skills to play a synaptic role between its countries of origin, primarily Morocco, and the global community.

The last issue is with respect to the countries of return. Obviously the effective utilization of returnees is predicated on addressing the underlying microeconomic impediments to economic activity. Conditional on these being addressed, returnees could be a source of revitalization. The example of Taiwan suggests that Jeffersonian democracy is not a necessary condition for luring expatriate talent home. Political stability, protection of property rights, physical safety, and a supportive policy environment probably are.

The same sorts of considerations enter into the decision making of the third source of supply response, foreign firms and investors. Faced with a variety of locations to choose from, the apparent ambivalence prevalent across the Middle East with respect to cross-border economic integration and globalization more broadly appears to raise the subjective assessment of risk that foreigners attach to economic interaction with the Arab economies. We have shown that in some cases reductions in risk might lead to increases in FDI of 30 percent or more. Political liberalization and a more secure and predictable domestic policy environment could contribute directly and indirectly to increased trade as well. Admittedly much of this evidence is more fragmentary, indirect, and circumstantial than we would like. That said, it all points in the same direction: Risk significantly reduces the volume and implicitly the terms on which cross-border economic exchange occurs. Reducing this risk premium would contribute to regional prosperity.

Political liberalization could contribute to such an outcome. However, while there are rising demands within the region for political liberalization, and indeed considerable ferment within some countries of late, it is not clear that these demands for greater internal political openness encompass economic reform or embody greater receptivity to foreign influences on a variety of dimensions.

The problem for any incumbent government is the lack of obvious policy instruments to address these underlying popular concerns on the one hand and reduce the perceived risk of the local business environment on the other. Public campaigns to stress the opportunities presented by globalization could be aimed at the former, while receptivity to the latter could be signaled by participating in preferential trade agreements as discussed in the previous chapter. Needless to say, neither are panaceas. And while in the long run democratization may reduce the likelihood of instability and indeed contribute to a virtuous circle of reform and prosperity, piloting the transition is not simple, particularly in societies in which political opposition is increasingly expressed in religious terms. We turn to this issue in the next chapter.

Appendix 9A

Table 9A.1 Lower-bound estimates of Arabs in Europe (thousands)

Country	Year[a]	Number of Arabs
Austria	2001	8
Naturalized citizens from:		
Egypt		5
Iraq		2
Tunisia		1
Belgium[b]	2000	96
Denmark	2002	56
Morocco		8
Iraq		22
Jordan		2
Lebanon		21
Syria		3
France[c]	1999	3,380
Foreign citizens, immigrants, and foreigners by origin from:		
Algeria		1,776
Morocco		1,604
Germany	2001	198
Immigrants from:		
Morocco		79
Lebanon		49
Tunisia		24
Naturalized citizens from:		
Morocco		30
Lebanon		16
Italy[b]	2001	197
Netherlands	2002	340
Immigrants from:		
Morocco		159
Iraq		41
Egypt		16
Foreign-born parent:		
Morocco		124
Spain[b]	2001	247
Sweden (foreign-born, Iraq)	2003	63
Implied total		4,585

a. Latest year for which data are available.
b. Implied total based on data in ICMPD (2003, tables A1 and A2).
c. Percentages of Algerian and Moroccan immigrants are applied to foreign citizen and foreigner by origin totals to estimate the number of Arab immigrants in France.

Notes: Countries reported in this table use different protocols for counting immigrants, so the format differs from country to country. Subtotals may not add up due to rounding error.

Sources: Austria: Ludwig Boltzman Institute (2003, table 9); Denmark: Documentary and Advisory Center on Racial Discrimination (2004, annex 3, table 1); Germany: Hönekopp, Will, and Rühl (2002, table 9) and Will and Rühl (2004, table 33); The Netherlands: Schreimer (2004, table 1); Sweden: Mulinari (2004, table 13).

10

Authoritarianism, Uncertainty, and Prospects for Change

The Arab world is unique in the prevalence of long-lived, undemocratic regimes consisting largely of monarchies exhibiting varying degrees of liberalism and authoritarian states applying repression of varying intensities. These governments face rising internal demands for political liberalization. The period 2005–06 witnessed an "Arab Spring" illustrated by general elections in Iraq, Lebanon, and the Palestinian Authority; municipal elections in Saudi Arabia; women's candidacies in Kuwait; and the establishment of a truth and reconciliation commission in Morocco, among other developments. This flowering was followed by retrenchments in Egypt, Syria, and a number of other Arab countries. This "two steps forward, one step back" pattern is consistent with quantitative modeling of political regime scoring systems such as those of the Polity IV Project or Freedom House, which can be used to calculate the timing and magnitude of political change. As discussed in detail in appendix 10A, these models point to rising (though nonmonotonic) odds on the probability of liberalizing transitions as illustrated in figure 10.1, derived from a fairly standard model from this genre.[1]

---

1. Such episodes are typically defined as a three-point or more *positive* (though not necessarily irreversible) change in the democracy score over a period of three years or less, at any given point in time. Examples of such liberalizing episodes in the sample would include Spain's transition from the Franco regime to parliamentary democracy in 1975, the 1985 end of military rule in Brazil, South Korea's transition to civilian government in 1987, the 1989–90 collapse of the Ceauşescu regime and the beginning of democracy in Romania, and South Africa's postapartheid transition during 1992–94. Among Arab countries, past examples of such episodes would include political reforms initiated in Tunisia in 1987 and in Algeria and Jordan in 1989. See Carothers (2002) for a thoughtful critique of the assumptions underlying the democratic transition literature. For expositional convenience, "liberalizing" and "democratizing" will be used interchangeably, keeping in mind Carothers's admonition that the two are not identical.

Figure 10.1   Likelihood of liberalizing transition, 1970–99

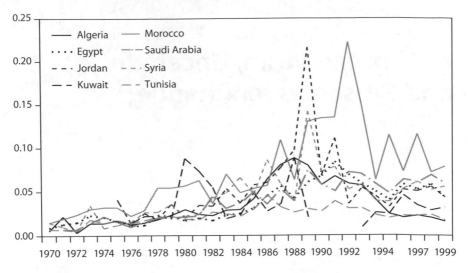

Source: Noland (2005c, figure 3).

The statistical models, however, cannot speak to the nature of such transitions or the character of successor regimes. It is almost a truism that most of the countries in the region, including large, important nations such as Egypt and Saudi Arabia, face deep uncertainties about their political futures.

How might it matter for economic performance? Political liberalization could affect performance through multiple channels. Perhaps the most profound effect would be by empowering constituencies in favor of dismantling the rent-creating distortions that underpin many incumbent Arab governments, along the lines discussed in chapter 7. But this is not the only avenue. A more liberal polity, generating greater popular consent, even if not necessarily fully democratic, may be a requirement to make commitments to future policies more credible and to reduce political and security risk assessments.

These considerations are economically relevant. Investment by its very nature involves irreversibility, and fundamental uncertainty about the future environment impedes it. Who would invest in tourism facilities, for example, if a future government might close down the tourism sector as un-Islamic or if such assets become a primary target of opposing sides in a violent political struggle? Or given a choice between locating a multibillion-dollar computer chip fabrication plant in a politically stable country like Costa Rica or a Middle Eastern country characterized by fundamental questions about the viability of the political regime, who would choose the Middle East? In societies that do not possess technical abilities in manufacturing or services, a reversal of the considerable brain drain that has occurred could fill a major gap. Foreign direct investment (FDI) and foreign consultants could also supply missing skills. The presence of buyer- and seller-led international production networks can be critical components of a development strategy (Gereffi 1999). The willingness of foreign and local actors to undertake long-term commitments will be enhanced by a democratic regime that is less likely to encounter violent opposition and may be more likely to live up to its commitments, whether tariff reforms or levels of taxation. External terrorism, which has often had the backing, explicit or not, of governments as a method of defusing internal opposition in the absence of a democratic process, has had underappreciated negative effects on the perceptions of investors and potential returnees.

In this chapter we address a series of issues relating to the nature of the Middle East's political regimes and how the region's political evolution could affect its economics. We first sketch out alternative reform paths, then assess the implications for external exchange and integration, and finally confront the bottom-line question: What are the prospects for change?

Path to Political Reform

In the long run, political liberalization could contribute to a virtuous cycle of reduced subjective assessments of risk and yield globalization on improved terms. However, as documented in chapter 7, today local attitudes toward enhanced cross-border economic integration are at best ambivalent, and the legacy of Arab socialism has created an unusual situation in which the middle class may be in favor of political liberalization but skeptical about the benefits of economic reform. A minority of the respondents in Arab countries supported the closure of large inefficient factories, even if it led to improved outcomes in the future.

Sufficiently creative and entrepreneurial political regimes may initiate reforms to increase their domestic legitimacy as in the case of the Asian countries of the 1960s, China in the late 1970s, and perhaps Chile after the dictatorship established by Augusto Pinochet in 1973. Others such as India in 1991 and many of the Latin American reformers of the 1980s responded to requirements by either the international financial institutions or other creditors. In many Arab countries, the quest for greater internal support has been relatively muted, perhaps reflecting the very strength in many social indicators ranging from income distribution to life expectancy (tables 3.1 to 3.5). On the other hand, there has been considerable grumbling about unemployment (table 3.7), stagnating urban wages (table 3.8), and more recently, corruption, nepotism, and democracy.

One problem in the Arab countries is that external events and their history have not catalyzed a political agenda for improved economic policy but are utilized precisely to offer excuses for the difficulty of reform. For decades governments have partly deflected attention from low income levels by focusing popular attention on external issues: colonialism, the Arab-Israeli conflict, the Egyptian–Saudi Arabian war in Yemen in the 1960s, pan-Arabism, the conflict in Western Sahara between Algeria and Morocco, the Iraq-Iran war of the 1980s, Libya's war with Chad, and the Iraqi invasion of Kuwait (used by Kuwait to partly explain its declining real GDP per capita), and now the US-led invasion of Iraq.[2] In contrast, successful countries have often mobilized their populace around economic growth, putting adversity to good use.[3] As illustrated by the cases of Eastern Europe with the breakup of the Soviet empire or Latin America with its financial crisis and "lost decade," a decisive political break may be needed to dislodge or overwhelm the coalitions in favor of status quo protections.

How moderate Islamist political parties and movements fit in is a matter of considerable controversy (Hamzawy 2005). Incumbent governments in the region may attempt to forestall the development of democratic, liberal, or secular alternatives, so that their publics face a "binary solution" in which the only choices are the relatively soft authoritarianism of the incumbent regimes or an Islamist opposition, betting that when confronted with such a choice, the majority, with resignation, will back the devil they know. Such a gambit may work. Or it may not, and given the possibility of abrupt transition and the pervasive restrictions on free expression that exist in the region, it is no mean task to infer the economic policies of potential successor regimes.

---

2. Gause (1995, 286) is representative of scholarly observers: "Wars tend to concentrate power in the hands of the executive, a power most leaders are loath to give up. Wars make it easier to stigmatize as treasonous, and then suppress, opposition forces. War preparation leads to greater state control over the economy, limiting the power and autonomy of private sector economic actors who might press for democratic reform. War preparation requires building coercive apparatus that then can be used internally. . . ." Eva Bellin (2004, 157) writes, "Besides providing rhetorical legitimization for coercive regimes, persistent conflict has rationalized the prolonged states of emergency that stifle civil liberties in many MENA countries." With respect to the Arab-Israeli conflict, Lisa Anderson (2001, 56) observes, "It may be no coincidence that the prospects for democracy seem to increase in direct proportion to the distance of a country from the Arab-Israeli and Persian Gulf arenas." The last statement has perhaps not aged well: Among Arab polities, Lebanon and Jordan have exhibited some of the greatest progress in political liberalization in recent years.

3. Japan after 1865 consciously tried to emulate and borrow from the West, particularly Prussia. Roughly a century later, South Korea set its sights on catching up with its former imperial master instead of bemoaning its fate under Japanese colonialism. Despite obvious threats from their neighbors, South Korean and Taiwanese leaders emphasized the importance of domestic economic growth as one response and systematically pursued good economic policies (Li 1988, Mason et al. 1980). Singapore under Lee Kuan Yew exceeded the income per capita of its former colonizer, Britain.

In an odd sense these observations echo the concerns expressed in the 1990s with regard to the transition from central planning to the market in Eastern Europe. The two regions exhibit some important similarities such as the existence of inefficient state-owned enterprises, the political dangers of privatization, and the need to introduce a regulatory environment if privatization takes place. There are significant differences as well, particularly that in the Arab countries a substantial percentage of productive assets are privately owned so that less attention has to be given to breaking up state-owned land or factories. Lessons derived from the now large literature on "transition" could be applied to the Middle East. What may be the single most salient lesson from the Eastern European experience is the sheer diversity of post-Communist outcomes: Some countries—the Central Europeans, the Baltics, and parts of Eastern Europe—have made relatively smooth transitions to market economics and democratic politics, while others—most obviously Belarus and parts of Central Asia—remain mired in populism, authoritarianism, and dysfunctional economics. There is nothing to say that the future economic and political trajectories of Arab countries might not be equally diverse.

For heuristic purposes, it might be useful to think about the political economy of reform as occurring through two paths, neither exhaustive nor mutually exclusive. One would be essentially an incremental reform model—essentially the continuation on the path that most of the countries have adopted with varying degrees of enthusiasm and success. Another path is the assumption of power by Islamists, though whether closer to the Turkish or Iranian model is an obviously critical distinction.

In the former case, one is essentially in a familiar pluralistic world where change is a function of the strength of contending forces, mediated by existing institutions. In this context it has been observed that there was a political bias toward maintenance of the status quo—because of the costliness of change and the uncertainty of benefits, even risk-neutral actors would forgo reversible policy changes under certain conditions (Roland 2000). This reluctance to change intensifies if outcomes are uncertain (Fernandez and Rodrik 1991) or obviously if decision making reflects aversion to risk.

Beyond the narrow economic aspects of globalization, however, the Pew data cited in chapter 7 depict societies that on a deeper level are discomfited by the cultural implications of globalization, and herein may lie the biggest differences with the Eastern European experience. One gets the sense that in the case of Eastern Europe, the Western model was attractive in both its political and economic dimensions, and in the realm of economic policy there was no real disagreement about the fundamental value of efficiency but rather a concern about the magnitude and distribution of the payoffs to reform. In the Arab world, the stakes may be higher.

For both the society and the state, aspects of opening could be threatening. Historically, the attitudes of governments in the region might be described as "information averse." Clement M. Henry and Robert Spring-borg (2001), for example, document the widespread abuse of journalists by governments in the region. This aversion extends beyond the human "software" to the hardware itself. The case of Syria is emblematic, if extreme: All typewriters had to be registered with the government and a sample of their typeface provided until the early 1990s, fax machines were prohibited until the latter part of that decade, and the Internet only became available in the country just before the death of strongman Hafez al-Assad in 2000.[4]

Better communications and greater access to the Internet, now part of the conventional wisdom about deficiencies that require improvement (UNDP 2002), also may threaten governments' ability to control the flow of information while increasing the possibility of coordination among opponents.[5] Well-trained software programmers are likely to be able to outwit government efforts to monitor or control e-mail or access to specific Web sites. There are widespread journalistic accounts of the unease with which governments view even the noninteractive availability of al-Jazeera. Satellite television, cellphones, and the Internet have replaced the 19th century's fear of the mimeograph machine as preferred methods of subversion.

Moreover, the history of aborted reform attempts in the Arab countries suggests that given the relative absence of civil society institutions through which to mobilize support, it would be difficult for would-be reformers from within the governing elite to gain backing for their reforms.[6] Instead, the repression of civil society and emasculation of the private sector have left religious institutions and underground groups as among the societal institutions with greatest autonomy from the state. Under such circumstances, it is perhaps not surprising that Islamists have emerged as

---

4. See Kalathil and Boas (2003) on the different responses exhibited by the governments of the United Arab Emirates, Saudi Arabia, and Egypt to the Internet. Daniel Lerner (1958) recounts the responses of Middle Eastern governments to the earlier technology of the newspaper.

5. This is true in democracies as well. The 2003 primary campaign of Democratic presidential contender Howard Dean was financed in large part by contributions solicited over the Internet and bypassed traditional sources of leverage of the Democratic National Committee.

6. For instance, both Algeria and Jordan experienced liberalizing episodes in the context of the worldwide democracy wave of 1989–90. In Algeria, reformers had "global institutional and juridical vision" to move to "contractual relationships between the administration and production of goods and services . . . and to a transparent 'commercializing' of economic transactions" in the public sector (Henry and Springborg 2001, 113). Constitutional changes, which involved a reduction in the dominance of the National Liberation Front and the introduction of multiparty elections, were subsequently reversed, however. Another move toward more representative government began in 1995, following a period marked by extra-constitutional government and widespread political violence. In recent years there has been continued political liberalization, though the armed forces maintain a dominant role in politics, which have arguably not lost their authoritarian character.

the primary locus of opposition to the status quo and the primary beneficiaries of electoral opening.[7] Antigovernment sentiment may have crystallized around the Islamists almost by default given the paucity of secular alternatives, or it may be that clericalism reflects the underlying preferences of the population as some polling data suggest or that in the absence of secular alternatives, the Islamists have succeeded in nurturing proclerical views among the public (Gause 2005).[8]

So while attention often focuses on the effects of reform on different income groups, between workers and owners or rural and city dwellers, and across different regions, in the Middle East political liberalization may raise more profound challenges to the interests of the dominant political, social, and religious institutions. We are not suggesting these are decisive, but surely they are as important as the purely economic issue as usually narrowly construed. The implication of these observations is that reform may be even more difficult in the Middle East than it has been in other countries or regions.

The Arab world as a whole has embraced the market less decisively than the more successful Central and Eastern European countries. The weakness of the domestic civil society institutions, including the media and private business, may inhibit their ability to identify and seize emerging opportunities made possible by reform. The response is likely to be weak, absent a willingness to accept the disruption to well-established networks to extract and allocate rents, foreign collaboration, or both. In a number of the countries, the former importantly rests on political arrangements involving minority groups, which may feel very threatened by alterations in the status quo. Foreign collaboration may be viewed as threatening socially, religiously, and politically. Some Muslim-majority countries in Asia have done very well, particularly Indonesia and Malaysia. Both considerably relied on Chinese entrepreneurs and their substantial international marketing and financial networks. But despite considerable success, un-

---

7. Gause (2005) catalogues recent Islamist electoral triumphs: Morocco (2002), Bahrain (2002), Yemen (2003), and Saudi Arabia (2005). Kuwait (2006) could be added to this list. One observer writing in 2006, argues, "Now, the most vocal supporters of democratization are conservative Islamist politicians, the very people the United States most opposes. The detractors of democratization are liberal voices, the very people the United States most supports" (Alterman 2006, 2).

8. A 2006 poll conducted by the Ibn Khaldun Center of Cairo asked 1,700 Egyptians to identify the most important regional figures (Saad Eddin Ibrahim, "The 'New Middle East' Bush Is Resisting," Washington Post, August 23, 2006). No Arab head of government made the list. Islamists occupied the top five places. In rank order they were Hasan Nasrallah, the leader of Hezbollah; Iranian President Mahmoud Ahmadinejad; Khaled Meshal of Hamas; Osama bin Laden of al Qaeda; and Mohammed Mahdi Akef of Egypt's Muslim Brotherhood. The two secular figures to make the top ten, Palestinian Marwan Barghouti of the Al Aasa Martyrs Brigade and Egyptian politican Ayman Nour.

ease with the Chinese minority is still great, and government policies are undertaken to placate the majority.

The economic implications of xenophobia—in the absence or presence of reform—should not be ignored. Increased foreign interaction is almost surely a necessary condition for generating rapid employment and output growth in the industrial sector, and the global environment in which the Middle East is operating is an increasingly competitive one. The great strides that China has made, and now India, suggest that firms considering FDI, joint ventures, or licensing have a safe, historically tested alternative that benefits from large agglomeration economies (Harrigan and Venables 2004). The special economic zones (SEZs) in China have a quarter century of history, and India is a stable democracy that now provides an inviting climate. Moreover, both countries offer the attraction not only of an export platform, given their relatively low wages, but also huge domestic markets as well, something that Arab countries, even Egypt with the largest population (roughly 65 million), notably do not have. Thus these countries not only are late to globalization but also may suffer disadvantages that are not easily overcome even if there are comprehensive reforms and the anti-Western views can be attenuated or mollified.

The Eastern Europeans were obviously drawn by the cultural, political, and economic centripetal pull of Western Europe. But more broadly, one of the characteristics of reforms in other regions has been the demonstration effect exerted by regional champions. Having noted the success of Japan, South Korea, and Taiwan followed many of its policies once they were independent. In turn, Indonesia, Malaysia, and Thailand followed many of the Korean and Taiwanese policies along with emulation of Singapore's efforts to recruit FDI. Arguably China learned from its Asian neighbors— SEZs, for example, were close replicas of the export processing zones established in South Korea and Taiwan in the 1950s and 1960s. In Latin America, while many reforms were forced by the debt crisis of the early 1980s, the relative success of Chile's liberalization may have played a role in strengthening internal support for reform. From this perspective the Middle East faces the unenviable situation in which its arguably most progressive country and potential model for emulation, Israel, is widely regarded as a pariah, and the natural leader of the Arab world, Egypt, is actually a reform laggard in comparison to some of the smaller Arab states.

In sum, the constraints facing Arab reformers, while more severe, are not that much different from the problems faced in Europe in which reformers have to worry about resurgent Communist or neofascist parties. If much of the support of these extremist groups stems from dissatisfaction with economic outcomes, then they can be kept marginalized by the maintenance of acceptable economic performance. The increasingly religious coloration of opposition in the Middle East, and the centrality of cultural or social issues in the political discourse, suggests that one might imagine heated politics even if economic performance is satisfactory, and especially if that economic success is perceived to be heavily dependent on foreigners or contributing to the erosion of traditional values. Both Malaysia and Indonesia continue to have significant Islamist opposition despite their impressive growth, though this opposition has been expressed overwhelmingly though peaceful and legal channels.

This is the key difference with the Middle East. In Southeast Asia, there is a broad internal consensus about these countries' openness and role in the world—measured by the share of trade in national income, Malaysia is one of the world's most open economies, and when Abdurrahman Wahid (Gus Dur), the leader of the 45-million-member Nahdlatul Ulama, was elected president of Indonesia, he did not engage in radical social engineering. Across the Middle East both the degree of effective pluralism and the legal tolerance of the Islamist opposition vary—sometimes inversely, as in the case of Morocco—as does the zealotry of the Islamist opposition. As a consequence, one can envision much more abrupt transitions, as one of several possible trajectories, and in all likelihood not all countries in the region will follow the same path. Intriguingly, Jordan's Islamic Action Front, the political arm of the Muslim Brotherhood, has cited Malaysia as a model for emulation.[9]

Suppose such an abrupt transition were to occur. Is there anything that can be said about the character of economic policy or outcomes that would be associated with such a transition? There are two ways to go about answering this question. One is to examine the public statements of opposition groups. The other is to derive these prospective policies inductively, under the assumption that their policies would reflect the interests of their core political base.

One possibility is that a newly installed regime would have a fair amount of latitude to change policy, which, if used wisely, could significantly advance reforms. Given what appear to be fairly pervasive attitudes supporting a central role for religion in education among the general public (Zogby International 2005), political opening could empower groups favoring greater reliance on religious education and memorization and less on the cultivation of a questioning mode of thought. Yet a greater emphasis on high-quality technical education, the type needed for absorption of new technology and advocated by the recent *Arab Human Development Reports,* presupposes improved earlier training.

As one might expect, economic policy does not figure prominently in the manifestos of Islamist groups that tend to be more concerned with religious and social policies. Economic positions range from the relatively soft (supporting the development of Islamic financial institutions while grandfathering existing non-Islamic institutions and practices) to the relatively hard (closure of tourism, at least of the non-Islamic sort). Contem-

---

9. Sharmila Devi, "Jordan Turns Its Sights on Muslim Brotherhood," *Financial Times,* June 23, 2006.

porary Iran could probably be taken as a reasonably good approximation of the "hard" position.[10]

Support for this opposition appears to be disproportionately young and urban. As discussed previously, this group has borne the brunt of these countries' inability to generate employment opportunities to match the rapidly growing labor forces. Also, this group does not pay many taxes. Under these circumstances, an Islamist opposition coming to power in one of the relatively resource-scarce Arab economies might well pursue Keynesian-cum-populist fiscal policies to generate a rapid increase in employment, a pattern that would be familiar to students of Latin America or France during the early days of the François Mitterrand presidency. Such initiatives might include both public works projects as well as an expansion of employment in state-owned enterprises or quasi-public religiously controlled conglomerates (*bonyad*) as has occurred in Iran. Such policies could provoke balance-of-payments problems or a collapse of the exchange rate, necessitating an appeal to the International Monetary Fund (IMF), putting into political play domestically the issue of globalization and these newly emergent regimes' relationships to the international economic institutions.

Presumably, these economic developments would be paralleled by discord over domestic social issues. The combination of macroeconomic instability and social unrest would presumably deter new foreign investors from committing and might even spur some incumbents to divest. These actions might be accompanied by capital flight and, in the extreme case, emigration by the elites of the *ancien régime*. Beyond specific issues such as cross-border migration, which could affect particular countries under certain scenarios (i.e., if Morocco experiences upheaval, Spain will be affected) from the standpoint of the economic, as distinct from political, interests of the rest of the world, such developments in the resource-poor

---

10. Iran supports some insurgent groups either out of Shia solidarity or in pursuit of regional hegemony, so the connection is not purely theoretical. Michael Slackman ("Beneath the Rage in the Middle East," *New York Times*, February 12, 2006) provides a detailed account of the economic policies favored by Iranian President Mahmoud Ahmadinejad: "He ordered the banks, for example, to lower interest rates, and was rebuffed by the head of the central bank. He offered to give inexpensive housing loans to the poor—but with only 300,000 available, more than 2 million people applied. The program will cost the government more than $3 billion. He has traveled around the country, promising to dole out development projects the government can hardly afford. In the last year, the cost of construction materials has jumped 30 to 50 percent, and prices of dairy products have increased by more than 15 percent. Many people are asking how this can happen when the price of oil is so high. Without a strong grasp of economics, and an economy that is almost entirely in the hands of the government, Mr. Ahmadinejad has grappled with ways to inject oil revenue into the system without causing inflation to soar. At the same time, the volatile political situation has caused capital flight and limited foreign investment as the needs of the public continue to grow alongside the president's promises." Thus, Ahmadinejad is pursuing a standard inward-looking policy that would have been familiar to Juan Perón in Argentina in 1946.

Arab economies would not be of great consequence—they are not quantitatively important to the world economy. The same is not true for Saudi Arabia, and arguably, Kuwait, Qatar, and the United Arab Emirates, due to the systemic implications of energy supply disruptions emanating from internal political instability.

This negative interpretation of the developments under a sudden transition from one of today's secular authoritarian regimes to an Islamist regime should not be interpreted as a wholesale indictment of Islamism as a political movement—abrupt change is disruptive, and given the political stasis of the Middle East, it would be remarkable if crockery were not broken. The primary economic shock—the fiscal shock—is directly derived from the interests of the movements' core supporters. What distinguishes the Middle Eastern case is the greater stakes invoked when political action is couched in religious terms.

Implications for International Exchange

A less repressive political environment would presumably increase the likelihood of reversing the brain drain and retaining talented people, though it is difficult to document the quantitative impact. Beyond the economic effects, there could be additional social and political effects of an influx of educated risk takers from the West. Perhaps at the most profound level some have argued that it is possible that the Muslim communities of the West could be a source of theological innovation within Islam itself that might even begin to reduce the incidence of domestic terrorism, ultimately contributing to reductions in political and security risk. The results presented earlier on FDI suggest that the impact could be nonnegligible.

Another route of prospective benefits could be through the impact on trade with the United States. As observed in chapter 9, holding fundamentals constant, the United States trades more intensively with countries with which it has greater affinity, which in turn is partly a function of democracy. In the standard gravity model of bilateral trade, where trade volume is a function of income levels and transaction costs, an increase in a trade partner's Polity IV democracy score by one standard deviation (a standardized measure of statistical dispersion) translates into a 5 to 7 percent rise in trade volume (Noland 2005d).[11] Presumably, this is due to the greater ability of democratic governments relative to authori-

---

11. However, one standard deviation in the polity score amounts to more than two successive liberalizing transitions as defined in the previous section. How would a single democratizing episode affect US public attitudes? Not much: It would imply an increase in the Chicago Council on Foreign Relations temperature of less than 2 degrees and an increase in trade of 2 to 3 percent.

tarian ones to make credible precommitments to sustain policies and institutions. It may also reflect the greater comfort level that businesses have with their peers from countries that share similar characteristics.

The good news is that the Arab countries have a lot of upside potential in this dimension. To get a sense of how big this effect might be, if Egypt or Morocco were to achieve the degree of democracy of South Korea, Taiwan, or Turkey, it would imply a sustained expansion of trade with the United States on the order of 12 to 15 percent.

Presumably, there would be additional economic payoffs to democratization, if, as would seem likely, it is associated with an increased likelihood of sanctions removal or the initiation of preferential trade relations. The latter effect could be very important—one study found that a free trade agreement (FTA) between the United States and Morocco might increase trade volumes by anywhere from 15 to 50 percent depending on specific assumptions and modeling approaches, with the possible impact of a US-Egyptian agreement being even higher (DeRosa and Gilbert 2004). And additional gains would likely be captured through investment and other channels as well.

In short, democratization might contribute to larger trade and increase the likelihood of securing preferential access, which could have even greater impact. The magnitude of such gains is highly uncertain and from the standpoint of accelerating per capita income or employment growth may not be of overwhelming significance, but neither are these gains trivial politically. Nor are they the only channel—the increase in credibility of commitment would presumably reduce risk embodied in the local business environment with implications for both domestic activity and nontrade forms of international exchange such as FDI.

Prospects for Change

The question is what stands in the way of initiating a virtuous circle of economic and political reforms? For its part, since the September 11, 2001, attacks on New York and Washington, the US government has argued that democratization is a key to eliminating terrorism and has elevated the spread of democracy, the Freedom Agenda, to a primary national goal, manifested in initiatives such as the Middle East Partnership Initiative and the Broader Middle East and North Africa Initiative (Wittes and Yerkes 2006). Yet many analysts argue that this Wilsonian commitment is quixotic.

We focus on the antinomy between democracy and authoritarianism because we associate democratic regimes with greater popular legitimacy and policy stability, recognizing that this mapping is not simple, and one can point to counterexamples. Indeed, in Tunisia, arguably the most economically successful of the Arab countries, convergence on OECD income levels has not been accompanied by convergence on their political practices.[12]

Disagreements among economists about the policies that may be necessary to accelerate growth are minor compared with attempts to understand the development of democracy. Yet the importance is not limited to internal policies of nations—evidence suggests that democracy itself affects external perceptions of the desirability of economic interaction with them. The analysis of such issues has obviously filled a library of books and journal articles. In the last 50 years there have been analyses with a sweeping historical panorama. For example, Barrington Moore (1966) in a seminal volume attempted no less than an explanation of the "social origins of dictatorship and democracy" concentrating on the historical evolution of five nations—China, Britain, France, India, and Russia. At the other end of the spectrum many recent efforts have downplayed the historic evolution and the specific conditions of individual countries and utilized a growing body of data for a large number of countries to test a variety of hypotheses. As in the case of the cross-country growth regressions discussed in chapters 5 and 6, we interpret statistical exercises summarized in appendix 10A as a kind of intellectual sieve, informing one's prior expectations about reality. After reviewing the anecdotal and statistical evidence, persuading someone that all things being equal having a British colonial history increases the likelihood of a country being a democracy should be the intellectual equivalent of running downhill. Convincing someone that the Middle East's democratic deficit is explicable in terms of adherence to Islam should be the opposite.

The results from these models point to a rich and complex set of possible determinants of democracy in the region and the possibility of liberalizing transitions. A number of hypotheses regarding the nature of the state as well as characteristics of the citizenry find support in the statistical modeling: Modernization, national ethnolinguistic fractionalization, polity scores of neighboring countries, average world polity score, Arab ethnicity population share, British colonial history, and share of taxes in state revenues (an inverse indicator of the presence of rents) are robust correlates with democracy.[13] A measure of cultural comfort with hierarchy is inversely correlated with democracy in a relatively small sample of countries. Similar sorts of results are obtained with respect to the likeli-

---

12. Tamara Cofman Wittes and Sarah E. Yerkes (2006, 7), for example, argue that "Tunisia's impressive economic growth and attraction of foreign investment have not loosened the grip of one of the region's most effective police states, because of the dependence of private-sector actors on the munificence of the government."

13. Other characteristics including the Muslim population share, oil exports per se as distinct from the broader concept of rents, and general and Israel-specific conflict variables do not appear to be strongly correlated with democracy, conditional on the variables mentioned above.

hood of a democratic transition or the waiting time for such a transition to occur. On these statistical norms, the Arab countries as a group do not appear distinct, though admittedly there is a chicken and egg problem with respect to the neighborhood effect (Noland 2005c).

To get a sense of the magnitude of these effects, one can calculate how much the democracy score would be affected if each correlate was changed by a standardized magnitude, in this case one standard deviation, a common statistical measure of dispersion. In these terms, the single most important determinant of democracy is British colonial origins, which alone is worth more than three points on the −10 to +10 Polity IV scale. The next three largest effects come from modernization, regional spillovers, and Arab ethnic share. This neighborhood effect is much more important than the impact of worldwide democracy waves—the influence of a one standard deviation change in the average level of democracy among bordering countries has more than four times the impact of a similar magnitude change in the average level of democracy worldwide. Looking forward, the advent of pan-Arab media such as the television stations Al Jazeera and Al Arabiya may magnify this regional spillover effect even further, contributing to a more genuinely pan-Arab consciousness in which developments in one country have a more immediate and profound influence on outcomes elsewhere within the region.

Some commentators have argued that Islam may confer additional legitimacy to Arab political regimes despite their questionable ability to deliver material progress or political liberty. This argument is sometimes couched in terms of an Islamic juridical tradition of quietism, though in fairness, scholars who have documented these cultural antecedents (e.g., Lewis 1993b, Crone 2004) have done so in the context of 11th century jurisprudence, not contemporary political culture, and have acknowledged the existence of activist traditions as well. Others have been less circumspect (e.g., Huntington 1984, 1996).[14] M. Steven Fish (2002) makes the intriguing argument that the negative influence of Islam on democracy is due to the subjugation of women, which he implies is some innate aspect of Islam, citing Fatima Mernissi (1987), Hisham Sharabi (1988), the UN Development Program's *Arab Human Development Report 2002*, and other sources. And as documented in chapter 3, historically the status of women in the Arab world has been unenviable, though it has improved greatly over the past generation, and some of the evidence presented in chapter 9

---

14. For example, Samuel P. Huntington (1984, 208) writes, "Confucianism and Buddhism have been conducive to authoritarian rule. . . . Islam has not been hospitable to democracy. . . . The one Islamic country that sustained even intermittent democracy after World War II was Turkey, which had, under Mustafa Kemal, explicitly rejected its Islamic tradition and defined itself as a secular republic. The one Arab country that sustained democracy, albeit of a consociational variety, for any time was Lebanon, 40 to 50 percent of whose population was Christian and whose democratic institutions collapsed when the Moslem majority asserted itself in the 1970s."

suggests that these practices have carried over into the European Arab community. Yet the two notions—the impact of Islam and the impact of the status of women—are separable: The link between democracy and the status of women may hold whether it is related to Islam or not. One can accept one part of the argument without necessarily buying into the other. The proof of the pudding is in the eating, and Noland (2005c) fails to generate any robust support for these propositions. Contemporary Muslims do not appear to be particularly quiescent.

The most problematic result to interpret is the negative correlation between Arab ethnicity and democracy. Some scholars such as Hisham Sharabi (1988) have argued that elements of Arab culture are authoritarian, which would lend an essentialist causal interpretation to this result. There is evidence that political choices of the Arab governments are indeed distinct and nonsupportive of democracy, relative to either other former British colonies or other Muslim-majority countries. Among the 19 Muslim-majority former British colonies, the 8 non-Arab countries all joined the Commonwealth, while none of the 9 Arab countries did (Stepan and Robertson 2004). This is particularly intriguing in light of former British colonial status being among the most robust correlates with democracy. With respect to more recent behavior, Alfred Stepan and Graeme Robertson document the very different behavior of the Arab and non-Arab Muslim-majority countries with respect to the use of international technical assistance in holding elections and foreign election monitors.

The question is what explains this apparent exceptionalism. In at least one poll Arabs listed "civil rights" as their primary political concern (Zogby 2002), and data from the World Values Surveys and other sources indicate that large majorities of Arabs support democracy (Tessler and Gao 2005). It could be that the interests of the governing elites and the man on the street diverge. The observed result—ubiquitous authoritarian regimes—reflects elite preferences, which may represent particular historical circumstances and political choices and are not intrinsic characteristics of Arab culture per se. This could be related to the relatively common occurrence of governments based at least partly on narrow confessional or tribal allegiances, for which a change in regime might lead to physical danger to the members of the group or close relatives—for example, Iraq under Saddam Hussein or Syria under the Assads. Even in the relatively small, repressive security state of Libya, tribal affiliations are thought to form one basis of loyalty to the regime. Such societies may exhibit complex transitional paths, which may not be well captured by statistical models.

A third possibility is that this result is correct in a statistical sense but in a deep sense really represents a historical artifact—it is correctly capturing a particular historical moment in a geographically defined region but that moment is itself transitory and the identifier "Arab" has little long-run explanatory power.

Along with authoritarianism, another key characteristic of these regimes has been their striking longevity, which can hardly be attributed to demonstrable popular support (figure 1.5). The Arab population share is associated with lower probabilities of liberalization. Obviously this demographic variable changes slowly, and if one takes the result at face value, it suggests that Arab democrats and their supporters may have long waits, indeed. However, if the Arab population share is really a proxy for something that we cannot observe directly—such as antidemocratic preferences among the elites, reliance on narrow constituencies, and/or expenditures on internal repression—then politics in turn may exhibit more abrupt change than the slowly evolving Arab ethnic population share, and plots such as those reported in figure 10.1 may be downwardly biased indicators of the true odds on change. Only time will tell.

In terms of economic policy and outcomes, the impact is ambiguous. Long-lived governments could have low rates of time discount: Confident that they will remain in power for a long period, they may be willing to undertake "patient" policies, expecting that they would be in power when the benefits of a reform begin to accrue and erase from minds the initial hardship imposed by, say, a reduction in tariffs or a devaluation. In the Arab world, Tunisia might be held up as an example of this tendency.

However, in the absence of political competition, dysfunctional choices— at least from a societal standpoint—may represent a stable political equilibrium: Governments may have little to fear from a continuation of bad policies as long as these continue to benefit the groups supporting the government. So while it is logically possible that the absence of political competition could deliver long-term gains to far-sighted governments, our sense of the reality of the Arab world is closer to the case of a lack of political competition enabling substandard practices. The fundamental challenge for the Arab world today is to introduce political competition in a way consistent with the maintenance, indeed improvement, of economic policy. The current trajectory in a number of Arab countries arguably reduces the likelihood of this outcome.

Appendix 10A
Quantitative Modeling of Political Regimes

The character of political regimes is obviously less amenable to quantitative analysis than prices and quantities, which are more naturally expressed in numerical form. Nevertheless, statistical analysis can be useful in weighing the explanatory power of competing and complementary explanations. One can examine these hypotheses in light of summary indicators of regime type and assess how the Arab world stacks up. Analogous to the case of foreign direct investment (FDI) discussed in the previous chapters, one might expect that the Middle East would exhibit low levels of democracy "on the fundamentals," or it could be that the region's authoritarianism was truly aberrant relative to a well-conceived international norm.

A large literature on the determinants of democracy offers a number of relatively uncontroversial hypotheses such as the importance of national identity and "modernization," as manifested in economic and/educational attainment as precursors to the establishment of stable, democratic polities (Lipset 1959, Rustow 1970).[15] A second common set of explanations about democratic performance involves the historical origins of a country's political institutions. Lipset et al. (1993), for example, have argued that democracy is associated with British colonial rule, a proposition that has generally found empirical support.[16] Subsequent arguments about democratic waves (Huntington 1984, 1993) and regional spillovers or neighborhood effects (Solingen 1998, Gleditsch 2002) have generally been substantiated empirically, and one could think of these explanations—"modernization," colonial origin, and contemporary regional and global external influences—as forming the core of an analysis of democratic attainment across countries and over time. Analyses also examine the Middle East's democratic deficit from a regional perspective emphasizing distinctive social or economic at-

---

15. For a recent review of the literature, see Levine (2005).

16. See Barro (1999), Przeworski et al. (2000), Fish (2002), and Noland (2005c). Per the discussion in chapter 5, Daron Acemoglu, James A. Robinson, and Simon Johnson (2001) argue that the degree of success in transferring metropole institutions to colonies was essentially a political investment decision driven by the presence of colonial settler populations, which were significantly constrained in some locales by tropical diseases and other environmental influences. Unfortunately, their instrument for institutional development, settler death rates, is available for only a limited number of countries, and more easily available, though crude, proxies, such as tropical climate or latitude, were not significant. Other characteristics distinguishing the historical origins of contemporary polities, such as origins of their legal systems, were generally insignificant once colonial origins were taken into account. In other contexts, some have argued that the British colonial effect is derived from the inclusion of small Caribbean island democracies. This argument is not applicable to the results in Noland (2005c), where those small island democracies were not in the sample.

tributes, such as the role of oil and/or rents (e.g., Ross 2001, Herb 2005) or the impact of Islam (e.g., Fish 2002).

All of these approaches, while informative, cannot be definitive because they cannot adequately weigh competing explanations. Although we have no illusions that the examination of data can fully resolve issues that will be turned over and over for years to come, some statistical tests may help to guide thinking on the issues and suggest new possibilities.

Statistically, the only way to parse these competing explanations is to specify a general model and test the nested hypotheses, modeling some summary quantitative indicator of political liberalism such as the Polity IV scores introduced in chapter 1 or similar ratings produced by Freedom House.[17] We review these hypotheses, first examining those related to the role of the state, then more fundamental cultural determinants, with the aim of identifying a synthetic model that would allow us to evaluate the region's democratic deficit. Having identified the determinants of the level of democracy, we then move on to evaluate prospects for change and how such changes could affect the extent of cross-border economic integration.

Hypotheses Relating to the Structure of the State

It has been frequently argued that the existence of large rents that can be captured by the state impedes democracy through such channels as absolving governments from taxation (and accountability), enabling patronage to relieve discontent, and financing institutions of internal repression. In the Middle East, oil production is the dominant, though not exclusive, source of such rents, which do indeed appear to be correlated with authoritarianism and extralegal internal repression. With respect to coercion, ideally one would want data on internal security services, though in real-

---

17. Among the variables that have been examined include ethnic fractionalization as an inverse proxy for national identity, log real per capita income, log literacy, and log urbanization, representing "modernization," average world level of democracy, average level of democracy of bordering countries (the neighborhood variable), GDP per capita, a dummy for OECD membership, literacy rate, educational attainment measured in terms of years of schooling, life expectancy, telephones and televisions per 1,000 people, college enrollment, population density, urbanization, growth rate of the urban population, international trade openness, a tropical climate dummy, latitude, area, agricultural employment as a share of the labor force, the literacy gender gap, the sex ratio, ethnolinguistic fractionalization, neighborhood and world polity scores, general conflict and Israel conflict dummies, colonial history dummies, legal origin dummies, legal transplant dummies, Hofstede and McClelland cultural indicators, religious affiliation and Arab ethnic population shares, Muslim and Arab population majority dummies, regional dummies including an Arabian peninsula dummy, tax revenue as a share of government revenue, government consumption, rents as a share of government revenue, grants as a share of government revenue, aid as a share of government revenue, a fuel exporter dummy, fuel exports as a share of GDP, an OPEC membership dummy, military expenditure as a share of GDP, and military personnel as a share of the labor force.

ity the distinction between the internal and external security services may be more theoretical than actual. And the Middle East is highly militarized: The Middle East accounted for 9 (10 if Israel is included) of the top 20 countries ranked either by military expenditures as a share of GDP or soldiers per 1,000 persons (US Department of State 2003). These indicators are weakly associated with authoritarianism. The direction of causality is debatable, however—while a history of colonialism or the presence of oil could be regarded as predetermined, whether authoritarians are the patrons or the products of the military is less obvious.

A related explanation might be called the "wag the dog" hypothesis—governments use internal and external conflict to foster undemocratic rule. In the case of the Arab countries, this argument is most often made with respect to the Arab-Israeli conflict, but one could think of it in more general terms, encompassing other conflicts such as Morocco's fight with the Polisario or Libya's incursions into Chad. General or Israel-specific conflict variables are occasionally statistically significant in these models but are not robust explanatory variables of the level of democracy.

In sum, the presence of rents and the maintenance of a large military apparatus appear to inhibit democracy through one or more distinct channels. The efficacy of "waving the bloody shirt" is less clear.

Cultural Explanations

One might regard the hypotheses examined thus far as being "structural" in the sense that they relate the degree of democratization to historical origins, external relations, and the structure of the state or the economy. Another class of explanations might be thought of as "internal" or cultural in nature. We start at the level of the individual psyche and then consider hypotheses relating to broader group identity.

At the most basic level, some have argued that the prevalence of particular personality attributes, belief systems, or cultural tendencies make some societies more compatible with democracy than others. This line of thought goes back almost a century to Sigmund Freud's *Civilization and Its Discontents*, which attempted to explain the origins of World War I. Other connections were made about the origins of totalitarian government by Erich Fromm (1941) and, more generally, by Harold Lasswell (1930). Harvard political scientist Samuel Huntington has forcefully applied this analysis and is a particularly visible, though not singular, contemporary advocate of the psychological view, though hardly a Freudian one. He posits that the prevalence of certain values and beliefs made some societies more compatible with democracy than others, citing David C. McClelland's (1961) attempt to measure the "need to achieve" based on an analysis of third- and fourth-grade school readers for a sample of countries in 1950 (Huntington

1984).[18] Huntington subsequently argued that the cultural origins of the democratic West lay in its globally distinct emphasis on individualism, invoking the work of Geert Hofstede (1983, 2001), who as part of an IBM management program over 1967–73 administered two rounds of survey questionnaires to 88,000 IBM employees (Huntington 1996).[19] In fact, one of Hofstede's measures is statistically correlated with democracy—not cultural individualism, the one that Huntington identified, but rather power-distance, a measure of comfort with hierarchy, which is inversely correlated with democracy in a data-constrained sample.[20] Such "theories" of democracy have virtually no overlap with the view of Barrington Moore (1966) that the initiation of democracy required an urban middle class that overwhelmed a landed aristocracy, a view not inconsistent with the emergence of democracy in Japan, South Korea, and Taiwan.[21]

Accepting for the sake of exposition the view that polities are individual psyches writ large, the obvious question is, Where do these politically relevant cognitive patterns and beliefs arise from? One controversial answer has been "religion" in general, and Islam in particular, and again Huntington advocates this view, arguing that specific religious or cultural traditions are good or bad for democracy—for example, Confucianism is bad, Buddhism is bad, Calvinism is good (Huntington 1984, 1996). Islam, he argues, is bad, a view that finds support in the writings of scholars such as Elie Kedourie (1992, 1)—"Democracy is alien to the mind-set of

---

18. Perhaps surprisingly, McClelland's measure is in fact correlated with democracy in a sample significantly limited by data availability (Noland 2005c).

19. According to Hofstede, statistical analysis of the responses suggested that they could be characterized along four dimensions: a power-distance index ("the extent to which the less powerful members of institutions and organizations within a country expect and accept that power is unequally distributed"); an uncertainty-avoidance index ("the extent to which the members of a culture feel threatened by uncertain or unknown situations"); an individualism-collectivism dimension ("individualism stands for a society in which the ties between individuals are loose. . . collectivism stands for a society in which people from birth onwards are integrated into strong, cohesive in-groups"); and a masculine-feminine dimension ("masculinity stands for a society in which social gender roles are clearly distinct . . . femininity stands for a society in which social gender roles overlap: Both men and women are supposed to be modest, tender, and concerned with the quality of life"). It is fair to say that this research is controversial. See McSweeney (2002) for a critique.

20. See Noland (2005c). Ironically, in earlier work Huntington correctly identified comfort with hierarchy as an antidemocratic cultural attribute: "A political culture that highly values hierarchical relationships and extreme deference to authority presumably is less fertile ground for democracy than one that does not" (Huntington 1984, 209).

21. The triumph of democracy in Japan can be partly attributed to US pressure in the postwar period while that in South Korea and Taiwan may have reflected the emergence of a middle class that increasingly demanded greater freedom, akin to Moore's (1966) urban bourgeoisie, with this group having to force the hand of governments that were not backed by large landowners. The latter had been marginalized in the reforms of the 1950s, which were urged by the United States.

Islam"—and Stefan Voigt (2005), and the statistical analyses of Robert J. Barro (1999) and M. Steven Fish (2002, 4), who argues that his analysis provides "strong support for the hypothesis that Muslim countries are democratic underachievers."

This argument is problematic on a variety of levels. First, if the religion hypothesis is correct, it would be helpful, though not essential, to the argument if religious affiliation were the primary characteristic of self-identity. But in general this does not appear to be the case: According to polling data, religious orientation is generally only a secondary source of personal identity in most Arab countries in the Middle East—rather, Arab ethnicity is the primary identifier, followed by religion and nationality (Zogby 2002).[22] Likewise when polled, Muslims in general do not express particular hostility to democracy (Tessler 2002, 2003; Pew Global Attitudes Project 2003; Tessler and Gao 2005). Finally, as Alfred Stepan (2001) points out, a close reading of Huntington suggests that he has fallen into the common trap of conflating "Islam" and "Arab."[23] Arabs make up a minority of Muslims globally, and depending on how one parses individual cases, perhaps 40 to 60 percent of the world's Muslims live in at least partly democratic countries.

The direct statistical evidence on this point is ambiguous, turning on the subtle issue of who is the relevant comparator group.[24] Moreover, Islam, like other religions, is open-ended, subject to interpretation, and widely varying in practice across the dimensions of both time and distance, and the category "Muslim" may be too broad to be analytically meaningful (Zubaida 1995). In particular, other cultural influences in non-Arab Muslim societies, such as pre-Islamic local traditions or the influences of non-Muslim groups such as the Chinese in Southeast Asia or the French in West Africa, may attenuate the impact of Middle Eastern traditions, a proposi-

---

22. Zogby polled respondents on the importance of family, city/region, country, religion, ethnicity, and social background in self-identity. He did not ask about tribe or clan as such.

23. In the first paragraph of analysis on Islam in Huntington (1996, 174–75), the word "Arab" appears eight times and "tribe" nine times, but there is no mention of South or Southeast Asia.

24. When population shares ascribed to major world religions are added to the core statistical model in Noland (2005c), the coefficients on the Hindu, Buddhist, Jewish, and Protestant Christian population shares are all positive and significant. The coefficient on the Muslim share is insignificant. However, these coefficients are all significantly greater or less than zero relative to the omitted group. If the definition of the omitted group changes, then so will the estimated coefficients. If only the Muslim population share variable is included, it is estimated with a statistically significant negative coefficient—that is to say, if Muslims are compared with all non-Muslims, then they appear distinctly undemocratic. However, if Muslims are compared with a group consisting of agnostics, atheists, Confucians, animists, Shintoists, Bahais, and Rastafarians, among others, then they are not. Fish (2002) argues that what is important is not the Muslim share but whether Muslims are a majority. The results reported in Noland (2005c) do not support this distinction.

tion that finds support in the statistical modeling (Noland 2005c, de Soysa and Nordås 2006). In fact, this modeling suggests that the salient analytical category is "Arab," not "Muslim," in explaining the region's democratic deficit.[25] James Zogby's finding that Arab ethnicity is the primary self-identification category in most Middle Eastern countries lends some plausibility to this conclusion.[26]

Liberalizing Episodes

The results discussed thus far pertain to the level of democracy in the Arab countries. Another characteristic has been the stability of the region's authoritarian governments. A number of nonmutually exclusive hypotheses explain stability: relative absence of economic or social change that would generate demands for alterations in the status quo; unusual quiescence on the part of the populace; distinctively effective investment in instruments of repression by the elites; and prevalence of governments with narrow bases of support in tribal, ethnic, or religious minorities. Some of these theories are more amenable to modeling than others (in particular, theories that focus on country or regime characteristics as opposed to those that emphasize a country's relation to the world system), and even among explanations centering on internal characteristics, there are issues of data availability, at least at the cross-national level.[27]

---

25. When the Muslim population share of each country was weighted by dividing by the distance between the national capital and Mecca (i.e., the weighted Muslim share declines with distance), the distance-weighted variable had a higher statistical significance. Moreover, when the ethnic Arab population share was added to the model and estimated with a negative coefficient more than twice as large as the Muslim population share coefficient, and when entered jointly, the Muslim population share variable lost its statistical significance—suggesting that the relevant variable is "Arab," not "Muslim."

26. Many Muslims and Arabs live in oil-exporting countries. As a consequence, it is important to model the potential relationships among these variables carefully; otherwise one runs the risk of misattributing the influence of one variable to the other. For example, Fish (2002, tables 2 through 5), after appearing to establish that OPEC membership is a robust negative correlate with democracy, inexplicably drops the OPEC variable when analyzing the influence Islam and the status of women have on democracy (Fish 2002, table 10). This is practically a textbook example of probable omitted variable bias. When in Noland (2005c) the Muslim population share and oil exporter variables are entered jointly, both are significant. When the Arab population share is entered jointly with the oil exporter dummy, the coefficient on the oil exporter variable becomes insignificant. When all three are entered together, only the coefficient on the Arab ethnic share is statistically significant. Indra de Soysa and Ragnhild Nordås (2006) do not do a comparable nesting, so it is impossible to know whether they would obtain the same result.

27. For example, many commentators emphasize the role of worsening income or wealth distribution or perceptions of relative deprivation in political motivation (e.g., Gurr 1970). However, historical, cross-country comparable income distribution data are not widely avail-

As in the previous section one can think of the drivers of political change as coming in the form of environmental or structural characteristics, specific country characteristics, and particular attributes that might have particular salience in the Middle Eastern milieu.[28]

The statistical analyses suggest that the global political environment and individual countries' past political histories have a significant impact on the likelihood of political liberalization at any given point in time. With respect to the former, political liberalization comes in waves: the greater the worldwide level of democracy, the greater encouragement of and shorter waiting time for a liberalizing breakthrough in any particular country. As for the latter, the more a country has liberalized in the past, the less likely it is to experience further liberalization as it encounters a kind of democratic asymptote.

The other robust correlates are variables that relate more directly to country performance or characteristics. Since we are now considering the likelihood of change at a given point in time, drivers that vary temporally are of greater interest. It has been argued that economic crises can be destabilizing for authoritarian regimes in general (Haggard and Kaufman 1995) and Middle Eastern regimes in particular (Lust-Okar 2004). In fact, conditional on the other variables, the more rapid the growth of per capita income growth, the longer the waiting time for transition—i.e., in the short run economic performance buys a certain degree of popular acquiescence, though in the long run rising incomes augur against authoritarian rule. This effect could be particularly salient for the oil exporters, which experience substantial volatility in income growth associated with swings in the price of oil, or countries like Syria and Yemen where oil reserves are expected to be exhausted in the relatively near future. Likewise, more educated populations are more demanding. The statistical results indicate that the higher the rate of literacy, the shorter the waiting time for a democratic transition.

Surprisingly, the degree of international trade openness is associated with longer waiting times for liberalizing breakthroughs, though some might point to the history of East Asia, where countries democratized at relatively high levels of per capita income after adopting an outward-oriented development model. It would be erroneous to conclude from

---

able, and data on wealth distribution or subjective appraisals of relative deprivation even less so, and existing research on this fragmentary data does not yield robust conclusions. See Perotti (1996), Drazen (2000), and Przeworski et al. (2000) and sources cited therein.

28. So as a starting point, the variables employed in the previous section to predict the level of democracy were used to model its advent. Appended to this list were other variables such as prior history of liberalizing transitions, population density, growth rate of urbanization, country size, international trade openness, dependency on trade taxes, and inflation, which in previous studies had been found to be statistically associated with the likelihood of political regime change.

these results that as a policy matter one should oppose economic growth or support closure to trade as a means of encouraging democratization—we still drive cars even though they contribute to traffic accidents. Both trade and growth are themselves desirable, and in the long run, prosperity contributes to expectations of political liberalization. However, in the short run, these forces may act as a kind of safety valve for discontent.

The previous discussion of the level of democracy pointed to several hypotheses derived from Middle Eastern studies that suggested that particular characteristics associated with the region might impede democracy. In some previous research, trade taxes have been shown to be associated with political instability—imposing trade taxes and delinking from the world economy encourages lawlessness in forms such as smuggling and underinvoicing and contributes to the delegitimization of the political regime. (Though it could be argued that causality runs in the other direction: Weak regimes rely on trade taxes because they are relatively easy to collect.) And indeed there is some evidence that the imposition of trade taxes is associated with a shorter waiting time for a democratic transition. Think Boston, circa 1773.

However, paralleling the results discussed in the previous section, the Arab population share is associated with significantly longer waiting times for liberalizing transitions. Again, one can think of multiple interpretations of this statistical result: that it reflects some essential characteristic of Arab culture or that the Arab population share variable is acting as a proxy for omitted variables, such as expenditure on internal security forces, the ruthlessness of minority-based regimes, or the political economy of rent-based patronage. But in this context, the Arab population share changes only slowly—it amounts essentially to a fixed effect that reduces the probability of liberalization but does not have much of an impact on changes in its likelihood from year to year. In this sense the difference of the two interpretations of the Arab population share variable is potentially important, with the former implying a semipermanent drag on democratization, while the other indicates that the statistical models may not do a good job of predicting the timing or extent of political change looking forward. The expected likelihood of a liberalizing transition for the eight large Arab countries is plotted in figure 10.1. If it is the case that Arabs are unusually quiescent, then figure 10.1 may provide a credible indication of the level and evolution of the likelihood of a liberalizing breakthrough.

In figure 10.1 it is apparent that the likelihood of a liberalizing transition in these countries was quite low at the beginning of the sample period and generally increased to something like 5 percent in any given year for the group as a whole. However, this increase has not been monotonic. For several countries there was a noticeable spike in the probability of a liberalizing breakthrough in 1989 or 1990, during a worldwide democracy wave, a period in which Algeria and Jordan experienced openings.[29] According to Thomas Carothers (2002), the relatively tentative (and possibly reversible) process of liberalization in the Arab countries may be more typical of the worldwide experience in political development over the past generation than the more well-known and decisive breakthroughs previously cited such as occurred in Spain, Brazil, South Africa, and Romania.

---

29. The spike for Morocco came later, primarily a product of the world conditions together with poor economic performance in Morocco during the early 1990s. In both cases the likelihood of a breakthrough in a particular year peaked at more than 20 percent, a substantial likelihood, though one well under a 50 percent probability. Morocco, which did not experience transition, adhered to the prediction of the model, whereas in some sense Jordan beat the odds. The models could be interpreted as indicating that the odds on liberalizing episodes occurring in any given year are generally low but rising, as relatively poor economic performance combined with increasing levels of educaation erode popular acquiescence to authoritarian governance.

11

Conclusion

The central economic challenges confronting the Arab world are to provide employment for its rapidly growing labor force and raise living standards. Continuation of past performance will not be sufficient to accomplish these goals: Achievement of these objectives requires rapid, sustainable expansion of labor-intensive activities and growing labor productivity, which necessitate a more successful integration into the global economy than has been witnessed to date.

The region's reputation as a risky business environment, due in part to deep uncertainty about the future of many of the region's political regimes, inhibits successful globalization. Economic and political uncertainty and risk thus lie at the heart of the region's challenges. The central role of oil in the economic and political life of a number of these countries creates additional opportunities—and potential pitfalls.

These societies are not without achievement: As documented in chapters 2 to 4, in a number of the Arab countries economic growth has been steady, albeit inadequate to generate the employment opportunities to absorb their rapidly growing workforces. In recent decades, advances in fundamental indicators of social welfare such as life expectancy, childhood mortality, and literacy have been impressive for the region as a whole, and in some cases spectacular. On poverty incidence and many social indicators of health and education, most of the Arab countries are at, or above, the achievements of other states with similar per capita income. However, this performance is not uniform: The experience of Yemen has not been encouraging, and Iraq and the Palestinian Authority territories face extraordinary problems. Nevertheless, for the region as a whole, the improvements have been substantial, considerably exceeding widely held impressions. At issue is not the extent of past achievements, which look similar to many other middle-income developing countries, but rather whether the existing economic and political models that delivered these gains in past decades are adequate to successfully address the current demographically driven pressure to deliver jobs in the context of an increasingly competitive global economy. The answer is almost surely no.

Fortunately, many in the region recognize the need for change, indeed with a nuanced understanding born of daily experience that those of us from beyond the region cannot hope to match. They face a situation in which the required policy adjustments are complex, the payoffs uncertain, and the potential political risks enormous. Yet, one important insight emerging from our analysis is that the substantial intraregional variation in achievement in many of the relevant benchmarks that we identify suggests that these outcomes are not determined by intrinsic cultural factors. The influence of Islam or the anthropology of Arab culture may have many effects on local institutions and practices, but they cannot explain why it takes 15 times as long to enforce a contract in Egypt as it does in Tunisia. This simple example is emblematic of a very important point that we have tried to convey in our analysis, namely that considerable improvements in economic efficiency are consistent with the maintenance of fundamental aspects of local identity, and indeed, in many cases, significant improvements in economic outcomes could be achieved by simply matching the best practice standard established by others within the region. Egypt need not turn into Norway.

Identifying the Constraints

If the growing labor force is to be absorbed productively, an acceleration of aggregate growth will be necessary, and this growth will have to be labor-intensive in nature. Given the growing competitiveness of low-income rivals, the existing economic, political, and social practices may inhibit or preclude the type of growth necessary for these economies to succeed or indeed for their governments to maintain political viability. The task is to identify the most acute constraints on development whose relaxation might accelerate growth in the short run (i.e., pick the low-hanging fruit) while a long-run strategy is formulated.

We begin by identifying what is not the problem. As alluded to earlier, the evidence that we have reviewed indicates that Islam is not the issue, at least not in a simple sense that the adherence to the faith encourages behavior antithetical to economic development. Neither the simple observation of relatively strong performance among some predominantly Islamic countries such as Indonesia and Malaysia nor the econometric evidence summarized in chapter 5 supports the notion that adherence to Islam is a drag on development. Islam is relevant, however. It is the spiritual prism through which many in the region interpret existence; many adherents increasingly regard it as being under threat; and for a variety of reasons, political opposition to the region's ubiquitous authoritarian regimes has an increasingly Islamist bent.

Turning to more conventional economic explanations, our analysis suggests that macroeconomic instability is not the main culprit in slowing growth either. While macroeconomic policy management may not be perfect, and the presence of oil and other natural resources may present "Dutch disease" challenges for some of the countries of the region, macroeconomic management is sufficiently good that, as the analysis presented in chapter 6 suggests, alterations in macroeconomic policies are not likely to deliver large improvements in outcomes.

However, the portrait derived from a variety of measures on microeconomic policies and institutional characteristics presented in chapters 5 and 6 is less positive. The Arab countries, with some exceptions, generally do not score highly on these measures (though in many cases they do not appear to be distinctly weaker than the relevant comparators from outside the region) and do not appear to have made significant progress over time—at least relative to their extraregional competition.

Specifically, the Arab countries score poorly on a nexus of indicators relating to cross-border economic integration and transfer, dissemination, and application of technological knowledge and innovation. Outside of the special cases of the extractive industries (such as oil) and tourism (where geology or special assets like the Pyramids confer unique and irreproducible advantages), as a group, the Arab countries appear to have weak linkages to the outside world, whether measured in terms of merchandise trade, import of capital goods (which embody technological advances from abroad), cross-border investment, integration into transborder supply networks, technology licensing, patenting, and internationally recognized intellectual achievements, as well as a number of other indicators that we have reviewed. In short, the neural synapses that would link the latent productive possibilities of the Arab people with the goods and services demanded by the rest of the world appear to be weak or nonexistent.

Building such links presents a formidable challenge. Unlike issues of macroeconomic policy management—where policy change can be implemented by a relatively small number of centrally placed technocrats and is subject to relatively straightforward feedback mechanisms to facilitate benchmarking progress (i.e., one can observe changes in inflation, the money supply, the exchange rate, or the budget deficit fairly rapidly and alter policy in response)—addressing the institutional weaknesses that we have identified requires a much more prolonged and uncertain slog.

Moreover, while lessons can be derived from the experiences of other countries, at this level of microeconomic and institutional reform the particular priorities and constraints, much less the specific political tactics needed to achieve reform, will differ country by country and will require sustained diligent activity by a broad group of actors. Long-run progress is likely to reflect the cumulative impact of many small reforms and innovations over a protracted period, rather than a small number of bold moves. Indeed, one of the themes that we have emphasized is the region's diversity, and while there are important commonalities, there are obvious differences as well. Formulating detailed country-specific prescriptions lie, beyond the scope of this book. Instead, we point at some general issues and tendencies, recognizing that their salience will vary across countries, and emphasize that addressing them is neither straightforward nor trivial in either a programmatic or a political sense.

Designing Solutions: An Example

One of our fundamental contentions is that education and technology are complements. To take a simple illustrative example, the returns to a country training software engineers may not be very high in the absence of computers; conversely, building or importing computers may not have a high payoff if no one knows how to operate them or if local conditions prevent their efficient usage. Properly measured, the social returns to education in the Arab countries may not be particularly high in the absence of complementary technology and an enabling business environment. However, there is often a high private return to education, inducing individuals to obtain more schooling than can profitably be deployed. One understandable, if regrettable, response by local governments to this circumstance has been to warehouse college graduates in public-sector employment to buy social peace. A second salient point is that much of the relevant technology, defined broadly, originates outside the region and will continue to do so for the foreseeable future.

These two facets of the economic landscape suggest that the Arab countries face a coordination task that is more complex than the simple example above suggests. At the first level, educational and training programs need to be coordinated with the skills demanded by the market—but even this may not be easy to accomplish, as the example of garment factories in Jordan, recounted in appendix 8B in chapter 8, illustrates. In this case, the supply of adequately skilled local workers has been problematic, and the newly created jobs in large part have been filled by migrant workers from South Asia. The coordination problem is particularly difficult in situations where the emerging industries and occupations do not yet exist, and hence the market is not signaling to either students or administrators into which activities resources should be deployed.

Even if countries are successful in addressing these initial tasks, the payoffs cannot be realized in the absence of commercial activity. The experiences of Taiwan, South Korea, and more recently China have been that the initial response to the expansion of science and engineering education was the emigration of a substantial number of highly skilled workers. Ultimately some of them returned, in effect creating a critical connection between the local economy and technological development abroad, but the initial social return on this human capital investment was not high. In the case of the Middle East, this particular trajectory may be impaired by the post-9/11 diplomatic environment and restrictions on cross-border movement—i.e., at present it may be difficult for graduates to emigrate to seek greater returns on human capital. The absence of this option may pose a particularly acute dilemma for local governments insofar as educated but underemployed young people may pose a significant latent threat to domestic political stability.

A complementary strategy, perhaps more feasible given current diplomatic realities, would be to educate the domestic labor force and encourage foreign firms to establish production locally. This strategy immediately runs into the problem documented in chapter 7, namely that Arab attitudes, both popular and elite, appear to be ambivalent on this score. In this sense, the task is not only a "technical" one of how to marry local capacities to technology derived from abroad but also a political one of how to open up—how to make globalization acceptable to skeptical elites, a dubious "Arab street," and overcome entrenched special interests in an environment in which the high-stakes political conundrum will encourage policymakers to be cautious, hesitant, and risk-averse.

Political Economy of Reform

Local Dimension

The political and economic consequences of the reforms discussed in this volume will lead governments, authoritarian or democratic, to carefully evaluate the prospective benefits and costs before embarking on the path, unless the governments have no choice due to a financial or economic crisis, an outcome less likely in a world of $60 to $70 per barrel of oil, whose rents are widely dispersed. Yet the benefits of reform may be small in the short run if supply response is limited due to a shortage of necessary local skills. It is widely believed that the outcomes in relatively reformist countries such as Jordan and Morocco have fallen short of expectations. Accepting for the sake of argument that these impressions are correct—that the economic response to policy reform has been disappointing—one can posit a variety of responses and explanations, such as the reforms were insufficient, poorly implemented, or poorly designed. Each is possible. Yet other interpretations, emphasizing the absence among local producers of the industrial competence or capacity to take advantage of the opportunities created by policy change, may be germane. However, greater reliance on foreign skills might compensate in the latter case, but such a tack raises another concern, namely, is the added foreign presence socially and politically acceptable?

Both paths—one emphasizing the development of indigenous capacities, the other emphasizing foreign engagement—present their own unique challenges. In reality, the two strategies are complementary, not mutually exclusive. Increasing domestic supply capacities is likely to be a relatively long-term endeavor, and the region's demographic clock is ticking. Although this approach may be desirable in the long run, it may be inadequate in light of the immediacy of the problem.

Nor is it simple—it requires both technical upgrading of skills and complementary improvements in the institutional functioning of the business environment to facilitate the economic mobilization of those skills. With respect to the first challenge, the evidence reviewed suggests that there is considerable scope for improving the quality of education in the Arab world. There may also be a need to establish or improve existing institutions along the lines of India's Institutes of Technology or Taiwan's Institute for Technological Research and Innovation, which closely tie education and research with their ultimate commercial users, recognizing that most attempts to emulate these success stories have failed. Moreover, this local skills–based approach may require controversial changes in education and social organization, for example, a reordering of priorities to place a greater emphasis on science in schools at the cost of religious education. Even in the United States, such measures are not without difficulty—witness the increasing demands for the teaching of "intelligent design." Moreover, improvements in "inputs" may not manifest themselves in better outcomes in the absence of complementary changes in the business environment to support local innovation and entrepreneurship—from improved access to capital and dispute adjudication to improved property rights protection.

If such changes could be implemented, the benefit could be substantial, in essence manifested in an increase in total factor productivity—a "free good" that would permit a permanent rise in income and consumption without necessitating a corollary increase in investment, either at the expense of consumption or through an increased balance of payments deficit. However, none of this is easy, and the payoffs are uncertain.

Alternatively, greater reliance on foreign sources of technology and marketing knowledge may have more immediate rewards but could also have unintended effects. The sorts of international agreements discussed in chapter 8 could considerably ameliorate the problem through the generation of jobs in labor-intensive activities in the industrial and internationally tradable service sectors. In the last 25 years, China has created tens of millions of jobs in the industrial sector, much of it due to direct foreign investment. Initially this strategy was undertaken in special economic zones, operating outside the rest of the economy, but the approach came to complete fruition only when these developments spilled beyond their geographical confines, establishing physical, economic, and ultimately cultural linkages with the broader Chinese economy. A similar transformation, if it were to occur in the Middle East, could imply significant changes in some aspects of these societies, in particular a greater presence of foreigners, who have been key participants in the extraordinary reversals of economic performance in many of the relatively successful Asian countries.

Yet in this connection, there is a deeper worry, rarely articulated, that the hesitancy to reform in the Arab world is driven by more fundamental concerns than the usual special-interest politics. Greater international trade typically involves greater contact between local citizens and foreigners. Exporters are often required to spend time overseas, obtaining firsthand knowledge of the types of goods in demand. Nationals must travel abroad to trade shows to evaluate the newest advances in technology in both capital and intermediate goods and to become acquainted with potential suppliers. At home, potential foreign importers will visit to assess the capabilities of local producers and to establish buying offices. In the case of local buying offices established by large multinational retail purchasers, a substantial group of conspicuously foreign personnel will be present, and if this occurs in the clothing industry, a likely sector of early comparative advantage, many will be young women dressed in contemporary styles.

Expanded foreign investment could augment the absent or critically scarce technical and marketing abilities, but it would be implemented by individuals who will be noticeably foreign not only in appearance but also in the different mores they follow, seen, for example, in their choices of clothing and consumption of alcohol. Such considerations do not necessarily preclude cooperation: Despite lingering hostility over Japanese colonialism and World War II, South Korea, in its early industrialization, depended partly on Japanese engineers, who commuted every weekend from Tokyo. The examples can be multiplied, but the general point about the potential social adjustments required for successful globalization should be evident.

The difficulty for the governments in question is whether they can withstand the inevitable, perhaps intense, opposition to very visible Westernization. Polling data discussed in chapter 7 indicate that local attitudes toward manifestations of globalization are ambivalent at best, a characteristic both limiting and informing government choices. The degree to which anti-Westernization feelings are sufficiently strong to make leaders cautious about such an opening is unknown. Anti-Western violence in countries such as Morocco and Egypt cannot be reassuring to the governments nor, very importantly, to prospective foreign investors or suppliers. With respect to the latter, the physical and financial risks will inevitably affect decisions. Whatever the objectives of terrorism in the minds of its proponents, it not only poses a threat to the polity but also severely undermines the likelihood of successful economic development.

Reductions in these risk perceptions would facilitate more genuinely successful globalization than has been witnessed to date. As we have argued, these risk assessments are rooted in reality, and for many of the

Arab countries, transforming public perceptions toward globalization could improve significantly the terms on which globalization occurs. Yet it is not self-evident how public policy can support such a transformation: Beyond public campaigns and high-profile promotional activity by societal elites, there are no obvious policy instruments for encouraging the public to be more tolerant or less xenophobic or to take a more positive view of change, especially change emanating from foreign or nontraditional sources. Moreover, evidence suggests that a self-reinforcing feedback loop from individual preferences to policies decays only slowly— once established, it can take generations for local beliefs to converge toward broader international norms. This raises the possibility that popular attitudes, both by conditioning local policies and by elevating the risk perceived by potential foreign investors, can contribute to long-lasting hysteresis and, in the extreme, to the formation of poverty traps, where a reputation-derived risk premium impedes cross-border economic integration and ultimately economic development.

As discussed in chapter 9, returnees, who presumably have a more nuanced understanding of these issues and perhaps lower subjective assessments of risk, could act as intermediaries in generating a solution to this conundrum, bringing back to the region innovative technology and ideas from abroad, and indeed, such returnees have been an important part of the development story in a number of countries. Taiwan, for example, proactively encouraged émigré scientists and engineers to return home and establish high-technology businesses, which had a significant impact on Taiwan's industrial development. However, for this strategy to succeed and induce individuals of considerable achievement in education and income to uproot their lives in the West, the returnees must be confident that the economic and social environment is fundamentally supportive and welcoming, that they and their families will be physically safe, and that they will not be subject to economic predation. These concerns go to the heart of the political economy challenges facing many of the countries in the Middle East.

Unfortunately, fear of fundamental political instability, accentuated by concerns over terrorism and the radical Islamist nature of some opposition groups, may discourage even the implementation of incremental reforms, contributing to a dysfunctional dynamic. Greater technological diffusion will require increased availability of computers for individuals, yet these also have obvious potential for allowing political opposition to organize. As another illustration of this tendency, one of the few variables that are routinely found to impede growth in econometric studies cited in chapter 4 is excessive government consumption. Yet, in the Middle East, government bureaucracies often serve as employers of last resort for university graduates, and reducing the drag created by unproductive public-sector employment might significantly accelerate growth in the long run. Under such circumstances, fears about the internal political ramifications of eliminating this social safety valve may overwhelm expectations of long-run improvement. Failure to reform contributes to slow growth, which in turn may make it more difficult to undertake policy changes involving short-run distress. And lurking in the background is the issue noted by a variety of commentators, namely that many terrorists have scientific or engineering backgrounds. Increases in education without addressing the underlying origins of disaffection, whatever their source, could actually increase the deadliness of terrorism, contributing to a vicious circle of terrorism impeding investment and growth, in turn contributing to more terrorism.

While the calculation of beneficiaries and losers from economic liberalization that help or harm particular income, regional, and sectoral groups and their relative political strengths is hardly simple, policymakers understand the rough parameters of the algorithm. The impact of policy changes on prices, wages, and profits—and hence the economic fortunes of different groups in society—is comprehensible, at least in principle. In contrast grasping the political opportunities and dangers created when reforms affect social-religious sensitivities may tax even the most adroit leader, and there is an understandable tendency toward caution that has contributed to the region's stultifying inertia. Yet despite the unknowns, many of the region's more successful countries—which tend to be underendowed in natural resources—have undertaken reforms, though perhaps not as substantial as countries elsewhere. These policy changes were implemented despite conventional special-interest political pressure, as well as more fundamental cultural considerations, which must have informed the calculation. It may be that rents, whether in the form of oil receipts, aid, remittances, or other revenues due to unique geopolitical circumstances, lessen the urgency of reform, while the absence of such financial cushioning encourages greater risk taking. If the historical analogy to European anarchism holds, this challenge may be multigenerational in duration.

International Dimension

Those who maintain that the potential of radical Islam to exploit any short-term problems is sufficient to preclude reform could be correct. If they are, there is a perverse dynamic. Reform is precluded by the fears of Islamic radicalism, which in turn feeds on the stagnation or inadequate growth generated by these fears. Economic growth is, in this view, not a formula for obtaining legitimacy. Some abhor the characteristics of modern economic growth including greater geographic and social mobility, greater participation by women, influx of foreign ideas and domestic effort to absorb them, growing high-quality education system, and less certainty about one's place in the economic and social system. The issues being contested are fundamentally "internal" in nature. In this case, the international community can do little.

Yet the international community has an enormous stake in the developments within the region and has no real alternative but to engage in the hope of reaching mutually beneficial outcomes. The United States bears special responsibility for the situation in Iraq and is often blamed for developments in the Palestinian Authority territories. Yet the advanced nations, particularly the United States, face deep skepticism within the region concerning their interests and motives.[1] Indeed, it is hard to overstate the depths to which America's image within the region has fallen. To cite but one recent piece of evidence, 85 percent of Jordanians—a "moderate" Arab country with which the United States has a free trade agreement—expressed unfavorable sentiments toward the United States (Pew Global Attitudes Project 2006a, 2006b). One might be tempted to dismiss the Jordanian response as reflecting its unusual position of being sandwiched between the conflicts in Iraq and the Palestinian territories. But 69 percent of Egyptians, the other Arab country polled, recipient of billions of dollars in US aid, also had an unfavorable assessment of the United States.

Under such conditions, the industrial nations, particularly the United States, have to tread extraordinarily carefully. As argued in chapter 8, the "deep integration" preferential trade agreements preferred by the United States may confer large benefits on Arab partner countries, particularly if these agreements are accompanied by complementary domestic reforms. Objectively, these agreements may be useful instruments to Arab governments seeking to accelerate employment and per capita income growth. Much of popular and elite opinion nevertheless regards such initiatives as "neoimperialism" aimed at undermining Arab societies, however, and the label "made in the USA" could be a death knell. It may be that the United States simply acts as a lightning rod for the discontent that seems disproportionate to the actual achievements of the Arab countries in income and welfare.

In this battle for a change in perception and commitment, which has a large noneconomic component, the United States is faring abysmally. Huge majorities in the Arab countries are aware of the abuses at Abu Ghraib and Guantanamo Bay (Pew Global Attitudes Project 2006a, 2006b). The Dubai Ports World debacle exposed US ambivalence in its self-professed support for free markets. In counterpoint to the complex, difficult, and uncertain tasks that the Arab governments face in improving the functioning of their local institutions, the United States faces a difficult path in repairing its standing in the Arab world, though one suspects the hostility would become more muted with more sustained growth in the

---

1. Such attitudes are manifest despite diplomatic and military efforts that benefited many Muslims: in the Balkans and the Sudan and the relief efforts following the December 2004 Indonesian tsunami and the 2005 Pakistani earthquake.

Arab countries and greater possibilities for political participation within these countries.

Such an initiative would have four components. The first component is regulatory and macroeconomic. Given the xenophobic reaction of some Americans to previous episodes in the 1970s and 1980s—when US external imbalances required substantial inflows of foreign capital and led to foreign purchases of highly visible trophy assets (i.e., Japanese purchases of Rockefeller Center or the Pebble Beach Golf Course)—and the more recent China National Offshore Oil Corporation (CNOOC) and Dubai Ports World cases, oddly enough, reducing the US balance of payments deficit, and hence the likelihood of future irritants such as the Dubai Ports World fiasco, would be a useful first step. Of course, a more careful regulatory process could more directly preclude such blunders. Serendipitously, this first step would largely be a function of US fiscal policy adjustment, which requires no foreign diplomacy and can be undertaken completely unilaterally. Such a policy would also have secondary effects that would be quite desirable, namely reducing the demand for oil.

A fall in the full employment deficit combined with a tax on the use of carbon fuels would reduce demand for oil, generating a variety of beneficial effects. For the United States, a reduction in the trade deficit is desirable on several grounds including the dangers posed to the US economy as a result of the accumulation of dollar-denominated assets in other countries and the danger that a sudden change in the economic prospects of the United States could trigger a dollar crisis. In the Middle East, given the likelihood that a higher price reduces the political interest in reform not only in oil exporters but also in other countries that receive remittances from nationals in the oil-exporting countries, attenuated American demand for oil could encourage reform broadly. Our point is that a reduction in the US trade deficit brought about by a more responsible fiscal policy could have underappreciated benefits for our relations in the Middle East. Resolution of the nettlesome US imbalances is difficult, and the impact on the Middle East will not constitute a major source of political support for the necessary fiscal changes. Nevertheless, it is worth noting the benefits to be derived from such contemplated policy changes.

The second component would be public diplomacy aimed at both improving the image of the United States and strengthening progressive, democratic political forces in the region, which are needed to liberalize their economies if growing unemployment is not to undermine their polities. The latter aspiration derives from the potential gains from greater openness of the economies and an enhanced receptivity to the transfer of knowledge. Such responsiveness might be enhanced if the Arab populations were not suspicious about the sources and implications of growing globalization.

The United States needs to greatly expand, strengthen, and reorient its public diplomacy toward the region in a variety of ways. America does not have powerful levers for achieving such objectives, but given the stakes, the effort is necessary. One possibility would be to redirect resources from the US government–sponsored satellite television channel al-Hurra, which has failed to attract a significant audience (Telhami 2005), and apply these resources to increasing the availability of Western news sources in the Arab world. Evidence suggests that there are not only profound divergences in opinion between Arabs and the West but also deep differences regarding the underlying facts linked to sources of news and information (Gentzkow and Shapiro 2004).

A complementary approach would be to expand two-way exchanges of opinion leaders through programs such as Fulbright exchanges, to revitalize support for engagement of US *nonofficial* opinion leaders in the region along the lines of the Amparts program formerly operated by the USIA prior to its merger into the State Department, and to create a Middle East Foundation along the lines of the existing Asia Foundation as suggested by Amr Hamzawy (2005). Conversely, the United States also needs to reconsider Department of Homeland Security policies that significantly impede the issuance of visas to legitimate Arab scholars and opinion makers, discouraging precisely the sort of contact that should be encouraged, and generally conveying a poor image of the United States.[2] To be clear, we do not believe that mere familiarity or the provision of more accurate and diverse information will breed love—but what is being communicated today is *so* negative that almost any kind of truthful and noncondescending engagement would represent an improvement over the status quo.[3]

The bottom line is that improving the image of the United States and indeed the West in general including Britain and France, the former colonial powers, and strengthening moderate elements within the Arab world are going to be long and difficult endeavors involving many people making

---

2. In this regard, a critical issue is identifying Arab counterparts in these endeavors. Maghraoui (2006) identifies four broad constituencies comprising "Islamic Renewal": civil society organizations; proponents of "Islam and Democracy," i.e., moderate Islamist parties; proponents of "reform within Islam," i.e., modernizing clerics; and "culturally modern Islam" trying to articulate "western Islamic identity" mainly in the diaspora. Maghraoui would count the Malaysian government as an example of Islamic renewal, and in certain respects, the Moroccan monarchy. Among the moderate, democratically committed Islamist parties, Hamzawy (2005) identifies the Moroccan Justice and Development Party, the Jordanian Islamic Action Front (IAF), the Yemeni Reformist Union, and the Egyptian not-yet-legalized Center Party (Al Wasat). Intriguingly, the leadership of the Jordanian IAF has cited Malaysia as a model.

3. In this respect, the nonofficial status of the US participants in such programs is critical since within the region, statements by US officials are almost entirely discounted. This runs against the alleged tendency of the current US public diplomacy effort to select participants in officially supported outreach efforts from the ranks of the politically reliable, narrowly defined. It would also be desirable to draw upon a pool of participants that goes beyond the regional specialists, who oddly enough may convey a skewed notion of American attitudes and interests.

incremental contributions, strangely reminiscent in its essence to the difficult and uncertain task facing the Arab countries in reforming their internal institutions. In the words of Abdeslam M. Maghraoui, "Prospects for an Islamic renewal across countries and regions remain slim, unless these scattered efforts and networks coalesce in a coherent movement that can articulate a common modernist vision and propose concrete reforms to achieve it" (Maghraoui 2006, 9). To be fair, since the December 2002 announcement of the Middle East Partnership Initiative, the US government has undertaken a variety of possibly underappreciated programs aimed at strengthening civil society and improving public-sector institutional capability (Wittes and Yerkes 2006). Pop music radio stations are not the answer, however.

The third component, as discussed in chapter 8, should be preferential trade agreements. In general, we believe that these could have a positive role to play, though obviously the impact of any specific agreement will depend on its particulars as well as complementary policy changes undertaken by the partner country. Robert Z. Lawrence (2006) presents a sophisticated analysis of the potential benefits and demerits of expanding US preferential agreements with countries in the region along the lines of the Bush administration's Middle East free trade area proposal. In this regard, he raises two ancillary, though important, points.

First, the way that the United States has gone about negotiating these agreements is effectively creating a "hub-and-spoke" system in which individual Arab governments have strong bilateral agreements with the United States but weak or nonexistent agreements between themselves. In part this would appear inevitable, if regrettable, reflecting both differences in capacity and orientation across the Arab governments and, in the specific cases of the militarily vulnerable Gulf oil exporters, a particular interest in deepening ties with a strategic partner. If it were just an issue of variable speed geometry, to borrow a European phrase, that would be one thing. The bilateral agreements themselves contain mutual inconsistencies, however, particularly with respect to "rules of origin," which make incorporating them into a single regionwide accord difficult. The situation is further compounded by the fact that the rules embodied in the US agreements are inconsistent with the agreements that the European Union is reaching with the Arab countries. It would be desirable to increase the internal consistency of these arrangements to facilitate integrating them together in the future, but frankly such coordination does not appear to be a particularly high priority of either the United States or the European Union and possibly of the Arab countries themselves.

However, a renewed emphasis on multilateral coordination should be the fourth component of US policy toward the region. As we have argued, much of what is needed amounts to institutional reform and capacity building. The United States as a national government obviously has a role to play in providing technical assistance and support—its US Agency for

International Development mission in Cairo is the largest in the world, and a new program, the Fund for the Future, emerging out of the Broader Middle East and North Africa Initiative (BMENA), will support small and medium-sized enterprises.

The United States should not limit itself to unilateral measures, however, and ought to make use of the whole panoply of international institutions including the World Trade Organization (WTO), International Monetary Fund (IMF), and World Bank, as well as cooperative institutions such as the G-8. The IMF and World Bank are ideally placed to provide such services, the former on macroeconomic and financial-market issues, affecting countries of the region, and the latter on a broader range of development issues that are particularly relevant for the poorer Arab countries, while the WTO has been expanding its capacity to offer technical assistance in the trade field. The Bank and Fund have received considerable criticism over the years, some of it deserved. Yet they are well suited for a patient process of engagement with the countries of the region, which given the profound uncertainties associated with reform, is precisely what is required. In essence what one is doing with the Bretton Woods institutions is buying an option on reform: maintaining contact and a local knowledge base in anticipation of the day when the host government will be ready to move forward, recognizing that at any given moment the payoffs to engagement will be low insofar as local governments are either incompetent, uninterested in reform, or simply too risk averse to pursue it.

The BMENA and its annual Forum for the Future meetings were unveiled during the US chairmanship of the G-8 in 2004. The financial contributions of the European Commission and its member states to the program have been small, however (less in total than that of Qatar), while Europe's own programs "give short shrift to advancing political freedoms or the role of civil society in EU-Arab relations" (Wittes and Yerkes 2006, 10). Nevertheless, given the problematic image of the United States in the region, pursuing constructive initiatives through multilateral channels is not a bad tactic.

Concluding Thoughts

The proof of the pudding is in the eating. The critical issue is whether sustained accelerated growth of employment and income is achieved or not. Realization of this outcome requires both supportive policies and sufficient local productive capacity organized by indigenous entrepreneurs or foreign investors to take advantage of the opportunities presented. The international community can certainly help with reducing the conventional redistribution costs of reform and thus its political riskiness. Broadly defined to include the private sector, it can also play a role in fostering the requisite supply response to reform to make faster growth a reality.

The most problematic scenario is created by the possibility that inefficiencies embodied in the status quo are not simply the outcome of standard interest-group politics, but rather reflect either a religious and social consensus that trumps economic efficiency, or that reform is precluded by fears of political radicalism unleashed by short-term dislocations. To the extent that such an outcome could be interpreted as accurately reflecting social preferences, there is little ethical basis for the international community to encourage changes that are contrary to local values. While there may be negative transborder externalities associated with slow growth in the Arab countries—such as the encouragement of illegal emigration to other regions or the externalization of political discontent—these cannot be the basis for advocating altered economic policies that are rejected by the countries themselves, though the representativeness of the political mechanisms that have generated the prevailing choices is admittedly questionable.

Though the prevailing situation could represent a religious-social equilibrium, we are skeptical. As observed in chapter 10, the Arab political elites have made far less use of international assistance in holding elections than other similarly situated countries and appear to have chosen a distinctly undemocratic path. More likely, these outcomes reflect the preferences of dominant, though possibly unrepresentative, groups within the society that may not reflect the true underlying preferences of the community more broadly. Perhaps the most likely interpretation is that the reluctance with respect to reform reflects simple apprehension that change could be profoundly destabilizing.

The Middle East has long been a politically contested region of global significance. The demographic pressures the region faces to productively absorb and employ its young people entering the labor force raise the stakes even higher. It is not difficult to envision the region caught in a downward spiral where impoverishment, discontent, militancy, and repression feed upon one another. Yet this is not the only possible future. If the region's daunting employment challenge can be successfully addressed, the region's demographics could turn from a potential liability to a valuable asset. Growing prosperity, confidence, and optimism about the future could underpin movement toward greater political openness and social tolerance. The recognition that neither of these alternatives can be excluded is both an antidote to despair and a call to action.

Postscript

The Arab Economies Seen Through the Prism of the "Arab Spring"

This postscript reproduces in reverse chronological order four pieces that the authors wrote together or separately for the RealTime Economic Issues Watch, the website forum of the Peterson Institute for International Economics. These pieces, which are reactions to events as they were taking place, echo and reinforce the messages of this book, demonstrate the continued validity of the arguments made in this book, and help convey a sense of the atmosphere—as seen by experts in the field—at the time.

Will Political Liberalization Produce a New Peronism in the Middle East?

MARCUS NOLAND, MARCH 7, 2011

Compared to other regions of the world, the Middle East was once unique in its combination of authoritarianism and stultifying stability. No longer. Beginning in Tunisia, a wave of political upheaval has rolled across the region, reaching Egypt, Bahrain, Libya and other countries caught between rising expectations and their antediluvian political systems, abetted by pan-Arab news channels and social networking media.

Political liberalization will not make the underlying economic problems disappear, and indeed, it could usher in an era of unprecedented instability.

Harnessing the energy of the region's millions of young people is the single most critical long-term challenge facing its governments. It is this generation that has risen up to change the status quo, and no wonder. Labor forces are growing at 3.5–4.0 percent annually. Past economic performance, while respectable by global standards, is inadequate to deal with demographic pressures on job markets. The region has the world's lowest employment rate—less than half of adults are formally employed—and youth unemployment is estimated at roughly 25 percent–double the world average.

The unemployment problem is concentrated among urban, educated youth. In contrast to the pattern in the US and elsewhere, joblessness *rises* with educational attainment. In Egypt, for example, a young college grad is nearly ten times as likely to be unemployed as a young person with only an elementary school education. And while Egypt is an extreme case, the same phenomenon is evident elsewhere: a young Moroccan college grad is five times more likely to be unemployed than is primary school educated neighbor, three time more likely in Iran, and 25 percent more likely in Jordan. This demographic imperative will remain a challenge however the current political struggles are resolved.

How, then, might the post-breakthrough dynamics play out in these countries?

Obviously there are profound differences between, say, Tunisia and Yemen, and events will be driven by local conditions and cross-border linkages. (Yemen receives little popular attention, but it is arguably the most dangerous case of all: it has weak institutions, multiple societal fissures, and a significant al-Qaeda presence. A collapse in Yemen, moreover, could induce a pre-emptive tightening of control in Saudi Arabia, and even endanger Oman.)

In the short-run, all these countries, particularly those without oil resources, could face financial crisis, capital flight, contraction, and the need for external balance of payments support, either from the International Monetary Fund (IMF) or some less conventional source like Saudi Arabia, perhaps channeled via the Gulf Cooperation Council, the Arab Monetary Fund or the Islamic Development Bank.. They could also turn to China, which presumably might be interested in seeking enhanced diplomatic influence and access to critical energy supplies.

In the medium- to long-run, however, the underlying structural challenges will return to the fore. There are two broad possibilities as to how these regimes might respond.

In the optimistic scenario, enhanced political legitimacy could create the political space for reform. In "normal" countries or those lacking rich resource endowments, such as Syria, a new government could begin dismantling the rent-creating economic distortions used to create political machines that have contributed inter alia to inefficiency and corruption. In countries of super-natural resource abundance, like Libya, resource-derived rents could be redirected away from vanity projects and in more constructive directions. Political liberalization could unleash entrepreneurship and dynamism, reversing the brain drain that has greatly afflicted many countries and drawing in new foreign investment and technology.

A more negative outcome is also possible, however. A newly responsive political system could actually impede or reverse reforms already under way across the region over the past decade, worsening the long-term prognosis. It is increasingly evident that, rightly or wrongly, these reforms, which have been undertaken with varying degrees of intensity, are widely regarded as contributing to inequality, corruption, and in the context of rising world food prices, poverty.

Which way might the emerging new political forces go?

If you listen to what the publics of the region say, they do not appear to be particularly anti-market. But they do appear to be skeptical of neoliberal reforms and globalization. In a Pew poll, for example, only about a third of Egyptian respondents indicated support for closing large inefficient factories—even if doing so brought greater prosperity in the future.

Islamist groups in most countries, which constitute the single most organized opposition faction, have varied economic views, ranging from moderate (encouraging Islamic finance while grandfathering existing secular institutions) to dramatic (banning tourism, at least of a non-Islamic sort).

Like everywhere else, people in the Middle East tend to vote their pocketbooks when given the chance. In the national capitals, a prime source of extra-electoral instability could be unemployed urban youth, and whoever ends up heading these new, less politically secure regimes would be sensitive to their needs, regardless of ideology. One obvious response would be Keynesian-cum-populist policies.

Despite a lack of populist tradition, it would be hard to imagine that no politician would advance a platform catering to unions, public employees, and subsidies for all (including those pesky students). Peronism of the East. The problem is that a key constituency to be mollified is urban educated youth, many of whom have majored in subjects that do not easily match the demands of private employers. While a Keynesian program of public investment might be defensible, and self-limiting, a natural temptation will be to permanently expand public employment and the size of government. And while macroeconomic management in the region has generally been good, countries without the resources to fund such binges could face a collapse of the exchange rate, bringing the IMF into play, along with revived concerns about globalization, neo-colonialism, etc.

(One interesting implication of the unrest is the employment potential latent in the role of social media, which has fueled the recent protests. The public employment possibilities from that phenomenon should not be discounted. Governments, ministries, and offices throughout the region are now busily constructing Facebook pages. Tweeting cannot be far behind. Such activities could be scalable, bringing in people to construct and maintain Facebook pages; tweeters; supervisors and editors to monitor the content of this activity; people to monitor and respond to the pages and tweets of rivals. The employment possibilities, especially for hard-to-employ literature majors, could be infinite.)

The internal discord that would likely accompany a macroeconomic crisis could work the other way, however, contributing to higher assessments of risk, more (not less) of brain drain, and reduced foreign investment.

The wild card in all of this is the path of commodity prices. Depending on how instability spreads (or does not spread) among the oil and gas suppliers, one can imagine a variety of paths for energy prices. If, for example, oil production in Libya is seriously disrupted, but other major producers are unaffected, world oil prices would jump significantly. But other producers could actually benefit. The price move would then generate greater revenues available to buy off local opposition—or help the state repress protests, and shore up shaky neighbors as Saudi Arabia is attempting to do in Bahrain. The region's oil importers could be made worse off. Second-order general equilibrium effects on the global economy could generate a slowdown in investment, remittances, etc., which would be felt unevenly across the region.

Rising food costs have contributed to discontent, but the region's governments exert little if any control over grain prices which are determined in global markets. Further increases could aggravate instability while declines could amount to a political windfall.

In short, the region faces real economic challenges. It is possible that the political honeymoons associated with the removal of longstanding authoritarians could create greater leeway for governments to implement reform. But it is at least equally likely that political disruptions could set off internal and external dynamics that would make addressing the underlying economic issues more difficult and contribute to an environment of political instability for a sustained period.

Dangers of Rapid Political Change in the Middle East

HOWARD PACK, FEBRUARY 9, 2011

World leaders are calling for Hosni Mubarak to either resign or to institute "political and economic" reform that will meet the demands of the demonstrators. Such calls show a large degree of ignorance about the needed economic reforms and the fact that increasing political participation may pose obstacles to reforms. While the maintenance of deeply unpopular autocratic regimes is undesirable, movement towards an improved economy will be considerably more difficult than the exhortations emanating from many leaders suggest.

The Arab economies, including Egypt and Tunisia, have not been notable underperformers in economic growth nor do they have an unusual amount of income inequality. This is not to say they are rich: Egypt's per capita income is roughly $5,700 per year, Tunisia's $8,300, and in both it has gone up by 50 percent since 2003. They exhibit poverty levels lower than many countries not undergoing revolutions, which doesn't not imply they are egalitarian societies. And both have benefitted from extraordinary growth in many measures of social welfare, such as life expectancy, infant mortality, and education rates. For example, life expectancy in Egypt is 72, Tunisia 76, comparable to that in Latin America. In both, the infant mortality rate is about 18, only slightly higher than that in Washington, DC. Thus they mimic the experience of earlier revolutions from the French to the Russian, which the historian Crane Brinton noted typically occur after considerable growth. What is unusual about these nations, and much of the Middle East, is the autocratic rule that has persisted for very long periods, most under one individual such as Mubarak or some dynastic such as the Assad government in Syria. The lack of political choice, the suppression of views, and an often brutal security state system are clearly major catalysts for the current demonstrations.

But a major factor contributing to the current unrest is the small number of job opportunities for the burgeoning labor force, which stems from historically high birth rates that have recently declined but whose effects will continue for another decade. As in the OECD countries such as Spain, youth unemployment is difficult to address, but for nations like Egypt and Tunisia a relatively straightforward solution lies in the emulation of Asian nations such as Korea and Taiwan that faced similar problems in the 1960s. More recently China and Vietnam have had spectacular success. These nations have used intensive international integration to foster the growth of national income as well as the generation of employment.

International links have taken two forms—exports of labor intensive manufactured goods such as clothing and sportswear to more advanced countries and the tapping of western technological knowledge to lower costs and improve quality. These nations signed foreign technology licensing agreements with firms from advanced countries, which taught them foreign technologies and production methods. Some encouraged multinational corporations to relocate or colocate, which brought investment finance, technical knowledge, managerial abilities, and critically, marketing networks that allowed the products to reach retailers' shelves. But such "globalization" is typically very unpopular in Arab countries as shown in many surveys of social attitudes. Similarly, the privatization of government-owned enterprises is not welcomed despite their inefficiency, although Egypt has been better than other Arab nations in this respect. The improvement of efficiency of government agencies that supervise transportation, ports, and airports would require firing existing staff and reorganizing production, always a painful process for those affected. Unlike East European nations that underwent revolutions two decades ago and had as their model the liberal economies of the adjacent European Union, the population of the Arab nations is deeply skeptical of globalization.

Thus, any government that emerges from the current turmoil will face a deep conundrum. The steps they need to pursue to increase income levels and employment will inevitably engender popular disapproval. Given the success of the current demonstrations, newly enfranchised leaders may hesitate to undertake necessary reforms. They cannot assume they will receive backing from the international community should there be demonstrations against desirable economic policies that inevitably are disruptive in the short term even if they have benefits in the longer run. Given the recent advice by the West to give in to the popular demonstrations, how can a new government assume Western leaders will have sufficient perceptiveness to distinguish dissatisfaction with new desirable economic policies from unhappiness with the new government? Economic reform can occur under political systems as disparate as India's and China's as long as there is strong domestic backing for it. But pronouncements from world leaders that contain the contradictory "enhance democratic transitions and undertake major economic reforms" are not a substitute for a domestic political constituency for deep economic restructuring with its attendant short-term disruptions. There is no evidence of widespread acceptance of this agenda.

Existing leaders may exit, but this may not usher in a new era of comity and growth. There is no iron law that Middle Eastern countries will not undergo the same traumas as many of the nations in the Soviet bloc in the 10 years following the demise of communism. Income per capita declined in some by 20 percent or more, inflation was severe, and life savings were wiped out. Establishing the institutions and policies to preclude such an outcome will require much more effort than calls for a change of regime from Western capitals. And if the East European experience is repeated, much of the blame will be shifted to others. Slower change, not the disastrous "big bang" of Eastern Europe, should be the goal of both the nationals of the countries and the international community.

Arab Revolutions of Fing Expectations

MARCUS NOLAND AND HOWARD PACK, FEBRUARY 1, 2011

As poor countries go, Egypt is not in the bottom rank even among nations in the Arab world. Measured by such conventional indicators as the percentage of population living on less than $2 a day, Egypt's poverty is not high by international standards. Incomes have steadily risen and progress on life expectancy, infant mortality, years of education, and other indicators there has been impressive. Why then has the lethal mixture of poverty, unemployment, and rising food prices come together to ignite antigovernment protests in its streets?

The answer is not simply that citizens have tired of a repressive regime. It is also that regime's inability to address high unemployment, particularly among educated urban youth.

Though birth rates have been declining, there is a huge population bulge of job seekers in Egypt and elsewhere in the region with few prospects, regardless of education. Youth unemployment in the Middle East is roughly twice the world average, exemplified by Mohamed Bouazizi, the college graduate fruit vendor whose suicide set off the conflagration in Tunisia. In fact, unemployment goes *up* along with educational attainment. Joblessness among Egyptian college graduates is almost 10 times that of people with primary educations. It is no surprise that many of the leaders of the current unrest are university graduates.

Egypt faces two fundamental imperatives. The first and most obvious is to allow greater freedoms to channel protest and dissent. But the second fundamental imperative is to create jobs, particularly among those who have striven to better themselves through education. Right now, some educated young people defect to the oil rich Gulf and to the West to seek careers. But there are things Egypt and other countries in the region can do to create jobs at home.

Fifty years ago East Asia faced similar demographic circumstances and harnessed it into a boom that continues today. The key task is to penetrate global markets in labor-intensive manufacturing and service sectors, which can rapidly generate large-scale employment. Yet despite proximity to Europe and free trade arrangements with the European Union, manufactured exports have been paltry. Thailand, with a population smaller than that of Egypt, exports 10 times as many manufactured goods.

How could the region's governments foster such a job-creating export boom? Success requires improving productivity, thus lowering costs. Upgrading roads and port facilities—making it easier to both import components needed by export industries and ship out the finished exports—would be a start. Special economic zones to facilitate processing for exporting firms have been used with success in nations as diverse as China and Mauritius, but are relatively rare in the Middle East.

But more fundamentally, increasing productivity requires Egypt and other countries to open their doors to foreign technology, technology licensing agreements, foreign direct investment, and the use of consultants from advanced countries. The widespread use of social media in the Tunisian and Egyptian protests demonstrates that these societies are adapting imported technology. But more could be done, particularly in industrial applications. The Philippines, roughly the size of Egypt, reports more technology royalty payments—an indicator of technology importation—than all Arab countries combined. In the Middle East, however, several *Arab Human Development Reports* have documented the dearth of incoming knowledge flows, such as translations of books into Arabic and the introduction of modernized school curricula.

Addressing the employment problem alone will not resolve political tensions; the dislocations caused by reform could actually be destabilizing in the short run. And while economic growth may be a short-term palliative, rising incomes in the absence of political liberalization will intensify discontent in the long run. But addressing this issue is a central challenge to the ability of Ben Ali's successors in Tunisia to establish a sustainable basis for governance in a more open political system, as it will be for their eventual counterparts in Egypt and elsewhere in the region. Whoever emerges on top will face the same labor unrest and need to implement changes ranging from education reform to economic policy. Americans should require little reminder of how difficult such changes are.

In Tunisia, an Uprising Spurred by Economic Advances

MARCUS NOLAND, JANUARY 18, 2011

The overthrow of Tunisia's longstanding Ben Ali dictatorship, sparked when 26-year-old vendor Mohamed Bouazizi set himself on fire in protest after his business was confiscated for lack of approved documents, has led many to wonder if these events may be a harbinger of the region's future. Lost in the descriptions of Tunisia's disaffected youth is that Tunisia is arguably the Arab world's most successful economy, the only one where over the last half century per capita incomes have steadily converged on those of the rich industrial democracies of the OECD.

Arab economies face daunting challenges, most notably with respect to unemployment—educated urban youth unemployment in particular. Yet as Howard Pack and I showed in our book, *Arab Economies in a Changing World*, across dozens of indicators of economic performance—including those relating to the ease of starting and maintaining a business, precisely the issues that led to Bouazizi's self-immolation—Tunisia was consistently at or near the top of the regional rankings. From a regional perspective this is clearly not a story of economic incompetence generating an uprising. If anything, it is the opposite: a steadily advancing society chafing under repression.

Tunisia may not be the model for developments elsewhere in the Middle East. Its small size, geographical proximity to Europe (some Tunisians are capable of receiving Italian radio and television broadcasts from

Sicily), and large tourism sector (and attendant exposure to Western cultural influences) set it apart from much of the Arab world. But the emergence of Al Jazeera and other pan-Arab broadcast media, together with the rapid expansion of internet-based social media, means that news spreads more quickly and with even greater intimacy than it did only a decade ago.

Many jihadist groups speak of martyrdom. Ben Ali raised political repression to an art form. His government has been brought down by very brave young men who took to the streets knowing that they would be fired upon by the police. The dozens who died are real martyrs.

References

Abadie, Alberto. 2006. Poverty, Freedom, and the Roots of Terrorism. *American Economic Review* 96, no. 2: 50–56.

Abadie, Alberto, and Javier Gardeazabal. 2005. Terrorism and the World Economy. Kennedy School of Government, Harvard University. Photocopy (October).

AbiNader, Jean. 2003. PTAs and Arab Regimes: Realities and Opportunities. Paper presented at the Trade Regionalism Conference, Airlie Center, Warrenton, VA, July 29–30.

Acemoglu, Daron, Simon Johnson, and James A. Robinson. 2001. The Colonial Origins of Comparative Development. *American Economic Review* 91, no. 5: 1369–401.

Adams, Richard, and John M. Page. 2003. Poverty, Inequality and Growth in Selected Middle East and North Africa Countries, 1980–2000. *World Development* 31: 2027–48.

Aghion, Philippe. 2006. Interaction Effects in the Relationship Between Growth and Finance. *Capitalism and Society* 1, no. 1, article 2.

Aghion, Philippe, and Peter Howitt. 1997. *Endogenous Growth Theory.* Cambridge, MA: MIT Press.

Aghion, Philippe, Peter Howitt, and David Mayer-Foulkes. 2005. The Effect of Financial Development on Convergence: Theory and Evidence. *Quarterly Journal of Economics* 120, no. 1 (January): 173–222.

Al-Atrash, Hassan, and Tarik Yousef. 2000. *Intra-Arab Trade: Is It Too Little?* IMF Working Paper WP/00/10. Washington: International Monetary Fund.

Albuquerque, Rui, Norman Loayza, and Luis Servén. 2005. World Market Integration Through the Lens of Direct Foreign Investors. *Journal of International Economics* 66, no. 2: 267–95.

Alesina, Alberto, and Allan Drazen. 1991. Why Are Stabilizations Delayed? *American Economic Review* 81, no. 5: 1170–88.

Alesina, Alberto, and Nicola Fuchs-Schuendeln. 2005. *Goodbye Lenin (or Not?): The Effect of Communism on People's Preferences.* Discussion Paper 2076. Cambridge, MA: Harvard Institute for Economic Research.

Alfaro, Laura, Areendam Chanda, Sebnem Kalemli-Özcan, and Selin Sayek. 2003. *FDI Spillovers, Financial Markets, and Economic Development.* IMF Working Paper WP/03/186. Washington: International Monetary Fund.

Alhadeff, Gini. 1998. *The Sun at Midday.* New York: Random House.

Alsan, Marcella, David E. Bloom, and David Canning. 2004. *The Effect of Population Health on Foreign Direct Investment.* NBER Working Paper 10596. Cambridge, MA: National Bureau of Economic Research.

Al-Suwailem, Sami. 2006. *Hedging in Islamic Finance*. Occasional Paper 10. Jeddah, Saudi Arabia: Islamic Development Bank.

Alterman, Jon B. 2006. After Liberals Back Down. *Middle East Notes and Comment*. Washington: Center for Strategic and International Studies (April).

Anderson, Lisa. 2001. Arab Democracy: Dismal Prospects. *World Policy Journal* (Fall): 53–60.

Angels-Oliva, Maria. 2000. *Estimation of Trade Protection in Middle East and North African Countries*. IMF Working Paper WP/00/27. Washington: International Monetary Fund.

Auty, Richard M., ed. 2001. Resource Abundance and Economic Development. *UNU/WIDER Studies in Development Economics*. Oxford: Oxford University Press.

Ayubi, Nazih. 1993. *Political Islam*. London: Routledge.

Baer, Werner, and M. E. A. Hervé. 1966. Employment and Industrialization in Developing Countries. *Quarterly Journal of Economics* 80: 88–107.

Balassa, Bela. 1989. My Life Philosophy. *American Economist* (Summer): 16–23.

Balasubramanyam, V. N., M. Salisu, and David Sapsford. 1996. Foreign Direct Investment and Growth in EP and IS Countries. *Economic Journal* 106, no. 434: 92–105.

Barlow, Robin. 1982. Economic Growth in the Middle East, 1950–72. *International Journal of Middle East Studies* 14: 129–57.

Barrett, David B., George T. Kurian, and Todd M. Johnson. 2001. *World Christian Encyclopedia: A Comparative Survey of Churches and Religions in the Modern World*. New York: Oxford University Press.

Barro, Robert J. 1991. Economic Growth in a Cross Section of Countries. *Quarterly Journal of Economics* 105: 407–43.

Barro, Robert J. 1999. Determinants of Democracy. *Journal of Political Economy* 107, no. 6: S157–S183.

Barro, Robert J., and Rachel M. McCleary. 2003. Religion and Economic Growth Across Countries. *American Sociological Review* 68: 760–81.

Barth, James R., Tong Li, Don McCarthy, Triphon Phumiwasana, and Glenn Yago. 2006. Economic Impact of Global Terrorism from Munich to Bali. Paper presented at the American Economic Associations meeting, Boston, January 6–7.

Beblawi, Hazem. 1990. The Rentier State in the Arab World. In *The Arab State*, ed. Giacomo Luciani. Berkeley, CA: University of California Press.

Bellin, Eva. 2004. The Robustness of Authoritarianism in the Middle East. *Comparative Politics* 36, no. 2: 139–58.

Bellin, Eva. 2006. The Political-Economic Conundrum. In *Uncharted Journey: Promoting Democracy in the Middle East*, ed. Thomas Carothers and Marina Ottaway. Washington: Carnegie Endowment for International Peace.

Benmelech, Efraim, and Claude Berrebi. 2006. Attack Assignment in Terror Organizations and the Productivity of Suicide Bombers. Department of Economics, Harvard University; National Bureau of Economic Research; and Rand Corporation. Photocopy.

Bergen, Peter L., and Swati Pandey. 2006. The Madrassa Scapegoat. *Washington Quarterly* 29, no. 2: 117–25.

Berman, Eli, John Bound, and Stephen Machin. 1998. Implications of Skill-Biased Technological Change: International Evidence. *Quarterly Journal of Economics* (November): 1245–79.

Berman, Eli, and Ara Stepanyan. 2004. How Many Radical Islamists? Indirect Evidence from Five Countries. University of California, San Diego; National Bureau of Economic Research; and Rice University. Photocopy.

Berman, Eli, and Laurence R. Iannaccone. 2005. *Religious Extremism: The Good, the Bad, and the Deadly*. NBER Working Paper 11663. Cambridge, MA: National Bureau of Economic Research.

Berkowitz, Daniel, Katharina Pistor, and Jean-François Richard. 2003. Economic Development, Legality, and the Transplant Effect. *European Economic Review* 47, no. 1: 165–95.

Berry, Christopher R., and Edward L. Glaeser. 2005. *The Divergence of Human Capital Levels Across Cities*. Harvard Institute of Economic Research Discussion Paper 2091. Cambridge, MA: Harvard University.

Bevan, David, Paul Collier, and Jan Gunning. 1999. *The Political Economy of Poverty, Equity, and Growth: Nigeria and Indonesia.* New York: Oxford University Press.

Bhagwati, Jagdish, and T. N. Srinivasan. 1983. *Lectures on International Trade.* Cambridge, MA: MIT Press.

Biers, Dan, and Sadanand Dhume. 2000. In India, a Bit of California. *Far Eastern Economic Review* 163, no. 44 (November 2): 38–40.

Blanke, Jennifer, and Emma Loades. 2005. The Executive Opinion Survey: An Essential Tool for Measuring Country Competitiveness. In *The Global Competitiveness Report 2005–2006.* Geneva: World Economic Forum.

Blomberg, S. Brock, and Gregory Hess. 2006. How Much Does Violence Tax Trade? *Review of Economics and Statistics* 88, no. 4: 599–612.

Blonigen, Bruce, and Miao Grace Wang. 2005. Inappropriate Pooling of Wealthy and Poor Countries in Empirical FDI Studies. In *Does Foreign Investment Promote Development?* ed. Theodore H. Moran, Edward M. Graham, and Magnus Blomström. Washington: Peterson Institute for International Economics.

Bolbol, Ali A., and Ayten M. Fatheldin. 2005. *Intra-Arab Exports and Direct Investment: An Empirical Analysis.* AMF Economic Papers 12. Abu Dhabi: Arab Monetary Fund.

Bolbol, Ali A., and Mohammad M. Omran. 2005. Investment and the Stock Market: Evidence from Arab Firm-Level Panel Data. *Emerging Markets Review* 6: 85–106.

Bosworth, Barry F., and Susan M. Collins. 2003. The Empirics of Growth: An Update. *Brookings Papers on Economic Activity* 2: 113–79.

Borensztein, E., J. De Gregorio, and J.-W. Lee. 1999. How Does Foreign Investment Affect Economic Growth? *Journal of International Economics* 45: 115–35.

Boroumand, Ladan, and Roya Boroumand. 2002. Terror, Islam, and Democracy. *Journal of Democracy* 13, no. 2: 5–20.

Branstetter, Lee, Raymond Fisman, and C. Fritz Foley. 2005. *Do Stronger Intellectual Property Rights Increase International Technology Transfer? Empirical Evidence from U.S. Firm-Level Data.* NBER Working Paper 11516. Cambridge, MA: National Bureau of Economic Research.

Bremer, Jennifer, and John D. Kasarda. 2002. The Origins of Terror. *Milken Review* (fourth quarter): 34–48.

Brenton, Paul, Eugenia Baroncelli, and Mariem Malouche. 2006. *Trade and Investment Integration in the Maghreb.* Middle East and North Africa Working Paper Series 44 (May). Washington: World Bank.

Brittingham, Angela, and G. Patricia de la Cruz. 2005. *We the People of Arab Ancestry in the United States.* Washington: US Census Bureau.

Campos, E. J., and Hilton Root. 1996. *The Key to the Asian Miracle: Making Shared Growth Credible.* Washington: Brookings Institution.

Cardoso, Fernando Henrique, and Enzo Faletto. 1979. *Dependency and Development in Latin America.* Berkeley and Los Angeles: University of California Press.

Carothers, Thomas. 2002. The End of the Transition Paradigm. *Journal of Democracy* 13, no. 1: 5–21.

Carr, David L., James R. Markusen, and Keith E. Maskus. 2001. Estimating the Knowledge-Capital Model of the Multinational Enterprise. *American Economic Review* 91, no. 3: 693–708.

Carstensen, Kai, and Farid Toubal. 2004. Foreign Direct Investment in Central and Eastern European Countries. *Journal of Comparative Economics* 32, no. 1: 3–22.

Cassing, James H., Samiha Fawzy, Denis Gallagher, and Hanaa Kheir-El-Din. 2000. Enhancing Egypt's Exports. In *Catching Up with the Competition,* ed. Bernard Hoekman and Jamel Zarrouk. Ann Arbor, MI: University of Michigan Press.

Caves, Richard. 1996. *Multinational Enterprise and Economic Analysis,* 2d ed. Cambridge, UK: Cambridge University Press.

CCFR (Chicago Council on Foreign Relations). 2004. *Global Views 2004.* Chicago, IL.

Chenery, Hollis, Sherman Robinson, and Moshe Syrquin. 1986. *Industrialization and Growth: A Comparative Study*. New York: Oxford University Press.

Cheong, Young Rok. 2003. Chinese Business Networks and Their Implications for South Korea. In *The Korean Diaspora in the World Economy*, ed. C. Fred Bergsten and Inbom Choi. Washington: Institute for International Economics.

Cheung, TaiMing. 2001. *China's Entrepreneurial Army*. Oxford: Oxford University Press.

Choi, Inbom. 2003. Korean Diaspora in the Making: Its Current Status and Impact on the Korean Economy. In *The Korean Diaspora in the World Economy*, ed. C. Fred Bergsten and Inbom Choi. Washington: Peterson Institute for International Economics.

Cieślik, Andrzej, and Michael Ryan. 2004. Explaining Japanese Direct Investment Flows into an Enlarged Europe. *Journal of the Japanese and International Economies* 18, no. 1: 12–37.

Clatanoff, William, C. Christopher Parlin, Robert Jordan, Charles Kestenbaum, and Jean-François Seznec. 2006. Saudi Arabia's Accession to the WTO: Is a 'Revolution' Brewing. *Middle East Policy* XIII, no. 1: 1–23.

Clerides, Sofronis, Saul Lach, and James R. Tybout. 1998. Is Learning by Exporting Important? Microdynamic Evidence from Colombia, Mexico, and Morocco. *Quarterly Journal of Economics* 113: 903–47.

Coe, David T., and Elhanan Helpman. 1995. International R&D Spillovers. *European Economic Review* 39, no. 5: 859–87.

Coe, David T., Elhanan Helpman, and Alexander Hoffmaister. 1996. North-South R&D Spillovers. *Economic Journal* 107, no. 440 (September): 134–49.

Collins, Susan M., and Barry P. Bosworth. 1996. Economic Growth in East Asia: Accumulation vs. Assimilation. *Brookings Papers on Economic Activity* 1: 135–92.

Combes, Pierre-Philippe, Miren Lafourcade, and Thierry Mayer. 2005. The Trade-Creating Effects of Business and Social Networks: Evidence from France. *Journal of International Economics* 66, no. 1: 1–29.

Council on Foreign Relations. 2002. *Terrorist Financing*. New York.

Council on Foreign Relations. 2004. *Update on the Global Campaign Against Terrorist Financing*. New York.

Council on Foreign Relations. 2005. *In Support of Arab Democracy: Why and How*. New York.

Creane, Susan, Rishi Goyal, A. Mushfiq Mobarak, and Randa Sab. 2003. *Financial Development in the Middle East and North Africa*. Washington: International Monetary Fund. Available at www.imf.org (accessed December 30, 2004).

Crone, Patricia. 2004. *God's Rule: Islam and Government*. New York: Columbia University Press.

Dasgupta, D., Jennifer Keller, and T. G. Srinivasan. 2002. *Reforms and Elusive Growth in the Middle East—What Has Happened in the 1990s*. MENA Working Paper 25. Washington: World Bank.

de Ferranti, David, Guillermo Perry, Indermit Gill, Luis Guasch, William Maloney, Carolina Sanches-Paramo, and Norbert Schady. 2003. *Closing the Gap in Education and Technology*. Washington: World Bank.

Deininger, Klaus W., and Lyn Squire. 1996. *Measuring Income Inequality Database*. Washington: World Bank.

de Melo, Jaime. 1985. Sources of Growth in Korea and Taiwan: Some Comparisons. In *Export-Oriented Development Strategies: The Success of Five Newly Industrialized Countries*, ed. V. Corbo, A. Krueger, and F. Ossa. Boulder, CO, and London: Westview Press.

Dennis, Allen. 2006. *The Impact of Regional Trade Agreements and Trade Facilitation in the Middle East and North Africa Region*. World Bank Policy Research Working Paper 3837 (February). Washington: World Bank.

DeRosa, Dean, and John P. Gilbert. 2004. Technical Appendix: Quantitative Estimates of the Economic Impacts of US Bilateral Free Trade Agreements. In *Free Trade Agreements: US Strategies and Priorities*, ed. Jeffrey J. Schott. Washington: Peterson Institute for International Economics.

de Soysa, Indra, and Ragnhild Nordås. 2006. Islam's Bloody Innards? Religion and Political Terror. Paper prepared for the meeting of Environmental Factors in Civil War Working Group, September 21, Oslo.

Dhonte, Pierre, Rina Bhattacharya, and Tarik Yousef. 2000. *Demographic Transition in the Middle East: Implications for Growth, Employment, and Housing*. IMF Working Paper WP/00/41. Washington: International Monetary Fund.

Djankov, Simeon, Rafael LaPorta, Florencio Lopez-de-Silanes, and Andrei Shleifer. 2003. Courts. *Quarterly Journal of Economics* 118, no. 2: 519–48.

Documentary and Advisory Center on Racial Discrimination. 2004. *Analytical Report on Education: National Focal Point for Denmark*. Vienna: European Monitoring Centre on Racism and Xenophobia.

Donovan, N., D. Halpern, and R. Sargeant. 2003. *Life Satisfaction: The State of Knowledge and Implications for Government*. Cabinet Office Analytical Paper. London: Prime Minister's Strategy Unit, Government of the United Kingdom.

Drazen, Allan. 2000. *Political Economy in Macroeconomics*. Princeton, NJ: Princeton University Press.

Duffy, John, Chris Papageorgiou, and Fidel Perez-Sebastian. 2004. Capital-Skill Complementarity? Evidence from a Panel of Countries. *Review of Economics and Statistics* 86, no. 1: 327–44.

Durlauf, Steven. 2003. Comment. *Brookings Papers on Economic Activity* 2: 180–89.

Durrell, Lawrence. 1957, 1958, 1960. *The Alexandria Quartet*. New York: Penguin Books.

Easterly, William, Michael Kremer, Lant Pritchett, and Lawrence H. Summers. 1993. Good Policy or Good Luck? Country Growth Performance and Temporary Shocks. *Journal of Monetary Economics* 32, no. 3: 459–83.

Easterly, William, and Ross Levine. 2001. It's Not Factor Accumulation. *World Bank Economic Review* 15, no. 2: 177–219.

Eaton, Jonathan, and Mark Gersovitz. 1984. A Theory of Expropriations and Deviations from Perfect Capital Mobility. *Review of Economic Studies* 48: 289–309.

Eid, Florence, and Fiona Paua. 2003. Foreign Direct Investment in the Arab World. In *The Arab World Competitiveness Report 2002–2003*, ed. Peter Cornelius. New York: Oxford University Press.

El-Gamal, Mahmoud. 2006. *Overview of Islamic Finance*. Occasional Paper 4. Washington: Department of the Treasury.

El-Hawary, Dahlia, Wafik Grais, and Zamir Iqbal. 2004. *Regulating Islamic Financial Institutions: The Nature of the Regulated*. World Bank Policy Research Working Paper Series 3227. Washington: World Bank.

El Qorhi, Mohammed, Samuel Muzele Maimbo, and John F. Wilson. 2003. *Informal Funds Transfer Systems: An Analysis of the Informal Hawala System*. IMF Occasional Paper 222. Washington: International Monetary Fund.

Engerman, Stanley L., and Kenneth L. Sokoloff. 2003. *Institutional and Non-Institutional Explanations of Economic Differences*. NBER Working Paper 9989. Cambridge, MA: National Bureau of Economic Research.

Enos, John, and W. H. Park. 1988. *The Adoption and Diffusion of Imported Technology: The Case of Korea*. London: Croom Helm.

Esfahani, Hadi Salehi. 2000. Political Economy of Growth in MENA Countries: A Framework for Country Case Studies. University of Illinois at Urbana-Champaign. Photocopy.

Evans, Carolyn L., and James Harrigan. 2005. Distance, Time, and Specialization: Lean Retailing in General Equilibrium. *American Economic Review* 95, no. 1: 292–313.

Fallon, P. R., and P. R. G. Layard. 1975. Capital-Skill Complementarity, Income Distribution, and Output Accounting. *Journal of Political Economy* 83, no. 2: 279–302.

Fanon, Franz. 1967. *Black Skin, White Masks*. New York: Grove.

Fanon, Franz. 1968. *The Wretched of the Earth*. New York: Grove.

Fernandez, Raquel, and Dani Rodrik. 1991. Resistance to Reform: Status Quo Bias in the Presence of Individual-Specific Uncertainty. *American Economic Review* 81, no. 5: 1146–55.

Ferragina, Anna, Giorgia Giovannetti, and Francesco Pastore. 2004. EU Integration with Mediterranean Partner Countries Vis-à-Vis CEE-10: A Gravity Study. Paper presented at the European Trade Study Group, ETSG2004 Programme, University of Nottingham, September 9–11. Photocopy.

Fidrmuc, Jan. 2000a. Political Support for Reforms: Economics of Voting in Transition Countries. *European Economic Review* 44, no. 8: 1491–513.

Fidrmuc, Jan. 2000b. Economics of Voting in Post-Communist Countries. *Electoral Studies* 19, no. 2/3: 197–217.

Finnish League for Human Rights. 2002. *Migrants, Minorities, and Employment in Finland.* Vienna: European Monitoring Centre on Racism and Xenophobia.

Fish, M. Steven. 2002. Islam and Authoritarianism. *World Politics* 55 (October): 4–37.

Fisher, F. M., S. Arlosoroff, Z. Eckstein, M. Haddadin, S. G. Hamati, A. Huber-Lee, A. Jarrar, A. Jayyousi, U. Shamir, and H. Wesseling. 2002. Optimal Water Management and Conflict Resolution: The Middle East Water Project. *Water Resources Research* 38, no. 11: 1243.

Fisman, Raymond, and Edward Miguel. 2006. *Cultures of Corruption: Evidence from Diplomatic Parking Tickets.* NBER Working Paper 12312. Cambridge, MA: National Bureau of Economic Research.

Florida, Richard. 2002. *The Rise of the Creative Class.* New York: Perseus Books.

Frankel, Jeffrey. 2003. Comment. *Brookings Papers on Economic Activity* 2: 189–99.

Fromkin, David. 1989. *A Peace to End All Peace: Creating the Modern Middle East, 1914–1922.* New York: Henry Holt & Co.

Fromm, Erich. 1941. *Escape from Freedom.* New York: Holt, Rinehart, and Winston.

Furman, Jason, and Joseph E. Stiglitz. 1998. Economic Crises: Evidence and Insight from East Asia. *Brookings Papers on Economic Activity* 30, no. 2: 1–114. Washington: Brookings Institution.

Galal, Ahmed, and Robert Z. Lawrence. 2004. Egypt, Morocco, and the United States. In *Free Trade Agreements: US Strategies and Priorities,* ed. Jeffrey J. Schott. Washington: Peterson Institute for International Economics.

Ganor, Boaz. 2002. Defining Terrorism: Is One Man's Terrorist Another Man's Freedom Fighter? *Police Practice and Research* 3, no. 4: 287–304.

Gao, Ting. 2005. Foreign Direct Investment and Growth Under Economic Integration. *Journal of International Economics* 67, no. 1: 157–74.

Gardner, Edward. 2003. *Creating Employment in the Middle East and North Africa.* Washington: International Monetary Fund. Available at www.imf.org (accessed December 30, 2004).

Gause, F. Gregory, III. 1995. Regional Influences on Experiments in Political Liberalization in the Arab World. In *Political Liberalization and Democratization in the Arab World, Volume I: Theoretical Perspectives,* ed. Rex Brynen, Bahgat Korany, and Paul Noble. Boulder, CO: Lynne Rienner.

Gause, F. Gregory, III. 2005. Can Democracy Stop Terrorism? *Foreign Affairs* (September/October): 62–76.

Gentzkow, Matthew A., and Jesse M. Shapiro. 2004. Media, Education and Anti-Americanism in the Muslim World. *Journal of Economic Perspectives* 18, no. 3: 117–33.

Gereffi, Gary. 1999. International Trade and Industrial Upgrading in the Apparel Commodity Chain. *Journal of International Economics* 48: 37–70.

Gerschenkron, Alexander. 1962. *Economic Development in Historical Perspective.* Cambridge, MA: Harvard University Press.

Gilbert, John. 2003. CGE Simulation of US Bilateral Trade Agreements. Background paper prepared for the conference on Free Trade Agreements and US Policy, Peterson Institute for International Economics, Washington, May 7–8.

Glaeser, Edward. 2004. *Reinventing Boston: 1640 to 2003.* NBER Working Paper 10166. Cambridge, MA: National Bureau of Economic Research.

Glaeser, Edward, and Albert Saiz. 2004. *The Rise of the Skilled City.* NBER Working Paper 10191. Cambridge, MA: National Bureau of Economic Research.

Glaeser, Edward, Rafael LaPorta, Florencio Lopez-de-Silanes, and Andrei Shleifer. 2004. *Do Institutions Cause Growth?* NBER Working Paper 10568. Cambridge, MA: National Bureau of Economic Research.

Glain, Stephen. 2004. *Mullahs, Merchants, and Militants*. New York: Thomas Dunne Books.

Gleditsch, Kristian Skrede. 2002. *All International Politics Is Local: The Diffusion of Conflict, Integration, and Democratization*. Ann Arbor, MI: University of Michigan Press.

GlobeScan. 2003. *19-Nation Poll on Global Issues*. Washington: GlobeScan Research Partners.

GlobeScan. 2004. *8-Nation Poll on Africa*. Washington: GlobeScan Research Partners.

Gollin, Douglas, Stephen L. Parente, and Richard Rogerson. 2004. *The Food Problem and the Evolution of International Income Levels*. Economic Growth Center Discussion Paper 899. New Haven, CT: Yale University.

Graham, Edward M., and David Marchick. 2006. *US National Security and Foreign Direct Investment*. Washington: Institute for International Economics.

Greif, Avner. 1994. Cultural Beliefs and the Organization of Society: A Historical and Theoretical Reflection on Collectivist and Individual Societies. *Journal of Political Economy* 102, no. 5: 912–50.

Grossman, Gene M., and Elhanan Helpman. 1991. *Innovation and Growth in the Global Economy*. Cambridge, MA: MIT Press.

Grubert, Harry, and John Mutti. 2000. Do Taxes Influence Where U.S. Corporations Invest? *National Tax Journal* 53, no. 4: 825–40.

Guiso, Luigi, Paola Sapienza, and Luigi Zingales. 2003. People's Opium? Religion and Economic Activities. *Journal of Monetary Economics* 50, no. 1: 225–82.

Guiso, Luigi, Paola Sapienza, and Luigi Zingales. 2004. *Cultural Biases in Economic Exchange*. NBER Working Paper Series 11005. Cambridge, MA: National Bureau of Economic Research.

Gurley, John, and Edward Shaw. 1960. *Money in a Theory of Finance*. Washington: Brookings Institution.

Gurr, Ted. 1970. *Why Men Rebel*. Princeton, NJ: Princeton University Press.

Haggard, Stephan. 1990. *Pathways from the Periphery*. Ithaca, NY: Cornell University Press.

Haggard, Stephan, and Robert R. Kaufman. 1995. *The Political Economy of Democratic Transitions*. Princeton, NJ: Princeton University Press.

Hale, David. 2004. *Jordan Trade Relationships in 2004: A Record of Remarkable Growth and Success*. Available at http://usembassy-amman.org.jo (accessed July 20, 2005).

Hallaq, Wael B. 1984. Was the Gate of *Ijtihad* Closed? *International Journal of Middle East Studies* 16, no. 1: 3–41.

Hallaq, Wael B. 1997. *A History of Islamic Legal Theories*. Cambridge, UK: Cambridge University Press.

Hamzawy, Amr. 2005. *The Key to Arab Reform: Moderate Islamists*. Policy Brief 40. Washington: Carnegie Endowment for International Peace.

Hansen, Bent, and Girgis A. Marzouk. 1965. *Development and Economic Policy in the UAR (Egypt)*. Amsterdam: North-Holland.

Hanushek, Eric. 2005. Why Quality Matters in Education. *Finance and Development* 42: 15–19.

Harrigan, James, and Anthony J. Venables. 2004. *Timeliness, Trade, and Agglomeration*. NBER Working Paper 10404. Cambridge, MA: National Bureau of Economic Research.

Harrison, Mark. 2003. *Suicide Terrorism*. Coventry, UK: University of Warwick.

Helliwell, John F. 2005. *Well-Being, Social Capital, and Public Policy: What's New?* Working Paper 11807. Cambridge, MA: National Bureau of Economic Research.

Helliwell, John F., and Haifang Huang. 2006. *How's Your Government? International Evidence Linking Good Government and Well-Being*. NBER Working Paper 11988. Cambridge, MA: National Bureau of Economic Research.

Hellman, Joel. 1998. Winners Take All: The Politics of Partial Reform in Postcommunist Countries. *World Politics* 50, no. 2: 203–34.

Henry, Clement M., and Robert Springborg. 2001. *Globalization and the Politics of Development in the Middle East*. Cambridge, UK: Cambridge University Press.

Henry, Clement M., and Rodney Wilson. 2004. *The Politics of Islamic Finance*. Edinburgh: Edinburgh University Press.

Herb, Michael. 2005. No Representation Without Taxation? Rents, Development, and Democracy. *Comparative Politics* 37, no. 3.

Hernander, Mark G., and Luz A. Saavedra. 2005. Export and the Structure of Immigrant-based Networks: The Role of Geographic Proximity. *Review of Economics and Statistics* 87, no. 2: 323–35.

Hill, Christopher. 1967. *From Reformation to Industrial Revolution*. London: Weidenfeld & Nicholson.

Hill, Hal. 1996. *The Indonesian Economy since 1996*. Cambridge, UK: Cambridge University Press.

Hobday, Mike. 1995. *Innovation in East Asia: The Challenge to Japan*. London: Edward Elgar.

Hoekman, Bernard, and Denise Eby Konan. 2005. Economic Implications of a US-Egypt FTA. In *Anchoring Reform with a US-Egypt Free Trade Agreement*, by Ahmed Galal and Robert Z. Lawrence. Washington: Institute for International Economics.

Hoekman, Bernard, and Patrick Messerlin. 2002. *Harnessing Trade for Development and Growth in the Middle East*. New York: Council on Foreign Relations.

Hoekman, Bernard, and Jayanta Roy. 2000. Benefiting from WTO Membership and Accession. In *Catching Up with the Competition: Trade Opportunities and Challenges for Arab Countries*, ed. Bernard Hoekman and Jamel Zarrouk. Ann Arbor, MI: University of Michigan Press.

Hofstede, Geert. 1983. *Cultures and Organizations*. New York: McGraw Hill.

Hofstede, Geert. 2001. *Culture's Consequences: Comparing Values, Behaviors, Institutions, and Organizations Across Nations*, 2d ed. Thousand Oaks, CA: Sage Publications.

Hönekopp, Elmar, Gisela Will, and Stefan Rühl. 2002. *Migrants, Minorities, and Employment in Germany*. Vienna: European Monitoring Centre on Racism and Xenophobia.

Horne, Alistair. 1978. *A Savage War of Peace: Algeria, 1954–62*. New York: Viking Press.

Hou, Chi-Ming, and San Gee. 1993. National Systems Supporting Technological Advance in Industry: The Case of Taiwan. In *National Innovation Systems: A Comparative Analysis*, ed. Richard R. Nelson. New York: Oxford University Press.

Houtzager, Dick, and Peter R. Rodrigues. 2002. *Migrants, Minorities, and Employment in the Netherlands*. Vienna: European Monitoring Centre on Racism and Xenophobia.

Hughes, Robert. 1986. *The Fatal Shore*. New York: Knopf.

Huntington, Samuel P. 1984. Will More Countries Become Democratic? *Political Science Quarterly* 99, no. 2: 193–218.

Huntington, Samuel P. 1993. *The Third Wave: Democratization in the Late Twentieth Century*. Norman: University of Oklahoma Press.

Huntington, Samuel P. 1996. *Clash of Civilizations and the Remaking of World Order*. New York: Simon and Schuster.

Hussein, Khaled A., and M. F. Omran. 2005. *Financial Development in Arab Countries*. Jeddah: Islamic Development Bank.

Ibrahim, Saad Eddin. 1982. *The New Arab Social Order: A Study of the Social Impact of Oil Wealth*. Boulder, CO: Westview Press.

ICMPD (International Centre for Migration Policy Development). 2003. *Migrants, Minorities, and Employment*. Vienna: European Monitoring Centre on Racism and Xenophobia.

IIF (Institute of International Finance). 2005. *Summary Appraisal Gulf Cooperation Council Countries*. Washington.

IMF (International Monetary Fund). 2001. *IMF Concludes 2001 Article IV Consultation with Saudi Arabia*. Public Information Notice (PIN) 01/119. Washington.

IMF (International Monetary Fund). 2002. *IMF Concludes 2002 Article IV Consultation with Saudi Arabia*. Public Information Notice (PIN) 02/121. Washington.

IMF (International Monetary Fund). 2003. *IMF Concludes 2003 Article IV Consultation with Saudi Arabia*. Public Information Notice (PIN) 03/143. Washington.

Iqbal, Farrukh. 2006. *Sustaining Gains in Poverty Reduction and Human Development in the Middle East and North Africa*. Washington: World Bank.

Iqbal, Munawar, and Philip Molyneux. 2005. *Thirty Years of Islamic Banking: History, Performance, and Prospects*. New York: Palgrave MacMillan.

James, Harold. 1996. *International Monetary Cooperation since Bretton Woods*. Washington: International Monetary Fund.

Joshi, V. J., and I. M. D. Little. 1996. *India's Economic Reforms, 1991–2001*. Oxford: Clarendon Press.

Kalathil, Shanthi, and Taylor C. Boas. 2003. *Open Networks, Closed Regimes: The Impact of the Internet on Authoritarian Rule*. Washington: Carnegie Endowment for International Peace.

Kamrava, Mehran. 2004. Structural Impediments to Economic Globalization in the Middle East. *Middle East Policy* XI, no. 4: 96–112.

Kardoosh, Marwan, and Riad al Khoury. 2005. *Quality Industrial Zones and Sustainable Development in Jordan*. Amman: Jordan Center for Public Policy Research and Dialogue (February).

Karsh, Efraim, and Inari Karsh. 1999. *Empires of the Sand: The Struggle for Mastery in the Middle East*. Cambridge, MA: Harvard University Press.

Kaufmann, Franz-Xavier. 1997. Religion and Modernization in Europe. *Journal of Institutional and Theoretical Economics* 153: 80–96.

Kaufmann, Daniel, Aart Kraay, and Massimo Mastruzzi. 2003. *Governance Matters III: Governance Indicators for 1996–2002*. Washington: World Bank.

Kaufmann, Daniel, Aart Kraay, and Massimo Mastruzzi. 2005. *Governance Matters IV: Governance Indicators for 1996–2004*. Washington: World Bank.

Kedourie, Elie. 1992. *Democracy and Arab Political Culture*. Washington: Washington Institute for Near East Policy.

Kee, Hiau Looi, Alessandro Nicita, and Marcelo Olarreaga. 2004a. Ad Valorem Equivalents of Non-Tariff Barriers. World Bank, Washington. Photocopy (March).

Kee, Hiau Looi, Alessandro Nicita, and Marcelo Olarreaga. 2004b. Estimating Mercantilist Trade Restrictiveness Indices. World Bank, Washington. Photocopy (March).

Kenney, Charles. 2005. Why Are We Worried About Income? Nearly Everything that Matters Is Converging. *World Development* 33, no. 1: 1–19.

Khan, Mohsin S., and Abbas Mirakhor, eds. 1987. *Theoretical Studies in Islamic Banking and Finance*. Houston, TX: Institute for Research and Islamic Studies.

Kheir-El-Din, Hanaa. 2000. Enforcement of Product Standards as Barriers to Trade: The Case of Egypt. In *Trade Policy Developments in the Middle East and North Africa*, ed. Bernard Hoekman and Hanaa Kheir-El-Din. Washington: World Bank.

Kim, J. I., and L. J. Lau. 1994. The Sources of Economic Growth in the East Asian Newly Industrialized Countries. *Journal of Japanese and International Economics* 8, no. 3: 235–71.

King, Robert, and Ross Levine. 1993. Finance and Growth: Maybe Schumpeter Was Right. *Quarterly Journal of Economics* 108, no. 3: 717–38.

Knack, S., and P. Keefer. 1995. Institutions and Economic Performance: Cross-Country Tests Using Alternative Institutional Measures. *Economics and Politics* 7, no. 3: 207–27.

Kögel, Tomas. 2004. Youth Dependency and Total Factor Productivity. *Journal of Development Economics* 76: 147–73.

Konan, Denise Eby. 2003. Alternative Paths to Prosperity: Economic Integration Among Arab Countries. In *Arab Economic Integration*, ed. Ahmed Galal and Bernard Hoekman. Washington: Brookings Institution.

Krueger, Alan B., and Jitka Maleckova. 2002. Education, Poverty, Political Violence and Terrorism: Is There a Causal Connection? *Journal of Economic Perspectives* 17, no. 4: 119–44.

Krueger, Anne O. 2002. *Economic Policy Reforms and the Indian Economy*. Chicago, IL: University of Chicago Press.

Kundera, Milan. 1984. The Tragedy of Central Europe. *New York Review of Books* (April 26): 33–38.

Kuran, Timur. 1992. The Economic System in Contemporary Islamic Thought. In *Islamic Economic Alternatives*, ed. K. S. Jomo. London: Macmillan.

Kuran, Timur. 1993. The Economic Impact of Islamic Fundamentalism. In *Fundamentalisms and the State: Remaking Polities, Economies, and Militance*, ed. M. E. Marty and R. S. Appleby. Chicago, IL: University of Chicago Press.

Kuran, Timur. 1995. *Private Truths, Public Lies: The Social Consequence of Preference Falsification*. Cambridge, MA: Harvard University Press.

Kuran, Timur. 2003a. The Islamic Commercial Crisis: Institutional Roots of Economic Underdevelopment in the Middle East. *Journal of Economic History* 62, no. 3: 414–46.

Kuran, Timur. 2003b. Islamic Redistribution Through Zakat: Historical Record and Modern Realities. In *Poverty and Charity in Middle Eastern Contexts*, ed. Michael Bonner, Mine Ener, and Amy Singer. Albany, NY: State University of New York Press.

Kuran, Timur. 2004. The Economic Ascent of the Middle East's Religious Minorities: The Role of Islamic Legal Pluralism. *Journal of Legal Studies* 33: 475–515.

Kurtzman, Joel, Glenn Yago, and Triphon Phumiwasana. 2004. The Global Costs of Opacity. *MIT Sloan Management Review* 46, no. 1: 38–44.

Kuznets, Simon. 1966. *Modern Economic Growth*. New Haven, CT: Yale University Press.

Lacoutre, Jean. 1973. *Nasser: A Biography*. London: Secker and Warburg.

Lal, Deepak. 1998. *Unintended Consequences: The Impact of Factor Endowments, Culture, and Politics on Long-Run Economic Performance*. Cambridge, MA: MIT Press.

Lall, Sanjaya. 1975. Is "Dependence" a Useful Concept in Analysing Underdevelopment? *World Development* 3, nos. 11&12: 799–810.

Lall, Sanjaya, and Donald Keesing. 1992. Marketing Manufactured Exports from Developing Countries: Learning Sequences and Public Support. In *Trade Policy, Industrialization, and Development: New Perspectives*, ed. G. Helleiner. London: Clarendon Press.

LaPorta, Rafael, Florencio Lopez-de-Silanes, Andrei Shleifer, and Robert W. Vishny. 1999. The Quality of Government. *Journal of Law, Economics, and Organization* 15: 222–79.

Laquer, Walter. 2003. *No End to War*. New York: Continuum International Publishing Group.

Lasswell, Harold. 1930. *Psychopathology and Politics*. Glencoe, IL: The Free Press.

Lawrence, Robert Z. 2006. *A US–Middle East Trade Agreement: A Circle of Opportunity?* POLICY ANALYSES IN INTERNATIONAL ECONOMICS 81. Washington: Peterson Institute for International Economics.

Layard, Richard. 2005. *Happiness*. New York: Penguin Press.

Lederman, Daniel, William F. Maloney, and Luis Servén. 2004. *Lessons from NAFTA for Latin America and the Caribbean Countries*. Washington: World Bank.

Lee Kuan Yew. 1998. *The Singapore Story*. Singapore: Simon & Schuster.

Lee Kuan Yew. 2000. *From Third World to First—The Singapore Story: 1965–2000*. New York: Harper Collins.

Lee, Martin A. 2002. The Swastika and the Crescent. *Intelligence Report* (Spring): 18–26.

Lerner, Daniel. 1958. *The Passing of a Traditional Society: Modernizing the Middle East*. New York: Free Press.

Levine, Ross. 1997. Financial Development and Economic Growth: Views and Agenda. *Journal of Economic Literature* 35, no. 2: 688–726.

Levine, Ross. 2005. Law, Endowments, and Property Rights. *Journal of Economic Perspectives* 19, no. 3: 61–88.

Levine, Ross, and Sara Zervos. 1998. Stock Markets, Banks, and Economic Growth. *American Economic Review* 88, no. 3: 537–58.

Lewis, Bernard. 1982. *The Muslim Discovery of Europe*. New York: W. W. Norton.

Lewis, Bernard. 1993a. *Islam in History*, 2d ed. Chicago, IL: Open Court.

Lewis, Bernard. 1993b. *Islam and the West*. New York: Oxford University Press.

Lewis, Bernard. 2005. Freedom and Justice in the Modern Middle East. *Foreign Affairs* (May/June): 36–51.

Lewis, W. Arthur. 1954. Economic Development with Unlimited Supplies of Labor. *Manchester School* 22: 139–91.

Li, K. T. 1988. *The Evolution of Policy behind Taiwan's Development Success*. New Haven, CT: Yale University Press.

Lipset, Seymour Martin. 1959. Some Social Requisites of Democracy: Economic Development and Political Legitimacy. *American Political Science Review* 53, no. 1: 69–105.

Lipset, Seymour Martin, Kyoung-Ryung Seong, and John Charles Torres. 1993. A Comparative Analysis of the Social Requisites of Democracy. *International Social Science Journal* 45 (May): 155–75.

Lord, Montague. 2001. *Economic Impact and Implications for Jordan of the U.S.-Jordan Free Trade Agreement*. Report for the US Agency for International Development for the Access to Microfinance and Improved Implementation of Policy Reform (AMIR) Program in Jordan (February). Available at http://usembassy-amman.org.jo/fta-usaid.pdf (accessed January 31, 2007).

Luciak, Mikael. 2004. *Migrants, Minorities, and Education*. Vienna: European Monitoring Centre on Racism and Xenophobia.

Luciani, Giacomo. 1990. Allocation vs. Production States: A Theoretical Framework. In *The Arab State*, ed. Giacomo Luciani. Berkeley, CA: University of California Press.

Ludwig Boltzman Institute of Human Rights. 2003. *Migrants, Minorities, and Employment in Austria*. Vienna: European Monitoring Centre on Racism and Xenophobia (January).

Lugar, Richard. 2004. *A New Partnership for the Greater Middle East: Combating Terrorism, Building Peace*. Washington: Saban Center for Middle East Policy, Brookings Institution.

Lust-Okar, Ellen. 2004. Divided They Rule: The Management and Manipulation of Political Opposition. *Comparative Politics* 36, no. 2: 159–80.

Lutz, James M., and Brenda J. Lutz. 2006. Terrorism as Economic Warfare. *Global Economy Journal* 6, no. 2.

MacGarvie, Megan. 2006. Do Firms Learn from International Trade? *Review of Economics and Statistics* 88, no. 1: 46–60.

MacKinnon, Robert. 1973. *Money and Capital in Economic Development*. Washington: Brookings Institution.

Maddison, Angus. 2003. *The World Economy: Historical Statistics*. Paris: Organization for Economic Cooperation and Development.

Magder, Dan. 2005. *Egypt after the Multi-Fiber Arrangement: Global Apparel and Textile Supply Chains as a Route for Industrial Upgrading*. Working Paper 05-8. Washington: Institute for International Economics.

Maghraoui, Abdeslam. 2006. *American Foreign Policy and Islamic Renewal*. Special Report 164. Washington: United Institute for Peace (July).

Mahoney, Paul G. 2001. The Common Law and Economic Growth: Hayek Might Be Right. *Journal of Legal Studies* 30, no. 2: 305–25.

Mankiw, G., D. Romer, and D. Weil. 1991. A Contribution to the Empirics of Economic Growth. *Quarterly Journal of Economics* 107, no. 2: 407–37.

Mason, Edward S., Mahn Je Kim, Dwight H. Perkins, Kwang Suk Kim, and David C. Cole. 1980. *The Economic and Social Modernization of the Republic of Korea*. Cambridge, MA: Harvard University Press.

McClelland, David C. 1961. *The Achieving Society*. New York: The Free Press.

McSweeney, Brendan. 2002. Hofstede's Model of National Cultural Differences and Their Consequences: A Triumph of Faith—A Failure of Analysis. *Human Relations* 55, no. 1: 89–118.

Mehanna, Rock-Antoine. N.d. A Quantitative Analysis of Middle Eastern Trade. Warburg College, Waverly, IO; and American University of Technology, Lebanon. Photocopy.

Memmi, Albert. 1965. *The Colonizer and the Colonized*. Boston, MA: Beacon Press.

Mernissi, Fatima. 1987. *Beyond the Veil* (revised edition). Cambridge: Schenkman.

Metcalf, Barbara D. 1999. Weber and Islamic Reform. In *Max Weber and Islam*, ed. Toby E. Huff and Wolfgang Schluchter. London: Transaction Publishers.

Miniesy, Rania, and Jeffrey B. Nugent. 2004. Egyptian Competitiveness in International Trade: Evidence from a Gravity Model of Bilateral Trade and Various Institutional Indicators. Paper presented at the CEFRS-USAID Conference on Revisiting Egypt's Competitiveness: The Road Ahead to Building New Sectors, Cairo, June 28–29.

Miniesy, Rania S., Jeffrey B. Nugent, and Tarik M. Yousef. 2004. Intra-regional Trade Integration in the Middle East: Past Performance and Future Potential. In *Trade Policy and Economic Integration in the Middle East and North Africa*, ed. H. Hakimian and Jeffrey B. Nugent. London: Routledge.

Momani, Bessma. 2004. American Politicization of the International Monetary Fund. *Review of International Political Economy* 11, no. 5: 880–904.

Moore, Barrington, Jr. 1966. *Social Origins of Dictatorship and Democracy*. Boston, MA: Beacon Press.

Mulinari, Diana. 2004. *Analytical Report on Education: National Focal Point for Sweden*. Vienna: European Monitoring Centre on Racism and Xenophobia.

Mutti, John, and Harry Grubert. 2004. Empirical Asymmetries in Foreign Direct Investment and Taxation. *Journal of International Economics* 62: 337–58.

National Center for Education Statistics. 2004. *Highlights from the Trends in International Mathematics and Science Study (TIMSS) 2003*. Washington (December). Available at http://nces.ed.gov/TIMSS (accessed March 23, 2007).

Najjar, Fauzi. 2005. The Arabs, Islam, and Globalization. *Middle East Policy* XIII, 3: 91–106.

Nehru, Vikram, and Ashok Dhareshwar. 1995. *A New Database on Physical Capital Stock: Sources, Methodology, and Results*. Washington: World Bank.

Nelson, Richard R., and Howard Pack 1999. The Asia Growth Miracle and Modern Growth Theory. *Economic Journal* 109, no. 457: 416–36.

Nelson, Richard R., and Edmund Phelps. 1966. Investment in Humans, Technological Diffusion, and Economic Growth. *American Economic Review* 56: 69–75.

Noland, Marcus. 2000. The Philippines in the Asian Financial Crisis: How the Sick Man Avoided Pneumonia. *Asian Survey* 40, no. 3: 401–12.

Noland, Marcus. 2005a. Religion and Economic Performance. *World Development* 33, no. 8: 1215–32.

Noland, Marcus. 2005b. Popular Attitudes, Globalization, and Risk. *International Finance* 8, no. 2: 199–229.

Noland, Marcus. 2005c. *Explaining Middle Eastern Authoritarianism*. Working Paper 05-5. Washington: Peterson Institute for International Economics.

Noland, Marcus. 2005d. *Affinity and International Trade*. Working Paper 05-3. Washington: Peterson Institute for International Economics.

Noland, Marcus, and Howard Pack. 2003. *Industrial Policies in an Era of Globalization*. Washington: Peterson Institute for International Economics.

Noland, Marcus, and J. Brooks Spector. 2006. *The Stuff of Legends: Diamonds and Development in Southern Africa*. Occasional Paper 1. Johannesburg: Business Leadership South Africa.

North, Douglass. 1991. Institutions. *Journal of Economic Perspectives* 5, no. 1: 97–112.

Nugent, Jeffrey B. 2000. Impediments to Dispute Resolution and Firms' Competitiveness in the MENA Region. University of Southern California, Los Angeles, CA. Photocopy (February 11).

Nugent, Jeffrey B. 2001. Explaining the Paradox: Generous Foreign Investment Laws but Little Foreign Investment in Arab Countries—The Role of Legal Shortcomings. Paper prepared for the conference on Arab Legal Systems in Transition, Washington, April 5–6.

Nugent, Jeffrey B. 2002. Why Does MENA Trade So Little? University of Southern California, Los Angeles, CA. Photocopy.

Nugent, Jeffrey B., and Fahyre De Alencar Loiola. 2003. Jordan's Patterns and Prospects of Trade and FDI: Some Implications of Euro-Med, GAFTA, and the QIZ Alternatives. Paper presented at the conference The Jordanian Economy in a Changing Environment, Amman, Jordan, May 12–14.

Olson, Mancur. 1982. *The Rise and Decline of Nations: Economic Growth, Stagflation, and Social Rigidities.* New Haven, CT: Yale University Press.

Pack, Howard. 1992. Technology Gaps Between Developed and Developing Countries: Are There Dividends for Latecomers? *Proceedings of the Annual World Bank Conference on Development Economics* 1992: 283–302.

Pack, Howard. 2001. Technological Change and Growth in East Asia: Macro versus Micro Perspectives. In *Rethinking the East Asian Miracle,* ed. Joseph E. Stiglitz and Shahid Yusuf. New York: Oxford University Press.

Pack, Howard. 2006. Econometric versus Case Study Approaches to Technology Transfer. In *Global Integration and Technology Transfer,* ed. Bernard Hoekman and Beata Smarzynska Javorcik. London: Palgrave.

Pack, Howard, and Larry E. Westphal. 1986. Industrial Strategy and Technological Change. *Journal of Development Economics* 22, no. 1: 87–128.

Page, John M. 1998. From Boom to Bust—and Back? The Crisis of Growth in the Middle East and North Africa. In *Prospects for Middle Eastern and North African Economies,* ed. Nemat Shafik. London: Macmillan Press Ltd.

Page, John M. 2003. Structural Reforms in the Middle East and North Africa. In *The Arab World Competitiveness Report 2002–2003,* ed. Peter Cornelius. New York: Oxford University Press.

Page, John, and Linda van Gelder. 2002. Globalization, Growth, and Poverty Reduction in the Middle East and North Africa, 1970–1999. Paper presented at the Fourth Mediterranean Development Forum, Amman, Jordan, April 7–10.

Pape, Robert. 2002. *Dying to Win: The Strategic Logic of Suicide Terrorism.* New York: Random House.

Park, Walter, and Douglas Lippoldt. 2003. *The Impact of Trade-Related Intellectual Property Rights on Trade and Foreign Direct Investment in Developing Countries.* Paris: Working Party of the Trade Committee, Organization for Economic Cooperation and Development.

Péridy, Nicolas. 2005. The Trade Effects of the Euro-Mediterranean Partnership: What Are the Lessons for ASEAN Countries? *Journal of Asian Economics* 16: 125–39.

Perkovich, George. 2005. Giving Justice Its Due. *Foreign Affairs* (May/June): 79–93.

Perotti, Roberto. 1996. Growth, Income Distribution, and Democracy. *Journal of Economic Growth* 1: 149–87.

Peters, Rudolph. 1999. Paradise or Hell? The Religious Doctrine of Election in Eighteenth and Nineteenth Century Islamic Fundamentalism and Protestant Calvinism. In *Max Weber and Islam,* ed. Toby E. Huff and Wolfgang Schluchter. London: Transaction Publishers.

Pew Global Attitudes Project. 2003. *Views of a Changing World.* Washington: Pew Research Center for the People and the Press (June).

Pew Global Attitudes Project. 2006a. *The Great Divide: How Westerners and Muslims View Each Other.* Washington: Pew Research Center for the People and the Press (June).

Pew Global Attitudes Project. 2006b. *America's Image Slips, But Allies Share U.S. Concerns Over Iran, Hamas.* Washington: Pew Research Center for the People and the Press (June).

Pipes, Daniel. 2002. God and Mammon: Does Poverty Cause Militant Islam? *National Interest* (Winter). Available at www.danielpipes.org/article/104.

Portes, Richard, and Hélène Rey. 2005. The Determinants of Cross-Border Equity Flows. *Journal of International Economics* 65(1): 269–96.

Pritchett, Lant. 1997. Divergence Big Time. *Journal of Economic Perspectives* 11: 3–17.

Pritchett, Lant. 2001. Where Has All the Education Gone? *World Bank Development Review* 15, no. 3: 367–91.

Pryor, Frederic L. 2006. *The Economic Impact of Islam on Developing Nations.* Social Science Research Network (August 18). Available at http://papers.ssrn.com.

Przeworski, Adam, Michael E. Alvarez, José Antonio Cheibub, and Fernando Limongi. 2000. *Democracy and Development.* Cambridge, UK: Cambridge University Press.

Quandt, William B. 1998. *Between Ballots and Bullets: Algeria's Transition from Authoritarianism.* Washington: Brookings Institution.

Racanelli, Vito. 2005. European Trader. *Barrons* (May 23).

Radelet, Steven, and Jeffrey D. Sachs. 1998. The East Asian Financial Crisis: Diagnosis, Remedies, and Prospects. *Brookings Papers on Economic Activity* 30, no. 1: 1–74.

Rajan, Raghuram, and Luigi Zingales. 1998. Financial Dependence and Growth. *American Economic Review* 88, no. 3: 559–86.

Ranis, Gustav. 1973. Industrial Sector Labor Absorption. *Economic Development and Cultural Change* 21: 387–408.

Rao, Kishore. 2000. Free Zones in the Middle East: Development Patterns and Future Potential. In *Trade Policy Developments in the Middle East and North Africa*, ed. Bernard Hoekman and Hanaa Kheir-El-Din. Washington: World Bank.

Rauch, James E. 2001. Business and Social Networks in International Trade. *Journal of Economic Literature* 39, no. 4: 1177–1203.

Rauch, James E., and Vitor Trindade. 2002. Ethnic Chinese Networks in International Trade. *Review of Economics and Statistics* 84, no. 1: 116–30.

Reuter, Peter, and Edwin M. Truman. 2004. *Chasing Dirty Money.* Washington: Peterson Institute for International Economics.

Reynolds, Paul D., William D. Bygrave, and Erkko Autio, with contributions from Pia Arenius, Paula Fitzsimons, Maria Minniti, Sinead Murray, Colm O'Goran, and Frank Roche. 2004. *GEM 2003 Global Report.* Global Entrepreneurship Monitor. Babson Park, MA: Babson College. Available at www.gemconsortium.org (accessed on February 2, 2007).

Rhee, Yung, Bruce Ross-Larson, and Gary Pursell. 1984. *Korea's Competitive Edge: Managing Entry into World Markets.* Baltimore, MD: Johns Hopkins University.

Richards, Alan. 2001. The Political Economy of Economic Reform in the Middle East: The Challenge of Governance. University of California, Santa Cruz. Photocopy.

Richards, Alan, and John Waterbury. 1996. *A Political Economy of the Middle East.* Boulder, CO: Westview Press.

Rigobon, Roberto, and Dani Rodrik. 2004. *Rule of Law, Democracy, Openness, and Income: Estimating Interrelationships.* NBER Working Paper 10750. Cambridge, MA: National Bureau of Economic Research.

Robalino, David A., and Tatyana Bogomolova. 2006. *Implicit Pension Debt in the Middle East and North Africa.* Middle East and North Africa Working Paper Series 46 (June). Washington: World Bank.

Rodinson, Maxime. 1973. *Islam and Capitalism.* New York: Pantheon Books.

Rodrik, Dani. 1994. *Has Globalization Gone Too Far?* Washington: Peterson Institute for International Economics.

Roland, Gérard. 2000. *Transition and Economics.* Cambridge, MA: MIT Press.

Rosen, Howard. 2004. Free Trade Agreements as Foreign Policy Tools: The US-Israel and US-Jordan FTAs. In *Free Trade Agreements: US Strategies and Priorities*, ed. Jeffrey J. Schott. Washington: Peterson Institute for International Economics.

Ross, Michael L. 2001. Does Oil Hinder Democracy? *World Politics* 53 (April): 325–61.

Rustow, Dankwart A. 1970. Transitions to Democracy: Toward a Dynamic Model. *Comparative Politics* 2, no. 3: 337–63.

Sachs, Jeffrey, and Andrew M. Warner. 1997. Sources of Slow Growth in African Economies. *Journal of African Economies* 6: 335–76.

Sadik, A. T., and A. A. Bolbol. 2003. Arab External Investments: Relation to National Wealth, Estimation, and Consequences. *World Development* 31: 1771–92.

Said, Edward. 1978. *Orientalism.* New York: Pantheon Books.

Sala-i-Martin, Xavier, Gernot Doppelhofer, and Ronald I. Miller. 2004. Determinants of Long-Run Growth: A Bayesian Averaging of Classical Estimates (BACE) Approach. *American Economic Review* 94, no. 4: 813–35.

SaKong, Il. 1993. *Korea in the World Economy*. Washington: Peterson Institute for International Economics.

Saxenian, AnnaLee. 2001. *Taiwan's Hsinchu Region: Imitator and Partner for Silicon Valley*. Stanford, CA: Stanford Institute for Economic Policy Research.

Saxenian, AnnaLee. 2002. Bangalore: The Silicon Valley of Asia? In *Economic Policy Reforms and the Indian Economy*, ed. Anne O. Krueger. Chicago, IL: University of Chicago Press.

Schreimer, Rita. 2004. *Analytical Report on Education: National Focal Point on the Netherlands*. Vienna: European Monitoring Centre on Racism and Xenophobia.

Sennott, Charles M. 2002. *The Body and the Blood: The Middle East's Vanishing Christians and the Possibility for Peace*. New York: Public Affairs.

Sharabi, Hisham. 1988. *Neopatriarchy: A Theory of Distorted Change in Arab Society*. New York: Oxford University Press.

Shaw, Edward. 1973. *Financial Deepening in Economic Development*. New York: Oxford University Press.

Shetty, Shobha. 2006. *Water, Food Security, and Agricultural Policy in the Middle East and North Africa Region*. Middle East and North Africa Working Paper Series 47. Washington: World Bank.

Shleifer, Andrei, and Robert W. Vishny. 1993. Corruption. *Quarterly Journal of Economics* 108, no. 3: 599–618.

Siddiqi, Muhammed Nejatullah. 1981. *Muslim Economic Thinking*. Jeddah, Saudi Arabia: International Centre for Research in Islamic Economics, King Abdul Aziz University.

Smith, Heather. 2000. *Industry Policy in Taiwan and Korea in the 1980s*. Cheltenham, UK: Edward Elgan.

Söderling, Ludvig. 2005. *Is the Middle East and North Africa Achieving Its Trade Potential?* IMF Working Paper WP/05/90. Washington: International Monetary Fund.

Solingen, Etel. 1998. *Regional Orders at Century's Dawn*. Princeton, NJ: Princeton University Press.

Solow, Robert M. 2001. Applying Growth Theory Across Countries. *World Bank Economic Review* 15, no. 2: 283–88.

Someya, Masakazu, Hazem Shunnar, and T. G. Srinivasan. 2002. *Textile and Clothing Exports in MENA: Past Performance, Prospects and Policy Issues in Post-MFA Context*. Washington: World Bank.

Srinivasan, T. N., and Suresh D. Tendulkar. 2003. *Reintegrating India with the World Economy*. Washington: Institute for International Economics.

Stepan, Alfred. 2001. *Arguing Comparative Politics*. Oxford: Oxford University Press.

Stepan, Alfred, and Graeme Robertson. 2004. Arab, Not Muslim, Exceptionalism. *Journal of Democracy* 15, no. 4: 140–46.

Stiglitz, Joseph E., and Shahid Yusuf. 2001. *Rethinking the East Asian Miracle*. New York: Oxford University Press.

Telhami, Shibley. 2005. *Arab Attitudes Toward Political and Social Issues, Foreign Policy and the Media*. College Park, MD: College of Behavioral and Social Sciences, University of Maryland. Available at www.bsos.umd.edu (accessed November 30, 2006).

Tessler, Mark. 2002. Islam and Democracy in the Middle East: The Impact of Religious Orientations on Attitudes Toward Democracy in Four Arab Countries. *Comparative Politics* 34, no. 3: 337–54.

Tessler, Mark. 2003. Arab and Muslim Political Attitudes: Stereotypes and Evidence from Survey Research. *International Studies Perspectives* 4: 175–80.

Tessler, Mark, and Eleanor Gao. 2005. Gauging Arab Support for Democracy. *Journal of Democracy* 16, no. 3: 83–97.

Transparency International. 2004. *Corruption Perceptions Index 2004*. Available at www.transparency.org (accessed February 1, 2007).

Turner, Bryan S. 1974. *Weber and Islam: A Critical Study*. London: Routledge & Kegan Paul.

UNDP (United Nations Development Program). 2002. *Arab Human Development Report 2002*. New York: United Nations.

UNDP (United Nations Development Program). 2003. *Arab Human Development Report 2003*. New York: United Nations.

UNDP (United Nations Development Program). 2004a. *Human Development Report*. New York: United Nations.

UNDP (United Nations Development Program). 2004b. *Iraq Living Conditions Survey 2004: Volume I Tabulation Report*. Baghdad.

UNDP (United Nations Development Program). 2004c. *Iraq Living Conditions Survey 2004: Volume II Analytical Report*. Baghdad.

United Nations. 1955. *Problems and Processes of Industrialization in Underdeveloped Countries*. New York: UN Department of Economic and Social Affairs.

US Department of State. 2003. *World Military Expenditures and Arms Transfers*. Washington. Available at www.state.gov.

USITC (US International Trade Commission). 2004. *U.S.-Morocco Free Trade Agreement*. Investigation no. TA-2104-14. USITC Publication 3704. Washington (June).

Venables, Anthony, and D. Puga. 1999. Agglomeration and Economic Development: Import Substitution Versus Trade Liberalization. *Economic Journal* 109: 292–311.

Voigt, Stefan. 2005. Islam and the Institutions of a Free Society. *Independent Review* 10, no. 1: 59–82.

Wade, Robert. 1990. *Governing the Market: Economic Theory and Taiwan's Industrial Policies*. Princeton, NJ: Princeton University Press.

Warde, Ibrahim. 2004. Global Politics, Islamic Finance, and Islamist Politics Before and After 11 September 2001. In *The Politics of Islamic Finance*, ed. Clement M. Henry and Rodney Wilson. Edinburgh, UK: Edinburgh University Press.

Wei, Shang-Jin. 2000. How Taxing is Corruption on International Investors? *Review of Economics and Statistics* 82, no. 1 (February): 1–11.

Will, Gisela, and Stefan Rühl. 2004. *Analytical Report on Education: National Focal Point for Germany*. Vienna: European Monitoring Centre on Racism and Xenophobia.

Williamson, John. 1990. What Washington Means by Policy Reform. In *Latin American Adjustment: How Much Has Happened*, ed. John Williamson. Washington: Peterson Institute for International Economics.

Wilson, Rodney. 2004. Capital Flight Through Islamic Managed Funds. In *The Politics of Islamic Finance*, ed. Clement M. Henry and Rodney Wilson. Edinburgh, UK: Edinburgh University Press.

Wittes, Tamara Cofman, and Sarah E. Yerkes. 2006. *What Price Freedom? Assessing the Bush Administration's Freedom Agenda*. Analysis Paper 10. Washington: Saban Center for Middle East Policy, Brookings Institution.

World Bank. 1993. *The East Asian Miracle*. Washington.

World Bank. 1995. *Claiming the Future*. Washington.

World Bank. 1998. *East Asia: Road to Recovery*. Washington.

World Bank. 2003a. *Trade, Investment, and Development in the Middle East and North Africa*. Washington.

World Bank. 2003b. *Better Governance for Development in the Middle East and North Africa*. Washington.

World Bank. 2004a. *Gender and Development in the Middle East and North Africa*. Washington.

World Bank. 2004b. *Unlocking the Employment Potential of the Middle East and North Africa*. Washington.

World Bank. 2004c. *Trade, Investment, and Development in the Middle East and North Africa*. Washington.

World Bank. 2004d. *Jordan Quarterly Update, Fourth Quarter 2004*. Washington.

World Bank. 2005. *World Development Report 2005*. Washington.

World Bank. 2006a. *Middle East and North Africa Economic Developments and Prospects 2006: Financial Markets in the New Age of Oil.* Middle East and North Africa Region, Office of the Chief Economist. Washington.

World Bank. 2006b. *Doing Business 2006.* Washington. Available at www.doingbusiness.org (accessed January 31, 2007).

World Bank. 2006c. *Morocco, Tunisia, Egypt and Jordan after the End of the Multi-Fiber Agreement: Impact, Challenges and Prospects.* Report no. 35376 (December). Social and Economic Development Sector Unit, Middle East and North Africa Region. Washington. Available at www-wds.worldbank.org (accessed February 2, 2007).

Zarrouk, Jamel. 2000a. Regulatory Regimes and Trade Costs. In *Catching Up with the Competition,* ed. Bernard Hoekman and Jamel Zarrouk. Ann Arbor, MI: University of Michigan Press.

Zarrouk, Jamel. 2000b. The Greater Arab Free Trade Area: Limits and Possibilities. In *Catching Up with the Competition,* ed. Bernard Hoekman and Jamel Zarrouk. Ann Arbor, MI: University of Michigan Press.

Zarrouk, Jamel. 2000c. Para-Tariff Measures in Arab Countries. In *Trade Policy Developments in the Middle East and North Africa,* ed. Bernard Hoekman and Hanaa Kheir-El-Din. Washington: World Bank.

Zarrouk, Jamel. 2003. A Survey of Barriers to Trade and Investment in Arab Countries. In *Arab Economic Integration,* ed. Ahmed Galal and Bernard Hoekman. Washington: Brookings Institution.

Zogby, James. 2002. *What Arabs Think: Values, Beliefs, and Concerns.* Utica, NY: Zogby International and The Arab Thought Foundation.

Zogby International. 2005. *Six Arab Nation Survey Report.* Submitted to the World Economic Forum's Arab Business Council (November). Available at www.zogby.com/abcreport. pdf (accessed February 1, 2007).

Zubaida, Sami. 1995. Is There a Muslim Society? Ernest Gellner's Sociology of Islam. *Economy and Society* 2: 151–88.

About the Authors

Marcus Noland, senior fellow, became deputy director of the Peterson Institute in September 2009. He has been associated with the Institute since 1985. He is concurrently a senior fellow at the East-West Center. He was a senior economist for international economics on the Council of Economic Advisers (1993–94); visiting professor at Yale University, Johns Hopkins University, the University of Southern California, Tokyo University, Saitama University (now the National Graduate Institute for Policy Studies), and the University of Ghana; and a visiting scholar at the Korea Development Institute. He is author, coauthor, or editor of *The Arab Economies in a Changing World* (2007), which was selected as Choice Outstanding Academic Title for 2007, *Witness to Transformation: Refugee Insights into North Korea* (2011), *Famine in North Korea: Markets, Aid, and Reform* (2007), *Korea after Kim Jong-il* (2004), *Industrial Policy in an Era of Globalization: Lessons from Asia* (2003), *No More Bashing: Building a New Japan-United States Economic Relationship* (2001), *Avoiding the Apocalypse: The Future of the Two Koreas* (2000), which won the 2000–01 Ohira Memorial Award, and *Economic Integration of the Korean Peninsula* (1998).

Howard Pack, visiting fellow, has been a professor of business and public policy and professor of economics at the Wharton School, University of Pennsylvania, since 1986. He was a fellow at the Harry S. Truman Institute for Peace Research, the Hebrew University, Jerusalem. He has been a consultant to the World Bank, the UN Conference on Trade and Development, and many other international development agencies. He is author or coauthor of *The Arab Economies in a Changing World* (2007), which was selected as Choice Outstanding Academic Title for 2007, *Industrial Policy in an Era of Globalization: Lessons from Asia* (2003), *Productivity, Technology and Industrial Development* (Oxford University Press, 1987), and *Structural Change and Economic Policy in Israel* (Yale University Press, 1971).

Index

inflows, 120, 121*t*
public welfare expenditures and, 73
foreign direct investment (FDI), 4–5,
111–19
best practice score in, 266
factors affecting, 174–75, 269–70, 299
gravity-type models, 261
growth strategy focused on, 159, 250,
250*n*, 260–66, 260*n*, 275, 304–305
horizontal, 261
inflows, 111, 112*t*
intraregional, 116
motivations for, 261–62
popular attitudes toward, 264–66, 269,
305
stock markets and, 131–32
technology inflows via, 175, 175*n*, 177,
304
underperformance in, 261
vertical, 261
foreigners. *See also* immigrants
acceptance of, 196
entrepreneurship by, 250–51, 252*b*
fear of, 279–80, 306
staffing of new enterprises with, 180–81
Forum for the Future, 312
France, Arab immigrants in, 257–58
Freedom Agenda, 284
free trade agreements (FTAs). *See*
preferential trade agreements; *specific*
agreement
Front Islamique du Salut (FIS), 81, 204
Fulbright exchanges, 310
fundamentalist movements, 79*n*, 80, 80*n*
Fund for the Future, 311–12

Gadhafi, Muammar, 249
GAFTA. *See* Greater Arab Free Trade Area
(GAFTA)
Gandhi, Rajiv, 57
garment manufacturing, 180*n*
gate of *ijtihad*, 140–41
GATT. *See* General Agreement on Tariffs
and Trade (GATT)
GCC. *See* Gulf Cooperation Council
(GCC)
GDP per capita
global rate of, 1, 2*f*
growth rate of, 47*t*, 48, 169, 170*t*, 171
happiness and, 73
investment ratio and, 48–51, 49*f*–50*f*
in local prices, 43–48, 44*f*
Mediterranean comparison of, 38*b*
OECD comparison, 39, 42–43

oil prices and, 34*b*
regional comparison of, 21, 22*t*
share of government wages in, 71
share of rents in, 26, 27*t*
GEM project. *See* Global Entrepreneurship
Monitor (GEM) project
gender differences. *See also* women
in Arab-European community, 257
in educational attainment, 91
in life expectancy, 61, 62*f*
in literacy, 69–70, 69*f*
General Agreement on Tariffs and Trade
(GATT)
Article XXIV, 217–18
membership in, 209–14, 210*t*–11*t*
generalized system of preferences (GSP),
230
geography
and economic development, 137
and free trade agreements, 221
Germany, Nazism in, 189, 191–92, 192*n*
Gini coefficients, 64–69, 67*t*
Global Competitiveness Report 2005–2006,
103–104, 104*t*, 108, 123, 146, 149–53,
175, 177, 180
Global Entrepreneurship Monitor (GEM)
project, 243, 245
globalization, 209–36. *See also* trade
liberalization
adaption to local values, 200
adverse effects of, 198
attitudes to, 12, 183, 193–96, 194*t*–95*t*,
206–207, 209, 305
and foreign investment, 264–66,
269, 306
and political reform, 277–78
challenge of, 11–13, 301
cultural impact of, 105
demographic crisis and, 85–135
economic effects of, 3–4, 96, 98, 108–11
obstacles to, 8–9, 86, 98–99, 105–108,
200, 299, 301
social change needed for, 305
Global Mediterranean Policy (EU), 219
GlobeScan surveys, 193*n*
governance
bad, deflecting attention from, 139,
139*n*, 276
effect on economic growth, 171
good, happiness and, 75–78
indicators of, 146
government burden indicators, and
entrepreneurship, 245
government officials, favoritism by, 153

government revenue, share of rents in, 26, 27t
Greater Arab Free Trade Area (GAFTA), 215, 217, 225–26
Groupe Salafiste pour la Prédication et le Combat (GSPC), 80
Group of 20, 212
growth accounting
  Bosworth-Collins model of, 164–72, 166f–67f, 168t
  Nelson-Phelps model of, 172–74, 172n, 184–85
GSP. *See* generalized system of preferences (GSP)
Guantanamo Bay, 308
Gulf Cooperation Council (GCC), 98, 226
  capital-market development, 127
  financial-sector development, 123–26
  free trade agreements, 218–19, 219n–20n
Gulf War of 1990-91
  aid inflows after, 120, 161
  economic effects of, 44f, 45, 161

Hamas, 82, 85n
happiness, 73–78
  employment and, 75, 78
  good governance and, 75–78
  income levels and, 73–74, 78
  lack of (*See* discontent)
  self-assessment of, 73, 74t
hawala, 118b
health care services industries, 111
hetistes, 82
Hezbollah, 82
homosexuality, acceptance of, 193, 196, 196n, 207
Hong Kong, 157
Hsinchu Science Park, 258
human capital, 33–37, 35f. *See also* labor force
  entry barriers to, and popular attitudes, 196
  regional comparison of, 24, 25f, 26
  technology and, 173, 302–303
  total factor productivity and, 51–52, 52n, 56
Hungary, 188
Hussein, Saddam, 267

ICOR. *See* incremental capital-output ratio (ICOR)
IGAD. *See* Intergovernmental Authority on Development (IGAD)

IMF. *See* International Monetary Fund (IMF)
immigrants. *See also* foreigners
  acceptance of, 196
  in Europe, 256–59, 269, 271t
  in North America, 251–56, 269
  return of (*See* repatriation)
immigration, 93–94, 93n, 93t
  of educated workers, 180–81 (*See also* brain drain)
  to Europe, 256–59, 269, 271t
  to North America, 251–56, 269
immunization, childhood, 64, 65f
imperialism, 191–92
import customs clearance, 107–108
imported equipment, cost of, 176t, 179
import liberalization, benefits of, 109
import substituting industrialization, 158, 187, 202
income inequality, 64–69, 67t
  land reform and, 66–67
  social indicators and, 70–71, 70n
  sources of, 71–73
income levels, 19–57. *See also* per capita income; poverty
  happiness and, 73–74, 78
  of immigrants, 253
  international comparison of, 39, 40t–41t
  in oil-exporting countries, 1, 6b
income per worker, growth in, effect of policy variables on, 164–68, 168t
incremental capital-output ratio (ICOR), 28, 29t
  calculation of, 28n
  investment to GDP ratio and, 51
India
  business climate in, 243, 245
  corruption in, 153, 155
  economic growth in, 24, 48, 157, 163, 169, 170t, 171, 187
  economic strategy in, 280
  export orientation in, 109–110
  human capital in, 180
  immigrants from, 252b
  political economy of, 57
  returnees to, 251, 259
  Trade Expansion and Cooperation Agreement with, 226
Indian Institutes of Technology, 260
Indonesia
  Chinese business community in, 43n
  economic strategy in, 157, 159, 162, 281
  legal system in, 146
  manufacturing exports, 102–103

in OECD, 140
oil rents in, 26–27, 42
resource curse in, 30
industrialization
delays in, 105
import substituting, 158, 187, 202
repatriation and, 260
technology inflow and, 179
industrial sector, labor deployment to, 67
infant mortality, 2, 61–62, 63f, 63n, 87
inflation measures, 165, 166f
information channels, and political
reform, 278, 278n, 306
information technology sector, 46
initial public offerings (IPOs), 127, 127n,
131, 132n
Institute for Technological Research and
Innovation (ITRI), 258
institutional quality
economic growth and, 139–44, 248, 301
entrepreneurship and, 248
measures of, 165, 167f
worker income growth and, 168, 168t
intellectual property rights (IPR)
protection
technology licensing and, 178
US trade agreements and, 222
WTO regime, 211
Intergovernmental Authority on
Development (IGAD), 226
International Centre for Migration Policy
Development, 256
International Country Risk Guide, 146
international exchange, 283–84
International Finance Corporation, 131
International Labour Organization, 94
International Monetary Fund (IMF)
employment generation survey, 96
financial-market development
assessment, 123
involvement with, 211, 312
Islamic financial institutions report, 114
policy changes imposed by, 163
Internet access, 278, 278n, 306
intraindustry trade (IIT), level of, 103, 104t
investment. *See also* foreign direct
investment (FDI); incremental
capital-output ratio (ICOR)
economic growth and, 163, 171
in education, 173, 180–81, 302–304
financial-market development and,
122–23
Islamic financial system and, 115
for job creation, 86

political uncertainty and, 274–75
public sector, 71–72
riskiness of, 116, 262–65, 265n, 269–70
terrorism deterring, 78–79, 131, 261–64,
269, 305–306
investment ratios, 32–33, 32f
GDP growth and, 48–51, 49f–50f
IPOs. *See* initial public offerings (IPOs)
IPR protection. *See* intellectual property
rights (IPR) protection
Iran
economic policies in, 204, 282, 282n
as part of Middle East, 4b
war with Iraq, 160
Iraq
gender literacy gap in, 70n
infant mortality in, 63n
invasion of Kuwait, 44f, 45, 120, 161
US invasion of, 81, 308
US popular attitude toward, 268
war with Iran, 160
Islam
cultural tolerance and, 196
economic reform and, 204, 283, 300–301
European division based upon, 188–89,
189f, 191t
political attitudes and, 197–98, 286–87,
286n, 292–94
social processes and, 197–98, 283
as source of personal identity, 197–98,
293–94, 293n
Islamic Action Front, 281
Islamic bonds, 115, 119
Islamic Development Bank, 114–15, 126
membership in, 15t–17t
Islamic education systems, 141, 281, 304
Islamic finance, 113–15, 118b, 131, 140,
197, 202
Islamic Financial Services Board, 114
Islamic nations
Arab ethnicity in, 293–94
cross-country regression approach to,
142–44
economic comparison of, 26
economic growth of, 10, 12, 139–44
gender literacy gap in, 69–70, 69f
happiness in, 74, 74t
institutional environment in, 144
legal systems in, 145–46
Islamic political movements
differences between, 79n, 80, 80n
and potential for reform, 277, 281–83,
306–307
rise of, 279, 279n

Islamic Renewal, 310n, 311
Islamic Salvation Front, 81, 204
Israel
  economic effects of war on, 161, 276n
  economic integration and, 139
  as part of Middle East, 4b
ITRI. *See* Institute for Technological
  Research and Innovation (ITRI)

Jamahiriyah ideology, 249
Japan, 159
job creation. *See* employment generation
Jordan
  economic characteristics of, 21, 169, 303
  emigration from, 94
  fiscal deficit rate, 165, 166f
  foreign investment zones, 180, 180n
  market capitalization in, 127
  political reform in, 278n, 297n
  remittances to, 120
  unemployment in, 75
  US free trade agreement with, 108n,
    222, 222n, 223, 230–32
Jordan, Robert, 145
journal articles, technical, 178
journalists, abuse of, 278
JPMorgan Emerging Bond Index Global,
  132
judicial independence, 149

Kenyatta, Jomo, 199
Kestenbaum, Charles, 145
Khaled Sheik Mohammed, 81
knowledge acquisition, modes of, 173–74
knowledge generation, domestic, 178–79
knowledge transfer
  banking sector and, 126n
  by immigration, 252b
  measures of, 175
Kramer, Martin, 82
Kundera, Milan, 188
Kuwait
  demographics, 3
  economic characteristics of, 21
  FDI inflows to, 111n
  financial markets in, 119, 130
  Iraqi invasion of, 44f, 45, 120, 161

labor force. *See also* employment; human
  capital
  educational status of, 70, 180, 302–303
  immigration and, 93–94
  industrial sector, 67
  measurement of, 94, 94n

regional comparison of, 24, 25f, 26
total factor productivity and, 51–52,
  52n, 56
women in, 94, 95f, 96, 97n
labor force absorption, 96–98, 135
  alternative scenarios for, 97, 97t
labor force growth, 1, 3
  addressing, 11–13
  capital accumulation and, 33
  cohort bulge causing, 88
  obstacles to, 97–98
  in OPEC countries, 161
  rate of, 85
labor-intensive production
  export orientation resulting from,
    109–10
  job creation with, 86, 99–100, 132
labor-intensive service sectors,
  development of, 110–11, 132
land reform, income inequality and,
  66–67
Latin America. *See also specific country*
  debt crisis in, 158, 187
  economic strategy in, 158, 187, 198–99,
    280
  political reform in, 275
law enforcement, terrorist financing and,
  118b
Lebanon, 255
legal systems
  effectiveness of, 146, 147t–48t, 149
  impact on economic growth, 144–51
  origins of, 145–46
lending
  bank, 126, 126n, 131
  bureaucratization of, 125t, 126
less developed countries (LDCs), growth
  accounting model for, 184–85
Liberia, 162
Libya, 249
"license raj," 153, 155
life expectancy, 2, 60–61, 61f, 87
  gender differences in, 61, 62f
liquidity glut, 122
literacy gap, gender, 69–70, 69f
living standards
  changes in, 20, 299
  government policy affecting, 42
  international comparison of, 37–43
  population growth and, 1
  real domestic, 43–48, 44f
  regional comparison of, 23
  war and, 160–61
loans, bank, 126, 126n, 131

Lugar, Richard, 79
"lumpen capitalists," 248

macroeconomic policy
  deficiencies in, 12
  economic growth and, 301, 312
  entrepreneurship and, 248
  investment and, 282
  quality measures, 165–68, 168t
MAFTA. See Mediterranean Arab Free
  Trade Area (MAFTA)
Maghraoui, Abdeslam M., 311
Malaysia, 157, 159, 281
manufacturing exports, levels of, 100–103,
  101f, 102t
manufacturing value added, oil prices
  and, 34b
market capitalization, 127, 128f, 129
mass media, and political reform, 278,
  278n, 306
maternal mortality, 63, 64t
Mediterranean Arab Free Trade Area
  (MAFTA), 216n
Mediterranean countries
  economic performance of, 38b
  preferential trade between Europe and,
  219–21
middle class, rise of, and democratization,
  200–201, 201n
Middle East. See also Arab economies;
  specific country
  definition of, 4b, 15t–17t
  map of, 3f
  population of, 22t
  trade shares, 216–17, 216t
Middle East Economic Research Forum
  (World Bank), 159, 159n
Middle East Foundation, 310
Middle East Free Trade Area (MEFTA),
  216n, 222, 311
Middle East North Africa (MENA) region
  definition of, 4b, 15t–17t
  policy indicators, 163
Middle East Partnership Initiative, 284, 311
migration. See immigration
military-industrial complex. See also war
  economic reform and, 203
  global engagement and, 212
  political reform and, 291
mineral endowments, 24. See also oil
modernization
  as determinant of democracy, 286,
  289–90
  failure of, 38b, 42

Mohammed Atta, 81
monarchies, 6, 273
monetary policy
  in Arab economies, 159–62
  financial-market development and,
  123–26
money laundering, 118b
Morocco
  business climate in, 242–43
  demographics, 2–3
  economic characteristics of, 21, 303
  immigrants from, 256–58
  political reform in, 297n
  returnees to, 258
  stock market in, 132
  US free trade agreement with, 222,
  232–34, 284
mortality, 2, 88
  child, 64
  infant, 2, 61–62, 63f, 63n, 87
  maternal, 63, 64t
MSCI Emerging Markets equity index, 127
Mubarak, Hosni, 42
Multi-Fiber Arrangement, phaseout of, 220
multilateral agreements, versus
  preferential agreements, 214, 311–12
multilateral institutions. See also specific
  institution
  membership in, 209–14, 210t–11t, 312
Muslim Brotherhood, 10, 80, 192n, 205,
  281
mutual funds, Islamic, 114–15

Nahdlatul Ulama, 281
Nasser, Gamal Abdel, 42, 199
NATO. See North Atlantic Treaty
  Organization (NATO)
natural resources, 26–33. See also oil
Nazif, Ahmed, 243
Nazism, 189, 191–92, 192n
necessity index, 243–45
Nehru, Jawaharlal, 199
Nelson, Richard, 172
Nelson-Phelps growth accounting model,
  172–74, 172n, 184–85
neoimperialism, 308
newly industrialized countries, economic
  strategy of, 158
Nigeria, 26, 120, 162
Nkrumah, Kwame, 199
nonperforming loans (NPLs), 126, 126n
North American Free Trade Agreement, 51
North Atlantic Treaty Organization
  (NATO), 191

policy inertia, 8, 59
political economy
constraints caused by, 13, 160
of economic reform, 5, 57, 99, 200–205,
270, 273–97, 303–12
of entrepreneurship, 249–50, 304
of Europe, 189, 191
versus Arab economies, 191–92
of intraregional trade, 217–18
of multilateral institutions, 212–14
oil rents and, 30–32, 31t
of preferential agreements, 215
productivity growth and, 99
public-sector employment and, 159
religion and, 9
and rise of middle class, 200–201,
201n
statistical modeling of, 285–86
of trade barriers, 202
political equilibrium, 288
political geography, 137, 139
political leaders, lack of focus on
economic issues, 199–200
political reform. See also democratization;
regime change
binary solution to, 276
demand for, 273, 273n, 295
economic effects of, 274–75, 295
episodes of, 294–97
international exchange and, 283–84
Islam and, 286–87, 286n
lack of, 276
path to, 273, 274f, 275–83, 313
prospects for, 284–88
political structures, 5–9, 7f. See also specific
structure
cultural factors affecting, 286–87,
291–94, 296
happiness and, 75–78
impact of religion on, 144, 197–98
oil rents and, 290–91
popular attitudes toward, 7, 197–98
quantitative modeling of, 289–97
political uncertainty, 6, 8f, 14, 299. See also
war
economic effects of, 44f, 45–46, 116,
274–75
versus need for equilibrium, 288
and prospects for change, 273–97, 306
religion and, 9
political voice, lack of, 80–81
polity scores, 5–6, 7f, 31–32, 31t, 259, 273,
283, 286, 290

popular attitudes, 193–98. See also
discontent
American, 266–67, 268t
anti-Western (See anti-Western
attitudes)
on civil rights, 287–88
on cultural tolerance, 193, 196
on economic markets, 193
on education, 196, 303
on entrepreneurship, 249
European, 268n
on foreign investment, 264–66, 269, 305
on globalization, 12, 183, 193–96,
194t–95t, 206–207, 209, 305
effect on foreign investment,
264–66, 270, 303, 305–306
and political reform, 277–78
information-averse, 278
living standards and, 57
on multilateral institutions, 213–14
on politics, 7, 197–98, 275, 313
on terrorism, 80
on trade liberalization, 183, 187
population growth. See demographic
crisis
portfolio investment, 132, 133t, 261
poverty
absolute, 66, 68t, 72–73, 161
strategies to combat, 72–73, 299
terrorism and, 79–82
poverty traps, 306
PPP. See purchasing power parity (PPP)
preference falsification, 201
preferential trade agreements. See also
specific agreement
as anchor for reform, 224, 311
"deep integration," 223, 234–35, 308
with European Union, 219–21, 224
harmful effects of, 217–18
intellectual property rights and, 178
Mediterranean, 219–21
multilateral, 214–15, 311–12
versus multilateral agreements, 214
pan-Arab, 215–16, 311
participation in, 227t–29t
regional, 215–19, 225–29, 311
role of, 214–23
with United States, 108n, 178, 218–24,
223n, 230–36, 308, 311
prices
asset, 127
local, GDP per capita in, 43–48, 44f
oil (See oil prices)

Saddam Hussein, 70*n*
Salafist Group for Preaching and
    Combat, 80
satisfaction. *See* happiness
Saudi Arabia
    business climate in, 243
    economic characteristics of, 21, 203
    happiness in, 74–75
    immigration to, 93
    income levels in, 20, 43
    Islamic banking in, 114
    oil rents in, 30
    stock market in, 119, 127, 129, 129*n*,
        130*f*, 130*n*
    terrorist financing from, 118*b*
    terrorists from, 80
    US popular attitude toward, 267–68
    war with Egypt, 160
    WTO accession, 145, 149, 212
savings ratios, 32–33, 32*f*, 99
science and engineering education, 33,
        36*t*, 37, 70, 304
    economic growth and, 173, 281, 302–303
    terrorists with, 307
sea freight, 107–108, 137
second-generation reforms, 158, 248
September 11, 2001. *See* terrorism
service sector
    labor-intensive, development of,
        110–11, 132
    trade liberalization in, 234, 234*n*
SEZs. *See* special economic zones (SEZs)
sharia law, 145, 200
    financial systems compliant with, 114,
        118*b*, 131
    versus WTO rules, 212
Shi'ism, 141
Shuaa Capital Arab Composite index, 129
Sierra Leone, 162
Singapore, 157, 159, 250*n*
small and medium-sized enterprises
        (SMEs)
    and business climate, 238
    discrimination against, 169, 171, 171*n*
Smith, Adam, 77
social change
    discontent and, 59–60, 282–83
    needed for globalization, 305
    religious belief and, 197–98
social environment
    employment opportunities and, 5
    religion and, 77, 141, 197–98
    variety in, acceptance of, 196

social indicators, 60–73, 299
    income levels and, 70–71, 70*n*
    political reform and, 275
    of well-being, 77
social insurance
    and entrepreneurship, 245
    happiness and, 75
    provided by authoritarian
        governments, 88–89
socialism, Arab, 275
socioeconomic factors, and
        entrepreneurship, 244
Solow-Swan model, 142
South Korea
    business climate in, 242–43
    economic growth in, 23, 23*n*, 171
    economic strategy in, 157, 159–61, 182
    foreign investment in, 113*n*, 126
    human capital in, 173, 180, 302
    income inequality in, 68, 72
    land reform in, 66–67
    legal system in, 146
    returnees to, 251, 255, 258
    trade liberalization in, 109
sovereign ratings, 265*n*
Soviet Union, 191–92, 212–13
special economic zones (SEZs), 280
state-owned sector. *See* public sector
stock markets, 127, 129–30, 130*f*
Sufism, 141
suicide bombing, 82
Sukarno, 199
sukuks, 115
supply response, 237–71
Syria
    business climate in, 242–43, 249,
        249*n*
    economic characteristics of, 21
    information-averse attitude in, 278
    oil rents in, 30*n*

Taiwan
    business climate in, 242–43
    economic growth in, 23, 23*n*, 171*n*
    economic strategy in, 157, 160–61, 182
    foreign investment in, 113*n*
    human capital in, 180, 302
    income inequality in, 68, 72
    land reform in, 66–67
    legal system in, 146
    returnees to, 251, 255, 258–59, 269, 306
takaful, 115
Tamil Tigers, 82

returnees to, 259
US free trade agreement with, 222
Turkey
  business climate in, 242–43
  as part of Middle East, 4b

unemployment, 3
  entrepreneurship and, 245
  happiness and, 75
  measurement of, 94, 94n
  rates of, 75, 76t, 85
unhappiness. *See* discontent
United Arab Emirates
  demographics, 3
  market capitalization in, 127, 129n, 131
  services sector in, 110–11
  US free trade agreement with, 222, 232
United Nations
  definition of Middle East under, 4b,
    15t–17t
  Development Program (UNDP), 199
    (*See also Arab Human Development
    Reports* (UNDP))
  Educational, Scientific, and Cultural
    Organization (UNESCO), 15t–17t
United States
  Agency for International Development,
    311
  Arab immigrants in, 251–56, 269
  balance of payments deficit, 309
  business costs of terrorism in, 263
  Dubai Ports World controversy, 116,
    117b, 308–309
  economic reform initiative led by,
    309–12
  foreign opinion of, 117b, 308–11
  happiness in, 73
  Middle Eastern trade with, 216t, 217
  Patriot Act, 118b
  popular attitudes toward foreign policy
    issues in, 266–67, 268t
  preferential trade agreements with,
    108n, 178, 218–24, 223n, 230–36, 284,
    308, 311
  public diplomacy effort, 310–11,
    310n
  spread of democracy as goal of, 284
  trade with, effect of political reform on,
    283–84
universities
  quality of, 37
  science, 173
  women at, 70
Unocal, 117b

urbanization
  discontent and, 60, 77, 79, 89
  female labor force participation and, 94
Uruguay Round, 220

vaccination, childhood, 64, 65f
Venezuela, 14, 146
Vietnam, 161
Vietnam War, 161

wages
  real, 75, 85
    employment generation and,
      96–98, 135
  repatriation and, 258–59 (*See also*
    repatriated earnings)
war. *See also specific war*
  of attrition, 201–202
  economic effects of, 44f, 45–46, 63n,
    160–61, 191–92, 203
  political reform and, 276n, 291
Washington Consensus, 158–59, 162, 182,
  199–200
water supplies, 64, 137, 138b
welfare, 59–83
well-being. *See* happiness
Western culture
  adoption of, 141, 141n–42n
  attitudes toward (*See* anti-Western
    attitudes)
Williamson, John, 158. *See also*
  Washington Consensus
Wolfensohn, James D., 79
women. *See also* gender differences
  educational attainment, 91, 94
  entrepreneurship by, 244
  labor force participation, 94, 95f, 96, 97n
  life expectancy, 61, 62f
  literacy gap, 69–70, 69f
  status of, 286–87
World Bank
  corruption index, 151
  employment generation survey, 96
  governance indicators, 146
  involvement with, 211, 312
  Middle East Economic Research Forum,
    159, 159n
  regulatory burden index, 149, 151
  rule of law index, 149
  sukuk issuance, 115
  World Development Indicators, 94
World Economic Forum, 126n
  Global Competitiveness Report, 103–104,
    104t, 108, 123, 146, 149–53, 175, 177,
    180

Other Publications from the Peterson Institute for International Economics

WORKING PAPERS

Completing the Uruguay Round: A Results-Oriented Approach to the GATT Trade Negotiations*   Jeffrey J. Schott, ed.
September 1990   ISBN 0-88132-130-3
Economic Sanctions Reconsidered (2 volumes)
Economic Sanctions Reconsidered: Supplemental Case Histories
Gary Clyde Hufbauer, Jeffrey J. Schott, and Kimberly Ann Elliott
1985, 2d ed. Dec. 1990   ISBN cloth 0-88132-115-X
                         ISBN paper 0-88132-105-2
Economic Sanctions Reconsidered: History and Current Policy   Gary Clyde Hufbauer, Jeffrey J. Schott, and Kimberly Ann Elliott
December 1990   ISBN cloth 0-88132-140-0
                       ISBN paper 0-88132-136-2
Pacific Basin Developing Countries: Prospects for the Future*   Marcus Noland
January 1991   ISBN cloth 0-88132-141-9
                      ISBN paper 0-88132-081-1
Currency Convertibility in Eastern Europe*
John Williamson, ed.
October 1991   ISBN 0-88132-128-1
International Adjustment and Financing: The Lessons of 1985-1991*   C. Fred Bergsten, ed.
January 1992   ISBN 0-88132-112-5
North American Free Trade: Issues and Recommendations*   Gary Clyde Hufbauer and Jeffrey J. Schott
April 1992   ISBN 0-88132-120-6
Narrowing the U.S. Current Account Deficit*
Alan J. Lenz
June 1992   ISBN 0-88132-103-6
The Economics of Global Warming
William R. Cline
June 1992   ISBN 0-88132-132-X
US Taxation of International Income: Blueprint for Reform   Gary Clyde Hufbauer, assisted by Joanna M. van Rooij
October 1992   ISBN 0-88132-134-6
Who's Bashing Whom? Trade Conflict in High-Technology Industries   Laura D'Andrea Tyson
November 1992   ISBN 0-88132-106-0
Korea in the World Economy*   Il SaKong
January 1993   ISBN 0-88132-183-4
Pacific Dynamism and the International Economic System*   C. Fred Bergsten and Marcus Noland, eds.
May 1993   ISBN 0-88132-196-6
Economic Consequences of Soviet Disintegration*   John Williamson, ed.
May 1993   ISBN 0-88132-190-7
Reconcilable Differences? United States-Japan Economic Conflict*   C. Fred Bergsten and Marcus Noland
June 1993   ISBN 0-88132-129-X
Does Foreign Exchange Intervention Work?
Kathryn M. Dominguez and Jeffrey A. Frankel
September 1993   ISBN 0-88132-104-4
Sizing Up U.S. Export Disincentives*
J. David Richardson
September 1993   ISBN 0-88132-107-9

NAFTA: An Assessment
Gary Clyde Hufbauer and Jeffrey J. Schott, rev. ed.
October 1993   ISBN 0-88132-199-0
Adjusting to Volatile Energy Prices
Philip K. Verleger, Jr.
November 1993   ISBN 0-88132-069-2
The Political Economy of Policy Reform
John Williamson, ed.
January 1994   ISBN 0-88132-195-8
Measuring the Costs of Protection in the United States   Gary Clyde Hufbauer and Kimberly Ann Elliott
January 1994   ISBN 0-88132-108-7
The Dynamics of Korean Economic Development*   Cho Soon
March 1994   ISBN 0-88132-162-1
Reviving the European Union*
C. Randall Henning, Eduard Hochreiter, and Gary Clyde Hufbauer, eds.
April 1994   ISBN 0-88132-208-3
China in the World Economy
Nicholas R. Lardy
April 1994   ISBN 0-88132-200-8
Greening the GATT: Trade, Environment, and the Future   Daniel C. Esty
July 1994   ISBN 0-88132-205-9
Western Hemisphere Economic Integration*
Gary Clyde Hufbauer and Jeffrey J. Schott
July 1994   ISBN 0-88132-159-1
Currencies and Politics in the United States, Germany, and Japan   C. Randall Henning
September 1994   ISBN 0-88132-127-3
Estimating Equilibrium Exchange Rates
John Williamson, ed.
September 1994   ISBN 0-88132-076-5
Managing the World Economy: Fifty Years after Bretton Woods   Peter B. Kenen, ed.
September 1994   ISBN 0-88132-212-1
Reciprocity and Retaliation in U.S. Trade Policy   Thomas O. Bayard and Kimberly Ann Elliott
September 1994   ISBN 0-88132-084-6
The Uruguay Round: An Assessment*
Jeffrey J. Schott, assisted by Johanna Buurman
November 1994   ISBN 0-88132-206-7
Measuring the Costs of Protection in Japan*
Yoko Sazanami, Shujiro Urata, and Hiroki Kawai
January 1995   ISBN 0-88132-211-3
Foreign Direct Investment in the United States, 3d ed.   Edward M. Graham and Paul R. Krugman
January 1995   ISBN 0-88132-204-0
The Political Economy of Korea-United States Cooperation*   C. Fred Bergsten and Il SaKong, eds.
February 1995   ISBN 0-88132-213-X
International Debt Reexamined*
William R. Cline
February 1995   ISBN 0-88132-083-8
American Trade Politics, 3d ed.   I. M. Destler
April 1995   ISBN 0-88132-215-6

Transforming Foreign Aid: United States
Assistance in the 21st Century   Carol Lancaster
August 2000   ISBN 0-88132-291-1
Fighting the Wrong Enemy: Antiglobal
Activists and Multinational Enterprises
Edward M. Graham
September 2000   ISBN 0-88132-272-5
Globalization and the Perceptions of American
Workers   Kenneth Scheve and
Matthew J. Slaughter
March 2001   ISBN 0-88132-295-4
World Capital Markets: Challenge to the G-10
Wendy Dobson and Gary Clyde Hufbauer,
assisted by Hyun Koo Cho
May 2001   ISBN 0-88132-301-2
Prospects for Free Trade in the Americas
Jeffrey J. Schott
August 2001   ISBN 0-88132-275-X
Toward a North American Community:
Lessons from the Old World for the New
Robert A. Pastor
August 2001   ISBN 0-88132-328-4
Measuring the Costs of Protection in Europe:
European Commercial Policy in the 2000s
Patrick A. Messerlin
September 2001   ISBN 0-88132-273-3
Job Loss from Imports: Measuring the Costs
Lori G. Kletzer
September 2001   ISBN 0-88132-296-2
No More Bashing: Building a New Japan–
United States Economic Relationship
C. Fred Bergsten, Takatoshi Ito, and Marcus
Noland
October 2001   ISBN 0-88132-286-5
Why Global Commitment Really Matters!
Howard Lewis III and J. David Richardson
October 2001   ISBN 0-88132-298-9
Leadership Selection in the Major Multilaterals
Miles Kahler
November 2001   ISBN 0-88132-335-7
The International Financial Architecture:
What's New? What's Missing?   Peter B. Kenen
November 2001   ISBN 0-88132-297-0
Delivering on Debt Relief: From IMF Gold to a
New Aid Architecture   John Williamson and
Nancy Birdsall, with Brian Deese
April 2002   ISBN 0-88132-331-4
Imagine There's No Country: Poverty,
Inequality, and Growth in the Era of
Globalization   Surjit S. Bhalla
September 2002   ISBN 0-88132-348-9
Reforming Korea's Industrial Conglomerates
Edward M. Graham
January 2003   ISBN 0-88132-337-3
Industrial Policy in an Era of Globalization:
Lessons from Asia   Marcus Noland and
Howard Pack
March 2003   ISBN 0-88132-350-0
Reintegrating India with the World Economy
T. N. Srinivasan and Suresh D. Tendulkar
March 2003   ISBN 0-88132-280-6

After the Washington Consensus: Restarting
Growth and Reform in Latin America
Pedro-Pablo Kuczynski and John Williamson, eds.
March 2003   ISBN 0-88132-347-0
The Decline of US Labor Unions and the Role
of Trade   Robert E. Baldwin
June 2003   ISBN 0-88132-341-1
Can Labor Standards Improve under
Globalization?   Kimberly Ann Elliott and
Richard B. Freeman
June 2003   ISBN 0-88132-332-2
Crimes and Punishments? Retaliation under
the WTO   Robert Z. Lawrence
October 2003   ISBN 0-88132-359-4
Inflation Targeting in the World Economy
Edwin M. Truman
October 2003   ISBN 0-88132-345-4
Foreign Direct Investment and Tax
Competition   John H. Mutti
November 2003   ISBN 0-88132-352-7
Has Globalization Gone Far Enough? The
Costs of Fragmented Markets
Scott C. Bradford and Robert Z. Lawrence
February 2004   ISBN 0-88132-349-7
Food Regulation and Trade: Toward a Safe and
Open Global System   Tim Josling,
Donna Roberts, and David Orden
March 2004   ISBN 0-88132-346-2
Controlling Currency Mismatches in Emerging
Markets   Morris Goldstein and Philip Turner
April 2004   ISBN 0-88132-360-8
Free Trade Agreements: US Strategies and
Priorities   Jeffrey J. Schott, ed.
April 2004   ISBN 0-88132-361-6
Trade Policy and Global Poverty
William R. Cline
June 2004   ISBN 0-88132-365-9
Bailouts or Bail-ins? Responding to Financial
Crises in Emerging Economies
Nouriel Roubini and Brad Setser
August 2004   ISBN 0-88132-371-3
Transforming the European Economy
Martin Neil Baily and Jacob Funk Kirkegaard
September 2004   ISBN 0-88132-343-8
Chasing Dirty Money: The Fight Against
Money Laundering   Peter Reuter and
Edwin M. Truman
November 2004   ISBN 0-88132-370-5
The United States and the World Economy:
Foreign Economic Policy for the Next Decade
C. Fred Bergsten
January 2005   ISBN 0-88132-380-2
Does Foreign Direct Investment Promote
Development?   Theodore H. Moran,
Edward M. Graham, and Magnus Blomström,
eds.
April 2005   ISBN 0-88132-381-0
American Trade Politics, 4th ed.   I. M. Destler
June 2005   ISBN 0-88132-382-9
Why Does Immigration Divide America?
Public Finance and Political Opposition to
Open Borders   Gordon H. Hanson
August 2005   ISBN 0-88132-400-0

DISTRIBUTORS OUTSIDE THE UNITED STATES

Australia, New Zealand,
and Papua New Guinea
D. A. Information Services
648 Whitehorse Road
Mitcham, Victoria 3132, Australia
Tel: 61-3-9210-7777
Fax: 61-3-9210-7788
Email: service@dadirect.com.au
www.dadirect.com.au

India, Bangladesh, Nepal, and Sri Lanka
Viva Books Private Limited
Mr. Vinod Vasishtha
4737/23 Ansari Road
Daryaganj, New Delhi 110002
India
Tel: 91-11-4224-2200
Fax: 91-11-4224-2240
Email: viva@vivagroupindia.net
www.vivagroupindia.com

Mexico, Central America, South America,
and Puerto Rico
US PubRep, Inc.
311 Dean Drive
Rockville, MD 20851
Tel: 301-838-9276
Fax: 301-838-9278
Email: c.falk@ieee.org

Asia *(Brunei, Burma, Cambodia, China,*
Hong Kong, Indonesia, Korea, Laos, Malaysia,
Philippines, Singapore, Taiwan, Thailand,
and Vietnam)
East-West Export Books (EWEB)
University of Hawaii Press
2840 Kolowalu Street
Honolulu, Hawaii 96822-1888
Tel: 808-956-8830
Fax: 808-988-6052
Email: eweb@hawaii.edu

Canada
Renouf Bookstore
5369 Canotek Road, Unit 1
Ottawa, Ontario KlJ 9J3, Canada
Tel: 613-745-2665
Fax: 613-745-7660
www.renoufbooks.com

Japan
United Publishers Services Ltd.
1-32-5, Higashi-shinagawa
Shinagawa-ku, Tokyo 140-0002
Japan
Tel: 81-3-5479-7251
Fax: 81-3-5479-7307
Email: purchasing@ups.co.jp
For trade accounts only. Individuals will find
Institute books in leading Tokyo bookstores.

Middle East
MERIC
2 Bahgat Ali Street, El Masry Towers
Tower D, Apt. 24
Zamalek, Cairo
Egypt
Tel. 20-2-7633824
Fax: 20-2-7369355
Email: mahmoud_fouda@mericonline.com
www.mericonline.com

United Kingdom, Europe
(including Russia and Turkey), **Africa,**
and Israel
The Eurospan Group
c/o Turpin Distribution
Pegasus Drive
Stratton Business Park
Biggleswade, Bedfordshire
SG18 8TQ
United Kingdom
Tel: 44 (0) 1767-604972
Fax: 44 (0) 1767-601640
Email: eurospan@turpin-distribution.com
www.eurospangroup.com/bookstore

Visit our website at:
www.piie.com
E-mail orders to:
petersonmail@presswarehouse.com

.